ASCENT

By Laurence Leamer

THE PAPER REVOLUTIONARIES
PLAYING FOR KEEPS IN WASHINGTON
ASSIGNMENT
MAKE-BELIEVE
AS TIME GOES BY
KING OF THE NIGHT
THE KENNEDY WOMEN
THREE CHORDS AND THE TRUTH

ASCENT

/\

*The Spiritual and Physical Quest
of Legendary Mountaineer
Willi Unsoeld*

Laurence Leamer

Quill
William Morrow
New York

PHOTOGRAPHY CREDITS

National Archives: 1; Isabel Trehearne Unsoeld: 2, 3; UPI: 4; Barry C. Bishop ©
National Geographic Society: 5–11, 13; Jim Lester: 12; Lila Bishop © National
Geographic Society: 14; Jim Lester: 15; UPI: 16, 17; Bill Turange: 18, 19, 21; Wide
World: 20; John V.A.F. Neal/Photo Archives: 22; The Seattle Times: 24, 25.

First published in hardcover in 1982 by Simon & Schuster.

Library of Congress Cataloging-in-Publication Data

Leamer, Laurence.
    Ascent : the spiritual and physical quest of legendary mountaineer Willi Unsoeld /
Laurence Leamer.
        p.   cm.
    ISBN 0-688-16543-5 (alk. paper)
    1. Unsoeld, William Francis, 1926–   . 2. Moutaineers—United States—
Biography.   I. Title.
GV199.92.U57L4 1999
796.52'2'092—dc21
[B]   99-12031
                                                                                      CIP

Printed in the United States of America

First Quill Edition 1999

1 2 3 4 5 6 7 8 9 10

BOOK DESIGN BY EVE KIRCH

www.williammorrow.com

To Daniela Leamer, my daughter
and
Laurence E. and Helen Leamer, my parents

There are nowadays professors of philosophy, but not philosophers. Yet it is admirable to profess because it was once admirable to live. To be a philosopher is not merely to have subtle thoughts, nor even to found a school, but so to love wisdom as to live according to its dictates, a life of simplicity, independence, magnanimity, and trust.

—Henry David Thoreau, *Walden*

Whoever gets around you must be sharp
and guileful as a snake; even a god
might bow to you in ways of dissimulation
You! You chameleon!
Bottomless bag of tricks! Here in your own country
would you not give your stratagems a rest
or stop spellbinding for an instant?

You play a part as if it were your own tough skin.

No more of this, though. Two of a kind, we are,
contrivers, both. Of all men now alive
you are the best in plots and story telling
My own fame is for wisdom among the gods—
deceptions, too.

—Athena to Odysseus, *The Odyssey*

The mountain rests on the earth.

—*The I Ching*

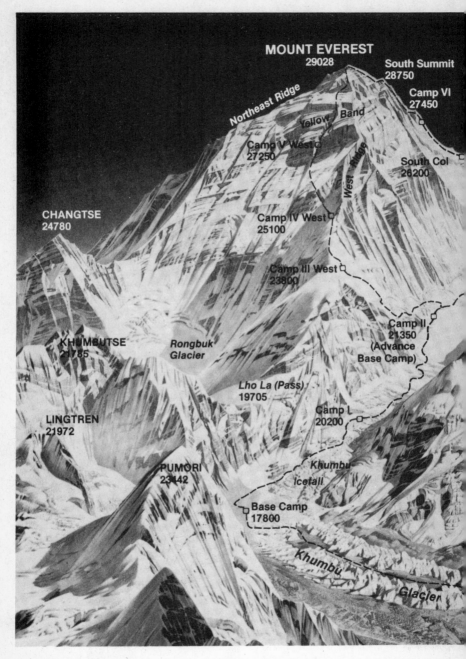

MOUNT EVEREST
29028

South Summit
28750

Camp VI
27450

Northeast Ridge

Yellow Band

South Col
26200

Camp V West
27250

West Ridge

CHANGTSE
24780

Camp IV West
25100

Camp III West
23800

Camp II
21350
(Advance
Base Camp)

KHUMBUTSE
21785

Rongbuk
Glacier

Lho La (Pass)
19705

LINGTREN
21972

Camp I
20200

PUMORI
23442

Khumbu
Icefall

Base Camp
17800

Khumbu

Glacier

On May 22, 1963, Willi Unsoeld and Tom Hornbein reached the summit of 29,028-foot Mt. Everest by the uncharted West Ridge and came down the other side. This was the first traverse of a major Himalayan peak and one of the great feats of American mountaineering. Below the summit the two Northwest

LHOTSE
27923

Camp V
26200

Geneva Spur

Camp IV
24900

NUPTSE
25726

Western Cwm

Camp III
22900

BARUNTSE
23688

CHO POLU
22093

Imja
Glacier

Namche Bazar,
18 miles

mountaineers joined up with Barry Bishop and Lute Jerstad who had reached the summit by the more familiar South Col route. The four climbers bivouacked at 28,000 feet, higher than anyone had ever survived overnight in the open.

Illustration by Heinrich C. Berann © National Geographic Society

Introduction

The new group of volunteers sat waiting for the arrival of Willi Unsoeld, director of the Peace Corps in Nepal. Practically everyone had gut-wrenching diarrhea. I was giddy from sleeplessness, the strangeness of Katmandu, and anticipation about where in Nepal I would be spending the next twenty-one months.

Suddenly, Willi stood before us, his face flushed and excited. It was as if an elemental force had burst into the long narrow chamber. He stood gazing out at all these young faces, bright with hope. With tan muscular arms he swept the room.

"So this is Nepal IV," Willi said, shaking his head, the phrase resonating with special meaning. He stopped a moment and looked around the room once again. He seemed to know each one of us, what we were, what we were capable of becoming.

"I hear you're having some trouble with the food," Willi said slowly, his small blue eyes twinkling impishly. Everyone laughed. Willi exuded health and energy. He rocked back and forth on feet that the year before, on May 22, 1963, had stood on the summit of Mount Everest, the highest peak in the world. Willi had lost nine of his toes, but he looked impervious to Asian diseases and other mortal maladies. To most of us Willi was not only a conqueror of Everest but a hero, a mountain mystic, a philosopher, a legend about whom we had already heard endless stories.

In Nepal dysentery was as much a standard subject for Willi's jokes as breasts are to a burlesque comedian. As he talked in graphic detail about diarrhea, laughter rolled through the room. Then when he had us relaxed, Willi led us on his own guided tour of Nepal. Willi had been to many of the hill posts. He talked about the tough treks. As he spoke I was ready to strap on my new Kelty pack and head out. Willi said that at the end of the trail stood these fascinating, exotic villages and towns.

"Now Chainpur is the real plum," Willi sighed, as if he wished he were going there himself. "It's a day to Dhankuta and then maybe a day and a half more. It's the loveliest little town you've ever seen. When I was there I was sleeping on the second floor of this house. I woke up at dawn and put my arm out the window."

As he spoke he reached out his hand in a gesture that was refined, almost delicate.

"And I plucked off a *suntala,* a tangerine, right off the tree. And you know, it was the best, the juiciest tangerine I ever ate."

I believed that it was my destiny to go to the hills. As Willi continued, I grasped the side of the rickety fold-up chair, hoping desperately for Chainpur.

"Now some of you, I'm afraid, a few of you, are going to the Terai," Willi went on in ominous tones, his voice dropping half an octave. As he spoke about the southern plain, a deadly silence came over the room. "I got to tell you it's dry most of the year down there, so dusty you wouldn't believe it, and when the monsoon comes, why there's water up to your ears. But you gotta stick it out."

To Willi the Peace Corps was a form of moral witnessing. He wanted us to get out there, out in life. That was the great glory of the Peace Corps. He couldn't stand all this endless intellectualizing, planning, testing, retesting. Just get the volunteers out there. Let them be. Let them *become*.

It was time for Willi to give us our assignments. Although the nearest I had gotten to mountains was driving through the Rockies once, I wanted very much to go to the high Himalayas. I had just graduated from Antioch College in the flatlands of southern Ohio. My father was a college professor. I wanted to seek out what was real, profound and manly, as I had decided mere ideas were not.

Willi reeled off the names and assignments like a judge announcing prizes. I didn't get Chainpur. Then Willi began tolling the names of those being sent to the Terai, his voice like a funeral bell. When Willi called my name, I began to swoon. I grabbed the chair even tighter. I tried to control the expression on my face. I didn't want anyone to know how desperate I felt.

Narhineghat, my station in the Rapti Valley, wasn't the real Terai, but some of the last real jungle in South Asia. There were tigers, rhinos, crocodiles, and myriad birds. I made the most of it but my roommate and I didn't get along. He was an easy going sort who ironed his T-shirts, talked of good times on the beaches of southern California, and didn't care about the mountains. I was sloppy and intense, forever looking up where the foothills rose out of the jungle mists. It was clear that one of us would have to be transferred.

After several months our group came into Katmandu for a conference. I went to see Willi in his office. Whoever Willi spoke to felt that he had a special relationship with him. I was sure that Willi understood me as few people ever had. I wanted to be like Willi, to live life to the hilt.

"Ron's right! I wouldn't want to live with me either, Willi," I said as I paced back and forth. "I want the hills. I want you to send me to the most remote place you can find. *Alone*. That's what I'm here for, Willi."

"You know we just can't give out transfers like postage stamps, Larry," Willi said, stroking his chin.

"I need the hills, Willi," I said, leaning over his desk. "I can do a real job up there."

"Yeah, the hills," Willi said, a far-off look on his face. He thought a minute. "Well, I guess maybe you should have your chance."

Willi lined things up for me to go teach in a tiny village in eastern Nepal, two days' walk from a road, a day's walk from any radio or telegraph communication. Not only would Willi come down to Narhineghat to pick me up, but he was going to let me travel with him visiting other volunteers before I headed off alone to my new post. A village in the hills. A trip with Willi. I couldn't have asked for anything better.

When Willi came tromping in to my school, the children placed *malas* of fresh flowers around his neck. The gawky, insecure young headmaster stammered a greeting in high-pitched, ungrammatical English. Willi was a master at these scenes. He didn't know much Nepali, but he soon had the headmaster giggling away, the two men shamelessly exchanging compliments.

Then it was time to visit my classroom. Like so many of the early volunteers, I was teaching English, a task whose most noticeable effect on Nepal was that out of the mouths of children came such noble phrases as "What is your name?" and "How are you?" I thought that Willi would discuss the Peace Corps, or John F. Kennedy, or development. Instead, he launched into a talk about the Everest climb, a subject almost as strange to my students as baseball.

"Why did I climb Everest?" Willi asked, hovering over my ninth-graders, who sat wearing white shirts, long pants, and bewildered looks that attested to my achievements as a language teacher.

"Why did I climb Everest?" he asked again, this time speaking far more slowly. I stood beside Willi knowing that only the son of the town's richest merchant would understand.

The tiny boy popped up, his head reaching hardly above the top of the scarred, ink-stained desk. "Because you want to be famous, sir."

"Ah, but I'm not famous," Willi said, puckering his face up in a gesture of feigned disgust. "Tenzing Norkay is famous. Sir Edmund Hillary is famous. But Willi Unsoeld. No! Who ever heard of Willi Unsoeld?"

The student thought a moment. "But you're famous to us, sir," he said brightly, and sat down.

Now, Willi and I were barreling back up the valley, a great plume of dust trailing behind the blue jeep. Further south Willi turned eastward onto the road the Chinese were building, a dusty track across the virgin jungle. As we jostled along, bouncing up and down, fording streams, roaring up inclines in low gear, I felt like Jim Corbet or Kim of the Jungle. Willi had never been through here either and was as much into the adventure as I was.

We finally made it out, onto a washboard road. In the villages of the eastern Terai, dust lay as fine as baby powder, half an inch deep on the baked, cracked earth. In the pre-monsoon it was so hot that the villagers got up before dawn to shop and chat in the dark streets, retreating as the sun rose into the heavens. We stayed with a Peace Corps couple stationed in one of the larger towns. In the evening we walked with them through the fetid bazaar, picking our way around the garbage. Next morning we drove on to visit a woman volunteer stationed in a village of mud huts so empty of people that it seemed a plague had been visited on the place.

The woman wanted to get out for the weekend. Willi was not about to deny her that. The three of us headed back. In the green depths of the jungle, Willi was in high spirits. As he drove he told stories, gesturing with one hand. At a fork in the road, he went up the branch that seemed to lead more directly west. Several hundred yards ahead water buffalo were lying in the muddy water. He roared down the river bank in low gear, churning across the water—only the buffalo weren't lying down but standing up. The jeep conked out.

"Oh, shoot, must have taken the wrong turn," Willi said, slapping his knee. "You know something about cars, Larry?"

"Not really," I said, wishing for all the world that I was a master mechanic.

Willi pulled off his sneakers. His feet were two stumps with one sad little toe sticking out. Standing on the river bank, Willi looked like a broken toy soldier whom the murmur of a breeze would have toppled over.

Wading into the water, Willi opened the hood. He stared down at the motor like a New Guinea aboriginal seeing his first airplane. "It's got to be about twenty miles to the road," Willi said, giving up on the motor. "And this looks to me like a tiger watering hole."

"Are you sure?" the woman volunteer said, scrunching herself up in the back of the jeep.

"Well, Willi, I guess I better walk out," I said. Willi was in no condition for such a trip. The prospect of saving toeless Willi and this woman delighted me.

"No, I'll go," Willi said as he tied his shoelaces. "You two stay in the jeep together."

Willi charged up the road, disappearing into the dark jungle. The woman and I sat quietly for a while, contemplating our fate. Since we had no food, we decided to go foraging. We thought we were miles from any help. It turned out that we were very near a village. Some people killed and cooked a chicken for us. If Willi hadn't already left they would have gone for help. The next morning Willi returned in an AID jeep, having walked the twenty miles incredibly fast. The AID mechanic wiped off the distributor cap with a greasy rag and the jeep started up again.

The next week I left Katmandu for my new station in the eastern hills. I loved living in my village in the high Himalayas, teaching science and hygiene as well as English. I may even have done some good.

The next summer I decided to trek north to Thyangboche and beyond, coincidentally retracing much of the journey Willi had taken in 1954 on his way to climb Makalu. Then I planned to walk to Katmandu along the same trail Willi traveled on his way to climb Everest. I had a sense of almost limitless possibilities within myself. That was Willi's philosophy, not something you read, not some neat phrase to be taped to a door in a college dormitory. His philosophy was something you felt, and once you felt it, something you did.

I can see now how easily I could have gotten myself killed. I was by myself. The monsoon season had arrived. I traveled by canoe across rivers where many Nepalese were turning back. I forded rampaging streams. If I had slipped, I would have been swept downstream. Every day it rained. The trails were slippery. The dampness permeated my clothes. As I walked northward, I found it harder and harder to find anything to eat. One night all I had was a few boiled potatoes with a hill family. Then I picked up fleas sleeping on their floor. The next day the leeches were so bad that I gave up even trying to burn them off.

I could do nothing but go on. On the tenth day, when it was wetter and colder than ever, I walked over a high pass, down into the valley below Namche Bazar. It was sunny and warm. Flowers graced the sides of the wide trail. Above stood the Himalayas. Ama Dablam. Kantega. Thamserku. And above them, Everest. As I walked, I wanted to cry with sheer joy and ecstasy. I let tears form in my eyes, a watery prism, never letting the tears drop. I knew that I was feeling something of what Willi must have felt in the mountains. I knew that I was happier than I had ever been, happier than I would ever be.

I would have liked to have told Willi about my adventures. But by the time I arrived in Katmandu, he was gone. I never saw Willi again. Fourteen years later when I learned that he had died, the whole period when Willi was the great hero of my young life came back to me in a torrent of memory. Four months later I started work on this book, seeking to learn where Willi's ideas had led him and what his life had meant.

Part One

1

For days the weather on the mountain had been bad, but Sunday dawned bright and clear. Mount Rainier stood alone, sovereign over the northwestern skies. Passengers on the ferry north to Victoria looked back and saw rising beyond the blue waters of Puget Sound the peak many in Washington State call simply "the mountain." To city dwellers in Seattle heading out into the wilderness for the first sunny Sunday in weeks the mountain appeared a great white beacon eighty miles away. Further south in Tacoma the stench of the pulp mills blanketed part of the city, yet a person had only to look up to see the 14,410-foot peak way off there, so pure and clean. In Olympia, at the southern end of Puget Sound, Mount Rainier stood above the town to the east as if to remind the politicians that the state capital could never become a place where the monuments of mere humans rise above nature.

From a distance Mount Rainier appeared an exquisite, benign work of art. Six days before, however, on March 4, 1979, the mountain had taken the lives of fifty-two-year-old William F. (Willi) Unsoeld, a faculty member, and twenty-one-year-old Janie Diepenbrock, a student, at The Evergreen State College in Olympia.

"The eulogies that followed the news of Unsoeld's death are not the sort reserved merely for a man who was among the first Americans to conquer Mount Everest," the *Bellevue Daily Journal-American* editorialized. "They are reserved for a hero. A hero who taught—who virtually personified—the values of self-reliance and persistence in the face of discouragement."

Willi was a strong, redheaded son of the American Northwest. To some people he seemed a character straight out of a novel by Ken Kesey, the northwest novelist whom he physically resembled— Willie, the philosophy-spouting, back-slapping individualist. To others he was an American Odysseus on a journey to the unpeopled places. To still others he was a contemporary Captain Ahab: bearded, toeless old Willi out there with his plastic hips, searching for meaning and purity until white death dragged him down. Many heralded Willi as a saint, while some whispered privately that the man was virtually a murderer. Most considered Willi's concern for other human beings genuine and profound, while a few thought him a shameless manipulator.

Though the two bodies were still up on the mountain there would be a "memorable celebration" on campus this afternoon to commemorate Willi's and Janie's lives. On this fine day they had come from all over to tell tales of Willi, to sing the songs he sang, to remember what he had said and thought and felt, to laugh and to cry.

Some had known him when he had been a guide in the Tetons. Others remembered him as a philosophy professor to whom the mountains were not a weekend diversion but his crucible. A few had gone with him on the Everest expedition when he had climbed the Himalayan peak by the unknown, uncharted West Ridge, one of the great feats of mountaineering history. There was a contingent from his Peace Corps days when, as director in Nepal, he had been turned into a symbol for that idealistic young agency. Still others had met him while he was executive vice-president of Outward Bound, and he had seemed the embodiment of that organization. Some had climbed with him on expeditions, shared his triumphs, witnessed his tragedy. Many had studied under him, and whether the course was called outdoor education, philosophy, ethics, or wilderness consciousness, what they studied was Willi and his life.

While still a teenager Willie had sung a song of daring and danger that is now heard on every hill, highland and mountain in the American wilderness. Willi had been a backpacking sojourner when the rest of America was getting on with the business at home, a precursor of the millions of people who seek solace and spiritual rejuvenation in the wilderness. Willie was a teacher who believed in risk as other pedagogues believe in the rod, or Latin, or weekly essays.

The day was well on its way to becoming the warmest March 11 since the Weather Bureau started keeping records. The even rows of folding chairs (including special orange ones for smokers) set out in front of the portable stage were filling up. People sprawled on the cropped green lawns or squatted on the red-brick walk.

It was 12:30 by the time on the great gray rectangular slab clock tower that Willi and his students used to rappel down. The clock had no numbers. The clock appeared an abstraction, like Evergreen's burnished gray cement buildings designed as much for form as for function. Over six hundred people had arrived already and more were coming. They filled much of this square through which Willi had come bursting several times a day, as likely as not fifteen minutes late for his next meeting. Of course, it was different on the days when the pain in his hips was bad, and he moved along at a tortured uneven gait, struggling against his crippled self. In the end, moving across campus, he had looked like the old man of the mountain. He had a seer's deep, tiny, glowing eyes and an unruly nest of beard, only a few embers of reddish-brown left among the silver and gray.

Willi's wife, Jolene, and his surviving children, Regon, Krag, and Terres, had put this gathering together. Although all three children would speak, Jolene had chosen not to say anything. She was a woman with intensity and energy that burned off any extra flesh on her body. In recent years she had become a one-woman good government crusade in the state, a familiar figure striding single-mindedly through the marble corridors in the state capital pursuing malefactors of power.

Regon Unsoeld moved to the microphone. Off and on for a good number of years Willi's twenty-six-year-old son had been a student at Evergreen. He was well known on campus. He had a curly brown beard and long hair that wreathed his face, softening intense, earnest features that resembled his mother's. "We saw that people were starting to fall in the aisles 'cause of this weird weather so we're breaking with Evergreen tradition and getting started within an hour of the scheduled starting time," Regon began.

"Regon and I have been trying to figure out some way to introduce this event today," twenty-two-year-old Krag Unsoeld said in a folksy voice. He, too, had a full beard and, unlike his older brother, the more laid-back manner of the sixties. "And I guess in many ways there are some things that need to be explained maybe to a lot of people. And that's why this event is billed as a memorable celebration. And this is really something which is completely natural. This celebration is an attempt to represent that living is a full circle and that in dying there is both joy and sorrow."

"Two minutes!" Terres Unsoeld's voice shot out when Krag's monologue had exceeded the agreed upon time limit. Willi's diminutive twenty-year-old daughter, an aspiring actress, was not about to let her brother destroy the drama she had helped orchestrate.

"One point that Regon and Krag didn't mention," Terres said in a spirited, lively voice like her father's. "We have generations and eras of many different people here to speak and the first group is outdoor ed. This is the program Dad was teaching this year at Evergreen."

The students who had studied in Willi's outdoor education program stood at the back of the stage, their arms around one another. They wore rumpled rolled-up pants, sweat socks, jogging shoes, shorts, old long-sleeved shirts with arms rolled up, khakis, and one suit. The motleyness was a kind of uniform. In the early 1970s the word had gone out that while elsewhere the tide of experimentation was receding, beaching ideals and aspirations, here, in Olympia, a utopian institution was being built. Students had come from all over the United States to study at this new school set down among the forests on the edge of Eld Inlet outside the state capital. Many of the students were the burned-out survivors of more traditional schools and less traditional times. At Evergreen they found not a universe where they could become what they had always wanted to become, but a sanctuary.

In their stories and poems and lyrics the students sought to witness for Willi and for their group, and for Janie, who had died living Willi's teaching. A student read aloud something that Janie had written about Evergreen: "There is an almost frenzied expenditure of energy as individuals pursue hints and glimmerings of their potential. The power behind us could be so dynamic if this random movement could be directed, directed and centered toward a real and urgent mission. We are the age of future power."

The students talked not of a feeling of loss but of a spirit burning hot within them to carry on the message. They said that all the energy Willi had given out had flowed back, completing the circle. They talked of this spirit without which life could not be lived fully and how they would carry the spirit on. And they shared the sweetest of memories, gentle anecdotes of a man who mocked his ailments, a man who after operations that gave him artificial hip joints called himself "the bionic man."

Lynn Hammond moved forward to speak. She had come from Maine to teach with Willi. She had the lean, hard body of an outdoorswoman and a melodious, beckoning voice. "The man that I came to work with was characterized for me by a telephone conversation I had with him last spring," she said. "When I called after he had had his hip operation, I said, 'Well, Willi, how are your hips?' And he said, 'They're just fine.' He said, 'They don't work as fine as the original ones, but you know I wouldn't like it if all those smart doctors could outsmart mother nature.' And I thought this is a man with a positive attitude. And I suppose that's one of the things that really most characterized him especially in his public image was as somebody who never took no for an answer, who never gave up. He not only climbed mountains. He moved 'em.''

Then Hammond's voice changed, grew quieter, confidential. "But there was another part of Willi that became very important to me during this year as he came to know me better and to trust me

He let me see the person who was behind that mask. He let me see somebody who was vulnerable, who did have fears, who did hurt. . . . And I've had some solace from that, because I think he was about to have to accept that he was not going to be able to do the things he had done for so long and that were so central to his life. And although I personally, for myself and for all of you, feel a great deal of grief that he's not here to continue teaching us and to give us the joy that he gave, I really feel some gratitude that he didn't have to go through all the pain of the transition he would have had to make.''

A parade of those upon whose lives Willi had laid a hand came forward. Some of them told stories about Willi that had been related scores of times. Those anecdotes were like old friends. Others told new stories; those were fresh treasures. There was a story about Willi getting lost on a trail in Nepal and a tale of him leading a group of students at Evergreen on a year-long intellectual expedition. There were mirthful memories of his climbing days in college, and a poignant story of how on that last climb of Rainier he had promised his family that he wouldn't carry a pack. There was testimony about Willi's concern for preserving the wilderness and how that had led him to the Council of the Wilderness Society. Some commented on the Unsoelds as a family, how they all had a deep concern for social and political issues.

H. Adams (Ad) Carter, a teacher at Milton Academy in Massachusetts and the editor of the *American Alpine Journal,* stood. In 1936, Carter had been on the first expedition to climb Nanda Devi, the highest mountain in India. He had gone on to climb many other mountains, to lead his boys at school on many adventures. Like a football player who never again knows the public glory of his high school games, Carter knew that his identity as a climber was in good measure based on that youthful climb. In the 1950s Carter had first learned of the Teton guide Willi Unsoeld. He had heard a story that Willi had seen Nanda Devi from a distance in 1949 and found the mountain so beautiful that he decided to get married, have a daughter, and name her after the mountain. When Carter met Willi he found that the story was true, the daughter already existed.

"I guess I date from back at the time more or less that they invented the light bulb," sixty-four-year-old Carter said, in the voice of a Boston Brahmin. "We went together two and a half years ago to Nanda Devi. And Devi was with us. The Hindus were absolutely convinced that Devi was the reincarnation of the goddess, Nanda. The bliss-giving goddess is what it means. Devi was very blond and Gauri is another name for the goddess Nanda and it means the golden one. She certainly was that. So Willi was the father of a goddess. It gave him godlike qualities. But Willi was perhaps the most human person that I have ever known. Father of the goddess, he was also such a human person."

Carter stopped. On this day he would not go on and tell what had happened on the mountain. Surely everyone there before him knew that story and how it had changed Willi's life.

Other teachers, students, and friends got up to speak about Willi. For everyone who spoke a score could just as easily have told how Willi had affected their lives. Richard M. (Dick) Emerson, a sociologist and climber, considered Willi the most complicated person he had ever known. As he listened he thought about how over the years the Willi Unsoeld legend had grown up around his friend so that he wasn't sure he knew Willi anymore. Hearing speaker after speaker, Emerson began to feel once again the Willi he had known, Willi the nurturing shepherd, Willi, endlessly confronting people with life and its possibilities.

James Gulden, an Evergreen teacher, listened with dismay. Gulden had taught with Willi this quarter. The psychology instructor had thought Willi was deeply depressed. Gulden had been so worried about someone dying on Rainier that he had wanted to stop the climb; to him this so-called "memorable celebration" was an act of mythmaking pure and simple.

Standing on the fringe of the gathering was Worth Hedrick, an unemployed journalist. He had practically worshiped Willi and the family. For two and a half years he had been consumed with the Unsoelds. He had left his job to write a book about Devi. He had helped develop a Hollywood movie project about Willi's dead daughter. Now he had nothing—no book, no movie, no job, nothing—and he felt unwanted here today.

Terres finally introduced other members of Willi's family. "Both of Dad's sisters are here, Beryl and Isabel and his mother, Granny, who came up from California," Terres said, her voice charged with impish delight. "They're right over here. And I wanted Beryl or Isabel to tell one of her *Billy* stories." She said "Billy" as if the word were a wonderful private joke.

While Terres was talking, Willi's tiny, delicate mother rose.

"Granny, you want to stand up!" Terres exclaimed. "Eighty-five!"

Although Mrs. Unsoeld had been considered too upset and fragile to speak, she walked determinedly up to the microphone. Even before the applause died down, she began.

"I hope I won't shock a great many people," she said in a British accent that nearly seven decades in North America had hardly touched. "But when I got pregnant with Willi I seriously thought of an abortion."

A great wave of laughter.

"I had four children already and we were in very straitened circumstances and I thought I couldn't possibly afford any more. But I went to a doctor and I so despised that man I couldn't go to him again. So I had Willi. And I can only say that I *never* remember a time when he *really* upset me.

"When he first went to India with just another boy, with no money, no porters, really no anything. And my friend said to me, 'Aren't you petrified?' and I said, 'No, I'm not. If he should die on the mountain that's where he would want to go.'

"And to finish up with, a short while ago my two daughters were asking me what kind of funeral I wanted. They wanted to arrange it just the way I felt it should be done. And at that time Willi said to me, 'Mim, I would *love* to speak at your memorial service.'

"Now I am here."

The applause was not the clapping that had been heard before, at times cathartic outbursts, at times mere signals of approval. It was sustained, a salute. It ended finally, not petering off, but stopping in an instant as if the audience were one person.

A last large group moved up to the microphone. "We first have to take a consensus on who's going first," a young man said. The others laughed as if this were a secret that they shared.

"This is the group that was the expedition that was on Mount Rainier as the accident took place," a second young man said. "We were on Mount Rainier, a total of ten days. It was a very important time for us, an important time, I think, for everybody."

High on the mountain that great avalanche had come rolling down, killing Willi and Janie, leaving the students alone. They had fought their way through the blizzard to the cabin at Camp Muir. Three days later when they arrived back at Paradise they were singing. Whatever they had been before they headed up the mountain, they were different now.

Peter Miller stood silently before the microphone. The twenty-six-year-old student had met Willi in 1973 on the East Coast. Later he had traveled west to have Willi as his guide. He had a dark beard, deep close-set eyes, a face that could have been set down in the early American west, a young trapper, a mountain man. He had shared a tent with Willi and Janie that last night when the weather had turned so bad. In the morning he had been tied next to Willi and Janie on the same climbing rope. The avalanche had taken him. He had been buried over his head in the snow for fifteen minutes. He talked now as if he had come back from the dead.

"Saturday afternoon. A week ago. Sitting in a tent with Willie and Janie. The snow is falling very heavily. I remember how high Willi was. He'd mentioned that when he was a kid he wanted to be Peter Pan. And the only never-never land he'd ever found was over ten thousand feet. He had been to where they told him when they played with his legs he'd never be again."

Miller took quick, panting breaths, exhaling into the microphone. "I think the strength of Janie and Willi was something that amazed us all when we were up in the mountain," he gasped. "That's why it's so difficult to accept. That strength's still there and it's still going around 'cause it's in all of us now."

Other students talked about Janie's strength and Willie's toeless feet. Then twenty-one-year-old Ian Yolles moved forward. He was a lean, taciturn Canadian with eyes that seemed focused somewhere beyond the horizon. Yolles had been studying at Antioch College in Ohio but he had heard about Willi and had come west. He had a neat beard. Yolles, too, could have stepped out of the nineteenth century, a Quaker shopkeeper, a homesteader breaking sod on the frontier prairie. It was Yolles who had taken charge when Willi died.

". . . Yes, we left something on the mountain but we've come down from the mountain with a lot of strength," Yolles said evenly. "With something very, very, very special. And while we were up there for the two days after the accident each one of us experienced something just unbelievably intense . . . And during those two days we as a group developed a very, very unique closeness, a connection, a sense of camaraderie, a feeling of warmth, a feeling of sharing that Willie would have been exceptionally proud of. I think in a sense the experience we went through was perhaps the ultimate experience that Willi could have hoped for. And it was the kind of thing that we talked about, that we tried to generate during the entire quarter. And all of a sudden it became a very extraordinary reality for us. And as I look at these people now and as we look at each other, I think that we all sense that.

"And as I said I think that's the ultimate lesson that we could have learned from Willi and it also completes the circle that we've all been talking and thinking about earlier. And just one last thing. I think that for all of us now as a group of people, there's a lot of power. There's a lot of strength that we feel. And that what we as a group are grappling with now, and what we're struggling with now, and what we're attempting to learn and deal with is how to share that strength with you people, the people around us.

"Thanks."

Then the students who had been on Rainier with Willi began to sing the chantlike song they had sung as they had come back down to Paradise:

> *You can't kill the spirit*
> *It's like a mountain*
> *Old and strong*
> *It goes on and on*

The other students in the outdoor education program joined in. Soon everyone was singing.

You can't kill the spirit
It's like a mountain
Old and strong
It goes on and on

A few students took others by the hand, and then other students joined them.

You can't kill the spirit
It's like a mountain
Old and strong
It goes on and on

The young joined hands with the old, the easteners with the westerners, the mountaineers with the faculty. And the line moved beyond the red brick plaza, back into the trees. The line moved so far beyond its beginnings that anyone who could see one end could not see the other.

You can't kill the spirit
It's like a mountain
Old and strong
It goes on and on

The line curved back again, and the last hand clasped the first hand and formed a great circle. High above the trees stood Mount Rainier, the peak the Indians call Takhoma, the mountain that is God.

You can't kill the spirit
It's like a mountain
Old and strong
It goes on and on.

2

In the summer of 1939 Bill Unsoeld rode in the back of an open truck with a group of Boy Scouts toward the Cascade Mountains of Oregon. The only mountains twelve-year-old Bill had ever seen were the low-lying ones of the Coastal Range. Suddenly, the Three Sisters, the queens of the Cascades, appeared out of the haze, floating in and out of the mist. Bill thought that the ten-thousand-foot peaks looked as if they weren't even connected to earth. He felt himself being pulled toward the Three Sisters. He knew that it was up there that he, that man, belonged.

When Bill returned to the Cascades to climb with the Scouts, he was petrified. Bill was afraid of many other things. Until recently, he had fainted at the sight of blood. When he had been sick, he had terrifying dreams about a big ball coming down and rolling over him. But climbing was worse. He faced that pure fear when the body goes numb. He knew that if he didn't go on he would lose something that he would never get back. So he went on and turned that fear into one of the engines that drove him upward.

Climbing Bill felt things he had never felt before. He had a strong body. Climbing was a physical challenge beyond anything he had ever known. Tied to a rope with other boys, he felt a profound kinship. He was part of these boys and they were part of him, like a whole new family. Bill had always been a leader, up here even more so. He knew nothing about climbing, but he helped the weak and the fearful.

Bill felt God in the mountains too. The higher he climbed the closer he felt to God.

"I remember as a small Episcopalian boy being so shaken by the power and mystery of the communion," Willi said, years later when he had become one of America's greatest mountaineers. "I even remember trying desperately to cling to this awareness as I entered my mid-teens. But the harder I tried to induce such feelings, the faster they slipped away. For a period of years there was considerable competition in my life between attending church and attending to the mountains. Finally I was forced to admit that despite the tremendous sweep of Christian history, the power of its faith, the testimony of its martyrs, and the witness of its Book (as an Episcopalian I would also add the symbolism of its architecture and its vestments and the mystery of its rituals), for me God was no longer to be found in His traditional steeple houses, but rather seemed to dwell more vividly among the bare austerities of His earth's high places."

Then they came down the mountain, down through the lava bed, down through the virgin forests, down past the sparkling, surging McKenzie River, down to the gentle, pristine world of the Willamette Valley, down to Eugene where for days on end the sun might not shine, and a dampness penetrated the marrow of the bone. Bill didn't mind this climate that the outsiders cursed so. Like anyone whose roots are truly in the Northwest, he accepted inclement weather as part of nature's endless cycle, the rain a harbinger of sun, the sun a harbinger of rain.

What Bill dreaded was the climate inside his own family.

George Unsoeld, Bill's German-born father, had a thick red neck, broad shoulders, a fiery temper, and a taste for good music, good food, and good liquor. When Bill was born on October 5, 1926, in Arcata, California, his father was about to fulfill his one dream: to have his own store. In 1936 during the Depression Unsoeld's Department Store in Coquille, Oregon, failed. George turned more remote and morose than ever, sitting around the house drinking. Like his four grown-up sisters and brother, Bill was too afraid of his father to try to get close to him.

The burden of the family fell on Bill's mother. Isabel Trehearne Unsoeld had been born into a fine British family. Her parents had died when she was young, leaving Isabel and her brothers only a modest inheritance. Seventeen-year-old Isabel left England in 1911 for her brother's new ranch in western Canada. Two years later she found a job at House's Department Store down the road in Princeton, British Columbia. There she met and married another employee, George Unsoeld, who was twenty-one years her senior.

With the bankruptcy Mrs. Unsoeld had started taking in boarders. In Eugene the Unsoelds' rented house stood on Emerald Street near the one hundred-acre campus of the University of Oregon. The roomers moved in and out of the house as if it were a college dormitory. George sat in the kitchen during dinner, a brooding presence while the sound of laughter and easy conversation wafted from the boarders in the dining room.

Bill watched his father drinking more than ever. There was none of the joyous, rousing drinker in this man, and practically no one for him to drink with either. He came stumbling home, disappointment welling out of him. He had a gun that he brandished like a magical talisman, threatening first his family, then himself.

Disgrace hovered just above the home during the war years, waiting to descend like the rains that drenched the city. Bill's mother was a wisp of a woman with a proud carriage and a high-pitched voice. Manners and decorum were her bulwark against the ravages of life. Although Bill loved his mother, he enjoyed getting away from the enforced civility of the home. He liked saying words that he couldn't say in front of his mother, words like "shit" and "piss" and "snot" and "puss," words that he thought were real. He liked getting out in the woods and the mountains where life itself seemed more real.

Bill was quiet and reserved. He was small for his age, with

slicked-down red hair, freckles, blue eyes, and an earnest manner. He had a broad expressive face that telegraphed his emotions like a semaphore, a big mouth, and a tough muscular body that exuded health. Grace Scully, who boarded at the Unsoelds while in college, thought that Bill was about the laziest human being she had ever seen, lying on his back while his mother worked.

What Bill was doing was reading the greatest mountain-climbing literature. For the most part these climbers were Englishmen. During the second half of the nineteenth century, British mountaineers had largely invented modern climbing. They were an unlikely group for a youth in the Northwest to make his mentors: scholars, schoolmasters, scientists, ministers, Victorian esthetes, with tastes as refined in claret as in climbing.

When Bill read H. W. Tilman's book about the 1936 ascent of 25,645-foot Nanda Devi, he was transported to a hero's world. Nanda Devi was the highest mountain in the world yet climbed. Reading Tilman's account made him feel as if the greater the mountain the greater the heights of heroism that might be attained.

"Where each man pulled his weight each must share the credit," Tilman concluded. "For though it is natural for each man to have his own aspirations, it is in mountaineering, more than in most things, that we try to believe

The game is more than the players of the game,
And the ship is more than the crew."

Men like Tilman wrote celebrating a world of strong, simple virtues—of comradeship, of dangers real and immediate and bracingly clear, of sacrifice and self-denial; a world without women and family. Bill read Tilman's other accounts and anything else about climbing he could find. Nothing in mountaineering literature equaled the stories of George Mallory and his attempts on Mount Everest. Here was mystery, moment, and wonder.

Mallory's life was like a work of art against which all other artifacts of the period seem like prelude, all that comes afterward imitative or tainted by caricature. With his large, luminous eyes, fine, flaxen hair, sensitive mouth, and long arched eyebrows, Mallory didn't look like anyone Bill had ever known. Bill identified with the life the British climber led, and with the mountain with which Mallory's name would forever be linked.

Bill read in his books that at Oxford Mallory had at first planned to follow in his father's footsteps and become a minister, but decided on a career in teaching instead. He was a serious young family man but loved to climb, moving up the Alps with consummate grace. It was uncharted, unknown Everest that drew Mallory, and as it drew the British climber, so did it draw young Bill.

Bill knew all about Mallory's expeditions to Tibet to climb 29,028-foot Everest. He could talk about them in detail. Chomolungma, the Tibetans called her. Chomo-lungma, the Goddess-mother of the world. In 1924 Mallory was drawn back to the greatest of mountains for the third time. On June 8 Mallory and Irvine made one last try. The weather was magnificent, beckoning. They set out from Camp VI at 27,000 feet, two black specks moving slowly up against the immensity of time and space; two specks moving up to 28,200 feet, higher than man had ever climbed; two black specks moving toward the summit, from the unknown, through the unknown, to the unknown; two black specks . . . .

Bill dreamed of Everest, but much of his climbing was done just outside Eugene at Judkins Point. There Bill and his two buddies, Goodman Kaarhus and Robert Moffitt, discovered a cliff on which they could practice their techniques. The three high school students had no guide but themselves. They stood figuring it out as they went along. Finally Bill and his friends joined the Obsidians, the local mountaineering group.

"By the third trip up the Middle Sister there were three of us doing circles around the rest," Bill said later. "You were supposed to stay in rest step all the way, and we tried this on our hands for a while, but you are just obviously somewhere else than where they are. So they suggest that you are ready now and please get the hell out of their hair.

"Now you really enter the flirting with the limits where you seek the razor edge. You balance on it and the climb didn't really come off unless there was real doubt as to whether you were going to make it. You live that way. It is addiction.''

The Cascades were still young mountains—young in a climber's parlance—with unclimbed routes. Up here Bill did some strong leading, working his way up sheer cliffs, standing there exposed, the earth far below. Kaarhus and Moffitt were daring young climbers also but Bill had already moved beyond them, nudging his way further and further out onto the sheer edge of fear.

Bill did not talk to his friends about experiencing the sacred up on the mountains. He approached the Cascades like a lover. Up here he was free. There was no limit to life, no limit to Bill Unsoeld. His joy and enthusiasm poured over whoever was near him.

Down below Bill was full of stories about what he had seen and what he had gone through. Northwest climbers were known as terrible exaggerators. Bill's stories were another way of seeing. There was a difference between the true and the truth. True was a clerk's world, certifiable in a routine of columns, figures, and facts. Truth was the world as the poet created it, in images flashing with life and meaning. Wasn't it really the truth that he and his buddies had just had this incredible adventure up on the North Sister, coming within a hairsbreadth of getting killed? Now wasn't that the way it happened? Wasn't it? Anyone who thought otherwise just hadn't been there.

For all Bill's stories, back in University High School he was still reserved, and quiet, terribly shy around girls. He was an A student. Those who knew him in class thought him studious.

He was only 5 feet 7 inches tall and 117 pounds when he went out for football. Once, in scrimmage Richard Allison, a 180-pound fullback, came barreling through the line. Suddenly someone tackled him fiercely. Even before he hit the ground he knew it had to be Bill Unsoeld. Allison thought that Bill was strange. He mumbled, talking so low that Allison could hardly hear him. Bill was mild-mannered too, never getting mad at anyone. But let Bill loose on a football field and he would tear your head off.

Bill made the all-star team as end. He played all kinds of sports.

In the summer he worked for the Forest Service manning a fire tower in the Cascades. For his senior year he was elected captain of the football team.

Then Bill's father got a chance to go back to work in the store in Shafter, California, where he had started out many years before. Mrs. Unsoeld knew that she would have to go. George had to have something to do, some work. She was tempted to leave Bill boarding in Eugene, for this surely would be *his* year.

She went to see the principal of Uni High. "If I had a son who grew up like Bill, I'd be happy," the principal said. "But I think it would be unwise to leave him here alone."

In the summer of 1944 Bill went to Shafter with his mother and father. In school the students thought this Unsoeld was a strange character, so quiet, so interested in mountain climbing. He joined the football team and scored the winning touchdown against Shafter's great rival. Then he was a hero. In April, when he was still only seventeen, his mother signed the papers for him, and Bill enlisted in the Army's special reserve program for college-bound students.

ᴧᴧ

Bill put in his time in the Army studying electrical engineering at the University of Kentucky, then going to various Signal Corps Service schools. Wherever he had been stationed, he had managed to climb. In Kentucky, he had gone down in caves, though that dark, downward journey was not to his liking. Missouri almost stumped him, but he and his buddies found a big hole in the ground that they used as a practice cliff.

After the Army, Bill went climbing with his old army friends in the Tetons in the summer of 1946. Then he moved on to Oregon State University in Corvallis in the center of the Willamette Valley. Bill majored in physics and lived in a dormitory full of athletes. He was friendly, but didn't have the rah-rah Beaver spirit. As far as the other fellows in the dormitory were concerned, Bill was one of those quiet men who wanted to study.

On the weekends, up in the mountains Bill was transformed. Once a group of students went out hiking around Three Finger Jack in the Cascades. They made it up to the narrow saddle below the bulk of the mountain and were resting before heading back down. Suddenly they heard this incredible racket up above them, screaming, yodeling, yelling, a great cacophony of sounds unlike anything any of them had ever heard before in the wilderness. They looked up and saw climbers moving down Three Finger Jack like a race of crazed banshees. Leading them was a redheaded man rappelling crazily down the mountain on a rope, kicking his legs out in the air, letting out yet another war whoop, kicking his legs out again, sliding, slipping, jumping down the mountain. No one had to tell them that it was Bill Unsoeld.

Bill had grown to his full height of five feet ten inches and looked every bit the strong, young mountaineer. He loved taking novices up, being the guide and teacher. He didn't care if you were feeling sick. He didn't care how badly you were doing. He would get you up there. And he would show you a good time doing it. In the mountains Bill practiced getting along on very little. He ate oatmeal dry in the morning so it swelled up in the stomach, making him feel full all day. Climbing a mountain, he took a few dried prunes along, sucking on the pits to gain added nourishment.

Bill worked clearing tables in the cafeteria. If it was a night for pork chops, he scooped up all the uneaten meat off the plates and ate until he had stuffed himself. Then he took whatever pork chops were left, wrapped them in paper napkins, and carried them back to his room to make meals for another day.

Bill talked about his philosophy to his roommate, Bill Davidson. "I figure it this way," he said. "You can spend your life working like the devil to acquire all kinds of things, and not have any time to enjoy life."

"That's what most people do, I guess," his roommate said.

"Or you can settle for a lot less and have the time to do what you want to do," Bill went on excitedly. "I want to get everything I can out of life. I'm going to live simply."

On ski trips to Santiam Pass the students always stopped in a restaurant for breakfast. They ordered heaping stacks of pancakes soggy with syrup, mounds of scrambled eggs and buttered toast, big mugs of java and hot chocolate, to fuel a body for a long day on the mountain. Bill sat down like everyone else and ordered a glass of water. He took everything on the table—ketchup, syrup, salt, sugar, cream—mixed it all together and chugged it down. Then he went out and skied like the wild man of the mountains.

One day Bill received a letter from one of his old army climbing buddies, Herbert Rickert of Cleveland, Ohio. Rickert wanted Bill to get together whatever money he could, pack his climbing gear, and meet him in Zurich, Switzerland, in the summer. There they would whet their appetites on the Alps before taking on the Himalayas in India. In 1948 college students did not drop out to go traipsing around the world. The war had provided enough adventure and uncertainty. It was time to get on with life and work. Bill's mother was ambivalent about the trip. Bill's father, although he lived a few more years, was in no condition to give anyone advice.

On July 4, 1948, Bill stood on U.S. 66 outside Los Angeles with his friend John Barnes, holding a hand-lettered sign saying "Swiss Alps." Bill felt like a free man. All life lay ahead of him, the vast continental United States, the boat to Europe, the Swiss Alps, a Mecca that every true mountaineer wanted to climb at least once, and finally the Himalayas—those fantastic peaks that were not made of rock and ice but of his dreams. At the end of August, the two Northwest climbers linked up in Zurich with Rickert and his friend, Harold Jaeger.

Bill was used to wilderness climbing, trekking in through virgin forests. The Swiss, with their bourgeois fortitude, had set villages and towns at the very base of the great mountains. The three young climbers romped along past houses that looked like gigantic cuckoo clocks. They looked up to see peaks they could practically touch. Bill had a profound sense of climbing history. As he climbed the peaks—the Wetterhorn, the Jungfrau, the Matterhorn, and Monte Rosa—Bill knew that he was literally following in the steps of the masters.

Many of Bill's British mentors thought it unsporting to wear the strapped-on metal spikes called crampons. They considered it civilized and proper to climb only with Swiss guides. Even if Bill had had as much money as he had stories, he would never have hired someone to take him up. Half the joy and wonder of climbing was that you did it yourself with your friends; that way each climb was a virgin journey.

The old gentlemen climbers in their felt hats and natty wool clothes enjoyed nothing better up on the mountain than decanting some good wine and other delicacies carried skyward by their ruddy guides, then heading down to sleep at night in good warm Swiss beds. Bill and his friends, like so many climbers who followed them, had no money to squander on Swiss inns. They camped out. They made friends too. Bill met a Swiss girl and gave her the bulky wool sweater that a coed at Oregon State had knitted and sent him.

Tromping through the Alps Bill and his friends hefted sixty-pound packs containing all their belongings. When they weren't climbing the three men talked endlessly of their Asian venture. In Zurich, they went to the Swiss Foundation for Alpine Research where Herr Ernst Feuz helped them select a worthy peak. Though Everest remained the mountain of Bill's dreams, the climbers chose a more modest peak—Nilkanta, a 21,640-foot beauty in the Himalayan Garhwal. Bill had read all about this region in the accounts of the climbing of Nanda Devi. Nilkanta stood at the source of the sacred Ganges River, rising above the religious city of Badrinath. It was a worthy choice for a young man who sought the sacred in the earth's high places.

First there was a question of money. Bill had run out of his three-hundred-dollar grubstake. So had the others. Barnes decided to stay on in Switzerland to study the cello.

The one place where they were likely to find work and a ship to India in postwar Europe was Sweden. Northward they headed. In Göteborg, Sweden's largest seaport and second largest city, they got jobs in a foundry. It was immigrant's work, hard and dirty.

In their free time Bill and his friends haunted the offices of the ship companies seeking some kind of cheap passage to India. That did not appear a likely prospect.

The climbers had added an English climber to their party, Laurie French; at least, they could proudly proclaim themselves the Anglo-American Himalayan Expedition. Under that noble banner one day the climbers marched into the offices of yet another ship owner.

Bill had honed his rhetorical skills on a score of other magnates, clerks, and secretaries.

"Sir, it borders on an international disgrace that the Anglo-American Himalayan Expedition of 1949 is stranded in your fair city," Bill said.

The Swedish businessman decided that this thespian deserved a reward. He offered the expedition free first-class passage on the line's next freighter to India.

Bill, Rickert, and French (Jaeger stayed in Sweden) sailed eastward in civilized comfort. In Calcutta, they were plunged into the fervid life of the subcontinent: the rickshaw *wallahs* and the beggars, the pungent scent of sweets frying in *ghee* juxtaposed against the stench of offal; the clipped sounds of Indian English, the babble of Bengali; the exhausting, tedious business of transporting 240 pounds of baggage from the docks to a third-class train headed to Dehra Dun, a thousand miles to the northwest. At noon the furnace breath of the pre-monsoon already hung over the immense, fetid city. Calcutta was like a foundry.

This was an extraordinary time to be in the subcontinent. India had just gained independence from Britain. Hope and despair stood balanced. Freedom had been christened in the blood of over half a million Hindus and Muslims and in a war between India and Pakistan. Gandhi had been assassinated a year before. India throbbed with tensions and uncertainties. Bill was not interested in politics very much. He was journeying above all that.

From Dehra Dun, a temperate, civilized hill station, they traveled by bus past Rishikesh and the Alaknanda Ganga, a headwaters of the Ganges, to the town of Chamoli, where the road ended. On the fifty-mile walk up to Badrinath they were joined by Hindus journeying to the sacred shrines. The most devout prostrated themselves, measuring each step of the journey with their outstretched bodies. It was a strange humiliation these Hindu gods required, but no stranger than what the Hindus thought of these Western pilgrims, sahibs, rich men, walking to the sacred mountain without porters, carrying eighty-pound packs. "We were a constant source of curiosity to the pilgrim travelers as they were to us," Bill wrote, "but despite the language barrier it was seldom long before we had established contact through smiles and gesticulations.''

At Badrinath, the three climbers met a Hindu holy man, Swami Jnanananda. The Swami led them to the grotto that was his home and bid them stay. Bill had never had any real contact with Hinduism, the mother of religions. He was fascinated. Here was a religion without a Christ, a Buddha, a Mohammed, with gods within gods and meanings within meanings, existing outside time and beyond time. To the Hindu what mattered was the deed. According to the doctrine of Karma, by his own deeds a man was constantly determining his own future life. He would receive his reward in his next life on earth, as his present life was his reward for his last. He would be reincarnated again and again until he had worked his way up and out of the endless cycle of death and pain and suffering that was life.

Hinduism may not have seemed a religion to interest a son of the American West, full of life and its possibilities in this world. But if Hinduism was in some ways a religion of fatalism, justifying the world as it was, it also was a religion of action, guaranteeing reward for good conduct.

To the ascetic, the seeker, the mystic, to those who followed the lonely path of truth came great rewards. Casting off the gilded shackles of wealth and family, the seeker could win power that those still burdened with material things could never achieve. He could see tomorrow and yesterday. He could work miracles. Finally, he could solve the mystery within mysteries. He could stand beyond word and deed, birth and death, joy and sorrow. He was free beyond freedom. But it was a lonely route. In the words of the Hindu religious classic *The Bhagavad-Gita, The Song of God:*

> *Who cares to seek*
> *For that perfect freedom*
> *One man, perhaps,*
> *In many thousands.*
> *Then tell me how many*
> *of those who seek freedom*
> *Shall know the total*
> *Truth of my being?*
> *Perhaps only one.*

Swami Jnanananda talked to Bill about *The Bhagavad-Gita*. The holy man's mind sparkled with erudition. As a younger man he had lived in that world below. He knew English. Bill discovered that the Swami had "a true mountain man's appreciation of the grandeur of our natural surroundings." The Swami sensed a kinship with Bill and his friends as well. He helped them negotiate with porters and shopkeepers. "The secretary of the Hindu Temple was also of great service to us," Bill wrote, "donating our entire consignment of rice and dal (a total of 60 pounds) with the brief comment that he chose to consider us among the pilgrims whose welfare it was his duty to care for."

To the Swami the mountains were the abode of the gods. He traveled with the three westerners and their five porters up to the 14,000-foot Satopanth Glacier. There they set up what in climbing parlance is called Base Camp, the supply camp. The porters were supposed to carry their loads to the 16,500-foot western col, the saddlelike depression high on Nilkanta. But they did not have mountain boots and when they saw that massive slope of ice and snow, they turned back with the Swami.

For the next two days snow poured down upon the climbers. Then the weather cleared and the climbers moved readily up near the foot of the col. Down below, Bill and his friends had chugged down glass after glass of sweet milky Indian tea and devoured the sugary delicacies from the tea stalls while eating little protein. They had drunk all kinds of water, too. Now their stomachs had begun to act up. Dysentery had already weakened Rickert so badly that he simply could not go beyond 16,500 Camp I, named thus as the first camp above Base Camp.

French and Bill moved upward at dawn carrying 40-pound packs. Within an hour they had reached the bottom of the 1,000-foot slope up to the col. They forged a path along icy cliffs. That was difficult enough, but before long the slope grew ever steeper, the snow deeper and softer. There could be an avalanche at any moment. They hurried as best they could. The snow was up to their knees. Now it was above their hips, up to their chests. Only 300 feet more. They swam slowly through the snow like matrons doing breaststrokes in a heated pool. On top of the col, they set their packs down. It had taken eight and a half hours to move up the 1,000-foot slope. They needed a little rest. By the time they got up again four hours had passed. It was after six, too late to go back down.

Bill was never one to try to prepare for everything that might happen on a mountain; the gods of fate and destiny were not so easily assuaged. He and French had carried up their army surplus tent to pitch at their new camp, and five gallons of cooking gas. They had been planning to return to Camp I that same afternoon. They had no sleeping bags, mattresses, or stove. That night they lay freezing in their tent looking out on a full moon that washed Nilkanta in silver, the silence punctuated by the roar of distant avalanches.

In the morning the two climbers headed back down. They moved rapidly. The day before, a great avalanche had crossed this path only two hours after they had. At Camp I there was no danger of being swept away by a torrent of ice and snow, but Rickert was in such bad shape that he had left Nilkanta for good and "absconded with the only good food left." Three days later Bill and French tried one last time to push the route further up the mountain. They were beaten. They turned their backs on the unclimbed summit of Nilkanta and headed down.

When Bill looked back on his time on Nilkanta, what he remembered most was the night huddled high on the peak. The memory of cold had faded. For both Bill and French the night had become "one of the most beautiful of our existence."

The two young climbers were weak and half sick now. They had little money. They wandered down off the mountain not knowing how or when they would find their way home. As Bill told the story later, they were practically in rags, so dirty that even the villagers rejected them. They took some of their last rupees and bought a goat. The meat was so tough that one of them took a big piece, clamped his teeth into it, and gnawed away, trying to part the meat from the bone. When he had given up, he passed the meat to his partner who, setting his teeth into the bite marks, gnawed away some more.

Dr. Carl Taylor, a medical missionary, came upon the bedraggled, penniless climbers in the bazaar at Mussoorie. They were in what the doctor considered "the last stages of exhaustion." The missionary and his wife took the climbers in and gave them food and rest.

"The main thing about Bill at that young age was that he had this physical dynamism," Taylor said. "Once he had some food, he had this energy. When you were talking to him he was always going down duck walking around the room. He'd go over to this high doorway and jam his body up to the top. Most people would have thought that was strange but that was just the way he was. It didn't seem abnormal. The totality of him exuded this joy in life. It was the immediate thing that you felt.

"But when you got in discussions, especially when you'd be walking with him in the mountains, you'd see that he was looking for the deeper meaning in things. He was absolutely fascinated by the missionary orientation. But I remember it as a seeking. The dominant theme of the conversations was this wide-open seeking. He was trying to put it all in perspective. He was so far from having any clear dogma that I wouldn't say he had given up on anything."

Bill was not a great optimist about human beings and human life because he had had a childhood like Buddha's, shielded from ugliness, death, disease, and poverty. Nor had he gotten his beliefs from books or sermons. Bill's optimism was a great physical fury within him, a force that propelled him through problems, skepticism, and turmoil, a fury that his ideas only made more rational.

Whatever lay ahead, there were still more adventures to be had in India. Bill and French had almost no rupees left. Bill could conjure up money out of nothing. For three months they managed to travel through India, lecturing at schools and to embassy staffs. Along the route the two climbers sold their equipment item by item. They finally parted in Kashmir where French stayed on to teach chemistry at the Tyndale-Biscoe School.

Bill had only twenty rupees left when he arrived at the port of

Karachi in the new nation of Pakistan. He found work on a Swedish freighter as a deckhand, sailing along what he called the "underside of Asia." The ship steamed across the languid seas to the teeming, fetid ports of the Orient. For the sailors there were dark bars and dark whores, a man's carousing, but Bill had no interest in that.

Four months later the ship crossed the Pacific to the United States, sailing through a typhoon. Bill told his friend John Davidson that the freight had been so poorly secured in the hold that it started shifting, menacing the ship's stability. Only Bill had been willing to go into the hold, dancing among the moving crates, tying them down.

In the States Bill didn't boast about long nights in strange ports but only that he had kept his wages: $250 in all. He was back with almost as much money as when he had left a year and eight months before. He had had such amazing experiences, all for practically nothing.

This was the gods' little trick on the wealthy and privileged. Their money walled them off from the very experiences that they had the time and resources to seek. As far as an expedition went, there was less likelihood of reaching the summit on a ragamuffin affair like the Anglo-American Himalayan Expedition of 1949 but so what; they were closer to the rock and the snow, closer to the central core of the mountain experience.

When Bill left the States, he had been thinking of building his entire life in the mountains and of the mountains. The trip had convinced him that that was not enough. He was interested in theology and philosophy, putting some real substance on all he felt about life. He had an idea of perhaps becoming a missionary like Dr. Taylor. The doctor lived in the foothills of the Himalayas. In the name of God he did good work.

It had been a young man's odyssey. When Bill talked of reaching the top of the Matterhorn, that long night out on Nilkanta, the ports of Asia, the self-contained little Bill Unsoeld disappeared. He was a spellbinder. Each telling took him back, arms flapping, roaring with laughter in his rich tenor. He became his stories.

After recuperating, Bill and his buddy had gone trekking around the Himalayan foothills. From a windswept ridge Bill said that he saw this magnificent peak: Nanda Devi, the sacred goddess of the Garhwal. Looking up at this greatest of Indian mountains so far away, he decided that he would like to have a daughter and name her Nanda Devi, after this most beautiful of mountains. If he wanted a daughter then he better first have a wife. He had turned back from Nanda Devi determined to get married.

This was a story among stories. Each time he told about Nanda Devi, the story became more and more important to Bill and to his listeners. It became one of the tales by which Bill and his life were defined. In later years he suggested once that the story was "probably apocryphal." But usually he told the story as if it were the gospel truth. And as the gospel truth it was accepted.

Bill was like a tailor making a garment for himself, choosing the richest colors, cutting the cloth so that it covered any rudeness of form, seeing to it that it was nearly impossible to distinguish the threads that held the garment together. Then he would wear the garment for a while, making sure that this was a truth with which he felt comfortable. He didn't lie. The cloth was real, but it was cut to fit his pride and fancy.

Bill always managed to end up at his friends' houses around suppertime, paying for his meals with a slew of stories. As Kaarhus, Bill's high school and college friend, saw it, "Exaggeration was Bill's characteristic rhetorical ploy." Moffitt observed that Bill's stories and spirit cast a spell over people; almost despite himself he developed a retinue. Not many people glowed with life that way.

Bill had climbed great mountains, told great tales. What he needed now was a wife. He was, as he put it, "biologically ripe."

On one of the outings of the Mountain Club, Bill saw a woman in a man's G.I. issue mountain pants. He swore that he fell for her right then, as much for her pants as for her personality.

Girls simply didn't wear a man's pants at Oregon State University. Jolene Bishoprick was a thin, energetic young woman, as high-strung as a hummingbird. She had short brownish-blond hair, bright, darting eyes, and large white teeth. If she was not as pretty as the more favored sorority princesses, she pulsed with energy.

Jolene came from a prominent Northwest family that was in the lumber business. She had spent part of her childhood in China where her businessman father had prospered. She seemed destined for a proper marriage, to a businessman or a lawyer. But she was a bit of an outsider, both to her family and to the sorority world at OSU. She was an excellent student. She sometimes seemed plain, almost dour. But when she smiled, her protruding white teeth flashing, she glowed. She was a woman of enormous intensity. And she focused all that intensity on Bill.

Most of their courtship took place in the front seat of Bill's prewar Chevy coupe. It was a rattling, coughing excuse for a car, and Bill named it the Blue Jet. Whatever derision the Blue Jet drew, it got Bill and his friends up into the mountains. Bill never seemed to be able to afford antifreeze. At higher altitudes everyone but Bill worried whether the car would freeze up.

Bill had less and less time for his old friends. Kaarhus felt that Jolene's attitude had a lot to do with that. She had a strong, possessive love for Bill. She didn't seem to like him gallivanting off with his old buddies. Not only did Bill not have much time for his old friends, he had no time for serious climbing either. He didn't seem to care. He was so much in love that he even talked about giving up real climbing. When Bill and Jolene headed out with another couple to ski or climb, they often just sat around drinking hot chocolate, having a great time being together.

Bill had grown tired of physics. He was turning upward toward the worlds of religion and philosophy, thinking of studying theology. But Bill was not going to waste a fine spring day studying in the library. One afternoon he decided that he and his friends should rappel down Weatherford Hall. Some faculty members were not amused seeing students desecrating the building. Worse yet, the students were running an immediate risk of being killed. Bill could talk his way out of practically anything. He certainly could talk his way out of something as minor as this. His friend, Lee McFarland, was no so lucky. He was put on probation.

A couple of weeks later when Bill wanted to climb
of the Ag building, Lee knew that he was taking a double
they went. It was a romp up the building, but they were cau

"Lee and Bill, you promised me not to do that anymore,"
Darlington, the dean of men, told them sternly.

"Sarge," Bill said, "all we promised was we wouldn't go down
We didn't say anything about going up."

Young men often have a last wild, youthful romp before they
commit themselves to responsibility and routine—a bachelor party,
a drunken spree, or rappelling down a building. But Jolene appeared ready, eager even, to head out there into his life, a life of
adventure, idealism, purpose. In Bill, Jolene had found her special
man. She didn't want to waste either her life or Bill's. He was a
way for her to push off from all that was ordinary and banal around
her.

When Bill and Jolene announced their engagement, they did it
on top of Mount Saint Helens on a climb with the Mazama Club of
Portland. A picture of the happy couple was taken in May 1951
standing on the summit of the mountain. They wore old pants.
Jolene stood slightly behind Bill, as straight as the ice axe that she
held before her. Bill rested, slightly bowlegged, one arm around
Jolene's shoulder, the other holding a loose coil of rope. He looked
like a young Will Rogers.

It was a glorious day in a season of many glorious days. Later
that spring, at the age of nineteen, Jolene dropped out of college to
marry her mountain man.

\\

4

As the newlyweds drove across the flat sagebrush floor of the Jackson Valley, Bill saw the great panorama of the Tetons rising above. The Tetons were young mountains, abrupt, sharp pinnacles of rock that appeared to stand not only above nature but beyond it. An airplane had crashed up there the previous winter. Bill figured that he might be able to get a summer job packing out the bodies.

That hadn't panned out. Though he and Jolene had very little cash, Bill wasn't worried. He had learned in India and elsewhere that if you trusted in life things had a way of working out. He knew that something would turn up before the fall of 1951 when he began studying back east at Oberlin Theological Seminary. As for now he had everything he needed: the Teton range above, a tent pitched at the foot of the mountains on wooded, pristine Jenny Lake; and a climbing wife who shared his bed and rope.

Bill had married a woman who in many respects appeared his opposite. That took some getting used to. Jolene was the shrewd protector of the home. Bill was as undisciplined, disorganized, and spontaneous as a twenty-four-year-old Tom Sawyer. Jolene was disciplined, organized, and self-contained. Bill was funny as all get-out. Jolene had almost no sense of humor. Bill was a yea-sayer who had never met a man he didn't like; Jolene didn't trust people until she had good reason to trust them.

Although in the fall Bill was the one going on for a graduate degree, Jolene had a far more intellectual approach to life. She was a woman who saw and felt things in extremes of goodness and evil, of happiness and unhappiness, a woman of strong likes and dislikes. No one saw Bill standing quite so tall, noble, brave, and good as Jolene did; yet she could stand back and be harshly critical of her husband.

Free spirits like Bill were often pulled down shackled to a partner. "Most of us come to an accommodation with whatever forces are working on us," Bill told a group of climbers in Portland years later. "There, of course, is a developing career. There are usually family entanglements and this has an immediate and repressive effect on many people. For others it is the takeoff point. They may have just been lumping along and then they get married and suddenly they become tigers just escaping from the entanglements. So it can go either way."

It wasn't certain for a while which way Bill's marriage would go. Jolene loved Bill a great deal, and Bill loved Jolene, but he loved his mountains, too. He had thought he might give up mountain climbing for Jolene, but to give up the mountains was to give up life itself.

In the middle of the summer Bill was hired to become one of the four or five guides for the service run out of Jenny Lake by Paul Petzoldt and Glen Exum. Petzoldt and Exum figured they had hired a decent young fellow to do a decent job. They had gotten a living, breathing, three-ring-circus of a man who was better advertising than hiring someone to run through the streets of Jackson Hole with a bullhorn. Exum thought that there was a radiation coming from Bill that he had rarely seen, even on a preacher.

In the fall Bill and Jolene drove down into the Great Plains onto the flat, mundane landscape of northern Ohio. Bill was thinking about becoming a minister, a missionary maybe. He talked a lot about mysticism, Hinduism, Buddhism, and a Christianity that had direct and immediate meaning to each human being. He was searching for something here below that had the meaning that climbing mountains had for him above: the comradeship, the beauty, the intensity, the feeling, the energy.

On this greatest of his journeys, Bill had traveled to one of the noblest sources of American Protestantism. Sixty-four students entered the Oberlin Graduate School of Theology in 1951. Most of them had settled comfortably into their religious calling like country squires sliding into their pews on Sunday.

Americans generally were feeling satisfied with themselves and their country. Churchgoers wanted ministers who preached a satisfying sermon, then let them go home to their Sunday chicken, feeling spiritually well fed. In many Protestant churches, smoking cigarettes and drinking liquor were considered deadly sins; and rousing good times were themselves sometimes felt to be almost the work of the devil.

Bill fell in with the half dozen or so students critical of mainstream American Protestantism. They had many virtues, but these people also knew how to have a good time. For Bill, having fun, laughing, joking, talking was a kind of worship and fellowship. It was something that he hadn't found in many churches.

One evening the Unsoelds had some friends over for dinner. Everyone had a different kind of glass set out in front of his plate, from old peanut-butter jars to goblets.

"It would be nice to have glasses the same," Jolene said.

"What a waste!" Bill replied, and set off on a philosophical monologue about modest living that Thoreau could have given.

Bill was not seeking a dogma that he could proselytize in India or elsewhere, but a sacred religious experience. He appeared innocent and open. If he was afraid of seeming naive, he didn't let on. He approached each new idea as if he had been the first to discover it.

"What if you take Jesus and Jesus is fully human, not divine," Bill said excitedly, one evening.

"Yes, I understand," another student said, though the thought was virtual sacrilege at Oberlin.

"But Jesus would be more sensitive!" a third added.

"Or more prophetic!" someone else interjected.

"No," Bill said. "You're making Jesus superhuman. If you add more and more things like that the quantitative differences become a qualitative difference. That's divine again.

"Look at it this way. When you're rappelling the first time you're standing there on top and looking out and down and it's some kind of weird space out there. You're not certain you can get out in it. But when you do it, you find it's an ordinary world out there, ordinary space. Jesus lived in a space we all could live in. We can know what he knew. It would be natural. If we could just jump out into it."

Bill took away from the New Testament what he considered to be Christian ethics. To the world of his day "morality" meant first of all a person's sexual attitudes. Bill accepted the attitudes prevalent among most of the would-be ministers with whom he was studying: abstinence before marriage, fidelity within marriage.

Far more importantly, Christian ethics to Bill meant the idea of *agapeic* love. There were other kinds of love—the passionate, romantic *eros,* the brotherly and sisterly *philia*—but it was the all-encompassing love of *agape* that Bill considered the central core of Christianity. *Agape* was a love not only for friends but for enemies, a love for strangers as well as neighbors.

Bill was trying to live a life of love, to approach each act, each endeavor, each human interaction not with dogma or rules but with love. Paul, the disciple, said that Christ brought "faith which worketh by love" (Galatians 5:6). It was this love that Bill took on as his own, but he took it *without* the faith. He didn't accept Christ as his personal savior. For his faith Bill didn't look toward the hill called Calvary but high up in the mountains.

Bill was restless sitting in churches. He would rather be out with the Boy Scouts taking them into the Ohio wilderness or teaching them some knots, putting in that kind of service rather than dropping a few coins in the collection plate. Bill loved to teach his friends a little about climbing too, getting them to feel what he felt. He had them rappelling off the gymnasium until he found a marvelous sandstone quarry outside town.

While Bill was in class, Jolene worked in the dean's office. Early in the school year Jolene became pregnant. As Bill saw it, if you believed in life, life took care of you, and Bill was happy at the prospect of becoming a father. It did mean, however, that they would have to leave student housing. Vincent Hart, an Oberlin administrative employee, and his wife, Ruth, invited the Unsoelds to move in with them. When Jolene gave birth to a nine-pound three-ounce boy on May 30, 1952, Ruth Hart gave the baby its first bath.

As a name for his new son, Bill took the "O" off Oregon and called him Regon. The handmade birth announcements the Unsoelds sent out featured a drawing of a baby in diapers, a rope around his waist, a Tyrolean hat on his head, climbing boots on his feet, an ice axe held high, ready to go. The announcement read:

> Oh, 'twas on a lovely day in May
> When first I saw the light—
> Crawling forth just as would any little tyke;
> But, alas, my daddy met me with a 25-pound pack
> Saying, "Put it on—we're going for a hike!"

Bill was homesick for the mountains and the West. "We need a vertical dimension," Bill told friends. "Can't live only on the horizontal." That summer the Unsoelds headed west to spend the climbing season in the Tetons. Bill got right back into guiding.

That fall the three Unsoelds traveled to Berkeley where Bill continued work on a B.D. in theology at the Pacific School of Theology. To Dr. John D. Ottwell, his Old Testament professor, Bill was just another face in the classroom. On the day the students and faculty worked together cleaning up the campus, Ottwell could scarcely believe his eyes. Bill Unsoeld stood up on the roof clearing the gutters out, dancing along the edge like a tightrope artist.

Bill had some good professors and some good courses. But most of what he learned he considered intellectualized and dry. This deneutered, rationalized Christianity had none of the fire and fury of the Old Testament, none of the love of the New Testament. When Bill read of the wilderness in the Old Testament, however, he felt something real. This biblical wilderness was an inhospitable, isolated place, the opposite of the blessed Eden that man through his folly had lost. It was a place for pilgrimages, for prayer, for communion, a place to seek succor from God and to learn God's will. There were few seekers among the students and faculty at the Pacific School of Theology, few who would make journeys into the wilderness in search of meaning.

One book Bill read, Rudolph Otto's *The Idea of the Holy,* helped him understand what he found missing. Otto condemned this modern orthodox Christianity for failing to recognize the value of the nonrational element in religion and thus "gave to the idea of God a one-sidedly intellectualistic and rationalistic interpretation." Even language itself had been recruited into the service of this half religion. The word "holy" had come to mean merely the morally good when originally it suggested an ineffable, inexplicable quality.

At the center of this nonrational half of religion lay the *mysterium tremendum*. The *mysterium tremendum* was not to be described or understood in mere words and mere thoughts. It had to be felt. Otto wrote:

> The feeling of it may at times come sweeping like a gentle tide, pervading the mind with a tranquil mood of deepest worship. It may pass over into a more set and lasting attitude of the soul, continuing, as it were, thrillingly vibrant and resonant, until at last it dies away and the soul resumed its "profane," non-religious mood of everyday experience. It may burst in sudden eruption up from the depths of the soul with spasms and convulsions, or lead to the strangest excitements, to intoxicated frenzy, to transport, and to ecstasy. It has its wild and demonic forms and can sink to an almost grisly horror and shuddering. It has its crude, barbaric antecedents and early manifestations, and again it may be developed into something beautiful and pure and glorious. It may become the hushed, trembling, and speechless humility of the creature in the process of—whom or what? In the presence of that which is a *mystery* inexpressible and above all creatures.

This was what Bill had experienced in the mountains, a mere tremor of all of *this*. At its peak, it was powerful beyond power, wonderful beyond wonder, terrible beyond terror, awesome beyond awe. "In the face of the storm, the avalanche, or the power of the sea, the strongest human is keenly aware that he or she is simply no longer in charge of his destiny," Bill said later. "When one is acted upon with such towering finality, one is literally forced to say with Job that 'my mouth is stopped with dust and ashes' and 'I am as dust in Thy sight.' "

It was a fearsome experience, and it was absolutely fascinating. "In the midst of our primal fear and our agony at its alien tone, we drew near in fearful ecstasy," Bill said. "Which is why I feel that people climb mountains—and continue to do so long after they should have 'learned better.' "

Bill sought this experience with desperate hunger. He hadn't found it studying religion. Among philosophers Bill felt that he might discover what he had not found among theologians. He decided that in the fall of 1954 he would travel north to Seattle to take an advanced degree in philosophy at the University of Washington.

In the meantime Bill had been invited to become a member of the California Himalayan Expedition to Makalu in Nepal. Never before had he had such an opportunity: to climb one of the five highest mountains in the world. The expedition would be a formidable challenge at a time of great climbing opportunities in the Himalayas. Nepal, a hidden kingdom of adventure, had opened up to expeditions. The great 8,000-meter peaks had begun to be climbed. First 26,504-foot Annapurna in 1950 to the French; then 29,028-foot Everest to the British in 1953. America was still a climbing backwater. If the expedition reached the summit of the 27,790-foot Makalu, it would be the greatest international climb Americans had ever made. The climb would set a new standard, dramatically announcing the emergence of a strong new generation from the American West, a world away and above those gentlemen who still dominated mountaineering from places like Boston and New York. It would be a place for twenty-seven-year-old Bill to prove how good he was, to continue his spiritual quest on a plane higher than he had achieved before.

Bill would have his bachelor of divinity degree wrapped up in time for the February 1954 departure. The problem was that the Unsoelds' second baby was due in May when Bill was supposed to be high in the Himalayas. Bill was not about to let the tangles of domesticity ensnarl him. He left for Nepal, leaving behind a very pregnant Jolene.

Of the eight climbers and two scientists on the expedition, only Bill had previous experience in the Himalayas. He and two climbers left Calcutta to prepare the way for the others. Bill had traveled this sea of land before, the train moving slowly northward across the Indian plains, the engine's black smoke hanging in the hot dry air.

No land so intrigued Bill as did the tiny 500-mile-long, 100-mile-wide kingdom of Nepal, home of most of the world's highest mountains. The eastern Nepal that greeted Bill when he crossed the border at Biratnagar, however, was an extension of north India. Walking through the bazaar he saw scenes familiar from his trip to India a half decade before. Merchants sitting crosslegged in their shops, stroking their bellies, surrounded by bolts of cloth, pots and pans, matches, cigarettes and tiny cigar *bidis,* tins of spices and kerosene. Barefoot farmers in gray *dhotis,* wandering through the dusty streets, a few rupees clutched in their hands. Crippled beggars. Hindu priests. Schoolboys in blue shorts.

Not until he had traveled by truck thirty miles inland to Dharan with the other climbers did Bill catch his first glimpse of the verdant hills of Nepal rising behind town. No roads penetrated these hills. Man himself remained the main beast of burden. Bill met the 250 porters who would carry the expedition's goods northward to the base of Makalu. A hundred of the porters were from the hill villages, little men with coppery skins, walking on bare feet, their skin as thick as cartilage. These Nepalese were Hindus. They were the gentlest of peoples. Violent crime was rare in the hills. These tribesmen journeyed south to become Gurkha mercenaries, among the most feared and fearless soldiers in the world. In Dharan the shy, young recruits, mere boys, mingled for a moment with the veterans back on home leave. These proud British or Indian soldiers in stiff khaki shorts and brown sneakers marched into the hills trailed by their retinues—porters carrying the goods of Hong Kong and India, and usually a wife scurrying to keep up.

The other 150 porters were Sherpas and Sherpanis, men and women from the northeastern tier of Nepal. In the Tibetan language Sherpa meant southerner. The Sherpas were culturally Tibetan. It was a new idea to the Sherpas, as it was to most of the hill peoples, that they were all Nepalese, owing their identity not to caste or group but to nation.

Bill liked the porters from the hills well enough, but it was these Sherpas, a mountain people, whom he found special. They were taller than the hill Nepalese and far more gregarious. They might smell of smoke and rancid Tibetan tea, but Bill took to them as climbing brethren. Ten of these Sherpas were high-altitude climbing porters who would go high up on Makalu with the Americans. The year before, one of their number, Tenzing Norkay, had climbed to the summit of Mount Everest in full, equal partnership with Edmund Hillary, a New Zealander.

Now that Nepal was opening up to climbs, the same kind of romance and fame was developing about these climbing Sherpas and their sahibs as about the Gurkhas and their British officers. Back in 1949 when Bill had been called sahib, a term that literally meant master, by Indians full of deference, he had cringed. At first, Bill had found it vaguely embarrassing having his own Sherpa blow up his air mattress each evening and bring him tea in the morning. He had never had a servant in his life. After a while he decided that it was fine. There was a certain playful quality among the Sherpas, an egalitarianism, and Bill decided that he didn't mind being called sahib.

On their first days up in the hills, Bill had thought he might see Makalu, and above that Everest, his childhood dream. The farmers were burning off their fields, and a haze hung over the horizon. Bill moved through Dhankuta, a bazaar town controlled by the Newars, a shrewd, subtle people who combined business acumen with high cultural traditions. The Newars kept their houses so whitewashed that they stood there along the main street as if covered with snow. Here the Bara Haken, the local governor, greeted the Americans and gave them a formal permit to climb Makalu.

In the hills of Nepal generations went on like the seasons, blending almost imperceptibly one into the other. The trails grew narrower, snaking their way over and around undulating hills scalloped with terraces. Behind rose the Himalayan peaks, twice as high as the Tetons. Bill hadn't trained for the climb, immersing himself in a tedious routine of chin-ups, push-ups, and other exercises. The mountains did their own training. As the expedition moved northward, Bill surged with a sense of physical well-being.

Crossing the Arun River on the two hundred-foot-long bamboo suspension bridge, Bill and the others could have been spilled into the bubbling torrent below. From here the trail moved rapidly up to the snowline. In a swirling snowstorm they could not find their way. The one hundred hill porters, shivering in their bare feet and threadbare shirts, turned back, dumping their loads in a cache for the Sherpas and Sherpanis to carry north later.

After a day struggling in the snow the climbers found an opening into the Barun Valley, a funnel that would carry them on to Makalu. Here in the very shadow of the Himalayan peaks there was less snow. At a crook in the trail, for the first time Bill saw the great peak, the immense southwest face filling the horizon. He looked at Makalu with a pristine wonder and awe. He saw the mountain with a vision similar to Mallory's thirty-three years before, who seeing it the first time had said that "among all the mountains I have seen . . . Makalu is incomparable for its spectacular and rugged grandeur." Bill was as much an innocent in this expedition game as Mallory had been back in the early 1920s. He was moving toward a great mountain that was not only unclimbed but untouched.

On April 11 the climbers broke into two parties to probe a route onto the mountain. It soon became clear that the Southeast ridge offered the best prospects. Bill often said that it was the mountain that decided, not the men. Bill was clearly one of the two strongest climbers. A week later he and Allen Steck, a twenty-seven-year-old Berkeley sporting goods manager, began to climb Makalu in earnest.

The careers of many fine climbers are smothered by their inability to acclimatize at high altitudes. But Bill was sucking in enough air to maintain his vitality. Bill and Steck pushed on, developing a route that led directly to Camp II at 18,000 feet. Bill rested while other climbers established Camp III at roughly 21,500 feet. No longer was there any clear spot to pitch a tent: out of the ice and snow the men hacked a flat place. Trying to push the route up to

Camp IV, Bill and Richard Houston, a thirty-two-year-old high school teacher, reached about 23,000 feet, the highest point anyone attained until the very end of the expedition.

Time was running out. The monsoon would be sweeping down the mountain in a few days. If they were going to have a shot at the summit, it would have to be now—damn the weather. Once again it was Bill and Steck. May 19 dawned a clear, brilliant day. The two Americans and two Sherpas headed upward once again. The next day they made Camp III. The weather still held, one good day after another. They carried a load up to Camp IV, a small snow cave, not as high as the point Bill and Houston had already reached. Bill had a bout of dysentery, and he had to come down. It was about what had happened on Nilkanta. This time, though, it hardly mattered. The weather had turned foul. Nobody would be doing any climbing for a while.

By the end of May everyone had accepted the inevitable: they would not reach the summit, not this year. They still hoped to push the route up to a more respectable level. Bill was feeling better now. In a snowstorm, he and William Dunmire, a twenty-three-year-old zoology graduate student, moved back up to Camp IV. With them came two Sherpas carrying most of the equipment. The next day the four men worked hard putting up a rope ladder over a section of smooth rock. The effort so exhausted the two Sherpas that the following day Dunmire had to take them back down the mountain.

That same day twenty-five-year-old William Long, an Air Force survival instructor, moved up with three fit Sherpas. On the first of June, Bill, Long, and the Sherpas set out from Camp IV. Bill's stomach was aching badly. He couldn't get rid of the dysentery. It was snowing heavily. Long took the lead breaking trail in what Bill later called "a magnificent demonstration of endurance." They slogged upward past the point that Bill and Houston had reached so many days before. Finally, at something over 23,000 feet, they staggered to a stop. Here would be Camp V.

While the sahibs rested, the Sherpas set up the two tents and prepared dinner. The two Americans could hardly swallow. After a while, Bill pushed the instant potatoes and tuna aside. That night, helped by sleeping pills, Long slept. Bill, wracked with dysentery, tossed and turned.

In the morning, they made their final thrust up this mountain that had so thoroughly repulsed their attempt at its 27,790 foot summit. Bill swam through the waist-deep snow, resting a minute after each couple of steps. He had gone only two hundred feet when he looked down at Camp III, and thought he heard shouts wafting upward on the winds. "Come down! Come down! Come . . . ."

They had had it anyway. That night they slept at Camp V. The next morning Bill and Long began their final descent, not yet knowing that the radio below was reporting that the monsoon was moving immediately onto the mountain. Bill fought his way through a white whirlwind, stumbling in the loose, freshly fallen snow. Long fell and got up, only to fall again. As Bill fell he drove his ice axe into the snow. Pulling himself up, he felt his way forward, tumbling earthward again. Again and again the two men fell. To steady themselves they hammered pitons into the rocks as anchors, moving even more slowly down Makalu, through the driven snow like blind men feeling with canes. Finally, out of the whiteness appeared the tents at Camp IV.

High on the mountain Bill picked his way through the gray rocks. He looked out and saw Everest standing far above him. He stopped and looked down at his feet. There, growing out of the broken, lifeless rock was a tiny flower. Suddenly, everything fit. Life in the midst of death. Peace in the midst of chaos. Joy in the midst of pain. Finally, life made sense. Everything. The transcendent unity of the universe. He did not see it or feel it or think it. He was *it*. He was the universe. He stood looking at a tiny wisp of a flower, a tiny wisp of life that was everything and nothing. And he laughed. He laughed. He was filled with a joy and ecstasy that he had never known.

Bill headed down the mountain. He had reached the real summit. He had seen what he was meant to see, what he had sought all his life to see. He cherished the moment, not unfolding it to every person, every audience like some snapshot of a memory, but holding it close, cherishing it, turning it over and over again, gaining strength and knowledge. He had had a mystical vision. He had had it not wandering in the desert, or standing in some great cathedral, but up in the mountains, up where he belonged, up at the source of all his life and strength.

On Makalu Bill had touched eternity and found it beckoning. But he was drawn back to earth. Waiting there for him in America was his daughter, Nanda Devi, whom he had dreamed of for so long. Devi was a boisterous, beautiful baby. Nanda Devi was indeed like her name, Bill's bliss-giving goddess. Holding her he touched the finite and found it good.

Part Two

∧∧

5

He was Willi now. Willi was the name his climbing friends at Oregon State had given him. Now he was as flamboyant and out-going below as above, and almost everyone called him by his mountain name.

Willi had been refused a teaching assistantship at the University of Washington because he had no formal background in philosophy. Then he arrived in Seattle, stomping around campus in his old jeans and Pendleton shirts, telling climbing stories. After Willi spoke to the philosophy club about climbing, the department chairman said that Willi could have his assistantship; he might not know formal philosophy but at least the students wouldn't be bored.

As a graduate assistant, Willi lectured about classical western philosophy to undergraduates who thought they didn't care about such things. When Willi stood in class, arms waving while he talked about how the sheer presence of Socrates inspired people, one student, Kirk Smith, thought that Willi was like Socrates.

When Willi told the students about Plato's famous allegory of the cave in the seventh book of *The Republic,* not only could they understand the ideas, they could feel them. For two thousand years most philosophers had sought to make the journey upward out of Plato's dark cave in search of truth, goodness, and wisdom. In the twentieth century, though, truth did not seem to live in sunshine anymore but in shadow. In their own pursuits of truth most of the modern philosophers Willi dealt with in class and in his studies did not try to move upward to a world of pure light and beauty. Instead, they plunged even further down into the depths of the cave. Willi, for his part, didn't have the slightest interest in heading further down into this modern darkness in pursuit of truth.

No matter how much theology he learned, how many philosophy books he read, Willi still found his most profound faith, his deepest ideas in the mountains. Each June the Unsoelds packed up and headed out once again for a season guiding in the Tetons.

The guides Willi worked with in the 1950s were graduate students, scholars, teachers, and scientists to whom climbing was a glorious summer avocation. It didn't cost anything to pitch a tent in the pines behind the guides' shack. But food was expensive, and it certainly wasn't for the wages that the men returned year after year. It was a great life.

Willi would not have been happy guiding all year round, but he planned his life around the summers in the Tetons. His four children were born every other May, in time to go to the Tetons (except in Devi's case): first Regon, 1952; Nanda Devi, 1954; Krag, a son, in 1956; and finally, Terres, a daughter, in 1958. To some of the more conservative residents of Jackson Hole the idea of Willi and his wife living in a tent with a slew of babies was appalling. Willi was sure that it was good for his children; when he wasn't guiding he popped the littlest one into his pack and headed up into the mountains.

The other guides were drawn to Willi and Jolene. Most nights a group sat at a campfire in front of the Unsoelds' tent. As the flames died away, people moved closer and closer, not leaving until the last embers died away. "Back in my army days I went down into this cave in Kentucky," Willi said, his eyes glowing like coals. "We had these candles and when we got back in this narrow cavern we blew 'em out.

"It was the essence of blackness," Willi dramatized, pressing down on each syllable. "The essence of blackness."

The guides were very alive to ideas. Many evenings there were long, intense discussions.

"People just shouldn't be up in the mountains if they don't have the proper equipment," one guide asserted. "It's as simple as that."

"Every last one of us has a right to go up there any way he wants," Willi said pointedly.

"That's fine, Willi," another guide chimed in. "But we're the ones that have to go up and bring 'em down when they get in trouble—risking our necks."

"People have a right to go up there and kill themselves, or get themselves where either they work their way out or they die," Willi argued passionately. "Nobody, not us, not the Rangers, nobody has a right to stop 'em. That's what freedom's all about. You can't have it part way. For a man to know what he is, to find out, he's got to be free, absolutely free. And he's got to know it."

The other guides enjoyed taking people up the mountains to have a good time and learn better techniques. Willi led people up into the Tetons to experience life at what he considered its highest, its most profound. What Richard (Dick) Emerson, a climbing Ranger, noted about his friend was that Willi took dependent people, indeed he needed dependent people. In interpreting the mountain experience for his clients, he taught them to be independent. On a gray, menacing day when other guides were dubious about heading out, Willi was raring to go. He loved getting his charges into dangerous predicaments, then getting them out again, leading them back down the mountain with an experience they would never forget.

Emerson was a student, later professor of sociology, a gentle, introspective sort. To Dick a climb was in part an intellectual exercise, a puzzle. He enjoyed figuring out how to do a climb and then doing it. Richard (Dick) Pownall, a guide and junior and senior high school teacher, had an esthetic approach; he moved up a mountain as if it were a ballet, climbing with enormous grace. Willi's climbing was like a down-home hoedown, a sweaty, jumping, exuberant, all-join-in kind of dance, with Willi standing there slapping his knees, calling out the steps.

Paul Petzoldt, Willi's boss, was scared of his popular guide. He considered Willi "a great guy but with less judgment than any climber . . . [he] ever met." Yet Willi was so alert that he always got away with it. The story was told of the time that up at the summit during one guided climb his clients were walking blithely along unroped. Willi was up in front, laughing, talking, whistling with all his might. Suddenly, inexplicably one of the clients began to slip. Willi turned, jumped through the air, and caught the man by his heels.

In the morning his clients usually found Willi sitting on the bridge over Cottonwood Creek playing the *Colonel Bogey March* on his harmonica. He looked as if the slightest nudge would send him toppling over into the stream. But he never fell off. Before long the last of his charges came straggling in. Off they went following this Pied Piper with his harmonica.

"No matter how commonplace the climb may seem to the guide, it is always a test of his constant attention, skill, and ingenuity to make sure that the various party members enjoy it," Willi wrote in 1960, as his guiding summers in the Tetons drew to a close. ". . . To watch the reaction of the cocky young prepper who suddenly realizes that in order to cope successfully with some situations mere breeding, brass, and bank account are not always sufficient. Or to watch the slow dawning of appreciation in the eyes and actions of anyone who is making his first acquaintance with the mountains—an appreciation of the sublime intricacy of the minute structure of a great peak, of the overwhelming fascination which lies in the growing ability of the human form to successfully adapt itself to that structure, and finally an appreciation of the deep affinity possible between the mood of the mountain itself and that of the human soul!"

From Cottonwood Creek the route up the 13,766-foot Grand Teton, the highest and most frequently climbed peak in the range, led through the Lupine Meadows, up a series of long switchbacks.

At about 8,400 feet when many novices had begun to wish they had never left the comforts of Jenny Lake, the trail leveled off, the left fork moving into Garnet Canyon. By now Willi had a fair idea of his clients' abilities. A wobbly rock in the middle of a little stream was one of his gauges. If a client danced across there easily, it didn't matter whether he had never been outside Manhattan, he would probably be okay. But if a fellow teetered on the rock before jumping across, or worse yet, stumbled and got his feet wet, Willi knew he would have to watch out.

As Willi and his charges moved upwards they picked their way around a group of immense boulders. The air grew colder, sweaty bodies growing chill. Out came ponchos and down jackets. They moved along the glacier moraine, a long tongue of ice licking its way down the valley. Using the hundred-foot fixed rope that the guides had put in there, the group climbed up across wet rock to an icy path to the lower saddle. Here in this barren concave, between the Middle and Grand Tetons, the wind the only constant, they made their way to the eight-man tent, throwing themselves down while Willi got the two-burner Coleman stove going.

In five hours or so, Willi and his clients had traveled upward a good 5,000 feet to the 11,644-foot base of the high mountain, from the pristine meadows to the harsh alpine world. Among the major American mountains, the Tetons are unique in their accessibility and in the immediate, dramatic contrast between the worlds below and above. For Willi that was part of the mystical magic of the mountains. He celebrated that contrast. For the novice climber, his teeth chattering, his head throbbing from the altitude as he imbibed the cup of tea Willi thrust at him, this exuberant man bouncing around the tent seemed to be of some other race, a species whose natural habitat was this austere world.

Each client was supposed to bring some soup. Willi dumped the contents into a big pot, the Campbell's tomato melding with chicken gumbo, a Knorr's dried onion, and then, God forbid, some black bean or oxtail. As his charges sat back, their eyes still half glazed, he mumbled some strange incantation over the motley brew, stirring it like the witches of *Macbeth*. Then finally he pulled the cover off, took a deep whiff of the aroma, sighing with ecstasy as if he had struck upon some culinary sensation, and doled it out.

"With supper out of the way (either internally or otherwise), the next job is to secure the party for the night [Willi wrote in the

American Alpine Journal] . . . the employment of a large eight-man tent (known to have accommodated 15 upon occasions) . . . provides a snug shelter for the collection of sleeping bags maintained by the guide service. The last duty of the guide before turning in himself, then, is to crawl along the row of mummified forms, funneling a dipper of water into each parched opening. Now, with the pot scrubbed, the soup cans rinsed out, and with a pot of water on the stove ready for a cocoa breakfast, he is ready to avail himself of some well-earned sack time—barring the occurrence of some midnight emergency. One memorable night I was jerked back rudely from the edge of sleep by a gurgling cry from a client who had succeeded in tucking his wad of White Star chewing tobacco into one cheek long enough to whisper, 'Guide, oh guide!! Where do I spit?' Ah well—and some people sneer at the climber's hat as being merely decorative.''

At 3:00 A.M. or so, Willi was up and raring to go. When the last of his five or six clients had poked his wary head out of a down cocoon, the cocoa would be brewing away, steaming hot. Groups of people were the clay Willi worked with. By the time the group was moving up through the rock-strewn passage, Willi usually had them pretty well molded into a working unit. If they seemed weak, he carried all the sandwiches and extra gear in his pack as well as all their cameras strung around his neck like a bead necklace.

The guides almost always took the Exum route up the Grand. It was not a difficult route for an experienced climber. There were, however, several places where the climbers were highly "exposed," and a fall would be a serious business indeed. And there were enough interesting pitches to provide a decent challenge.

As a cold dawn seemed to be seeping up out of the rocks, the group moved along "Wall Street," a ledge that ran the whole length of the west face of the Exum Ridge. They stopped to rope up. The novices felt a surge of security as this mountain man passed from client to client checking the knots with his nimble fingers. The new climbers also were suddenly aware of the seriousness of their adventure.

Willi made this roping up a sacrament. Men and women climbed together, their fates linked to one another by a bond of rope. He believed that here on these windswept peaks they discovered each other, and in discovering each other, they discovered themselves. They worked as a team or they worked not at all.

There was a profound simplicity to this kind of guided climbing. The guide went first, moving up the mountain one "pitch," the length of uncoiled rope between him and the second climber. As he moved upward the second climber "belayed" him, supporting the rope against the rock, a piton, or his own body. Thus if the first climber fell downward, he dropped the distance that he had climbed upward plus the length of rope between the two climbers before his body jerked taut.

Willi could not depend on these belays set by a novice. As much as he sang of cooperation and group spirit, he was alone leading a group. He climbed by an axiom that could have been chiseled into the very rock: The Guide Does Not Fall. When Willi had finished the "pitch," braced himself, and called out "belay on," the second climber moved upward. If the second climber fell, he dropped merely the length of rope between his waist and the guide's belay point up above. He knew, moreover, that it was Willi holding onto him.

At the end of "Wall Street" came a break approximately five feet wide. Willi went flying into space. Then he set up his belay point around the corner. To a young woman petrified at having to jump across *space,* hardly daring to look up, or God forbid down, he tickled her out of her fears with sweet, gentle encouragement. If need be, he sent neat little barbs into the flanks of a smart-alecky young client, pricking him into a new sensitivity.

Willi was full of constant, bantering good cheer. Soon his clients had put that pitch behind them. Then came a series of chimneys, vertical indentations in the rock, nature's idea of a ladder. This didn't take bravado, but a fairly decent pair of arms and legs. Willi often had some cheerleading to do here before the party could move on. Then came the most difficult pitch of all: the Friction Pitch. Willi acted as if it was about as hairy as going out on the front porch to get the afternoon paper. He moved up on this smooth knobby rock that was like a giant's bald pate. His rubber-soled shoes grasped onto the rock. He moved easily up the convex surface.

To Willi rocks were almost alive, each full of its own character and idiosyncrasies. At the top of the pitch came a yodel, and possibly a serenade from a harmonica. If the summit still seemed too high, too distant, he shrunk it with his words until his clients could reach out and almost touch it. No matter how menacing the weather, how dark the clouds, how wet the rocks, Willi had seen it worse, ten times worse. This was nothing.

The clients still had a lot of scrambling to do, moving up and over the rocks, and there were some more long pitches with belays. Sometimes up there the weather got so foul that just short of the crest they had to traverse over and go back down by the old Owen-Spalding route. Most of the time, though, suddenly there they were on top of the Grand, the daddy of them all, looking out on half the world.

The route down the Grand was a long, unroped hike. It had a spectacular beginning that provided Willi with a fitting end to his day's derring-do, a 120-foot-long rappel, from almost the summit all the way down to the upper saddle. Willi loved to rappel and this was a beauty, the last 60 feet hanging free out in space, Willi moving down looking like a fireman on a brass pole.

Successfully reaching the summit of the Grand was adventure enough for some clients. The idea of heading out over that cliff, regulating the friction on the rope by one's arms, then suddenly finding one's feet crawling in space, took some getting used to. On one climb a boy had stood for fifteen minutes unable to move. It was a frigid day and the other climbers were half frozen.

"Willi, what do we do?" asked the second guide.

Willi took his ice axe, set the point nearly against the boy's breastbone, and said: "Why, run him through!"

When the last client had rappelled it was Willi's turn. He came roaring down, riding an imaginary bicycle, his legs pumping. It was a wonderful thing to behold, not only funny but a moment of pure and absolute exuberance.

Most of the other guides made sure that they were down on the far side of Jenny Lake by 6:00 P.M. so they could catch the last trip that Mann McCann and his boat made across that blue jem of a lake. But, as often as not, Willi and his clients came charging down in the gloom. Then good old Mann, a slim, grizzled Westerner with a voice as deep as a cavern, went back to get Willi and his charges. The guides didn't have to pay, but Willi shelled out his stories, carried on a sheer rush of energy. "You know, Mann, if I couldn't live in a tent for the summer and had to live in a house, I wouldn't even come out here," he said as the last rays of sunshine moved down below the panorama of the Tetons.

Willi couldn't understand why Mann wouldn't go on a climb just once. But Mann was like almost all the locals. As near to the mountains as he wanted to get was shuttling climbers and tourists back and forth across the lake.

The locals could understand the dude ranchers and the summer vacationers and what they were after. They could even understand old climbers like Paul Petzoldt who back in 1924 had made one of the earliest ascents of the Grand Teton wearing cowboy boots and a cowboy shirt. While still in college in 1931 Glenn Exum had climbed the Grand by a new route that bears his name. Back then people paid no attention to Petzoldt and Exum and a few others considered crazy enough to climb.

What the locals couldn't understand were the younger climbers. In the 1950s greater and greater numbers of climbers were journeying out to the Tetons. Many of these new climbers were an athletic counterpart to the Beat Generation. Down at Yosemite in California, these introverts, misfits, self-conscious ne'er-do-wells found what peace they had climbing. Without tents, down jackets, money or that other accouterment of the modern sporting life, the possibility of fame, they hung out in the mountains to climb the Big Walls.

It wasn't quite the same in the Tetons, but they were not a debonair lot. On the far side of Jenny Lake stood the climbers' camp. It was a motley array of tents, cook stoves, gear, and equally scruffy human beings. The Park Service itself thought the camp a terrible eyesore. The local people considered it tenfold worse than that.

It was experience these young climbers were seeking, experience, adventure, and risk. Their forebears had gotten enough experience milking cows on a winter's morn with frostbitten hands; standing in front of a spinning machine in a New England factory; plowing yet another acre of thick prairie sod. To such nineteenth-century Americans, experience was avoiding the mountains, not climbing them; getting through the desert, not journeying into it with breathless anticipation; cutting down the forests, not camping in them.

Some of the young climbers had ancestors who had pioneered the West. Then the best education was still obtained in the one school that always had open enrollment: the school of experience. Now education was often no wider than the pages of a book, no higher than a lecturer's lectern. In the atmosphere of sobriety and tranquility and caution that characterized the Eisenhower years, these young Americans felt boxed in. What they considered real life was not found in the schools, nor in the bureaucratic institutions where careers were made. If life was anywhere it was out here. These young men (and a few young women) headed up into the mountains, self-consciously creating risks and dangers.

Such climbers were the pioneers of experience, the beginning of a great rush to the mountains and the wilderness in search of the gold of challenge. Eventually they came carrying packs and freeze-dried food, toting kayaks and primus stoves. Most of them were happy to settle for a nugget or two of challenge. But these western climbers were the aristocrats of challenge. They cared little for appearances, pretense, or background. They hungered for the peaks.

In his own wildness, in his own deep visceral need for new experiences, Willi was one of their progenitors.

6

Willi always wanted to be out there in life, whether it was climbing in the Tetons or talking to students about philosophy. What he couldn't stand was sitting in graduate student housing, in one of those drab Quonset huts left over from the war, writing his Ph.D. thesis. As his subject he chose Henri Bergson, the French thinker who helped lead modern philosophy away from nineteenth-century determinism and positivism. Bergson was considered one of the precursors of twentieth-century existentialism. In 1950s America, his idealistic Christian-oriented philosophy was largely ignored.

When Willi first read Bergson, what he remembered were the metaphors the philosopher employed to try to describe his famous concept of the *élan vital* or vital impetus, the creative life force struggling upward against the material world. The *élan vital* was like a rocket blasting through the dead, fallen ashes. It was like a jet of steam bursting upward. It was like an invisible hand moving through iron filings, changing their pattern.

Willi was close to being the personification of Bergson's ideas. He felt this *élan vital* within himself. He set out to write a thesis elucidating his ideas: *Mysticism, Morality, and Freedom: The Idea of the Vital Impetus in Bergson's Theory of Ethics.* Mysticism, morality, freedom, and ethics were concepts profoundly important to Willi. But he wrote his 261-page thesis with all the deadly calculation of a graduate student, one eye on the thesis committee, the other on family bills.

Willi knew that Bergson's ideas couldn't be captured in mere words, a point that Bergson made himself. Willi didn't even try. He shuttled quotes from Bergson in and out of the pages like a switchman in a freight yard making up a train.

In places, though, Willi had his own bursts of illumination. Bergson saw an eternal evolutionary battle of life with matter. Willi called this the "cosmic struggle for freedom." In this struggle, intelligence, as Bergson defines it, is no help. Intelligence is always facing down toward those ashes of matter that the upward rocketing force of life leaves behind. Willi had read scores of philosophy books. For centuries philosophers had sought to understand life by mere intelligence; the more fiercely they attacked life with their pure intellects the further life moved away from them. As Willi writes, "Fairly bursting with articulateness, and (as the whole history of philosophy shows) just spoiling for a chance to untangle life's riddle, intelligence . . . is unfortunately ignorant of the critical answers."

Left to human intelligence alone man would never move upward risking the expanding, creative life that is the great glory of the human species. On the edge of intelligence, though, "there lingers a fringe of intuition, vague and effervescent," that is man's saving spark. This "intuition" rescues humanity from the earthbound realm of determinism and gives man the freedom to create. It is not intuition as the word is usually employed. It is not really instinct. It is not merely feelings or emotion. Yet it is something of each one of these concepts and more.

Willi believed with Bergson that intelligence had taken human-kind about as far as it could. This "intuition" was needed now. But how to teach that when, as Willi writes, "the only way to succeed in totally communicating an intuited concept to someone else is by successfully engendering the intuition in him, i.e., in helping him to have the intuition."

More importantly, how to live that? According to Bergson most people accepted a static religion that was no better than fairy tales. The philosopher believed there is also a dynamic religion, a religion of heroic mystical individuals. Willi writes: "The work of the moral creator is aimed at so influencing the wills of his followers through the inspiration of his own life and personality that they will be motivated to burst the bonds of physical necessity in which the species is held and to re-enter the on-going flow of life through the generation of the greatest possible amount of creative effort. . . ."

Life, then, is created by extraordinary men and women. Bergson's moral mystical heroes move higher than mere mountains, carrying humankind to heights beyond that of matter. Through their "intuition" they hear and feel things to which the masses of humanity are deaf and dumb. Then, amplifying what they have heard and felt, they invite the rest of humanity in, by so doing creating a richer, more complex life.

What sets Bergson's moral heroes so far apart is their love. It is a radical love for all humanity. The power of the moral pioneers, Willi writes, "stems from his contact with the vital impetus which pours itself into him as a veritable torrent of creative love. . . . The moral genius is able to pour out in action the dramatic products of that current of love by which the universe is created and explained. Through such demonstrations of the power of the human spirit to transcend the limitations imposed upon it by the demands of material nature, ever-broadening bands of imitators are inspired to follow the examples set by the gifted few." Christian mysticism is the highest form, for in it, Bergson believes, love and action are wedded. The true or highest mystic, then, does not sit alone in his mountain lair. He returns to humanity with his vision and humanity awaits him.

Bergson's ideas struck to the core of Willi's soul. He believed in the pure force of *agapeic* love. He had the French philosopher's "intuition." He was a true son of the American West, and he liked the idea of an individualistic moral hero leading humanity. Willi, himself, had gone up on Makalu and had a mystical vision.

Bergson believed that there are two ways to teach morality. By rigorous, intellectual discipline people can be taught "impersonal habits." By the higher mystical route the teacher's life itself becomes the moral lesson. This way people can "obtain the imitation of a person, and even a spiritual union, a more or less complete identification."

It was along this higher pathway that Willi was headed.

In the fall of 1958 Willi began teaching in the Department of Religion and Philosophy at Oregon State University, his old alma mater. He was Professor Unsoeld now, but he wasn't going to turn into one of those tweedy types when life was not in some book-lined study but out there in the mountains and wilderness. On campus he often could have passed for an athlete who had wandered over from the Phys. Ed. department or some fellow studying forestry.

In his classes the students looked up to this man who had seen the world, read the great books, wrestled with ideas as if they were living, breathing things. All bright-eyed and expansive, they asked, "How do I live a good life, Willi?"

Willi felt that the students were waiting for him to tell them the answers as if he had just come down from Mount Sinai. Willi knew that he had to shake them up. He threw the Bible at them, bruising their emotions, and tied them up in arguments so tightly that they didn't know where they stood. He stripped their beliefs away, until they stood there naked and shivering.

Teaching his course on the Sermon on the Mount, Willi stood in front of his class reading dramatically: "Therefore whosoever heareth these sayings of Mine and doeth them, I will like him unto a wise man, which built his house upon a rock." It was like being Jesus Himself. It was a heady business. He might have made a life of it, too, mellowing into the beloved Professor Unsoeld. But Willi decided there was something fraudulent about being this professor of virtue, lecturing year after year. At Oregon State, philosophy and religion were studied and experienced the same way as dental hygiene. There was something wrong, unauthentic about such an education. He developed what he called "a growing horror of the accumulation of facts for facts' sake. So much of what I found myself dispensing in my classes seemed aimed at having not even a passing effect on the student's personal economy. Temptation seems to be to confine the fragment of make-believe which constitutes the classroom situation with that living reality that is the world outside."

Dr. Warren Hovland, the department chairman, noted Willi's "tremendous enthusiasm for life, his great sense of the wonders of nature, together with the desire to communicate the thrill of mountain climbing and the fascination and grandeur of the climbing experience. His real life was this avocation." Willi's real life was, indeed, the mountains and all he found there. Down from the mountains Willi carried stories and lessons that he worked into his lectures. But that was not enough. Willi believed that it was not enough for his students, whose education was only half-education. And it surely was not enough for Willi.

Willi wanted his children to grow beyond the lives led by most of these Oregon State students. He wanted his children to choose their own lives, to dare, to experiment, to be free.

At home he was the same flamboyant, exuberant Willi, as much the star of the drama as he was in the classroom. He loved his children. He showed that love, hugging them, holding them to him. He loved Regon, the firstborn, who was such an outgoing child, running up to strangers and talking. He loved Krag and tiny Terres too.

But Devi was the blessed one. How often Willi told the story of seeing Nanda Devi and deciding to get married so that he could have a daughter to name after the mountain. In telling the tale it was as if he would have willed his daughter into existence without the bother of a wife and family. Though Devi was close to her mother, the relationship between Willi and Devi transcended the mundane categories of affection and love. Little Devi was good. She was a sweet blond child. When she wasn't laughing her lips were often pursed in an expression of curiosity and anticipation. She was Willi's child.

Willi loved Jolene too. They had an intense, demanding relationship. Jolene had graduated into motherhood before she had a chance to finish her undergraduate work. She poured all her fierce energy into being a good wife and mother. Whenever Willi and Jolene fought, they had only one rule. No matter the hour, they did not go to sleep until they had settled things. They had some late nights lying in bed next to each other. But they had a home now, a settled life, and some real stability.

They still went back each summer to the Tetons to receive more sustenance from the mountains. However, Willi was getting older. By the summer of 1959 he was already thirty-two, with four kids and an assistant professorship. Some of his old guiding friends were starting to do different things in the summer. Willi sensed that he was nearing the end of one trail. Willi told old Mann McCann that he wanted to give him some beer for all the times Mann had taken him across Jenny Lake. Mann thought Willi would give him a couple of six-packs, or maybe even a case. But when Mann got back to his house there near the boat dock, he found six cases sitting one on top of another on the kitchen table.

If there was one thing Willi wanted to do that summer it was to get Mann up for a climb. "I tell you, Mann," Willi said, surging with enthusiasm, "when you make the summit I'll set off a rocket."

Against his better judgment, Mann decided that he would go up in the mountains one time. On the third of September, the last guided climb of the season of what turned out to be Willi's last season as a guide, Mann, Willi, and four clients trudged up Garnet Canyon. Before dawn Willi got them up and moving. It was getting on to fall and the weather was rotten. Willi decided to take them up the old Owen-Spalding route. It wasn't half the fun of the Exum route but Willi took every variation, every side trip, and gave them the climb of their lives. When they reached the top and were sitting resting in that windswept sanctuary of rock, Willi took out a rocket from his pack and set if off. When they came down Willi signed a certificate for Mann saying that he had made it to the top of the Grand. Looking at the certificate, Mann knew that climbing was just as foolish as he thought it was; this was the only one of these things he'd ever get.

When Willi received an invitation to join the 1960 expedition to climb 25,660-foot Masherbrum in Pakistan's Karakoram range, he was a married man with four children, a heavy load of educational debts, a brand new Ph.D., and a promise to his wife that he would go on "no more major expeditions until she could go too."

At first Willi turned the invitation down. Willi credited Nick Clinch, director of the expedition, with getting him and the other climbers out of the loving clutches of their wives. "With infinite insight and delicacy, Nick finally managed to work himself around that perennial Himalayan problem—the Reluctant Wife," Willi wrote. "His use of enthusiastic propaganda, statistical safety demonstrations, and a downright deafness to repeated refusals finally won over an astonishing percentage of those married climbers whom he solicited as members."

Willi and his buddies could make the most wonderful heartfelt promises to their wives. There was no getting around the fact that they were going off to risk their lives on a grand adventure while their families stayed behind to wait and worry. To Willi, though, a climb was not just a climb, but a philosophical and moral quest. When he headed out it was as if he were doing this not only for himself but for Jolene, Regon, Devi, Krag, and Terres, for all humanity. It didn't matter that he had one son, Regon, who had broken a leg in January, a wife who had once again accommodated herself to her husband and his climbing, and faculty colleagues who had doubled their course loads. They were all glad for Willi, even Devi, who soon after her dad departed broke her arm shimmying across the parallel bars at school.

Setting off to climb Masherbrum, "Queen of the Peaks," Willi was as exuberant as a kid running out of school at the beginning of summer vacation. He loved being with groups and no group was like a bunch of mountaineers. Clinch had brought together some of the best climbers in America.

Willi was happy having Dick Emerson, his old Tetons buddy, on the trip. Dick McGowan was a quiet team player; he ran the Mount Rainier Guides' Concession. Willi had taught with McGowan at the University of Washington. George Bell, a scientist at Los Alamos, had already proven himself on K2 in 1953 and Lhotse in

1955. He was another good team player. Tom McCormack, a fine climber, had been on a Himalayan expedition in 1958. Willi had met Thomas Hornbein, the expedition doctor, when he was an intern in Seattle. He seemed a good sort too. There would be three Pakistani army officers joining as well. This would be a real international expedition.

In Pindi, fabled gateway to the Northwest Frontier Province, the climbers waited for the irregular plane service to Skardu. They stayed at the home of Colonel Eric Goodwin. When the British left the subcontinent they left behind a few characters who had all the dust and drama and dreams of the Empire in their blood. The colonel had served twenty-three years on the northwest frontier, a life of high adventure. His bungalow reflected that. Willi enjoyed simply being among the Persian rugs, leopard heads and a tiger's head on the wall, a library with books about adventures and mountaineering. The colonel himself was as much a relic as any of his souvenirs, padding around in ballooning shorts, a big gut rising up over his belt, playing Chopin on the piano and telling wonderful stories about the Pathans and the days of colonialism.

As a boy in high school Willi had read about this world. For once he sat quietly, absolutely mesmerized. When he wasn't listening to the colonel, Willi spent a lot of time with Dick Emerson and Tom Hornbein. Before long, Willi felt almost as close to Tom as he did to Dick. Hornbein was a spidery little man with the beaked face of an eaglet. He approached the mountains with intensity, leavened with what Willi considered a good sense of humor. He was a first-rate climber. Like Willi, Tom had not been slowed by four children. Tom's intensity and single-mindedness were hard to take at times. Among the other climbers he wasn't as popular as Emerson. Dick was gentle and noncompetitive, a sociological observer by nature as well as by profession.

When life was at stake men formed bonds that they had no other time. On the mountain everything was simpler, clearer, more profound. There were no wives, families, or other pursuits to pull them away. A man spent a few evenings with another man and saw through to his soul. A man saw another man's weakness but it was like looking through a pane of handmade glass where small distortions are not only accepted but appreciated. Willi's only problem was shutting off the talk so he and his two buddies could get some sleep.

Flying from Pindi to Skardu, the plane rose high over the brown plains and verdant hills, up into a world of ice and snow. The plane droned through narrow gorges with great 25,000-foot peaks such as Rakaposhi, Haramosh and Nanga Parbat on either side rising far above the foothills like sentinels. The Karakoram range was three hundred miles long, a mere fifth the sweep of the Himalayas, but there were over one hundred peaks in this one long rampart. Nothing like it existed in the world. The plane nudged over the icy spires, gliding around the edges of the gorges, finally diving earthward like a hawk after a rabbit, pulling up to land on the parched brown earth of Skardu.

In Baltistan water was the elixir of life. Without it there was only sand and dirt and brown hills. Where the ground was irrigated grew trees of apricots, apples, and peaches, and fields of millet, wheat, and barley. Whether one stood in dust or pasture, far in the distance loomed the vista of the Karakorams.

Few tourists came yet to Skardu. These Americans were among a handful of westerners who since partition had visited the scruffy town of less than ten thousand. This was not only a climbing expedition, then, but an exploration as well. Everything from the logistics to the scenery appeared new and unknown. For Willi and the others, every day was fresh and uncertain.

The eight high-altitude porters (HAPS) were not Sherpas, but Baltis from this mountainous region of Baltistan. So were the 180 porters who would carry the five and a half tons of food and equipment 100 miles into Base Camp. The "bandobast," porter caravan, moved out along the dusty banks of the Indus River. The porters wore Gilgit caps, baggy homespun pants, and shawls. Their faces had the history of Central Asia written on them: here an Aryan nose and there a Semitic nose, round Mongol eyes on a face with the expressive mouth that could have belonged to one of Alexander's soldiers. The porters had carried these loads for a thousand years and as far as they knew their heirs would carry them for a thousand more.

While the porters thumped ahead, many of them on bare feet, the sahibs moved painfully along trying to break in their new Bally boots. As Willi set out he was carrying a forty-six-pound pack, determined to carry more than any other sahib. He soon had the worst blisters he had ever had. But by the second day he was in incredibly good spirits that were infectious. He looked up at the rocky hillsides where the Baltis carried dirt by hand to grow a little wheat, and thought what a contrast between this and the green terraced hillsides of Nepal. He looked down at the children and saw diseases as omnipresent as the dust. He loved being with different peoples. When he burst into song he attracted a crowd of Baltis. Soon he had the scrawny, barefoot children singing their folk songs. He gave away combs to the tiniest children, running his finger along the teeth, the children jumping with excitement.

The expedition crossed the thundering, onrushing waters of the Shyok River on round rafts called *zakhs* made of a score or more of blown-up goat skins. As the *zakhs* shot down the Shyok, the boatmen danced back and forth blowing air into one skin then another, the raft bouncing downriver. For the Americans this was yet another adventure. To the Baltis the *zakhs* were part of their daily lives, the only way to get from here to there.

A day up the Hushe River valley, Willi looked up ahead and saw Masherbrum, its triangular shape thrust 25,660 feet into the sky. First, there lay the great Sérac Glacier, a band of glistening white ice; above, stood the Dome, the upper basin rising to the bottom of the southeast face; and above that 4,000 feet to the summit.

At Hushe, the last village in the valley, most men would have stopped at least long enough to watch a performance of the famed dancing girls. But Bell, McGowan, and Willi set off at dawn with Rahim Khan, one of the HAPS, to find a place for Base Camp. Two hours behind them came the rest of the party.

It was Regon's birthday, May 30, Willi realized as he walked behind the copper-skinned Khan, moving through deep cedar forests. Up and up the trail wound, across the rotten, broken rock of the Masherbrum Glacier, then up onto the snowfield itself. It was a day of purest sunshine, reflecting off the white snows. Willi was scorching hot. As they moved up the glacier, slogging through

deep, heavy snows, Willi was worried about the 150 porters following a couple of hours behind. They were carrying sixty to seventy
pounds apiece, not light packs like the sahibs. A lot of the Baltis
didn't even have shoes. At the site for Base Camp, Willi sat down
to rest. A half hour or so later the first of the porters appeared far
below. What impressed Willi so much about the porters was their
sheer stoicism. Most of them were full of good humor. It was as if
happiness grew out of pain and deprivation. He took some pictures
of the porters' bare feet. Then the sahibs paid the porters and they
hurried off through the snows, chasing the deepening shadows.

Now the climbing could begin. Down below Willi often surged
with playful, joyful life. Up here among the rocks and ice and cold
his exuberance was like a raucous laugh in a silent universe. For all
the glory of climbing, the everyday life of a climber on a large
expedition was about as romantic as hauling freight. Day after day,
carrying heavy loads, they slogged higher and higher up the mountain. At each camp, each level, the expedition shed equipment and
men, until finally it was lean enough and high enough for two or
three or four men to go to the summit.

Life was simple up here. If a man carried thirty pounds up a
camp, everyone knew it. If he carried forty pounds, everyone knew
it. If he stayed in his sleeping bag, pleading stomach trouble, everyone knew it too. If a man was smart he did his share, but no more
than his share. He was not a porter after all. He didn't want to burn
himself out, leaving the summit for someone else. Willi would not
let another man move up the mountain carrying a heavier load than
he did. If another climber picked up sixty pounds, then he picked
up sixty pounds too, feeding both his selflessness and his pride.

For Willi, part of what made this expedition so pleasurable was
that the group was working as an organic whole. The triumph
would go to the man who had struggled upward with fifty-pound
loads five times to Camp III as well as to the man who planted a
flag on the virgin peak. Willi wanted the summit badly, but he
wanted it the right way. As Bell observed, Willi "lived radically."
Up on Masherbrum he felt every act, taking his own triumph in the
moment.

The team was moving up the mountain so rapidly that Willi

found little time even to write Jolene. He carried many loads up to Camp I. Then while everyone else returned down to Base Camp to pick up more loads, Willi and Tom McCormack broke the route to Camp II. The sun burned down as the two men moved slowly through the upper icefall. With the sun reflecting off the snow, it was terribly hot. They trudged across precarious ice bridges, until they had reached the bottom of the Dome itself, at about 19,000 feet. Down below a group of sixteen porters had carried several loads up to Camp I so that Base Camp could be abandoned.

Almost everything was going well. Willi had an amazing ability to adjust to thin air. One of the few problems was Emerson who was suffering from altitude sickness and had to go down to the low camp to rest. Many inequalities separated men: among them, strength, stamina, and courage. On a mountain, no inequality was so unfortunate as the difference in the ability to acclimatize; it could be mistaken for those others, and a man came to doubt himself.

Willi and McGowan moved upward out of Camp II onto the steep side of the Dome. McGowan was a generation younger than Willi, but they were the two strongest climbers. They trudged slowly upward to about 21,000 feet where they established Camp III. Willi looked up and saw the summit. It stood nearly a vertical mile above, but the expedition had moved up the mountain with extraordinary dispatch. In a few more days they would be within striking distance. Then on the eleventh of June the sky darkened and the snows began. The weather reminded Willi of the snows on Makalu that had prevented the expedition from a summit attempt. Storms or no storms, for the next six days the climbers pushed up supplies, each day tromping a new trail through the fresh snow.

Not only Emerson now but McCormack was feeling the altitude; Jawed Akter Khan, one of the Pakistani officers, had become temporarily snowblind. The days were going by. If they were going to make the summit, the expedition had to move up to a new camp. Once again it was Willi and McGowan who moved up the mountain, taking three high-altitude porters with them.

It was tough going, moving through knee-deep powdery snow. The mist was just thick enough so that it was hard to see the peak above but not thick enough to prevent the sun from broiling them. The two men kept changing leads. By the middle of the morning, they had reached the sleek icy slope leading to the upper basin. By early afternoon, the weather had turned terribly cold. They couldn't see much of anything. There at about 22,000 feet, at the edge of the glacier, they placed Camp IV.

Setting down their loads, the porters turned back down Masherbrum. For Willi and McGowan the immediate problem was to get off their frozen boots and cloth gaiters that protected the boots from ice and wetness. They finally yanked them off in one piece. The next morning, the boots and gaiters were still frozen stiff; to separate them Willi and McCormack had to hold the boots over the flame of the butane stove for a quarter-hour.

After putting on their frozen boots, Willi and McGowan headed up to find a site for Camp V. The weather had worsened during the night. The two men could see only a few feet in front. Without a compass for direction and wands set into the snow forty or fifty feet apart to help them find their way back, they would surely have become lost. At times the route ahead disappeared in a whiteout, the snows enveloping the mountain. It made no sense going on. As the two climbers were about to turn around, they stumbled upon a flat snow crest at roughly 23,000 feet. They couldn't have done better in perfect weather. Here was the perfect jumping-off point for the climb to the southeast face.

When they got back down to Camp IV, Bell, Clinch, Hornbein, and the HAPS greeted them enthusiastically. All considered, it had been a good day. Then the skies above cleared. For the first time the climbers could see just what lay above them. The route from Camp V to Camp VI looked possible. Above that, though, lay unstable ice cliffs spread across the south face like a great wall set there to protect the summit. That would be especially dangerous. By the look of it, they would have to traverse a thousand feet before moving up toward the summit.

The eleven climbers all still dreamed of standing on the summit.

In the evenings, cramped together in the tents high on Masherbrum, the men talked about how hard they should push up along those unstable ice cliffs. These men were all physically brave by the standards used below. They had entered this game knowing that they might draw the black card. They knew that this game of Himalayan expedition climbing was not one that a person played many times. They had already taken chances that they would not have taken on a weekend climb in Yosemite or the Tetons or elsewhere.

Each man, however, played the game within limits. McGowan was a fine, strong climber, a powerful man. He had a pregnant wife at home. While remaining one of the strongest, most productive climbers, he played as carefully as he dared while still staying in the game. On the other extremes were Willi and Hornbein. They were for raising the stakes. They were for extending themselves on those dangerous ice cliffs, pushing upward with speed and determination.

When Willi felt risk sharply, he lost himself, all memory and obligation. It was just Willi and the mountain, his muscles and mind focused totally on the here and now.

Willi did not believe that he determined his fate on Masherbrum. "It's the mountain that decides," he kept saying. That mountain was made as much of fate and luck and destiny as of rock and ice and snow. That was the mountain the climbers struggled up while being pulled downward by fear, fatigue, reflection, and the sweet call of life as it was lived below. A climber lay there and didn't want to move. Then he looked at the man next to him getting up and putting on his boots. Neither man knew what the other felt and why. Neither man knew whether the load that pulled the other man downward, homeward, down to safety and security, was less than his or not.

When the assault team was chosen to climb to Camp VI and then on to the summit, it was Willi and McGowan. On June 22, the two climbers moved slowly upward. Behind them that same day followed Clinch and the four high-altitude porters carrying the camp supplies with them. Thus Willi and McGowan would be able to go on the next day to make their summit attempt.

Breaking the trail upward through the soft snow was a slow, brutal business. At places the two men had to stop to dig trenches into the snow, at another to put in fixed lines so that the porters would find it safer working their way up the steep sides.

So far they had been lucky in finding campsites. With the weather deteriorating again and the hour late, Willi and McGowan needed that same luck this afternoon. Pushing rapidly, almost desperately, ahead, they moved up to the towering Sérac, a great pinnacle of ice they had spotted from Camp V. At about 24,000 feet they came upon a tiny platform with crevasses on either side. To Willi the flat space looked positively cozy. There they placed Camp VI.

Nick and the porters appeared out of the gathering gloom carrying food and supplies. Willi was glad to be leading the way up Masherbrum, but he was doubly glad that it was a team moving up the mountain, a single organism with him and McGowan at its head. He was proud of the HAPS too. These four had proven themselves the equal of the Sherpas.

The next morning, Willi and McGowan headed out the sharply pitched route to the base of the couloir to prepare the route for their summit attempt the next day. As they moved ahead they put in fixed ropes as protection against getting swept away in an avalanche. The climbing was so steep, the danger of avalanches so extreme, that during the whole day the two climbers moved only about four hundred feet.

That afternoon Bell and Hornbein arrived in Camp VI to give their support for the summit attempt the following day, June 25. Willi was already higher than he had ever been before. He was feeling good and strong. In three trips to an Asian mountain this would be his first opportunity to go to the summit.

When Willi and McGowan woke at 1:00 A.M. and began to get ready, Willi was full of resolution. In the tiny tent, he put on the layers of clothing and equipment, the nylon pants and parka, mittens, piton hammer, lanyards, mitten cords, oxygen bottles, and mask. He looked less and less like Willi Unsoeld and more like some strange beast of Masherbrum. He moved laboriously, tangled in ropes and cords. Before he left he turned to McGowan.

"Let's get down and say a prayer, Dick."

McGowan was not a praying man but he admired Willi. He got down on his knees.

Then they set out, following the path they had forged the day before. Willi walked at a guide's pace, one foot always resting. He was living this pure, perfect moment, plodding steadily upward, sucking in pure oxygen, the only sound the oxygen equipment. Click, click, click. Click. Click, click, click. Click. . . . Willi realized that in trying to synchronize his breathing with the uneven tempo of the oxygen, he had started to hyperventilate.

The two men continued upward. Willi looked down at the oxygen balloon that hung beneath his chin like the enlarged thyroid glands he had seen so often in Nepal. The balloon had started to expand, growing bigger and bigger. He looked over at McGowan. His was growing bigger, too.

"We'll float up to the summit," Willi laughed as the two men stopped to readjust the equipment. They didn't need the oxygen anyway. Willi was glad when he could throw the empty bottle away.

Although the two climbers were making steady progress, the snow was so soft and heavy that it was almost impossible to move upward. Most of the time they were only traversing the bottom of the couloir. When they stopped at noon for lunch, Willi was still convinced that they would reach the summit; McGowan was not certain. He was not prepared to take the same risks as Willi. By two o'clock the toughest part of the climb still lay ahead.

"We could bivouac," Willi suggested.

"The weather, Willi," McGowan said. It had begun snowing.

"We need another camp. Better cache equipment here."

The two men headed back down, stumbling into camp at 6:00 P.M. Bell and Hornbein were there anxiously waiting.

The first days on Masherbrum the weather had been spectacularly good. Now the mountain was turning on them. Next morning the storm was blowing fiercely down the mountain. They had plenty of food at Camp VI, but so little Buta-gas for the cooking stove that the four men had no choice but to move down the mountain. Willi and Bell led the party, followed on the same rope by McGowan and Hornbein.

Willi had been in bad storms before high on Makalu, but this was as difficult a journey down a mountain as he had ever taken. The snow was so thick and enveloping that it was like swimming through an ocean of white. He couldn't see more than a couple of feet ahead. There were supposed to be wands to guide the climbers down, but Willi couldn't even see the confounded things. He realized that an avalanche had taken a big chunk of the snows down the mountain, carrying a bunch of the wands with it.

Willi stopped to discuss the situation with the three others.

"We better move there to the left. . . ."

The snows began sliding, moving down the mountain. The avalanche picked the four men up like twigs and tossed them head over heels down the mountain toward the ice cliffs.

Willi was all instinct. As he rolled downward he plunged his ice axe into the swirling avalanche, feeling the pick dig into the firm snow below, jerking him to a halt. The rope pulled taut, threatened to yank him loose. Willi held with all his might. Bell had managed to get his ice axe into firm snow too. Willi knew that if this had been a larger avalanche, nothing or no one could have stopped their downward plunge.

Hornbein had rolled two hundred feet and was lying far below the others. He was fine. So was everyone. As they continued down Masherbrum even more cautiously, McGowan keeled over, falling face down into the fresh snow. Hornbein hurried toward the injured climber, placing him on a shelf that Willi and Bell chopped out of the ice. Willi watched Hornbein working over McGowan, examining him with the same quickness and precision that he brought to his climbing. McGowan was sinking into delirium but Hornbein could find nothing wrong; the doctor decided that he must have inhaled ice crystals during the avalanche.

It would have been terribly difficult to move McGowan's inert form further down Masherbrum during the storm. Willi looked up and saw what he took as a miraculous sign. Not only had the storm ended suddenly, but the sun was shining. Far below Clinch and Jawed were breaking a trail up the mountain to their friends.

An hour and a half later Willi and the others sat safely in Camp V. Hornbein knelt in the tiny tent giving McGowan penicillin and injecting a salt solution. McGowan regained consciousness and was able to make it down to Camp III. But for him the climb was over.

On June 29 Willi and five other sahibs moved up again to Camp V. That night a storm once again descended. The wind picked up, rattling the center pole. Snow drifted up against the tent. Day after day the storm lashed at the tent while the climbers huddled together knowing their dream of the summit was probably over. It could have been a remorseful, bitter time, but hardship was the favored source of Willi's humor. He joked about the too small Bally boots that on the trek in had produced monumental blisters. He joked about the wonderful Budd Davis packs that had turned out to be instruments of torture. He joked about the wonderful "boned chicken" that Clinch had ordered from a Swiss company. The cans contained some meat on the necks and wings but mainly hundreds of little bones. Willi had stories to tell about his first trip to India and about Makalu, too. He had the climbers convulsed in laughter and good cheer, their raucous sounds louder far than the storm outside.

The storm was no match for Willi. He could have told stories for a month. By the fourth day, though, the food was running low. The other four climbers moved down to the lower camps leaving only Willi and Bell.

Dawn brought one of those days of pristine clarity that in the Himalayas sometimes rise out of the night skies like pure and ancient light. Willi and Bell dressed and headed upward. Willi had been sitting around so long that with each step he felt fatigue. After the storm the snow had become so hard that the two men had to chop steps with their ice axes. Arriving at Camp VI Willi had expected to find that the storm had taken its toll. What he looked at was simple savagery. The aluminum poles and fiberglass sticks of the Gerry Himalayan tents had been smashed, the tents lying in heaps on the ground.

Willi and Bell were still digging their way out when late in the afternoon Emerson and Jawed arrived in camp loaded with supplies. It had taken Emerson a long time to get used to the altitude but he was in fine form. Willi was glad that his old friend was up here now. Willi and Bell would make the first summit attempt. Then Emerson and Jawed would have their chance.

The next afternoon the four climbers reached the 25,000-foot level where days before Willi and McGowan had cached supplies. Whatever the storm had accomplished below at Camp VI, at least there something remained. But here not a piton was lying loose, not a piece of rope sticking out of the snow. Everything was lost, gone, swept off the mountain. While Emerson and Jawed hurried downward, Willi and Bell set up this new Camp VII.

At 2:00 A.M. Willi and Bell awoke. This would be Willi's second "summit day" on this expedition. They lay quietly talking, gathering strength. They forced down some Ovaltine and cornflakes and began the laborious process of dressing.

They were up here because they were the strongest. Willi was the leader heading upward. They were not using oxygen. They moved steadily ahead, Willi breaking the way in the fresh snow. The slope angled upwards at a 50- to 60-degree level and was covered with snow of uneven consistency. Willi had to improvise. He plunged the handle of the ice axe into the snow on one side, a snow shovel on the other. Then he heaved himself upward, kicking steps into the snow. It wasn't elegant, but it worked. As the sun beat down, Willi worked his way upward like a cripple on crutches. This was maddeningly slow work, but by eleven o'clock Willi and Bell were standing up on the summit ridge.

The northwest face dropped straight down to the Baltoro Glacier. Sitting on the tiny perch, Willi could have remained a long time, looking down on the camps so far below. But a strong wind was blowing from the southwest. Willi and Bell were soon driven from their icy resting place.

Above rose the rocks that they had seen from below, swept bare of snow and ice by the relentless wind. The rock was as rotten as a badly decayed tooth, but the wind kept the stone frozen solid. Wearing crampons, Willi and Bell continued their journey upward. Approaching the summit they came upon a chimney, a narrow cleft in the rock, that was almost as good as a staircase. The pack wouldn't pass through the thin gap. Willi and Bell hoisted it up on a rope. There, on a little platform where they couldn't even have pitched a tent, the two men stopped an hour for lunch.

Moving upward once again, Willi and Bell belayed each other up the last gentle slope that fell off thousands of feet to the west. Willi felt the ease of a fine athlete operating at his peak. He slogged upward as if he were on some foothill 20,000 feet below. Upward, upward he moved, until at 3:15 he and Bell stood on the highest of the summit crests, 25,660 feet above sea level.

It seemed so easy now. Willi looked out upon the panorama. To the north he saw the great wedge of K2 standing alone, rising even higher than Masherbrum. He turned eastward and counted the four Gasherbrums and Chogolisa and Broad Peak. Below he saw the silvery fingers of the glaciers feeding water to the parched flatlands that stretched to the horizon. He pulled out his camera and took pictures.

All his life Willi had wanted to climb to the summit of a great virgin peak, to stand arm in arm with Mallory, Tilman, Shipton. But now that he was here, why, he asked himself, why had he done it? What did it mean? What was this victory? Why did men climb mountains? Why did he climb? Why had he climbed Masherbrum?

Turning to Bell, Willi asked, "Why, George? Why are we up here?"

The tall scientist was having trouble enough even breathing without answering philosophical questions. He mumbled a reply that he forgot as soon as the words left his mouth. Whatever his own reasons Willi realized that they had been fulfilled. There were few virgin peaks in the world. He had done something few men had ever done—or ever would do. He knew that climbing had become an obsession with him, threatening his marriage and career. But it had been gratified for good, forever. He knew that it was time to quit, now when he was ahead of the game.

It was getting late but Willi had made a promise to Colonel Goodwin back in Pindi. He took the crucifix the colonel had given him and walked to the pinnacle of the mountain. He knelt and there he placed the crucifix. There he remained, as if in meditation.

"Well, Willi?" Bell asked. "Are you ready to go down now? Or shall we go up?"

Willi looked up at Bell as if he indeed were ready to climb up into the sky itself. Saying nothing, he tied in his rope with his companion's and headed down the mountain.

By eight that evening when the two men got back down to Camp VI they were terribly tired. During the night Bell began to cough. He said that he was feeling cold. Willi was afraid that the six-foot five-inch-tall scientist was on the verge of pneumonia.

Willi started the stove and heated some cocoa. He then began emergency treatment, plying Bell with antibiotics, giving him medicine to stimulate the heart, as well as diuretics. As Willi watched over him, Bell fell into near delirium, humming to himself. Outside the wind picked up, hurling snow and chunks of ice against the tent. Suddenly, Willi felt the tent itself sliding slowly down the mountain. The two men wrapped their arms around one another, preferring not to die alone. They then realized that the tent had not moved. Sheepishly, Willi went back over to the other side of the tent.

Later Clinch and Jawed also made the summit. Emerson had been scheduled to go with them but that morning he had awakened sick and weak. Willi thought of that and other things as the expedition headed from Camp I to Base Camp and away from Masherbrum for good. There were still crevasses but Willi saw no need to wear a rope any longer. The others had gone on ahead. Willi had chosen to pick his way down by himself. Although the route was well marked it was getting dark. It was hard following the path of the crampon points. Wearing his heavy pack Willi jumped over one deep crevasse after another, until he came upon one that was just too wide. At least there was a snow bridge. As Willi walked across, the snow gave way. He reached out and caught himself on the side of the crevasse. Hanging there by his arms, he knew that no one could help him now. He finally managed to pull himself up, and hurried ahead to catch up with the others.

"How'd it go?" Clinch asked as Willi appeared once again in view.

"Well, it doesn't go my way," he answered blithely, and walked on as if nothing had happened.

When the climbers marched down the Hushe, Willi felt sad.

McGowan couldn't wait to get home to see about his new baby. Many of the others had urgent matters carrying their minds back to America even before their bodies had reached there.

For Willi the climb had been almost perfect. They had climbed the mountain the right way. They had been a real team. Three Americans and a Pakistani had stood on the summit, but they had all shared the triumph. Willi liked these men immensely. They stood as high as the peaks they climbed. For Willi, human personality appeared almost as immutable as the mountains. He was proud to be one of this strong, good breed: a mountaineer from the American West.

Almost three weeks after his summit ascent Willi sat in the Hotel Metropole in Karachi. He had just two and a half hours before the plane back to the States. He decided to write a last letter home to Jolene, a Victory Installment for the newsletter she was mailing to family, friends, and anyone else who would send her postage.

"And so this particular 'Great Adventure' is successfully terminated," Willi concluded. "Four men stood a cumulative total of exactly one hour on top of a big heap of rock and ice in a far-off corner of Baltistan. The recurring question is always, 'So what'—and even in their hour of triumph the men themselves were asking each other, 'Why?' Inspiring answers could be offered concerning man's struggle for knowledge of himself and of the world in which he lives—of the adventurous flight of the human spirit . . . its refusal to stay satisfied with life on the beaten track . . . and its constant effort to broaden its own capacities. And there would be considerable truth in such answers. But in simplest honesty it would seem that some men are just built to respond to ridge of rock and crest of snow—there grows up an affinity between them as there does between some people—a need for further acquaintance and companionship between them. In the case of the 1960 Masherbrum party this relationship between man and mountain was realized to an unusually happy degree."

AA

In the summer of 1961 Robert Bates, president of the American Alpine Club, made a foray out west to meet mountaineers who didn't get back much to New England. Bates, a teacher at the exclusive Exeter Academy in New Hampshire, was an amateur climber of the old school. In his college days he had traveled across Canada on an immigrant train to climb in Alaska with other Harvard men from the east. Then, in the 1930s, there had been relatively few western climbers. The remote mountains largely sat waiting for young gentlemen who in the midst of the Depression had the time and money for such adventures.

Now climbing was moving away from the sedate, proper world of the American Alpine Club. In the west many mountaineers were, if anything, *anti*-gentlemen. At Yosemite National Park in California self-conscious outcasts and dropouts were, in a current phrase, "living at one with the dirt."

Bates was looking forward to meeting Willi Unsoeld, one of the big names among Northwest climbers. Willi had given up guiding in the Tetons and was spending the summer following the Masherbrum expedition in that most mundane of academic activities:

teaching summer school. He appeared to be settling down into the comfortable routine of hearth and home. Some of Willi's climbing buddies had talked him into coming along on this climb of Glacier Peak in the Cascades. Willi was supposed to meet Bates and the others at the trail head where his family would wait for him.

As usual Willi was late. By afternoon the mountaineers had given up on Willi and headed up the trail. Dusk was descending when the climbers looked back and saw this lone figure scampering toward them wearing shorts, a small day pack on his back.

"Willi, we're gonna climb a mountain!"

"My missus won't let me," Willi said baldly. He had created this public persona for Jolene. She was the caring, bossy woman out of whose loving clutches he always had to escape. "I've got to keep the peace. We had all kinds of car trouble. The car broke down en route."

"We're not leavin' you, Willi."

Bates and the other climbers weren't heading up the mountain without Willi. They decided to fool Jolene. By starting at midnight they could get up there and back so fast that Willi's wife wouldn't even realize that he had gone to the summit. It was a cold night when the mountaineers struggled into their gear. Willi hadn't brought any climbing gear. That would have signaled his intentions to Jolene. As an ice axe Willi used a tent pole with a nail in one end. To climb up the icy slopes, another climber gave Willi one of his crampons. Using just one was like hopping up the mountain on one foot.

Off they headed. When they reached the summit, the wind was howling, ripping across the glacier, raising the hairs on Willi's legs and setting them down again. As Willi arrived, some students from the University of Washington appeared over the rise. The students couldn't believe their eyes. There was this man standing, wearing shorts, playing a harmonica, then letting out this great whooping yodel that echoed halfway to Rainier.

"Is that Professor Unsoeld?" one of them asked incredulously.

"No, that's *Willi* Unsoeld."

Willi could not stay away from the mountains for long. Up there life was more real than it was below. The problem was still how to bring some of that reality down to earth before it melted into a puddle of memories. He was a popular professor, but his teaching was not going as he wanted it to. He surely wasn't going to spend the rest of his life cribbing from his old graduate student notes for his own lectures, standing spouting off to generation after generation of students.

All that could wait. When Willi received an invitation to join the American Everest Expedition, he knew that he had to go. He had said that Masherbrum was his last expedition, but this was Everest. "You place yourself in the footsteps of the great heroes of the past when you get an opportunity to take on Everest," Willi said. "It's not necessarily an ultimate in difficulty, but more a mystical ultimate."

In the period between Willi's sojourn on Nilkanta in 1949 and the successful ascent of Masherbrum in 1960, Himalayan mountaineering had passed through a golden age. At the beginning of the decade not one of the fourteen "eight-thousanders," peaks rising more than 8,000 meters or 26,250 feet above sea level, had been climbed. No where else in the world except along the 1,500-mile length of the Himalayas were there so many peaks that high.

These eight-thousanders were the great jewels of climbing. During the 1950s all but the lowest of the peaks was climbed. Everest was climbed twice, first by Sir Edmund Hillary and Tenzing Norkay in 1953, then by four Swiss climbers in 1956. Annapurna. Nanga Parbat. K2. Kangchenjunga. Makalu. Lhotse. Dhaulagiri. One after another they had fallen. Now when climbers looked up at the awesome panorama of the Himalayas they had to look down at lesser peaks to find challenges unsullied by predecessors. Still, Everest remained, as Willi said, the "mystical ultimate."

To set the American flag on Everest, Norman G. Dyhrenfurth began putting together the largest expedition in the history of American mountaineering. Dyhrenfurth was a tanned, handsome film producer-director. He looked as if he had been born to wear nothing but ski sweaters. He was the son of Gunter O. Dyhrenfurth, a Swiss geologist and one of the world's greatest Himalayan experts.

Dyhrenfurth had his choice almost literally of any climber in the country. The mountaineering fraternity was still so small that those climbers experienced enough to be considered for the Everest expedition knew one another, at least by reputation. Dyhrenfurth selected the finest group of American mountaineers ever to climb together.

From the outset, Willi was a dominant presence. Dyhrenfurth and the deputy leader William E. (Will) Siri, a biological physicist, were both in their forties. If they should fall through illness or accident, the full mantle of leadership would fall on Willi. Thirty-six years old at the time of the expedition, Willi was the old man among those climbers deemed most likely to reach the summit, the young man among those sought out for advice and direction.

Most of the twenty expedition members and strongest climbers were from the American West. Willi knew what they were like on a rope. He had guided in the Tetons with three of the men: James (Barry) Corbet, Richard (Dick) Pownall, and John "Jake" Breitenbach. When Breitenbach had been a student at Oregon State, Willi had spent hours with the young mountaineer helping him find a direction. Dick Emerson had been chosen too. So had Tom Hornbein, only this time, unlike Masherbrum, Hornbein wasn't getting stuck as expedition doctor. There were two other climbers from the Northwest, James W. Whittaker and Luther G. Jerstad. Whittaker was sales manager of an outdoors store in Seattle; Jerstad taught speech at the University of Oregon. Willi knew them as guides on Rainier.

Willi could have sat down around the campfire in the Tetons with most of these men discussing climbing, philosophy, religion, or raising kids. None of the Americans made their living climbing. Only four were bachelors. Five had Ph.D.s, three were working on their doctorates. There were three medical doctors, too.

To these men climbing was only an avocation, a summer pursuit. None of them had experienced anything like the sheer magnitude of the expedition. As he received letters typed on the fancy letterhead stationery, Willi was simply amazed at this gargantuan enterprise of which he had become a part. It was a far cry from the philosophy motivating Mallory on Everest or Tilman on Nanda Devi in 1936.

Dyhrenfurth was consumed with the idea of Americans standing on the summit of the world's highest mountain. When Dyhrenfurth first went looking for funds, he was turned away at the portals of the great foundations. They were not about to fund such a dubious venture as a mountain climb. It was, however, a time in America when leisure had become the midwife of adventure. The whole idea of sports was expanding. The new young President, John F. Kennedy, wanted the nation to be fit; he had even initiated fifty-mile hikes.

If climbing still might appear an eccentric, inbred sport, it was Everest after all, and these were Americans. Dyhrenfurth received some initial funding from *Life,* the picture magazine. What Dyhrenfurth was promising was a Grand Slam: not only Everest, but Lhotse and Nuptse, her sister peaks, and major scientific research as well. With that vision in mind, he went to the National Geographic Society. Both scientific and editorial departments at the Society became interested, promising over $100,000 for, among other things, a movie. The government came through as well: the National Science Foundation ($36,300), the Air Force Office of Scientific Research ($10,000), the Office of Naval Research ($25,190), and the U.S. State Department ($82,000).

Willi was amazed at the goods that Dyhrenfurth had persuaded more than 190 companies to contribute. As the outdoors became a great playground, a symbiotic relationship was developing between manufacturers and expeditions. A family might only be going out to the state park camping, but it was nice to know that the company that made the tent had also made the tents on the Everest expedition. Willi was glad that Dyhrenfurth had conjured up down sleeping bags, socks, aluminum ladders, medical supplies, boots, winches, crampons, climbing ropes, ice axes, and down clothing. But there were some items that didn't quite jell with the old climbing life: Woolite, Franco-American dinners, canned fruit cakes, electric toothbrushes, tapioca, Cara-Coa fruit brownies, puddings, beer, artichoke hearts, canned nuts, Metrecal cookies, Kwik-shakes, Quik-Eggs, deviled ham, chocolate bars, fig bars, meat bars, and Foam-ettes brushless dentifrice.

In all, the expedition received over $400,000 in funds, goods, and services. Although Willi wasn't totally happy that the 1963 American Everest Expedition was turning into such an extravaganza, he still wanted to go. He knew it was the men and the mountain that would decide whether they reached the summit, not Kwik-shakes and Cara-Coa brownies. He wanted to climb where Mallory had climbed, to climb beyond him, to stand on the summit of his dreams.

One morning the phone rang in Corvallis. Bob Bates was calling long distance. Bates had received a one-year leave of absence from Exeter to go to Nepal as first director of the Peace Corps.

"Willi, how would you like to go to Nepal as my deputy?" Bates asked.

"Sure, I'll go," Willi said as if Bates had asked him to waltz up the Grand. "But first, I have to ask Jolene."

Willi still wanted to climb Everest. He would find a way to do that. But this was just too good to be true. If Everest was the great physical adventure of his time, the Peace Corps was the great moral adventure. The Peace Corps had been Senator Hubert Humphrey's idea originally, sending secular missionaries to live and work among the poor, carrying the torch of American concern to distant corners. Kennedy had taken up the idea during the presidential campaign. Now Sargent Shriver, his brother-in-law, had set out to implement it. Some critics derided Shriver's Peace Corps as a Kiddie Korps, nice middle-class kids, plopping themselves down among poverty and disease. Willi, who knew something of youthful sojourns, never doubted the Peace Corps could succeed.

Jolene was a pushover, all for going. Shriver, however, didn't hire anyone he hadn't personally interviewed. Some candidates had done everything but pack before being turned down by Shriver.

When the call came through on Tuesday saying that he was to be in Washington, D.C., to see Shriver the following Thursday, Willi was sure they meant a week from Thursday. That wasn't the way Shriver's Peace Corps worked. When Willi realized his mistake, he had to rush around to get to Washington in time.

The Peace Corps was in an old downtown office building. Dressed in a suit, Willi got on the elevator that groaned and strained its way slowly up to the fourth floor. As he got off the elevator, he was plunged into a scene of holy disorder. Everyone was working with a sense of urgency. Whereas other agencies wrote letters, the Peace Corps sent telegrams. When bureaucrats deemed it necessary to send a telegram, the Peace Corps would have already called long distance.

While Willi waited for his interview with Shriver, he sat in the large long office of Timmy Napolitano, the Indian desk officer. As usual, Shriver was running late. Finally, a call summoned the candidate up to the fifth floor. An hour later, Willi returned.

"How'd it go?" asked Napolitano, a tiny, feisty woman exuding enthusiasm.

"Well, I haven't seen him yet," Willi said, a bit uncertainly. "I'm going to ride in the limousine with him to the airport."

The Chicago plane was being held for Shriver. While the limousine cruised toward National Airport the Peace Corps director had dozens of letters and memos to deal with and to sign, all the pesky little business he handled as he moved from place to place.

Shriver was a Kennedy by marriage, but he was more Kennedy-esque than the President, exuding a macho idealism and enthusiasm. As *his* representatives in Africa, Asia, and Latin America, Shriver sought people who had "good judgment and élan." It was a belief of the Kennedy people that judgment and élan went together.

When it came to judging people, it was not bloodlines Shriver was looking for but energy and daring. He wanted individuals. He wasn't about to load the Peace Corps down with a bunch of pale bureaucrats and pallid careerists, those traitors to life who would bank the fires of commitment that now burned so brightly.

Back in Corvallis Willi was the extrovert, but sitting here he hadn't said a word. The black Cadillac cruised up to the terminal at National.

"And who are you?" Shriver asked, finally noticing his muscular passenger.

"I'm Bill Unsoeld. I'm a candidate for Bob Bates' deputy in Nepal."

"Well, come along now," Shriver said, in that brisk Kennedy parlance as if he were about to lead a platoon up the beaches of Normandy. "We'll talk on the plane to Chicago."

After exchanging seats with another passenger, Willi sat down next to Shriver. The Peace Corps director knew all about Willi's career from his application, but a man was more than a résumé. This Unsoeld fellow had already been to Nepal. That was good. He was a mountain climber, virile and strong. That was good too. What impressed him particularly was that Willi had named his daughter after a mountain in India and his son after the state of Oregon. That was the kind of imagination he needed in the Peace Corps.

The two men talked intensely and earnestly as the plane soared westward. As soon as the wheels touched ground at O'Hare airport in Chicago, Shriver was off and running.

"Can you get back to Washington all right?" Shriver asked as he rushed out of the plane.

"Sure," Willi asserted enthusiastically, looking out at the maze of an airport. If he wanted to get to Nepal, he better be able to find his way back to the capital.

Willi knew that he had done well. Soon afterwards he learned that he had the job. Eventually, he learned, too, that he would be given leave to climb Everest. After he got back to Corvallis, on April 19, an editorial appeared in the *Oregon State Daily Barometer* entitled "Mixed Feelings." "The person who is about to leave the OSU faculty is unique," the student paper said. "We are confident that Dr. Unsoeld, with his keen intellect and affable personality, would make a fine Peace Corps representative. Our feelings concerning the possibility of him leaving are mixed. We hate to see him go, but we like to see Oregon State students and faculty fulfill themselves in bigger and better things."

Bob Bates flew over to Nepal that summer to get things ready for the first group of volunteers. That would take some doing since for so long Nepal had been sealed off from the rest of the world.

While Bates worked in Katmandu, Willi went through the train-

ing program at George Washington University in Washington, D.C.
Among the seventy volunteers who eventually went to Nepal, a
large number were mountain climbers and outdoor lovers who had
joined because it was Nepal and either Bates or Willi was involved.

There were young men and women who carried the names of old
American families like Saltonstall and Bingham. An elderly retired
schoolteacher had joined, an eighteen-year-old who had just graduated from high school, a middle-aged working class mechanic,
and even that rarest of Peace Corps finds—a black. They came
from little towns in upstate New York and Minnesota and from the
great American cities. A disproportionate number had graduated
from Harvard, Yale, and other Ivy League schools. It was not a
cross section of America, but the image that Kennedy's America
liked to project of itself: youthful, bright, idealistic, interesting,
and daring. During training the volunteers talked with Shriver. In
July, along with some Ethiopian trainees they met President Kennedy in the Rose Garden of the White House.

Few Americans had ever been to Nepal. No westerners had lived
there on the modest level as would these Peace Corps volunteers.
What the volunteers learned about Nepal during the training program often sounded like a fairy tale. They were told that the kingdom of Nepal had come into being in the second half of the eigh-
teenth century. Then Prithvi Narayan Shah, the ruler of the kingdom
of Gurkha in western Nepal, had won sovereignty over the three
separate kingdoms in the central Katmandu valley, then over the
eastern part of the country. During the early years of the nineteenth
century, the kings had fought the Chinese in the north in Tibet and
the English in the south in India. These disputes were settled in
1816 when the modern boundaries of Nepal were drawn. In the
1840s the Ranas, a noble family, gained control of the government,
instituting a hereditary prime minister. In 1950–51 a popular upris-
ing restored King Tribhuvan to power. The current ruler, his son,
King Mahendra, had decided to open his land up to the light of
modernity, but Nepal was still as backward and isolated as any
country in the world.

The academic lecturers at George Washington University did

their best. They took abstractions about the underdeveloped world and India and tried to make them fit all the subtle realities of Nepal. It didn't quite work. Nepal seemed even more remote, more exotic. Willi had been in Nepal only a few weeks while climbing Makalu, but he became one of the resident experts.

The volunteers went through language training in Nepali and political training as well. The Peace Corps was sending volunteers out into the Cold War. They didn't want Americans unprepared when they faced tough questions. They learned what to say about Red China and Mao's brand of Communism. With the Tibetan border so near, there were bound to be questions about China. They had to be able to ward off Communist agitators. When they were asked about the racial problem in the South, they had to be ready too.

The trainees got to know Willi and his family best when they went rappelling on some cliffs near Washington. Soon everyone went to Colorado to attend Outward Bound. The Outward Bound program, based on the ideas of Kurt Hahn, the German-born educator, had just begun in America. In Britain during the Second World War, Hahn had seen many young sailors die awaiting rescue in the open sea after their ships were torpedoed. Hahn's program involved a physical and moral toughening up, which challenged the sailors to go beyond themselves, beyond anything they ever imagined they could do. One of the main pedagogical tools was risk, used with psychological calculation.

Shriver liked the idea of schools for "character building," before sending his volunteers out into a tough world. He wanted them ready. Had Outward Bound been able to handle the numbers, Shriver would have had eight schools set up just for Peace Corps trainees. He settled for one Peace Corps Training Center in Puerto Rico, and the use of the new Colorado Outward Bound School for the first groups of Nepal-bound volunteers.

Out here was the real Willi surging with life. He carried seventy-pound packs on treks. He led the way rappelling off cliffs, plunging into an icy pool at dawn, walking across a high log bridge. At night he told wondrous stories about Nepal and the Tetons. To the volunteers Willi appeared a one-man Outward Bound.

The gung-ho outdoor types loved Outward Bound. Some of the others found the program as edifying as boot camp. One volunteer, Carl Jurgenson, thought that he knew something about survival from his experiences as a black at Harvard. As far as he was concerned, the idea that physical training and artificial risks created people who could survive out in the world was absurd. One particularly cold morning he refused to take the morning plunge in the pool. It took all Willi's powers of persuasion to get Jurgenson to go back and jump into the frigid water.

Other volunteers flared up, objecting to such indignities as an attempt to split up the married couples, and to declare the whole camp off limits to smoking. Willi became the mediator, soothing the volunteers, calming them down, ultimately saving several from being "de-selected" from the program.

Willi still found time to do some climbing. One day Willi took a fall that hurt his leg seriously enough to require medical attention.

Willi cared about the Peace Corps, but he cared even more about climbing Mount Everest. Since he was still involved with the training program he missed the expedition shakedown climb on Mount Rainier in September 1962. He arrived the day the climbers were coming off the mountain. The weather had been so bad on the 14,410-foot peak that the climbers didn't reach the summit.

"That's a great sign, fellows," Willi joked. "It's half the size of Everest and you can't even get up it."

Willi was such a natural leader that the other climbers came to him with their problems. Several members of the expedition thought that Willi should formally be named climbing leader, the crucial role up on Everest. Nothing came of the idea. Dyhrenfurth and Siri were not about to abdicate. Moreover, Willi would be in Nepal during the final planning.

Willi got together with Emerson and Hornbein to discuss the forthcoming expedition. Emerson didn't like Dyhrenfurth's idea of a grand slam of Everest by the South Col route that the British had used in 1953 and the Swiss in 1956, plus Lhotse and Nuptse. Another run up the South Col wasn't a fair game with the outcome uncertain enough. Maybe the American public would eat it up, but the climb would be a charade. The thirty-eight-year-old Emerson wanted a real climb. That meant an attempt at the summit by the uncharted, unexplored West Ridge. Dyhrenfurth had already talked to Hornbein about this as a distant possibility. Willi and his two friends knew that if the expedition made it up by the West Ridge, it would be one of the greatest things ever done in the Himalayas. If they didn't make it, and they probably wouldn't, it would still have been a great game. They talked some more and the idea just stayed there.

In October Willi and Nepal I, the first group of volunteers to go to the country, flew to New Delhi on a chartered Constellation airplane. The four Unsoeld children had the run of the plane as the propeller-driven craft lumbered eastward for thirty-six hours. At the New Delhi airport the female volunteers were asked to raise their skirts so that officials could do a proper job of spraying them with DDT. On the street, the Indians stared at the Americans as if they had been set down in Delhi for their edification.

The plane was supposed to fly on to Nepal. But no one had realized that the Constellation was too large to land at the airport in Katmandu. Willi had his first major problem as Deputy Representative. While waiting for DC-3s chartered from Royal Nepal Air Lines, the group stayed in the Oberoi Swiss Hotel, a bungalowlike establishment that became a favorite with the Peace Corps. The volunteers needed per diem in Indian rupees. Willi ended up the reluctant banker. He had dollars in one pocket, Indian rupees in another. By the time he had the mess straightened out he ended up losing money.

Finally, they were off to Nepal. Rising out of the squalor of Delhi, the plane cruised above the plains of North India. Engine throbbing, the small silver plane moved up through the tunnel-like passes, the great hills rising on both sides of the plane. Below, the Katmandu valley spread out before them, wearing the lush green of the post-monsoon season when green appears not a color but a spectrum of hues.

Landing here in this blessedly temperate clime, they saw Nepal as pristine and pure. The Nepalese put *malas* of fresh flowers around their necks. They were a small, sturdy race. The few women greeting the volunteers wore Indian saris. The men mainly wore the official Nepali dress—the *daura surwal;* the white pants fit at the ankles as snugly as ballet tights, then billowed out; on top a long vestlike shirt tied around the chest with strings; over that a suit jacket, and as a hat the pillbox *topi*. One of Willi's favorite movies was *Lost Horizon,* and Nepal appeared like the Shangri-La of James Hilton's novel, a hidden kingdom existing far above the plains of mundane life.

For the orientation period everyone stayed in the Royal Hotel, an old Rana palace that Boris Lissanevitch, a White Russian, had turned into the best hotel in Katmandu. During their hegemony the Ranas had attempted to mimic European royalty. Architecturally what they had achieved was neither East nor West but a bizarre rococo fantasy that would have fit neatly into *Alice in Wonderland*. Portraits of the Ranas lined the halls: All puffed up, wearing more medals than an Eagle scout has merit badges, they looked disdainfully down on this beachhead of tourism. Boris had hauled in old cots and beds with mattresses that had terrains as varied as Nepal, and set them there in the cavernous, high-ceilinged rooms. The holes in the ceilings were to let out spirits. The plumbing was as temperamental as a diva, and the guests the most eclectic group imaginable. It was a marvelous place, but it wasn't Nepal.

One volunteer, the middle-aged mechanic, had already had enough. "Ain't nothin' worked out the way they said it would so you best send me home right now," he told Bates. But the Nepal director talked the man into staying for a while.

Until their house was ready, the Unsoelds camped out at the Peace Corps offices. Like most of the houses in which the embassy and AID people lived, the Unsoeld residence was surrounded by a large wall. The house itself was a sprawling, two-story structure, large enough to provide quarters for servants in the back. Out of the compound Willi and his family ventured in the blue Peace Corps jeep.

". . . the wildest dreams of Kew are the facts of Katmandu . . ." Kipling wrote. Down the narrow streets of the city the sacred cows ambled unperturbed, moving languidly away from the bicycle rickshaws with their tinkling bells and the autos nudging through the crowds. The smell of garbage and offal mingled with that of wood fires and charcoal and the hundred other scents so strange and strong. It was a city of temples. Hindu temples to Shiva, and to lesser gods like Hanuman, the monkey God, and Ganesh, the elephant god. Buddhist temples, great Bodhnath and Swayambhunath, the Eyes of God staring from the four-sided tower.

Katmandu was a city of life; of hill women carrying their babies on their hips; of children running shrieking through the afternoon; of wedding processions, the bright colors of the saris and *malas* shining bright through darkened streets lit by kerosene Petromaxes, glowing like fireflies; of a thousand *pujas* and religious gatherings and feasts and rituals. It was a city where death walked in the streets, jostling with life, the hill people carrying wrapped bodies swinging on poles down to the river; corpses swathed in white burning on piles of fagots along the river bank. It was a city of disease, the pockmarked ravages of smallpox like biblical curses; the madmen roaming the city in their rags, as free as the dogs and the cows; the bent old men, shivering with fever.

Only for the last few years had there been even a road into Katmandu. To the hill people coming into the valley for the first time, these Land Rovers, open American jeeps, big Russian jeeps, were as strange as horses were to the Aztecs in the sixteenth century when the Spanish arrived in Mexico. Here men and women were the main beasts of burden. Along the dirt roads out of the valley porters padded along on bare feet, legs marbled with muscle, the weight of their loaded wicker baskets borne by a rope around the forehead. They were the colors of the bronze plates from which they ate their rice and vegetables. The Newars sat in their shops crosslegged. A shrewd cultivated race, they controlled most of the commerce. The Tibetans strolled arm in arm in heavy robelike coats, smelling of smoke and fire and rancid butter. Here in Katmandu diplomats of East and West jostled in close, if uneasy, proximity. Chinese diplomats in Mao coats and Russians in rudely cut suits rode past US AID officials and German technicians, and their walled homes.

No wall stood between the volunteers and Nepal. They were given goods to protect them, like modern amulets. Each volunteer received a bounty of US AID furniture that had been shipped into the country—beds, chairs, tables, an enormous wooden clothes closet. When the trucks pulled up in front of the little house where a volunteer named Bob Murphy lived, he cringed. What did he want with chairs? The Nepalese sat on the floor. His Nepalese friends stood watching this oversized furniture being squeezed into the house. Volunteers stationed in the Terai, the hot southern plain of Nepal, received large kerosene-run refrigerators that they couldn't afford to run on their 350-rupee-a-month ($47) salaries.

The volunteers soon discovered that all their training about Communism and political issues was as useless as the clothes closets. Most of the Nepalese had no idea where this great Peace Corps United States America country existed, over which hill, how many days walk. The Nepalese were wonderfully gracious but they didn't know quite what to do with these Peace Corps *sewaks*. One Peace Corps shop teacher found no equipment in his school. He did the best he could drawing saws, vices, and hammers on the blackboard. The headmaster was so impressed that he converted the young man into his art teacher.

Willi himself was an ebullient presence. He often wore shorts and sneakers. From his shoulders hung a canvas bag that was totally impractical for keeping papers and memos. He didn't like being stuck in the dank, white Peace Corps office down the street from the palace. He preferred to be off visiting volunteers.

Fleming Heegaard and Greg Pack were volunteers stationed at a school five miles outside Katmandu. When they needed a big table for the school, Willi didn't worry about paperwork. He took one of the tables that the Peace Corps had for their offices and homes, put it in his jeep, and drove it out there. At the school, Willi picked up the 150-pound table and carried it upstairs on his back.

In those early days Willi's main Peace Corps problem was Bob Bates. Willi considered Bates a good man but too much the prep-school master. Bates tried to hold the volunteers on too short a leash. He wouldn't delegate authority. He even managed the petty cash. Willi didn't openly criticize the director. Eventually, he leveled with a Peace Corps evaluator. "Bob ran practically a one-man show," Willi said. "I had to more or less snatch authority here and there . . . we as a staff failed the volunteers in two ways: at first we coddled them too much. Then, later, we did not maintain enough contact with them in the form of visits and plain interest in what they were doing."

Most of the volunteers were underemployed. Some had almost nothing to do. Each person had to make what he could of the job. It was never easy. Willi was a ready, sympathetic ear to the teaching and agriculture volunteers. To Willi Nepal meant mountains. He couldn't help but feel that the five volunteers stationed in the hot, humid plains of the Terai weren't really living in Nepal. About half of the volunteers were stationed in the 230-square-mile Katmandu valley. These volunteers Willi talked to regularly. For him, though, the real Nepal and the real Peace Corps lay out in the hills and mountains. In the west, Tansing lay a two- or three-day walk from the nearest airport. In the east Bhojpur stood a four-day trek from the closest road.

When Willi thought of a volunteer and how he was doing, he thought of a story or two. He loved to tell of the epic journey of Sarge, Bobby, Ethel, Barry, Rocky, and Romney to Bhojpur. For the centerpiece of his animal husbandry demonstration project, one volunteer, Dave Towle, had gotten together through US AID a herd of American livestock. From them Towle envisioned siring a whole new breed that would dramatically improve livestock in eastern Nepal. Towle named the bull "Sarge," the two rams "Bobby" and "Ethel," and the three ewes "Barry," "Rocky," and "Romney." To help Towle shepherd his herd to Bhojpur, Bob Murphy, another volunteer, went along.

Willi told how the two Americans and their American animals traveled by truck down the Raj Path, the twisting, rock-strewn, road that was royal only in name. Fifty miles south at the Indian border they caught a train. For five days they rode eastward in a cattle car, "Sarge" tied securely to Towle's Peace Corps book locker. As Willi told the story his listeners could smell the dung, taste the dust, and feel the frustration as the closed car sat for hours on sidings. At Biratnagar, in southern Nepal, the volunteers took another truck thirty miles north to Dharan, the jumping-off point into the hills. There another volunteer, John White, joined them.

Bhojpur was only 35 miles from Dharan. But a range of 4,000- to 6,000-foot hills lay between them and Bhojpur. The paths were slick from the monsoon rains. Journeying northward they forded one river a half dozen times. At the crossing of the great Arun River the volunteers and all their animals except the bull joined the six boatmen in a dugout canoe. As soon as Sarge was tied to the side, the boatmen began paddling upstream, keeping to the calm waters near the river bank. Suddenly, the boated surged out into the bubbling, frothy torrents. The boatmen paddled frantically. The dugout angled across. Willi made his listeners sigh with relief as the boat finally landed far downstream. Willi loved to tell how the volunteers thought their difficulties were over now but a tiger moved down toward them. By shouting and throwing stones, they drove the tiger off. A full ten days after leaving Dharan the volunteers and their ménage slogged up the last hill to Bhojpur.

Willi wanted to be around volunteers who grasped life joyfully and squeezed everything they could out of it. He enjoyed talking about Mac O'Dell, a smiling little dynamo who walked through the bazaar in Dhankuta saying hello right and left, making friends with everyone. Franqui Scott was stationed in Dhankuta in the eastern hills also. Willi told how she had learned that Nepalese girls during their menstrual periods sat at home supposedly meditating about "the seeds of life," the price of being female. She explained to her female students that menstruation was natural and taught them how to make sanitary napkins. Before long some of the girls told Scott privately that they had started coming to school all month long.

In the Katmandu valley lived one volunteer about whom Willi could tell stories for hours: Barbara Wylie. Like Willi, Barbara Wylie had an aura about her that a pallid term like charisma could not begin to capture. At the age of thirty-three, Wylie was older than most volunteers. Wylie had taught elementary school in Michigan. Riding her bicycle through the narrow streets of Katmandu, she looked like Katharine Hepburn. She glowed with not only physical but moral beauty.

Each afternoon she taught English at Padmor Kanya Girls School.

Willi liked to talk most about Wylie's morning project. She had
noticed that in her neighborhood many parents didn't have enough
money to send their children to school. With the help of a Nepalese
family she started a school. It was nothing but a big yard with some
tables and a book cupboard knocked together from discarded Peace
Corps crates; to the thirty to fifty Nepalese who showed up each
day, it was "The Happy Free School."

In the early years the best of the volunteers seemed almost a
superrace to the Nepalese. Unshackled by tradition, unspoiled by
the prejudice of caste and class, these young Americans appeared
to be free men and women, free as the Nepalese could never be.
Barbara Wylie was always smiling. The Nepalese saw this bright-
ness and cheer and loved her. Willi thought Barbara was simply
wonderful. But Willi and volunteers like Barbara got on the nerves
of some volunteers who looked more somberly at Nepal and the
Nepalese.

"I like the Nepalese," one early volunteer wrote home. "But
Katmandu is no peaceful village. Many people are very poor, and
many of those seem happy: that is they smile more than we (by
'we' I mean most Americans) do. But I am not sure just what that
means. The servants, here, say 'Nepal naramro dhash ho, America
ramro' (translated: 'Nepal is a terrible country, America is a good
place to live'). And no wonder. One little fellow is in the seventh
grade, and had agreed to pay his school fees, but this boy has no
shoes, no scarf, no clothes, save for the flannels of his Nepali
dress, and he has only a meager quilt to sleep in at night. And I
sleep in my insulated underwear, under quilt, sleeping bag, etc.
. . . I am discovering certain cultural differences in empathy. We
seem to like sad songs, the Nepalese do not. At this point, I can
only guess why."

Willi's home was a gathering place for volunteers in from the
hills or in need of a weekly shower. Willi and Jolene didn't seem
that much older than the volunteers. Jolene served big mounds of
American-style food, an antidote to the rice and vegetable curry of
Nepal. Willi served big mounds of enthusiasm, to fill a deflated
volunteer up before he headed out again.

To Willi and Jolene the unresolved question of the Everest climb loomed above all else. Willi was thirty-six years old. He would almost centainly take over for Bates when the director left in mid-1963. Yet Willi still insisted on going off on the climb, to risk his health, his career, his life, to make it up Everest.

Jolene understood what Everest meant to Willi. She also understood all that she and the family had sacrificed for Willi's climbing. She had had enough. Yet Willi insisted that he was going. He argued with his wife. She had known what he was when she married him. Hadn't she? Wasn't she asking him to become something different?

While they were arguing Willi tried one last time. If Jolene would let him go, he promised that he would return. Jolene took this not as a mountaineer's bravado, a fool's optimism, but the very measure of Willi. If he said he would return, then he would climb the mountain a safe, certain way. Then Willi said that this would be his last major expedition. Willi had said that before but there was only one Everest. Jolene said that yes, Willi could go. She and the children would wait for him.

‎MMMMMMMMMMMMMMMMMMMMMMMMMMMMMMMMMMMMMMM

On February 13, 1963, Willi drove to the airport to greet his comrades flying in from Calcutta on a chartered DC-3. He had often
gone out to the airport to meet dignitaries, Peace Corps staffers,
and others. Rarely had there been such palpable excitement and
anticipation. Willi didn't rush up to the plane, though, for the
climbers were greeted first by the snout of a camera filming for the
National Geographic special.

For sheer size the American Everest Expedition far surpassed
anything Willi had ever seen. Climbing expeditions had always
been something Willi did almost privately, at most afterwards writing an article for the *American Alpine Journal*. This wasn't only a
mountaineering expedition, though, but a great American venture.
Kennedy's America was showing the world what it could do,
climbing all kinds of mountains. With Willi and Bates mountaineers themselves and Shriver taking such an interest, the Peace
Corps seemed part of the expedition. Willi was going off to climb
the world's highest mountain not only for himself and for Jolene,
but for the Peace Corps.

Though Shriver had personally said that Willi could take leave without pay to climb Everest, the formal permission didn't arrive until the last moment. On February 20 as the expedition was heading out, seen off by what appeared to be most of the American community, Willi finally joined the group. As Willi trudged out of the Katmandu Valley he could hardly believe the spectacle of which he was a part, a four-mile-long centipede that took two hours to pass any given point. There were 909 porters carrying over 29 tons of goods, 30 high-altitude porters strutting along trying out their fancy new clothes and boots, as well as the expedition members.

Willi plodded along, following the trail of the nearly thousand people who had gone ahead of him that day. He and Tom Hornbein discussed why they had come on this expedition. Just going had nearly meant a divorce for Willi. Yet now both men weren't sure why they had come. Reaching the top of the first hill and walking along the ridge, the two friends sat down alongside pools of brilliantly clear water. From the first hours' walking their feet were blistered. They took off their boots and plunged their feet into the cool water.

"One thing that bothers me is that I've been working so darned hard lately I'm just about run down," Willi said. "I'm exhausted when I climb into bed at night. Maybe the old guide's too far along for this sort of thing."

"Cut it out," Hornbein said. "All I hope is you're washed up enough that I can keep up with you."

Like Willi, thirty-two-year-old Hornbein had dreamed of climbing Everest since his youth. As a boy of fourteen he had climbed Signal Mountain in northern Colorado. Standing on the summit feeling this wondrous, burdenless freedom, he knew that he had to return.

"I guess I'm hunting for some answers too," Willi said. "Where do I go after the Peace Corps? Philosophy, foreign service, or what? That's the big thing I hope this trip will clarify."

Dick Emerson watched ironically the developing relationship between Willi and Tom. On the whole trip through Asia, even in Katmandu, Emerson felt that Hornbein was clinging to him. Emerson had wanted to defuse the whole situation. Soon after Willi arrived, though, Hornbein turned all his attention and energy to Willi. Emerson was not only noncompetitive but he rebelled at competition, whether for Willi's attention or for anything else. Two-man teams would go to the summit. Emerson was sure that Hornbein was choosing the partner with whom he was most likely to get up there.

Other climbers also observed what Hornbein was doing. He was a man of narrowed, focused energy. When Hornbein set his mind on something he was hard to stop. He became so involved in his efforts that he forgot not only those around him but himself. At times like that he appeared selfish.

Willi took pleasure in the daily routine, feeling his body respond once again. It was good walking these hills of eastern Nepal. Every day Willi and the others passed from the lush green of the valley floors where rice and bananas grew among thickets of green bamboo, moving upward along winding trails past terraced paddies of rice and grain, through tiny villages, up higher still to the wooded or sparse slopes of the high ridges, above which stand the white spires of the Himalayas. Then down again, passing back through the same spectrum of geography. For hundreds of years the people here had terraced the land, this their only mild quarrel with what nature brought them, creating a second nature of gentle contours complementing the first.

After a day on the trail, Willi had his own Sherpa bringing his battered sneakers and pumping up his air mattresses. While the climbers sat at the fancy folding tables drinking their daily rationed can of warm Rainier beer, Willi regaled the men with stories. He loved talking about Buddhism and Hinduism, but whatever the subject Willi was ready with a spiel. The other climbers had begun to look at Willi in a special way. Not only did he know so much about Nepal and the East, but he possessed the climbing expertise needed. He was different from Will Siri, an aloof, distant man almost impossible to get to know. The nearer the expedition got to Everest, the more tense and nervous the deputy expedition leader appeared.

As Dr. James T. Lester, Jr., a clinical psychologist and the one nonclimber on the expedition, was discovering, Siri's behavior was unusual. Lester had thought that Everest would be a laboratory for stress. As he interviewed the climbers, he realized that for Willi and many of the others everyday life was the real laboratory of stress, all the dangers and rigors of this expedition a relief. The prospect of life in a tent on an icy ridge was not half so punishing to these men as getting up in the morning, dragging through the quotidian routine. They were men of what Lester called "assertive individuality." Within them there was "a yearning toward the ideal of *wholeness*. . . . It seems, paradoxically, this straining toward wholeness in itself reflects the inner division from which the climber seeks escape; he seems often to be trying to 'lose' himself by strenuously asserting himself. This poignant conflict is one source of the inner drama inherent in mountaineering, the drama inside the equally real adventure of the external events."

Marching toward Everest, Lester talked to Willi. "There was this girl back in Paris in Forty-eight," Willi confided. "Oh she was something, Jim. And I never made anything out of it. I did nothing. *Nothing*." In Willi's voice Lester heard poignancy, and not only about his lost love in Paris. Willi's life seemed full of much unfinished business. All of the climbers were telling Lester their dreams, but Willi's were all terribly frustrated. In one he was playing basketball when the ball turned to dust.

The third night out the expedition stopped on the slopes of the ridge at Chaubas. The eight burnt-orange tents blended into the red clay soil and appeared as natural a part of the scene as the reddish, terraced hills above. In the evening the climbers gathered in the largest tent to discuss their plans for the ascent.

In his mind's eye, Willi saw 29,028-foot Everest, straddling the frontier between Nepal and Tibet. The first obstacle would be the Khumbu Glacier, an immense wasteland of yawning, shifting crevasses and towers of ice. Above that lay a great ravine or valley that Mallory on his first reconnaissance in 1921 had named the Western Cwm, using a Welsh word for valley. It was an extraordinarily benign piece of nature to be found in this setting, a gentle sloping carpet leading up from 19,000 to 24,000 feet, at the very foot of the high mountain. Above lay a hard climb over snow and ice to the South Col, the depression between Everest and Lhotse. From there the route led directly to the summit. It was a formidable climb, and only six men had ever reached the summit, but technically it was not that difficult. Willi knew that as much as anything else it was a matter of good logistics—getting enough food and oxygen and equipment up to the South Col—then moving forward with great stamina and good luck. The year before the Indians had gotten within 500 feet of the summit before being driven back by the brutal winds.

Climbing the West Ridge was an entirely different matter. At the middle of the Western Cwm, nature's gift to the Everest climber, that uncharted route split off and headed directly up the steep snow and icy sides and sheer rock of the West Ridge, upward for almost 8,000 feet. The first task would be simply to get out of the Western Cwm, moving over abrupt cliffs and up a narrow gully. There, at around 28,000 feet, stood sheer cliffs, a formidable challenge at any elevation.

Willi had heard people call the West Ridge route impossible. Even if one day a team of climbers might get up there, it would only be after several reconnaissance trips. As it was now, the West Ridge was 8,000 feet of unknowns within unknowns.

Lhotse and Nuptse had been climbed before. To Willi and most of the climbers Dyhrenfurth's Grand Slam seemed little better than an advertising gimmick. The West Ridge was real.

"To the mountaineering world, even a good attempt would be a significant achievement," asserted Dick Emerson, in his quiet, earnest manner.

"This may sound like Madison Avenue kind of talk," Dyhrenfurth said, perfectly aware of his Hollywood image, "but you know how long it took to raise our money and, I repeat, the Swiss have done Everest and Lhotse. If we do less than that as an expedition, to the world, not to mountaineers, we are less successful."

To pull together the expedition, Dyhrenfurth had quit his job and made large financial sacrifices. He was forty-four years old. All his life he had lived in the shadow of his father and his immense knowledge about the Himalayas. Dyhrenfurth, the son, was obsessed with reaching the summit of Everest. He had to justify the treasure of goods and money that he had collected. If no one reached the summit, the shame would be his. Dyhrenfurth planned to use the logistical support to get a whole slew of climbers to the summit. While that was going on the scientists would be busy analyzing blood, urine, and human behavior. It was fine for some of the climbers to promote the West Ridge so assiduously, but Dyhrenfurth knew that he didn't have that luxury.

"Why not just drop the Col route and put the entire expedition on the West Ridge," Hornbein said. From beneath his high forehead, Hornbein's gleaming narrow eyes seemed to shine out from the middle of his balding head. "This would give us the best possible chance of climbing it."

There was no end of reasoned arguments against Hornbein. He didn't change one bit. Willi wrote later that Tom Hornbein's "continued agitation in favor of an all-out ridge attempt soon won for him the designation of 'pathological fanatic'—a title which he wore with considerable flair throughout the rest of the expedition." In the end it was decided that there would be at least a major reconnaissance of the West Ridge.

Willi and Hornbein were formidable propagandists for the West Ridge. They wanted the strongest team possible. To get it they sang the glories of the West Ridge, using flattery when that worked, even using a bit of shame.

In the end seven strong climbers chose the West Ridge: Willi; Hornbein; Emerson; two other old Tetons guides, John E. (Jake) Breitenbach and Barry Corbet; Barry C. (Barrel) Bishop, a geographer doubling as the *National Geographic* photographer; and David L. Dingman, a young Baltimore physician. The South Col team included Dyhrenfurth and Siri, the leader and deputy leader; Jim Whittaker; Lute Jerstad; Dick Pownall, a former Tetons guide; and Dr. Gilbert Roberts, a Berkeley physician. The support group of scientists and others consisted of Allen C. Auten, a radio expert; Daniel E. Doody, a cameraman; James T. Lester, Jr., a clinical psychologist, and the only nonclimber; Maynard M. Miller, a geologist; Barry W. Prather, an aeronautics engineer and the only non-American; James Owen M. (Jimmy) Roberts, a retired British lieutenant colonel, a Katmandu resident and logistical genius.

Hornbein did nothing but talk, plan, and scheme. The porters were carrying a great bounty of goods. Each bottle of oxygen for the South Col meant one less for the West Ridge. Every porter run far up the South Col subtracted at least one carry from the West Ridge. While Hornbein tried to whittle down the resources that would go to the South Col, Dyhrenfurth kept pushing out more chips of goods and climbers toward his team. He simply had to have the summit. Hornbein pressed and pressed. He was without guile or manners. When it was necessary Willi mediated.

Willi was gung-ho for the West Ridge too, but he kept his enthusiasm muted. He tried to prevent Hornbein from making enemies. Willi was a natural conciliator because he saw value in many different ideas and different positions. He could never be a dogmatist like Hornbein. Yet Hornbein's dogmatism was the spice that seasoned the West Ridge position and made Willi and Hornbein so fiercely hungry for the new route.

Jim Whittaker best symbolized the South Col team. He stood six feet five inches tall. "Big Jim" was a man of the Northwest. Like Willi he had begun climbing in Scouts. He was sales manager of Recreational Equipment, Inc., in Seattle. With the surge of interest in the out-of-doors, the co-op stood poised to become the world's largest specialty retailer of climbing, camping, and backpacking gear.

Whittaker was among the least intellectual of the mountaineers. He was absolutely dedicated to reaching the summit of Everest. During the psychological testing in the States, the climbers had been asked if they thought they would reach the summit. Some said they hoped to, others had said perhaps, while still others said it depended. Only Whittaker had said, "Yes, I will."

The previous fall at his home in Redmond, Washington, Whittaker had gone into training like a heavyweight challenger, doing miles of roadwork, plunging each morning into the chill waters of Lake Sammamish. Walking toward Everest, he moved along with relentless energy, his great shoulders carrying his Kelty backpack like a knapsack, each afternoon finishing up his day by doing fifty or sixty push-ups. Whittaker treated himself as a fine machine to be tuned up and serviced, ready to perform for whichever team would get him to the top.

Willi was a natural leader and not only of his team. Although he was all out for the West Ridge, Willi could draw back from his own goals and see the group as a whole. To Willi the expedition was a growing, evolving human organism. It fascinated him. He worked with humor, insight, and comradeship trying to knead the group into a real team. On a large expedition that was always a crucial matter, even more so on this climb. For a mountaineer what greater honor was there than to say that he had stood on the summit of Everest. It was an achievement that practically everyone in the world could understand. Yet not everyone would make it up there. Some men would climb on the shoulders of others. If there were squabbling and bickering, the expedition could easily become like a group of tumblers unable to form a pyramid because no one is willing to carry the weight of anyone else.

Willi tried to keep his humor benign and gentle. Sometimes, like someone who starts a pillow fight and ends up slugging with his fists, Willi ended up making fun of others. It was all in the best of sport, but Barry Corbet, for one, didn't like it. Other climbers thought that Corbet practically worshiped Willi. He certainly didn't worship that part of him. One day Corbet told Willi that he was tired of his always playing the good guy Willi, entertaining constantly, sometimes at the expense of others. Willi was careful around Corbet for a while and soon the two men were close again.

Willi had been somewhat out of shape when he left Katmandu, but the trails themselves had worked him back into condition. A man like Whittaker climbed a mountain a step at a time. But Willi was like a trampoline artist who first bounced up and down, psyching himself up, before springing upward. He had to get his motivation and energy working rhythmically together. He needed to be up there climbing with his friends. He was still the seeker.

"Emerson, if you knew you would not make the summit, would

you still go on the West Ridge?'' Willi remembered asking, in one of numerous discussions.

"Well, yeah, I still would."

"Well, why?" Willi asked again, digging into Emerson's psyche.

"Well, there's the uncertainty, and I have a theory that energy release is maximized when the outcome is most in doubt. Besides, I would always think I still could make it."

"No, Dick, you're cheating."

The West Ridgers thought of themselves as an expedition within the expedition, an expedition in the pure tradition of Mallory. The modern expedition, from the post-World War I Everest expeditions on through the successful British assault on Everest in 1953 to the American Everest expedition, was a formidable logistical enterprise, with many porters and supplies. It was thought that mountaineers had to climb up great mountains slowly in order to acclimatize. As these expeditions moved up the Himalayan peaks they shed their bulk, with fewer climbers, fewer supplies at the higher camp. Distinguishing both the 1953 British climb and the American climb from Mallory's exploits were the number of nonclimbing reasons the mountaineers were up there: everything from nationalism and science to book and movie contracts. Willi and his team wanted to shuck much of that, to go for the pure mountaineering pleasure.

"The West Ridge advocates seemed to care less about rewards in the outside world and to be less sensitive to the possibility of objective failure, more willing to risk failure in favor of possible internalized or self-given rewards," wrote Lester, the psychologist. "I believe several of the South Ridge advocates privately felt guilty and conflicted because they recognized the apparently greater purity of motivation in the West Ridge team. Perhaps 'guilty' is too great a speculation; after all it might be said that the South Ridge advocates were simply responding to a more complicated reality than the others, both to the mountain and to their responsibilities to those who had put up the money. They certainly seemed to be responding more to factors outside the expedition proper, and par-

1

The classic photograph of the Wind River by Ansel Adams. In the background rises the panorama of the Tetons, the mountains that were a spiritual home to Willi Unsoeld.

2

The Unsoelds' 1959 Christmas card. Willi, Jolene and the four children (l to r): Krag, Terres, Regon and Nanda Devi.

In the summer of 1960 Willi reached the summit of 25,660 foot Masherbrum, "Queen of the Peaks," in Pakistan's Karakoram range. The climb established Willi as one of America's premier climbers.

Members of the unsuccessful 1956 expedition to 27,800 foot Makalu, in Nepal. Top (l to r): Willi, Dr. L. Bruce Meyer, Dr. Harry Swan, William Long and Fritz Lippmann. Bottom: William Siri, Allen Steck, Dr. Nello Pace, Richard Houston and William Dummire.

3

4

6. Norman Dyhrenfurth, leader of the 1963 American expedition on Everest; 7."Big Jim" Whittaker, who reached the summit of Everest by the South Col; 8.Nawang Gombu, Whittaker's Sherpa partner on the trip to the summit; 9.Lute Jerstad, one of the six 1963 Everest summiters; 10.Barry Bishop, Jerstad's partner on their successful Everest ascent; 11. Tom Hornbein, Willi's summit partner on the West Ridge.

6

7

Barry Bishop's stunning photograph of Willi and Tom Hornbein slogging up the West Ridge of Everest.

5

8

9

10

11

The great Khumbu Icefall. Here in this groaning, unpredictable chaos Jake Breitenbach lost his life when an ice wall collapsed.

Willi tying his outerboots. On Everest as on any peak, Willi seemed a creature of the mountain, living far above the plain of ordinary existence.

Jake Breitenbach

14

13

Willi being carried out from base camp after reaching the summit of Everest on May 22, 1963.

15

16

17

When John Roskelley reached the summit of Nanda Devi in 1976, he was well on his way to becoming America's outstanding Himalayan climber.

Sargent Shriver, first director of the Peace Corps. Willi personified perfectly the ideals of the volunteer agency.

Willi and Jolene Unsoeld. Jolene had spent much of her life watching out for Willi, allowing him to go on his eternal quest.

18

Willi

19

20

Nanda Devi. To Willi the 25,645 foot Indian peak was once the most beautiful peak in the world, the mountain after which he named his daughter. Here Willi had thought he might go to die. Here his beloved daughter, Nanda Devi, met her destiny.

Willi and Devi. Rarely had a father and daughter been so close, so much kindred spirits, as Willi and Devi Unsoeld.

Mount Rainier. In the state of Washington, Rainier is simply "the mountain," the highest, most visible geographic landmark in the Northwest where Willi led a group of students from The Evergreen State College in February 1979.

Through the fury of a winter storm, the students fought their way down Rainier to Camp Muir saying the spirit of Willi had led them.

22

23

24

In his last years Willi looked like the old man of the mountain.

The "memorable celebration" in honor of Willi and Janie Diepenbrock, killed in an avalanche on Mount Rainier.

25

ticularly to economic factors. . . . West Ridge advocates seemed more reflective and introspective, more inward-looking than South Ridge advocates, who seemed more practical, pragmatic, and outward-looking. The former seemed the more sensitive and perhaps creative in some sense, while the latter seemed the more obviously rugged and hardy, more well-fitted to the physical stereotype of the mountain man.''

There was another aspect that reached its epitome in Willi. ''The relationship of height to spirituality is not merely metaphorical,'' the fourteenth Dalai Lama of Tibet wrote. ''It is physical reality. The most spiritual people of this planet live in the highest places. So do the most spiritual flowers . . . I call the high and light aspects of my being *spirit* and the dark and heavy aspect *soul*. Soul is at home in the deep, shadowed valleys. Heavy torpid flowers saturated with black grow there. The rivers flow like warm syrup. They empty into huge oceans of soul. Spirit is a land of high, white peaks and glittering jewel-like lakes and flowers. . . . Out in the jungles of the lamasery, the most beautiful monks one day bid farewell to their comrades and go to make their solitary journey toward the peaks, there to mate with the cosmos. At these heights, spirit leaves soul far behind. . . . People need to climb the mountain not simply because it is there but because the soulful divinity needs to be mated with the spirit.''

Among themselves the West Ridgers said that the South Col route was not ''a climb.'' If it was not a climb, then it was not a journey upward. They derisively dubbed the Col route the ''milk run.'' The milk run was a mundane, earthbound trip, hauling up one of the essences of life below. Willi, and to a lesser extent the other West Ridge proponents, thought of Everest physically, spiritually, and metaphorically. They wanted to ''climb'' higher than anyone had ever ''climbed'' before. Slogging up the South Col would not get them high enough.

Day after day the climbers moved toward Everest. They were already in touch with danger and death, though it did not wear the silver mantle of the high Himalayas but a rude, humble garb. Crossing the crude chain bridge over the Those River, eleven porters moved together across the swaying structure. As Dyhrenfurth stood below filming the scene, a chain snapped. The porters tumbled down onto the rocks and water below. Dyhrenfurth plunged into the raging torrent, pulling one porter back while two others swept by, to be yanked out two hundred yards downstream. The other porters lay crumpled on the rocks, moaning or stunned. Within an hour, seven of the porters started off again, carrying their loads. The most bruised and battered ones moved on loadless, happy that they would be paid anyway.

The next day a grotesque and terrible apparition appeared in camp, a Sherpa woman who six days before had charged into a flaming shed to save her only yak. Her upper body and face were burned so badly that her eyes stared out as if behind a charcoal mask.

In the States life was pumped into a dying person, blood and plasma, oxygen and medicine. When the person died his relatives asked what else could *they* have done. In Nepal the forces of life often waged their struggle with death unaided, and when a person was dead he was dead and life went on. The Americans could not leave the woman to die like this. As much to pay obeisance to their own gods as to save the woman, they paid two thousand dollars to have the helicopter fly from Katmandu to get her. And they moved on once again.

On the thirteenth day the expedition crossed the Dudh Kosi, the Milky River, in Sola Khumbu, the home of the Sherpas, and turned north. All this trip they had been moving through country that suggested that the people there were born to live within their own natural surroundings. The tiny, feline Newars were a townspeople. The hill peoples, sturdy, small, bronzed Limbus, Rais, and Tamangs, fit into the contours of the uplands. The Sherpas were a highland people, strong and manly, warm and vigorous. They were a playful race. The Sherpas loved to drink *chang,* a barley beer, and dance their snakelike group dance until they dropped.

Willi knew only a smattering of Nepali, but it was enough to make him someone special to the Sherpas. Willi was their kind of sahib. Willi believed that the Sherpas had a spirit that modern man had lost. That spirit was found among the hill peoples too, but up here it seemed more intense, more immediate.

Willi's legs had ached greatly the first day. They were strong now and willing. The blisters had gone away. His boots were new no longer. On the last three days as the expedition headed almost due north over the last high passes before Namche Bazar, the weather turned foul, the trails slick as oil. This was a region of great rainfall. The forests, looming out of the mist and fog, were lush, rich in foliage. The rain turned to snow. Willi trudged upward, following the slippery trail, to camp at Puijan—damp, dark, moss-covered, like a forest in an old German fairy tale. On the sixteenth day of trekking the skies cleared. The weather was warm and good. Willi moved past familiar two-story Sherpa houses, the yaks and cattle, chickens beneath. Willi looked up. Above stood the great wall of the Himalayas. Thamserku. Kangtega. Ama Dablam. He knew them all. Above them Lhotse, Nuptse. There behind, a mere tip visible, Everest herself.

The expedition moved through the thick, richly forested gorge below Namche, where nature again seemed bountiful and benign. Walking there some of the climbers noticed a loadless porter, keeping back away from the others, his face covered with a burlap bag. When they saw the face, a swollen mass of pustules, they recoiled in horror. To the expedition doctors, David Dingman and Gilbert Roberts, smallpox was an almost medieval affliction that they had experienced only through textbooks. They ordered the thirteen-year-old youth isolated in a neighboring village. As the expedition moved onward, the mountaineers feared that they might leave as their lasting legacy a smallpox epidemic, carried into the ranks of the hundreds of porters, and passed over half of Nepal. As soon as the expedition reached Namche Bazar, the doctors began vaccinating as many porters and Sherpas as they could. By the time more vaccine arrived, the climbers were gone and so were the approximately four hundred Tamang porters who were paid off at Namche Bazar. In the end, in Sola Khumbu there were enough deaths and illness to have been considered an epidemic in the States. But in Nepal a reported forty deaths was considered lucky.

After nine years Willi was glad to be back in the land of the Sherpas. For a town so fabled in the lore of adventure, Namche Bazar had a stern, austere appearance. The 140 two-storied houses blended into the gray landscape. Inside they were dark and smoke-stained. This was a country where everything had its opposite. If the land up here at 12,660 feet was gray, then the mountains were white. If the women wore black skirts, they wore gay aprons striped with colors. If the houses were dark and smoky, then life often was bright and frolicking. The climbers drank *chang*, ate yak stew, and watched the Sherpas dance. The orange and blue and green American parkas that the high-altitude Sherpas wore as their badges of honor blended with the rugs, skirts, and bright hats.

Two days later the expedition moved on six more miles to the monastery at Thyangboche, one of the highest permanently inhabited places in the world. As Willi moved upward to this 13,000-foot high alpine pasture, it was snowing. Seeing Thyangboche Willi felt blinded by its beauty. To him this was the "center of the mountaineering universe . . . an extremely holy and electric spot."

"Never were there such fantastic peaks in such profusion," Willi thought. Thyangboche was a place like Chartres where, standing in the cathedral looking at the light streaming down through those great blue windows, it was hard not to believe in a God. At Thyangboche no mammoth buttresses rose heavenward. The great buttresses were the mountains themselves, so immediate, and yet so distant. This was no longer the Tetons, where the mountains were a backdrop to life below, a neat panorama to be captured in snapshot and climbing boot. The mountains were a mammoth, humbling presence. The monastery itself consisted of a group of long buildings and rooms set down one against another like a stack of dominoes, topped with prayer flags and surrounded by round *stupas*. Thyangboche had no architectural unity, yet there was a higher unity.

In the afternoon many of the climbers rested in the big shed that the Incarnate Lama had provided for expeditions and other visitors. Willi sat talking to Jim Lester, the psychologist, in whom he was confiding a great deal.

"You know, it wouldn't be a bad place to die up there."

"What do you mean, Willi?"

"I mean just not coming back."

Although Lester did not pursue the conversation, he believed that Willi was at least playing with the idea of suicide high on Everest, the mountain of his dreams. The psychologist wasn't sure whether Willi was serious or not. After that one exchange the subject was never mentioned again.

In the evening Willi and Hornbein walked and talked together, their feet crunching into the deep snow, leaving a trail behind them. From the monastery the chanting of the monks wafted upward, rising like a spark from a fire, toward the Himalayas, great crystal jewels shining in the clear night. From another house came the sounds of Sherpa songs and the rhythmic stomping of Sherpa feet. Those sounds too rose upward, blending with the chanting of the monks, as if one was as much a form of worship as the other.

Hornbein was a man who thought as much as he felt. He felt Thyangboche, but his head turned quickly downward to plans for the West Ridge. When Emerson saw Hornbein looking over a photo of the West Ridge in the account by Sir John Hunt, leader of the 1953 British expedition, he joshed him. They had already gone over this so many times that it was ridiculous. As for Emerson, he was enjoying himself looking at *Playboy*.

At Thyangboche the whole West Ridge team got together to decide who would make the reconnaissance climb. "Should we send up a bunch of old broken-down crocks on as vigorous a path as this one?" Willi joked. Nonetheless, it was quickly decided that the four men who had already climbed in the Himalayas should make up the reconnaissance team—Willi, Emerson, Hornbein, and Barry "Barrel" Bishop. Bishop was built like a good football guard, squat, thick, and immovable. His nickname helped to distinguish him from the other Barry on the team, Barry Corbet.

"You could burn yourself out on this reconnaissance," Willi said. "All I can say is that we had best depend on not burning out."

"The composition of the team is sound, I think, on the basis of experience," said twenty-six-year-old Dr. Dave Dingman, one of the younger climbers.

"What we decide on the recon will probably be the most important decision made on the entire expedition as far as we can foresee," Willi added. "Once we split into two routes we will have endangered the summit. The whole expedition could go down the drain."

"But it will be fun," Breitenbach said.

"I don't know about sending all these wild men up there," Barry Corbet kidded, feigning a frown.

"There's the urge as you approach the twilight years to go out in a blaze of glory," Willi said.

After five days they set out again trekking toward Everest. At the end of the first day the expedition camped at 14,000-foot Pheriche, a village of twenty empty stone houses. From there the route passed through high meadows where in the summer the Sherpas grazed their yaks, on past great masses of boulders lying there like refuse from the making of the Himalayas. Then the expedition moved onto the terminal moraine where rocks and stones spilled down from the glacier. Here on this natural junkyard at 16,200-foot Lobuje, the climbers and Sherpas set up tents for a temporary camp. For several days the sahibs rested while porters ferried up the rest of the goods.

On the twenty-first of March Willi set off with Dyhrenfurth, Siri, Whittaker, Jerstad, and twenty-three porters to find a site for Base Camp. For the first time Willi was walking on the glacier itself, moving on ice and snow, passing by what the French called *néves pénitentes*, slim ice pillars that looked like worshipers in prayer.

Willi climbed a mountain the way some men made love, taking keen pleasure in the texture of the rocks, the feel of granite against his Vibram soles, the myriad sensations of snow and ice. He realized that this climb would call for all the techniques he had ever learned, and then some. On those sheer rock cliffs high on the West Ridge he would have to hammer in pitons. Long stretches on ice and snow would require clawlike crampons to get anywhere. Willi knew he would have a lot of just plain slogging to do too, moving up at a guide's pace trying to suck in enough oxygen to keep going.

For Willi, Everest was not just one test, but a series of tests. Leading the porters onto the glacier itself was the beginning of the time of testing. Willi looked up. The Himalayas no longer stood in front, but loomed over him. Directly above stood Lingtren and Khubutse. To the right rose the 20,000-foot saddle known as Lho La. It was here forty-two years before that Mallory, climbing from the Tibetan side, had looked down right where Willi was walking now. From Willi's perspective it appeared that the Khumbu Glacier spilled right out of Lho La. But he knew that the Khumbu Glacier actually snaked its way around and beneath Lho La, rising a good thousand feet higher. Above the glacier rose the West Shoulder of Everest. Above that rose the West Ridge, in size and grandeur beyond comparison, beyond words, beyond description.

Willi and the others set Base Camp at the center of the glacier. It was a decent site, but a dull counterpoint to the world above. The dry moraine rocks themselves looked like chunks and flakes of ice sitting on the ice and snow. While the porters finished dropping their loads, Willi and his comrades set up what would be a lab for most of the scientific research as well as "Rest and Recreation" for climbers down from the high camps. At the center of camp stood two twelve-by-twelve-feet burnt-orange tents united by awnings. Here the team would eat, get their medical checkups, and have their discussions. A radio antenna and a homemade flagpole further set the tents off. To one side stood heaps of boxes. On the other side was the makeshift kitchen, the food boxes set neatly in a row to provide five-foot-high shelves, all covered by large tarps set out on tall poles. There was another cook tent for the Sherpas, three other large tents, a bunch of two- and four-man tents for sleeping, and the world's deepest latrine, a tent set over a foot-wide crevasse of unfathomable depth.

Above Base Camp lay the great Khumbu Icefall, a great white mile-and-a-half-long torrent of frozen water rushing down 2,200 feet, stopping just above the motley array of tents at Base Camp. Here in the Icefall the glacier spewed snow and ice, constantly pressing downward. The Icefall seemed a living thing, thundering when a wall fell, groaning as yet another blue-green crevasse opened up, playing havoc with those who thought its whims and ways were predictable. In 1953 Hillary thought the Icefall "tottering chaos" while Hunt considered it so ever-changing, so varied that every passage through was a first ascent. Mountaineers swallowed danger daily but as often as possible in clearly marked doses, not like this moving through constant uncertainty.

At 9:15 A.M. on the second day of spring three of the best ice climbers—Willi, Jerstad, and Whittaker—and three Sherpas entered the Icefall. For most mountaineers it would have been spooky enough moving through this icy maze just once, beneath ice blocks as big as houses. This was the grand highway up to the Col. They would have to pass through here again and again.

Jerstad considered it a "spine-tingling" business finding a route over which the heavily laden Sherpas could pass, hacking out steps, putting in ropes for support, setting down ladders across crevasses. But risk was like a lover to Willi. He felt alive out here at the front of the expedition, leading the way on the first dangerous assignment. What bothered him was the heat. With the bright sun reflecting off the snow, it was close to 90 degrees.

"We cached our ice screws, extra rope and unused marking wands and headed back at 3:15 P.M.," Willi reported. "On the way down we installed two fixed ropes and prospected for better alternatives for certain sections of the route. The worst spot, we felt, was the final ice wall leading up to the plateau on which the dump was located. This was a near-vertical 30-foot pitch on which we placed our upper fixed rope, and it had some nasty blocks balanced above the track which we thought might be removed by chopping. It took us only two hours to slog back to Base."

On Everest as on any other mountain Willi was almost always in a good mood. Willi had a way of bringing a person's spirits up, a way of sensing who needed a lift and why. For many of the other climbers, the process of getting acclimated had already taken its toll on their spirits. If it wasn't a headache, it was a sore throat. If it wasn't a sore throat, it was nausea. If it wasn't nausea, it was "Cheyne-Stokes breathing," waking up in the middle of the night gasping, feeling suffocated. There were giddy, euphoric moments too.

Early the next morning, Lute Jerstad and his buddy, Jake Breitenbach, were sitting around talking about avalanches. "Lute, if there is an avalanche, I'll be the one to get it," Breitenbach said fatalistically. Later Breitenbach, Dick Pownall, Gil Roberts, and two Sherpas, Ang Pema and Ila Tsering, headed out to improve the route Willi and the others had put in.

That afternoon a little after two o'clock Willi was sitting in camp when shouts from the Icefall were heard. Willi ran into the Icefall following the markers he had helped place the day before. The shouts grew louder. Breitenbach was the one carrying the walkie-talkie. It had to be Jake. Suddenly there Pownall was, standing bruised and shaken. Beside him stood Ang Pema, his head caked with blood, and Gil Roberts, whose shouts Willi had heard.

As Willi listened to their tale, he visualized what had happened. The accident had taken place at the ice wall that Willi had climbed yesterday. Pownall had been leading up the ice wall followed by Ang Pema and Breitenbach on the same rope. Roberts and Ila Tsering were behind on a second rope. A muffled roar rose up out of the Icefall. The earth shook. A great block of wall collapsed. Roberts was picked up and flipped backward, skidding downward thirty feet. But he was okay. So was his one rope mate, Ila Tsering. Pownall lay pinioned under a half-ton block of ice. For ten minutes the two men hacked away at the ice with their axes. Finally, Pownall was free. Roberts heard a voice and dug frantically into the mass of broken ice. It was Ang Pema. The Sherpa's legs were up in the air, head downward. The rope that tied him to Breitenbach led down into the very center of the rubble. To get Ang Pema out, Roberts cut the rope leading to Breitenbach. In fifteen minutes Ang Pema was free. But Jake was gone.

Pownall looked as if he had been in a car accident. Ang Pema sobbed uncontrollably. While the other rescuers turned back with the living victims, Willi, Whittaker, and Jerstad moved on to the accident site. As they trudged the last four hundred feet to the wall, they cried openly.

Whittaker and Jerstad lowered Willi down by rope into the crack of the glacier. *"Jake! Jake!"* Willi shouted. *"Jake! Jake!"* All Willi heard was the echo of his voice bouncing against the mute ice.

As they walked back to camp, Willi cried like a baby. It had been a clean, certain death. "The ice had been still. It gave a wiggle, then was still again." Willi believed that if "Jake could have chosen his final resting place, no improvement could be imagined."

In front of him Willi spied a gorak on the ice. He saw the black bird as a symbol of life, a symbol of Jake's spirit.

Jake lived on.

For two days the sahibs sat in camp. Some of them got drunk. Others lay quietly in their tents. The Sherpas did not understand. They were sad too, but to the Sherpas life and death were intertwined. When a person died he returned in another form.

Like the other sahibs, Willi talked of giving up the ghost and returning home. But Willi had seen the gorak. He believed in reincarnation. Willi talked of dedicating the climb of the West Ridge to Jake's memory and going on.

Slowly the shadows of mourning began lifting. When some of the expedition members entered the Icefall the first time they were weighted down by what they had seen and felt. They tested each foothold, each step as if it might be another messenger of death. Gil Roberts vowed to go into the Icefield only twice more, once to travel up to the Western Cwm, once on the way out for good. Others moved through the Icefall as if by going past Jake's grave they were moving not only beyond his death but beyond the possibility of their own. For Willi the only way to deal with the fear of dying was to face it down. He was ready to go through the Icefall.

On March 27 Willi, along with Jerstad, Whittaker, and the

Sherpa Nawang Gombu, headed out into the Icefield. In less than two hours they had reached the spot where five days before they had dumped supplies. At noon the four men stood before a seventy-foot-tall white wall, the last barrier before the Western Cwm. By any standard this was a formidable barrier. Whittaker led off. In one hour he put three long ice screws into the ice and attached fixed ropes.

Next, while Jerstad stood below belaying him, Willi worked his way further up the wall. For minutes at a time he hung, forcing the route. He had a hard time catching his breath. They were at 20,000 feet. Willi could tell that he was not fully acclimated to the altitude.

To climb the highest mountain in the world, the expedition had everything from metal ladders and ascenders to slings. Despite all that, it gladdened Willi that he was using only rope, a few ice screws, and a technique from his early climbing days, snapping in a second rope to the ice screws, then pulling himself up. After an hour Lute was supposed to take over. It was simpler, continuing on up. Willi worked a second hour. Finally, he was crawling over the top.

Willi stood looking up toward the summit. Directly above sloped the Western Cwm, the five-mile hollow that the Swiss had named the Valley of Silence. After the groaning, shifting uncertainties of the Icefall, the Western Cwm was a gentle place, where a human voice seemed an intruder. The summit lay hidden still, but the massive bulk of Everest's southern and western flanks stood above, the great white form dominating the skies. Willi could have stood there for hours, but it was late. The four men headed back to Base Camp.

"I have to admire both Unsoeld and Whittaker," Jerstad wrote in his diary that evening. "I wonder if I could have mustered the strength they did to manage such vigorous ice-climbing after such a tough day and in thin air. What powerful men! I was very impressed, if not a bit humble, after watching their performance."

Everyone had to carry big loads up to Camp I on the Western Cwm. Willi, though, was simply incredible. If everyone else was struggling to carry sixty pounds, Willi carried eighty and went through half the Icefall by himself, unroped. If most of the climbers made a carry in three and one-half hours, Willi made it in two and three-quarters. At night he lay wiped out in his sleeping bag.

Hornbein wondered if after Jake's death Willi thought he had to play cheerleader. Was this his idea of real leadership? Did he think this was the way to set an example? People were asking themselves how they could possibly keep up with Willi. Finally, Hornbein and Emerson went to Willi and got him to slow down.

For all Willi's talk of cooperation, he was as competitive as a person could be. He channeled that competitiveness into arenas where it had some higher usefulness. He wanted to get the others, as well as himself, successfully up Everest. He was morally competitive as well, seeking to be a better, more generous human being than his peers, judging himself by higher standards than he did others.

Camp II, or Advanced Base Camp, lay at 21,350 feet, halfway up the Western Cwm. This was the highest point above Base Camp where everyone could sleep and eat together, men from both teams as well as the high-altitude Sherpas. From here the path up the West Ridge veered leftward out of the Valley of Silence, while the South Col route continued upward on the Western Cwm.

Not only the climbers separated here but the food, equipment, oxygen bottles, and Sherpas. Every time a high-altitude porter arrived at Advanced Base Camp, Hornbein corralled whatever he could for the West Ridge team. Before long he had a four-man tent, twelve oxygen bottles, ice screws, and fixed ropes. Once he had a stove and three food boxes the West Ridge team would be ready for the reconnaissance that was scheduled before the big South Col climb. Watching Hornbein the South Col climbers became nervous. They didn't like Hornbein's attitude, watching over his supplies outside the mess tent so intently, oblivious to the other team.

Hornbein handled logistics, but Willi was the recognized leader of the West Ridge team. He knew that from the moment the West Ridgers stepped out of Camp II and began to move up the 2,400 vertical feet that stood between them and the West Shoulder of Everest, they would be on ground no foot had ever trod. It was uncertain whether they could even reach the West Shoulder.

On April 3, Willi and Bishop made the first journey up the new route. For Bishop it was sheer delight climbing with Willi. Four days later Hornbein, Bishop, and seven Sherpas established a camp called the West Ridge Drop a thousand feet above Advanced Base.

Now would come the major reconnaissance. It was to have been Willi, Hornbein, Bishop, and Emerson. Emerson was having a hard time acclimating. At Advanced Base Camp he came into the mess tent, looked at food, and took something as simple as a bowl of bouillon. As soon as he swallowed a few spoonfuls he ran out of the mess tent to throw up.

Willi saw that Dick wasn't up to going any higher now. Willi cared a great deal about Emerson. He had felt so bad about Dick's problem on Masherbrum, getting his body used to operating on reduced oxygen. Now this. Day by day Dick was losing strength. His body was growing thinner and thinner. Willi and Hornbein weren't hungry either, but they jammed the food down their throats like a couple of Strasbourg geese. "Tom and I had a death pact that read simply that eating is not a function of appetite," Willi said. "It is not even a function of emotion but of will. We swore to eat until we died. And every meal we came pretty close because we just forced it in."

Despite this Hornbein had begun to lose the first of about twenty pounds. Except for Willi, everyone else was losing considerable weight. The mountaineers were letting their beards grow too. Already the men appeared a different species from the fresh, clean-shaven Americans of the group picture in Katmandu.

Up here above 20,000 feet the mere act of existing took great energy. Every day took its silent toll. There were wrenching changes in climate and weather. One sunny day at four o'clock Willi was lying in his tent wearing only underwear. The temperature on the inside thermometer read 106 degrees. An hour later at dusk Willi noticed that the thermometer read 6 degrees below zero. He was already snuggled in his down sleeping bag.

Jake was dead. Dick was sick. Willi knew that he would have to martial his team carefully. He had only two climbers in reserve:

Dingman and Barry Corbet. Corbet was solid, but he was not fully acclimated yet. He would save Corbet for the Ridge. As for Dingman, Willi felt that since the accident the young physician's enthusiasm for the West Ridge had been badly deflated. He decided if he was going to use Dingman, he better use him now.

On April 9 the four team members—Willi, Hornbein, Bishop, and Dingman—set out along with seven load-carrying Sherpas. Willi led, followed by Hornbein on the same rope. The snow was solid. Willi could move more rapidly than Hornbein who had to coil and uncoil the rope, keeping it taut. Willi pushed relentlessly ahead.

"Damn it, Willi, what are you trying to do?" Hornbein yelled.

"Just testing you," Willi said as he looked back. Hornbein was his partner, but Willi constantly had to prove that he was in better condition.

"For what?" Tom asked, unsatisfied.

"Better things."

The other rope teams were soon far below. At roughly 23,000 feet, Willi was willing to let Hornbein lead. About 800 feet further up the mountain, at about 4:00 P.M., the two men called a halt. It was snowing and they couldn't even see the West Shoulder above them. This would have to be their camp. The Sherpas finally slogged into camp, dropped their loads, and hurried back down the mountain.

That night in their tiny tent, Willi and Hornbein ate curried shrimp and rice royally doused in ketchup. Even the most mundane tasks of living were fraught with difficulty. For the first time they used oxygen for sleeping. Willi and Hornbein fed off the same oxygen bottle. The masks were so uncomfortable that Willi yanked his off and slept with a tube up his nose. That way all the oxygen flowed freely to Willi. Whenever his nose filled, it all flowed into Tom's mask. The oxygen was like a glass of warm milk. Soon Tom was fast asleep while Willi, breathing heavily, wakened. That cleared his nose and he dozed off while Tom moved restlessly. So it went through the night.

Whether Willi and Hornbein were tied to one another by rope, oxygen tube, or aspiration, they were held close to one another by a strange, profound, imperfect bond.

The mountains often simplified a man, bringing out what was true and deepest within him. So Everest had already done to Hornbein. All his determination and single-mindedness had come to the fore. Hornbein was as focused as a laser beam. Willi respected his partner but saw him as a man who wore blinders. Hornbein was like a climber so focused on reaching the summit that he didn't even realize he was kicking rocks down below. To those who did not share Hornbein's obsession, the man could seem dreadfully boorish.

The next morning the team changed partners and moved up Everest wearing snoutlike oxygen masks, large goggles, and crampons. The four men looked like giant praying mantises. Willi led, followed by Dingman. Willi saw Hornbein and Bishop moving up rapidly behind him. Willi was sure Hornbein was trying to beat him to the West Shoulder. He would have none of that. He stopped and turned Dingman's oxygen up to a full blast of four liters per minute, giving him a jab of energy. Then Willi took off up the mountain. The eternal mists played back and forth across the great mountain. Willi still could not see what lay above.

The following day Willi and the others once again climbed up to the ice- and snow-covered West Shoulder. Above loomed the massive bulk of Everest's West Ridge, the blue-black stone not like a mountain, but a whole universe of rock, ice, and snow. Willi's head turned skyward, eyes sweeping the summit a mile above. The route was steep, outward slanting. Willi felt it was possible but that a real challenge lay in making the route safe for the Sherpas. It was hard to see how they could do it unless the whole expedition decided to go for the West Ridge, pouring Sherpas, oxygen, and climbers up that massive bulk. There was little choice but to give up the whole idea of a West Ridge climb.

The next morning Dingman felt sick and stayed in camp. Willi, Hornbein, and Bishop roped up for one final look at the West Ridge, and the possibility of finding a high campsite. They moved up rapidly to the West Shoulder. This day Everest stood clear against the blue sky, stripped even of its white plume. Down to the left lay the immense Rongbuk Glacier, its white tail like ruffled lace, snaking down toward the barren, brown hills of Tibet. Sweeping the scene with binoculars Willi saw the remains of the Rongbuk Monastery, from which Mallory had started out to climb Everest over forty years before.

Hour after hour Willi, Hornbein, and Bishop pushed ahead. Willi's crampons dug into firm snow and ice that was like a layer of Styrofoam against the bare rock an inch or two below. One o'clock. They were beyond their highest previous point. Willi knew they were walking in Tibet now, not Nepal. Two o'clock. No one had ever walked here before. That made the trip doubly sweet. It was getting late. Three o'clock. If they could only reach the point where the ridge ran up against the ore-like rock of Everest's peak. Twenty-five thousand feet. Four o'clock. They were standing now right at the end of the West Shoulder, looking up at the beginning of the West Ridge. The rock itself was rotten, crumbling, not at all what Willi liked to climb. But Willi moved upward to the crest of the ridge. Sitting right there was this beautiful little campsite, protected by rocks. They were now at 25,100 feet. Almost 4,000 feet below Willi saw Advanced Base Camp, a pebble sitting in the middle of the Valley of Silence.

The three men sat down to eat some rum fudge.

"All right, Willi, have you made up your mind?" Hornbein asked. Even now he pushed. "Or do we have to go higher still?"

"I'm convinced, Tom," Willi said.

"We have found it," they called down to Advanced Base on the radio they carried with them. "We have found it."

As Willi descended, "the unearthly light illuminated a veritable mountain kaleidoscope. Peaks appeared and vanished among the mobile clouds while the colors deepened till even the snow glowed a deep, golden bronze. Striding easily downhill . . . in the midst of such exhilarating beauty it was easy to overlook our lack of actual information as to route. By the time we reached 3W we were all firmly convinced that such a fine campsite as the one discovered for 4W really *deserved* to have a route extended above it. And so it was settled that the West Ridge would indeed go."

● ● ●

The next day as the four men slogged into Advanced Base Camp together, Willi and Hornbein's feeling of accomplishment and resolution tempered their fatigue. They had reached 25,100 feet and found a perfect campsite for the assault on the high mountain. As the West Ridge team reached Advanced Base the other climbers slapped their backs and squeezed their hands. The South Col group knew, however, that the success of the West Ridge contingent created more problems. While the four members of the West Ridge team were up above, the remaining climbers had voted to use four-man assault teams on the South Col, not two-man teams, as previously planned. Four-man teams would require so much oxygen and supplies that a parallel attempt on the West Ridge was out of the question.

It didn't take Willi and Tom very long to figure out what the added West Ridge votes might have done to Dyhrenfurth's exercise in democracy. To assuage them, the expedition leader offered to let the West Ridge team become the second four-man team to go to the summit on the South Col route. Willi's choice was clear. Either sign on for a highly probable climb to the summit by the South Col route and the prestige and honor of entering that exclusive fraternity, or simply wait, hoping that there would be time and resources for what at best would be a problematic uncertain climb.

If this was not bitterness enough for one day, Dave Dingman told Willi and Tom that he had decided to join the South Colers. He didn't feel the West Ridge was worth the risk. Privately, he thought Hornbein dangerously gung-ho. Willi hadn't been counting that much on Dingman anyway. Then in the evening Bishop came to the tent. "I got a letter from the *Geographic,*" the photographer/geographer said glumly. "They're paying my keep and they've got to have pictures as high on the mountain as possible. I've got to go on the South Col, Willi." As Bishop said the words, he knew that even if he reached the summit, he would still be denying part of himself.

"I can't risk it."

Willi stared at the stocky, intense mountaineer. Bishop was the kind of man you wanted to have with you.

"Sure, Barrel," Willi said, feeling the loss deeply. "We understand. It's tough. I don't envy you having to climb Everest by the Col."

There it stood. Bishop was gone. Dingman was gone. Emerson was hurting. It was just Willi, Hornbein, Corbet, and the two Sherpas. Eight climbers might reach the summit. Willi could be one of them. Willi knew, moreover, that with his weakened team and almost no logistical support from the main expedition, it was highly unlikely that any of the West Ridgers would reach the summit. Yet Willi would not give up the climb, for there was "the spiritual, moral and mountaineering correctness of the only route worthy of our efforts."

From the trek north to Sola Khumbu, the West Ridgers had been an expedition within the expedition. Now they were outsiders staring through the glass pane at the wealth of men and resources moving up the South Col route. Dyhrenfurth had promised that as soon as the South Col route was adequately supplied much of the energy and resources of the expedition would pour up the West Ridge.

While Willi tried to get used to the idea of waiting around, Hornbein spent hours in his sleeping bag at Advanced Base Camp figuring out logistics. Hornbein told Willi that no matter what Dyhrenfurth said, it would take until the end of April to supply the South Col for the four-man summit teams. It simply wasn't fair. The only good news was that Al Auten, the communications man down at Base, had agreed to come up and help.

To get supplies up the mountain the West Ridge team had to depend not on the muscles of Sherpas but on motor-driven winches. The "Tiny Tiger" motors used a special high-altitude fuel. They coughed and sputtered like an asthmatic child. Day after day the climbers worked with them, but it was hopeless. Then they turned to the hand winch. It was set up at a supply dump high on the West Shoulder, the airplane control cable running hundreds of feet down the mountain, leading to a special sled set on six Head short skis loaded with eighteen bottles of oxygen.

At the top Corbet and the two Sherpas took turns cranking away.

It was so difficult that a person couldn't crank more than half a minute before collapsing. Emerson, who was finally feeling okay, stood far below watching the heavily laden sled creep up the mountain a couple of feet at a time. To protect the precious cargo from veering off toward a crevasse, as a barrier Emerson stuck his ice axe into the snow hard against the cable. "Okay, anchor up," Emerson said into the radio. "It's coming . . . it's coming . . . oh shit." The ice axe had gone flying a hundred feet across the snow. The sled sidled off sideways into the crevasse.

Far above, Corbet and the two Sherpas continued cranking away, unaware that this crucial supply of oxygen had just fallen down a black hole and with it any hopes of reaching the summit. They just kept cranking and cranking away. As Emerson stood there unbelieving, the loaded sled nudged up out of the crevasse and started moving up the mountain.

Willi considered it something of a miracle. One fact remained though. In two weeks all they had gotten up the mountain were two sleds carrying thirty-six oxygen bottles.

The days turned into weeks. Soon the monsoon season would be upon them, bringing a season of storms. Willi felt that if the West Ridge team were ever going to make their move, they needed help *now*. But the final push for the summit by the South Col route had begun.

On April 25 Whittaker, the Sherpa Nawang Gombu, Dyhrenfurth, and his personal Sherpa Ang Dawa were scheduled to begin the five-day move up the South Col for the first assault on the summit. Morning dawned snowing and windy, the worst day yet on Everest. The next day was bad too. The climbers got together in the big mess tent at Advanced Base to discuss their prospects.

The people at Advanced Base Camp were using the rations up about as fast as they were carried up from Base Camp. As far as Dyhrenfurth was concerned, it was the five West Ridge climbers who were eating too much food and wasting supplies needed for the push up the South Col.

"If I had known some members of this expedition were going to be so fanatical about the West Ridge . . . ," Dyhrenfurth said.

Everyone knew the expedition leader was talking about Tom. "If we stay here any longer we'll never make it. We'll be too deteriorated, too far gone."

"One more day just sitting and we may be too far gone for the final push," said Will Siri, the deputy leader. "Tomorrow we either have to start the final assault or all go down to recuperate."

Hornbein bristled. "But, Will, four days ago you said there was no sign of deterioration!!"

"Be quiet, Tom," Willi, said, shushing his partner. Willi usually did not give in so easily. But in Hornbein he had a partner who was considered something of a fanatic.

As Willi looked out the tent flap in the morning, he saw that it was a beautiful day, so perfect that the white plume was gone from the summit. Willi said good-bye to the summit team. The next day he said good-bye to the second summit team of Bishop, Jerstad, Pownall, and Girmi Dorje.

On the thirtieth Willi, Hornbein, and Emerson retreated from a nearly deserted Advanced Base Camp to Base Camp to await the outcome of the summit thrust. Willi watched the shadows play across the bottom of the Western Cwm. Willi wanted the West Ridge as much as ever. "Yet there is a magic about the summit that makes it hard to turn one's back to it at almost the moment of its attainment; a moment so symbolic of the conquest by the best elements of the human spirit over the dross of laziness, timidity and selfishness."

At Base Camp Willi had time for a sponge bath with warm water, meals with real eggs and fresh vegetables and goat meat. On May 1 as he sat in the warm sun, Willi looked up at the looming bulk of Everest and knew that somewhere up there Dyhrenfurth, Whittaker, Nawang Gombu, and Girmi Gorju were moving up to the summit itself. When Al Auten made the 5:00 P.M. radio call to Katmandu he still had no news from the summit team to report. As usual Jolene had driven over to Colonel Bill Gresham's radio shack. Today she had the four children with her. As far as Willi was concerned the big news from the capital was that the Unsoeld cat had just given birth to kittens.

"Wonderful!" Willi enthused. "How are they?"

"Fine."

"Where are they?"

"In the bathtub."

The next afternoon the radio at Base Camp squawked alive. Gil Roberts was calling from Advanced Base Camp. "The big one and the small one made the top!"

Willi and Tom hugged one another. Willi was happy that Whittaker and Gombu had made the summit, doubly happy that now the West Ridge team would have its chance. Nothing stood in their way any longer.

That evening Willi and Hornbein lay next to one another in their sleeping bags planning the assault. Hornbein was the logistician for the West Ridge, as well as the oxygen expert for the entire climb. He knew how many cylinders of oxygen they needed, how much food and how many porter trips.

The voice of Maynard Miller wafted over from the mess tent. "Now that the mountain is climbed we've got to put our major effort into science," the geologist told Siri.

Strain as they did, Willi and Hornbein couldn't hear Siri's answer. They couldn't be sure whether science was their new opponent or not.

The next few days Willi learned that other events high up on the mountain had severely hurt their chances of a successful West Ridge climb. The summit triumph had been a victory over laziness and timidness but not over selfishness. Nothing was more precious, nothing harder to move up Everest than the cylinders of oxygen. To reach the peak the first team had used far more oxygen than they had any right to use. They had used so much that on the South Col at the 26,200-foot-high camp the second team discovered that instead of the twelve to fifteen full cylinders of oxygen that were supposed to be waiting for them, there were only four. That meant that only two men would be able to make the second summit attempt.

On the morning of May 2 when the four men set out toward Camp VI, they had decided that Bishop and Jerstad would go for the summit, Pownall and Girmi Dorje providing backup. They had scarcely gotten away when they ran into Whittaker and Gombu, stumbling down half exhausted. The second team had no choice but to go back to camp with the two men, brew up some tea, heat food, and wait for Dyhrenfurth and Ang Dawa. An hour and a half later the expedition leader arrived delirious, looking terribly old. As he mumbled senselessly, Jerstad laid him on the snow and gave him oxygen, knowing that for now the second team's summit attempt was finished.

Three days later Willi watched an aged, tired Dyhrenfurth walk slowly and deliberately into Base Camp. The man's veneer was gone now. His emotions stood out like the workings of a watch when the face is removed. Almost immediately the expedition leader called a meeting.

"If I had known Tom was going to be so fanatical about the West Ridge, I would have increased our budget, ordered three hundred oxygen bottles, and hired fifty Sherpas. If only Tom had been honest with me about his ambitions back in the States."

Hornbein couldn't quite figure out what Dyhrenfurth was getting at. "I'm sorry. I guess I wasn't aware of my own ambitions back then," Hornbein said.

The burden of financing and organizing the expedition had been primarily Dyhrenfurth's, as well as leadership on Everest. Tom, with his single-mindedness and impatience, had added more to that latter burden than anyone else. Dyhrenfurth suggested now that Tom was responsible for the one major logistical weakness as well: the lack of sufficient oxygen. The expedition leader believed that back in the States while in charge of planning the oxygen, Hornbein had seriously underestimated the amount needed. On Everest itself, Hornbein and the West Ridgers had squirreled away far too many cylinders for their own use.

As the expedition leader talked Willi clutched Hornbein's shoulder. Willi was afraid that at any moment Tom would explode. Willi and Hornbein were glad that Dyhrenfurth had reached 28,200 feet, higher than a man his age had ever reached. Unfortunately, to get him and Dawa that high and to get Whittaker and Gombu to the summit, seventy-five of the ninety bottles of oxygen up there had been used. They had been squandered on porter trips. They had been used not only for sleeping and climbing, but for sitting in the tents at Camp VI. They had been used, bottle after bottle, like a kid's soda pop. The victory went in part to the seventy-five bottles of oxygen. Willi knew that it wasn't Tom's fault that there was barely enough oxygen left up there for Bishop and Jerstad to have their chance.

Norman's face was gray, drained. Using so much oxygen he had gone beyond his own capabilities. Hornbein turned toward Willi, looking first at Willi's hands, then into his eyes. Willi relaxed his grip. They both knew there was no reason any longer to argue with Norman. What was the point? Now, finally, they would have the resources for the climb up the West Ridge.

Bishop and Jerstad still wanted the summit too. In their own frustration at a thwarted summit attempt, they were half-brothers to the West Ridge team. They were the poor kin of the South Col team, left with a bare minimum of oxygen and supplies.

The plan that was now coordinated with Dyhrenfurth at Base Camp was as daring and spectacular as anything that had yet been achieved in the Himalayas. There would be two summit attempts, one by the unknown West Ridge, on the same day. If all went well the four men would meet on the summit, Willi and Hornbein from the West, Bishop and Jerstad from the South. Then Bishop and Jerstad would lead the West Ridge team down the South Col. After that, Corbet and Emerson would have their summit day on the West Ridge route.

"All energy is being sucked together for the final sustained effort," Willi wrote Jolene, after meeting with Dyhrenfurth. "From tomorrow on there will be no let up in our drive; and on this drive are concentrated all our planning powers, imagination, physical sources, and incidental dreams and passing fancies. . . .

"In the midst of such all-consuming concentration, though, is the dim awareness of the background provided by you, Jo, and the kids and the Peace Corps job and the years that lie ahead for us.

The foreground of the all-out effort on the mountain gives depth and richness to this background; but without the background the mountain would lose all perspective, becoming a mere comet burst whose light fails to illumine the life that follows. . . ."

To Willi a wasted summit day was like a love lost forever. For the next three days the weather was bright and sunny, but the West Ridge team and five Sherpas were still 8,000 feet below the summit, hefting supplies upward. Further below in Base Camp, Bishop and Jerstad waited impatiently. On May 9 the weather turned bad once again, as Willi knew it would. The West Ridge team lost another day.

The next afternoon Willi and Hornbein were in Advanced Base Camp when Gil Roberts, the chief doctor, talked to Barry Prather in Base Camp about the summit plans. Willi didn't have to be told that many of the climbers down in Base Camp wanted to get going, to return to their families and normal lives. The scientific work was winding up too. None of those below had cared that much about the West Ridge; now they cared even less.

With the lost day the attempt on the West Ridge would come by May 20. That was pushing hard up against the beginning of the monsoon, but the supplies and oxygen wouldn't be high enough any earlier. Bishop and Jerstad had waited as long as they were going to in Base Camp; they were planning their summit day May

18. The porters were arriving to clear out Base Camp on May 21. As Willi saw it the expedition was willing to abandon the West Ridge. They would go home holding high a lone triumphant banner, one that by itself was unworthy and tawdry.

"The only conditions under which we can hit the summit on the nineteenth or twentieth are if we do not lose any more days because of weather," Hornbein said emphatically. Thinking he might be usurping Willi's role, Tom had foresworn talking on the radio. But this was different. "In other words, perfect conditions. Is this clear?"

"Roger, roger. Gotcha," Prather said. "It's just that time is running out. Over."

"May I talk to Norman, please?"

"Roger, he's listening," Prather said. The expedition leader's laryngitis was still so bad that he couldn't possibly talk over the radio. "Go ahead."

"Okay, we realize time is running out but we envisioned that there were a few more days beyond the twentieth or twenty-first, so far as summit attempts by our route are concerned. And even though this might retard at least part of the exodus from Base Camp, we would hope that we could pursue our attempt beyond the twentieth or twenty-second of May. How do you read that? Over."

Dyhrenfurth was still the leader of the expedition. He wanted the West Ridge too, but there were limits. The monsoon would soon be upon them. He had responsibilities to the whole team.

"Only comment is, there are three hundred porters coming in here on the twenty-first. Over."

"Well, I guess we'll see you in Katmandu then. Are we going to have any support for our traverse if we happen to get that far and it happens to be later than the twentieth of May? Over."

The idea that the West Ridgers might stay up there alone was unthinkable. Willi and Hornbein were capable of doing just that. That was the specter that had suddenly risen before Dyhrenfurth and the expedition members at Base Camp. A death or an accident up on the West Ridge, and nobody left to help bring them down. The press would never understand that they had brought it on themselves. The expedition would end not in glory but in disgrace.

In Base Camp, Bishop came on the radio next. As a former West Ridger himself, he understood Willi and Tom's feelings as well as anyone. "Tom, do you read me? Over."

"Yes, I do, Barrel. Fire away."

"Righto. Lute and I will delay another day. . . . But I think that's about it. How does that tie in with you, Tom?"

"As long as the weather is good, fine," Hornbein answered, not willing to concede an inch. "I would drop one other thought, though, that you consider leaving us a small nest egg if you really have to pull out on the twenty-second. In case we get out a little later than that, we can move out behind you and perhaps catch up. Over."

"Roger. We hope this doesn't happen, though."

The expedition had been on the mountain almost two months. Another week or ten days and the climb would be over. Willi had no time now to enjoy what he considered the pure mountaineering pleasure of the West Ridge route. At least, Dyhrenfurth had agreed to hold up the porters' arrival until the twenty-fifth while Jerstad and Bishop were willing to wait until the twenty-first for their summit day. If the two teams didn't meet on the summit, Dyhrenfurth and Whittaker had cautioned Willi about going ahead with the traverse, trying to climb down an unknown route.

All Willi was thinking about now was getting up high enough to have a real shot at the summit. The eleventh was another bad day. The twelfth was fine. On the thirteenth they were up again at Camp 3W, which now was fully stocked with oxygen and food. On the fourteenth Willi led a line of thirteen Sherpas up along the West Shoulder onto the West Ridge itself, higher and higher, up to the campsite at 4W that Willi, Hornbein, and Bishop had reached a month and two days before. Up there Willi was an engine of strength and resolve, never sparing himself.

The next day Willi headed back up to 4W again carrying another heavy load, this time with Hornbein and the Sherpas. While the Sherpas hurried back down the mountain, Willi and Hornbein set up a tent on what Tom thought the most beautiful spot in the whole

Himalayas. It was an exquisite moment standing there on the tiny platform where the snow of the ridge meets the sheer rock of the summit block, the two men looking out on Tibet.

That night in the tent Hornbein spilled two quarts of water. "You seem to be cracking under the strain," Willi said. "Maybe you'd better go down too."

"Drop dead, Unsoeld. Goodnight."

Even now, Willi was pushing Hornbein, digging at him. It was as if Tom was a side of Willi himself that he kept hidden beneath his gaudy cloak of humor and public goodwill.

The sixteenth was one of those blustery, marginal days. Willi and Tom decided to spend it in their sleeping bags. Wind or no wind, by noon Willi and Hornbein felt the inexorable pull of Everest. They headed up the mountain. They intended to go only a little way, but were drawn on and on, their crampons digging into the snow, scratching against the limestone. Finally, they reached 25,250 feet. Here would be the site for Camp 5W, the next-to-last camp before the summit. Above ran a gully for over 500 feet leading up to a band around which they could not see.

Moving back down to Camp 4W, they found the wind had already covered over their tracks. Willi and Tom felt their way down Everest. Willi looked down and saw two four-man Drawlite tents pitched at camp next to the two-man Gerry tent. Arriving in Camp 4W Willi found Auten, Corbet, and four Sherpas eating dinner.

What bothered Willi was that Emerson had not come up. Yesterday he had become sick again and turned back. He was supposed to try again today. Dick was a man of great feeling. He exuded a quiet humanity as rare among mountaineers as among those who inhabited the world's lower places.

At 7:00 P.M. Barry made the radio call.

"Norman and the whole gang down here say 'good deal on Camp 5W,' " said Prather, speaking from Base Camp.

"Those of us here at Two are jumping up and down," Bishop said from Advanced Base Camp, where he and Jerstad were spending the night on their way up to the South Col. "One last thing— you'd better not count on Emerson from the way things are going.

He's moving real slow. We can look up now and see he's just about at the New Dump, about three or four hours out at his present pace, and he said something about a possible bivouac on the way.''

Prather came on the radio again: "Norman says here, and it's agreed that Dick should not fiddle around anymore up there. Dick should come down.''

Except for not knowing what had happened to Emerson, it was a fine evening. Willi led the three Americans in song. There was no comradeship like this, four men together in a tiny tent in the dark night so far from life below, so close together.

As the climbers went to sleep, the wind began blowing furiously. At around midnight, Willi woke up. He decided to wake Hornbein.

"Tom, I had this weird dream,'' Willi mumbled.

"You mean the one about the head that comes into the tent?''

As Willi spoke, a bearded, frozen, windblown apparition appeared in front of them. "A couple of tents just blew away,'' Auten said, almost nonchalantly, his head poking through the tent door that he had just unzipped.

A few minutes before, Auten and Corbet had awakened to feel the two joined four-man tents sliding downward. Instinctively, they dug their fingers into the snow beneath the tent doors. The two tents continued rolling over and over. The six inhabitants tumbled like laundry in a clothes dryer. Suddenly, they stopped. They knew that at least they hadn't rolled southward or they would have been sailing 4,000 feet down to the West Cwm. It had to be toward the north. That was better but not that much better, a 6,000-foot drop, but not so vertical. While the wind blew in hundred-mile-an-hour gusts, the six pondered their position. The tents had ended upside down, encapsulating them like a body bag. If too many of them got out, the tent would probably go sailing off. While Auten and Corbet debated, fifty-five-year-old Tashi, the oldest and wiliest of the Sherpas, bit a hole through the side of the tent with his teeth. When Auten got out he was wearing two left boots, but was better off than the five others still in the tent.

"We're about one hundred fifty feet down the hill,'' Auten went on. "A real mess.''

Willi and Hornbein pulled on their outer gear, and with Auten stumbled down, their bodies pushed and pulled by the violent wind, their head flashlights cutting a narrow swath through the black night. The two tents lay in a jumbled heap. Corbet's air mattress was poking through the hole in the tent like a flag of surrender.

"Well, what'll we do?" Willi yelled over the storm, his voice almost cavalier.

"How about seeing we go no further," Corbet's muffled voice sounded out of the tent.

Willi, Hornbein and Auten lashed ropes around the big bundle and tied them to ice axes sunk firmly into the snow.

"Hey, that's my feet," Corbet yelled as Willi wrapped the rope around a promising protuberance.

"Well, they'll be there in the morning," Willi said, as he went looking for another likely anchoring spot.

"All okay? Nawang? Everybody comfortable?" Willi yelled into the tents when he was finished.

"OK, sahib," the Sherpas said.

"See you in the morning, Barry," Willi said as he, Hornbein, and Auten turned to fight their way up to their tent through the storm.

Morning dawned on a brilliantly blue sky, but the wind continued unabated. In Willi's tent, the three climbers took turns anchoring the two sides with their bodies. The great gusts beat against the frail yellow tent. The wind roared up and underneath the floor, lifting Hornbein and his sleeping bag off the ground. The three men grasped the aluminum frame and held the tent down. While this was going on, Willi was telling stories of other storms on other mountains. For him this night was an experience to be savored, to be put in a repository with other mountain memories and drawn on in the *next* storm. At 8:00 A.M. Willi got on the radio to Base Camp. The first voice he heard was not coming from Base Camp, but from Barry Corbet just 150 feet away.

"We're currently waiting rescue by Willi and Tom and Al," Corbet said, his voice crackling through the radio.

"Can you read 4W now?" Willi asked.

"I read you loud and clear, Willi," Prather answered from the radio tent at Base Camp. "Did you get what Barry wanted?"

"I think I did. Yes, it's going to be awhile yet . . . because we're just barely holding on to the Gerry tent. Here's a question, Bear. How's the wind down your way? Over."

"It's blowing a little bit down here, not very hard though—twenty or twenty-five miles per hour. Over."

"I see. Well, we may not be able to hold out here much longer. . . . Tent's taking a beating. Wind's blowing about a hundred pretty steady. Over."

The only good news was that up in Advanced Base Camp Dingman had spotted Emerson walking up the West Shoulder to Camp 3W.

"Holy cow. I can't believe it!" Willi exclaimed.

"That's great news, Dave! Great news! Now if we can get out of this mess we'll be fine. Over."

Corbet and the four Sherpas decided if they waited much longer for rescue, they would be blown right off the mountain. While the Sherpas headed down on their own, their backs braced against the wind, Corbet struggled up to the two-man tent. Auten left the tiny tent to look for his pack. At nine o'clock Willi got on the radio again.

"O.K. Here's the latest report," Willi said. As Willi spoke, the guidelines on the tent snapped. Despite the human ballast, the tent began to slide down the mountain. 'O——oo——v——e——e——e——r.'"

"You want the weather report? Over."

"God damn! The tent's blowing away," Willi said.

"Roger. The tent's blowing away. We'll stand by."

"*Stand by.* We're headed over the brink!"

"Roger."

"Tom. Barry! Get out! The tent's going."

Willi watched Hornbein jumping for the door. Half outside, Hornbein grabbed a long rappel picket and jammed it into the ground. With his feet spread-eagled inside he stopped the tent. Corbet piled out next, heaving boxes and oxygen bottles on top to weigh the tent down. Then Willi moved outside, walkie-talkie in hand, still talking almost casually to Base Camp.

"Well, we're all out, the tent's gone, and we're headed for Three as fast as possible. Over."

They couldn't follow the Sherpas back down the mountain without ice axes, and their ice axes were still supporting the wrecked tents below.

As they fought their way toward the broken tents, Willi felt the wind picking up even more. He watched as the wind heaved a food box off the mountain, tore a sleeping bag out through the hole in the Downlite tents, casting it upwards, lost in the mists of blowing snow. Willi grabbed his ice axe. He decided he wanted at least a picture to take down with him as a souvenir. He was wearing a heavy pack. He rammed his ice axe into the frozen surface. As he fumbled with the camera, the wind picked him off the ground. "Hey, man, you need an anchor," he thought. He reached out, grabbed the ice axe, hooked his leg around the shaft, and took his pictures.

The four climbers struggled down, pulled right and left by the violent wind. Only a hundred feet above Camp 3W did they reach the more windless side of the mountain. Willi's face was a frozen mask, his runny nose frozen into icicles on his ice-caked beard. Willi slumped down beside Hornbein in the snow. It was all over. They were finished. Everest had spit them out like pebbles.

Back in the tents Willi was at least relieved to see Emerson. He had slept out on the mountain. Against one of the cardinal rules of expedition climbing, Emerson had headed up alone. He had gone up with the idea that if he wasn't strong enough to make it all the way to Camp 3W, he would bivouac outside for the night. Even before leaving Advanced Base Camp he had chosen his spot for the bivouac, a crevasse near a dump on the West Shoulder. Emerson realized that he probably wanted to bivouac. At dusk, he had reached the dump, foraged around for the two extra bottles of oxygen there, and found the crevasse. With darkness descending he rappelled down thirty feet into the black depths where the sides narrowed to a mere four feet. With his ice axe he pounded the snow down into a bed tight across the abyss, blew up his air mattress and set it down, got his oxygen gear all regulated, and settled down for a night's sleep. Soon enough the wind picked up, blowing snow down into the crevasse, covering him with a blanket of white.

For Dick the expedition had been one frustration after another, not noble frustrations either. His battle had not been with the great mountain primarily, but with his body. He had lost forty pounds, more than any other climber. There were guideposts on a mountain. A man knew if he had reached 24,000 feet or 26,000 feet. There were no guideposts to tell how far Dick had come in this struggle, no way of knowing just what he had combated, no way of judging himself. He had lain there by himself alone in this black night, knowing that this was where he wanted to be.

If they had not been so tired, the West Ridge team would have trudged all the way down to Advanced Base Camp that afternoon on their way off the mountain. The climbers spent a last night high on the mountain dreaming as much of fresh eggs and meat as summit journeys. While Willi slept, Hornbein was still resolutely planning away, trying to come up with some scheme, any scheme that would get them to the summit. Even Hornbein realized that the idea of going back up again was "sheer fanaticism." Camp 4W was in ruins. Much of the food had blown off the mountain. The four strong Sherpas who had made it up there were already down at Advanced Base Camp, finished, worn out.

Lying in his sleeping bag, Hornbein had an idea. What if they didn't put in two more high camps, as they had planned, but only one more. That would make it five camps in all instead of six as on the South Col route. It was crazy. But if they could get the Sherpas to do one more high carry. . . . If the loads were kept light, no more than forty pounds. . . . If the route didn't prove too difficult. . . . If. . . .

At dawn Hornbein couldn't wait any longer. "I didn't mean to wake you up," Hornbein said as he nudged Willi in the ribs. "But since you are, what do you think of this?"

Willi could still draw on endless reservoirs of enthusiasm. He was soon pumping away with energy and resolution. Willi knew it would be tough. There would be enough supplies for only one two-man summit team. It was the one chance they had left. When Corbet, Emerson, and Auten heard the idea, they were all for it as well. Willi radioed the news down to Dyhrenfurth at Base Camp.

"Well, I'm delighted by your plan," the expedition leader said, all quarrels with the West Ridge team forgotten. "Willi, you've had a hell of a lot of tough luck. You've worked awfully hard. And we're all two hundred percent with you. We wish you all the luck in the world and hope you make it. Over."

"Thanks a lot, Norman," Willi said, equally excited. "Really this is probably a terrifically long shot."

"Willi, we all thank God, of course, that you are all alive, that nobody got hurt; and whether you make it or not, in any case you have accomplished miracles. I think the mountaineering world, I'm sure, will recognize that this is an incredible accomplishment on a long and difficult and unknown route. Over."

"Thanks a lot," Willi said. "We share your joy in all being alive, all right. There were a few times when things were flying around wildly that we weren't sure but that some of the objects were us. And, I don't know, if we just get one break in the weather now, it's entirely possible to go all the way. . . . The upper part of the mountain might give us something we can really sink our teeth in. Over."

"Willi, it sounds very, very good. All the luck in the world. As they say in German, *Hals und Beinbruch.*"

The plans were, if possible, for the two teams to meet on the summit. The South Col climbers would guide the West Ridge team down the southeast ridge to the high camp where Dave Dingman and the Sherpa Girmi Dorje would be waiting. If that didn't work out, the West Ridgers would go back down their route rather than attempt to descend by the far easier but to them unknown South Col.

For the next two days the West Ridge climbers looked up at the summit and saw that the weather was clear. They rested and prepared, waiting for the two fresh Sherpas and more supplies to reach them. Over on the South Col route, the other team had been held back by the storm as well. Both teams might try for the summit on the twenty-second of May.

In the afternoon Emerson was outside shoveling snow while the other climbers sat inside the tent. Willi was discussing his post-expedition plans. He was very excited about using Outward Bound as a tool to help juvenile delinquents, leading them into wilderness, into risk to help them develop a sense of themselves. "It can change their lives," Willi said enthusiastically.

"That's absurd, Willi!" Emerson said, his voice carrying through the walls of the tent. Emerson and Willi loved arguing with one another for the pure pleasure of it. Willi would take a position diametrically opposed to Emerson. This time Willi was serious. Emerson was all for the wilderness and climbing too, though he didn't see it as a solution to the problem of urban poverty. To Willi, however, there were no limits to what a person could learn in the mountains.

The one bit of business left before departing Camp 3W was what Willi called "the most crucial decision perhaps of the entire expedition." As climbing leader Willi had the right to choose the summit climbers. That was not how he wanted it done. The five members of the West Ridge team—Willi, Auten, Corbet, Emerson, and Hornbein—met to decide.

"I don't mind being outspoken since I'm not in shape for it anyway," Emerson said to the team members. "There's no question that Barry, Tom, and Willi are in the best shape. I think that is the first consideration."

By that criteria Corbet probably stood first. It had taken him a long time to acclimatize. Now he was strong and ready.

Corbet said, "I think Willi and Tom should go. For one thing, you've plugged harder on the route than any of the rest of us."

Willi said, "All the more reason for you to have a turn, Barry."

"Another thing," Corbet went on, "you two have been climbing together; you know each other, and you'll make the strongest team. What's more, you're both just about over the hump. This is my first expedition. I'll be coming back again someday."

As long as he lived, Willi would never forget how Corbet acted that day. At thirty-six, Willi was indeed the old man of the summit climbers. Willi and Tom were the logical team. That did not mean that Corbet had to see it that way. Corbet was as good as any rock climber on the expedition. So far he had experienced none of the joy of forging a new route. He had been weighed down with the mundane, often tedious business of getting the team up high on the mountain. Corbet was physically and mentally ready for a summit attempt. Willi knew that perfectly well. Willi considered Corbet's decision unselfish; Corbet figured this was just the nature of the game, nothing to get excited about.

On the afternoon of the twentieth of May the five members of the West Ridge team and five Sherpas moved back up to the wrecked, broken remains of Camp 4W. Only three of the twelve food boxes remained. The two-man tent had caught there on the frame of the larger tents below. It was whipping in the air like a yellow prayer flag. Salvaging whatever they could, the five Americans and the five Sherpas settled down for some sleep.

On the morrow the ten climbers set out for one of the most extraordinary one-day team efforts in the history of Himalayan climbing. If Willi and Hornbein were to have their shot at the summit, the five Sherpas and five Americans would have to climb up 2,000 vertical feet over unknown, uncharted, increasingly steep terrain, carrying heavy loads. This was twice the distance anyone had ever carried in a day that high on a mountain.

By any reasonable standard they were a motley crew even to attempt such a venture. Except for hemorrhoids that he called his "Achilles anus," Willi still appeared fit. At only 125 pounds, Hornbein was a bony runt of a man. Corbet was strong and willing but he had a certain melancholy quality. Auten had never been considered a summit climber. Among the Sherpas, Ang Dorje was the most experienced but he was in his forties, old age for a high-altitude porter. Ila Tsering was the only other Sherpa who had even gone on a big expedition before.

In the darkness Corbet and Auten rose, put on their boots and oxygen and set off, angling up the North Face, breaking a trail directly up the massive bulk of the West Ridge. Then they turned and moved directly up a couloir leading toward the summit.

At nine o'clock the last of the Sherpas stuck his head out of the tent. "All good Sherpas base camp, sahib," Tsering said. "All bad Sherpas here." Even the three inexperienced Sherpas, Tenzing Nindra, Passang Tendi, and Tenzing Gyaltso thought that was funny.

Willi helped the Sherpas with their loads. Hornbein fixed their oxygen. By 9:30 the Sherpas were off trudging slowly onward, weighed down by their heavy packs, sucking in oxygen. Then together on a rope came Willi, Hornbein, and Emerson. Willi and Hornbein carried the oxygen bottle that ran up to their face masks, flashlights, cameras, diaries, and a few personal belongings. Emerson lumbered behind carrying an extra cylinder of oxygen.

For the first time since Masherbrum, the three men were climbing together. When they had gone only a few hundred yards, Willi turned around. Emerson was hurting. Even now his old friend had not acclimated.

"Dick, for goodness sake, get rid of that bottle," Willi said through his mask. Emerson shouldn't even have been up here. He was there only through sheer willpower.

"No, no. That's why I'm here—because you guys need the bottle."

"Willi, you tell him why he's here," Hornbein said, turning toward Willi.

"Dick, we asked you to come with us today because we love you."

The three men stood there and cried. Willi took the extra cylinder of oxygen and threw it away, and they went on. It was as good a climbing day as they had ever spent together. When they reached the base of the couloir at 26,250 feet, ice was falling down the mountain. Looking upward they saw Corbet 800 feet above chopping out a staircase. There they stopped to have lunch. When the ice stopped falling, the Sherpas started up the route that Barry had prepared for them. Soon it was time for Willi and Tom to move up the couloir too. Dick was going to wait to help the Sherpas return. The three friends cried.

Willi said, "Must be the altitude."

Emerson said, "Don't do anything foolish, you nuts." Then Willi and Hornbein headed up Everest. For the longest time Emerson sat on the empty ledge looking out down the Rongbuk Glacier toward the brown hills of Tibet.

Willi and Hornbein moved slowly up the thousand feet of stairs cut out of ice. The Sherpas were moving even more slowly. Willi and Hornbein passed them. At about 27,250 feet Corbet and Auten stood on a ledge at the bottom of the Yellow Band, the wide strip of rock that girdles the uppermost region of Everest. Below, the Sherpas struggled up the 40-degree pitch.

As Willi pulled himself up onto the ten-foot-long ledge that at its widest was a bare twelve inches across, he was smiling. "Where did you find such spacious accommodations?" he asked Corbet.

"We knew you'd be satisfied with nothing but the best, but it's the only possibility we've seen all afternoon. Anyway you'll be able to keep warm digging a platform when we leave. Only don't knock any ice down on us."

The Sherpas reached the ledge anxious for at least some respite from their efforts. Standing perched on the West Ridge, digging in with their ice axes, they waited while the four sahibs cut a larger platform out of the snow. Then the supplies were passed up—high-altitude rations, oxygen cylinders, the tent—each item indispensable and irreplaceable.

It was late, no time for long good-byes. These were not sahibs and Sherpas any longer, not summit climbers and load haulers, but men who shared and felt and cared. They cried and grasped each other's hands and through the mittens felt each other's warmth. Each Sherpa said, "Good luck, sahib." Then Corbet tied the long climbing rope onto his ice axe anchored in the snow. Auten rappelled down into the gathering dusk. One after another the Sherpas followed him.

It was Corbet's turn. As he was leaving the ledge he called back, "Gee, Willi, just like guiding on Mount Owens." In the Tetons this was how they got their clients down. It was a gallant thing to say, a gift of the familiar, of the common, a gift of warmth.

As Corbet disappeared Willi turned toward Hornbein. "You know,

Tom, it's going to be lonesome up there." Then he looked up at the foggy summit of Everest and saw loneliness there like a physical presence.

For an hour the two men worked without oxygen, chopping a larger platform out of their snowy berth. By the time they finished the wind was blowing down the mountainside. As they grappled with the tiny tent, the gusts tore at them. The tent would not fit properly secured. The best they could do was to pitch it at an angle, about a foot hanging over the ledge; the ropes tied onto a piton driven a half inch into the rock, the sides held down by their ice axes and extra oxygen bottles; topped by the prayer flag Dorje had left. As they entered the tent, they could only hope that two hundred feet higher on the other side of Everest, Lute and Barrel were doing much the same thing.

On their tiny stove Willi and Tom cooked freeze-dried curried shrimp in tomato sauce and Campbell's Red Kettle soup together in the same pot, along with crackers, peanut butter, blackberry jam, and grapefruit sections washed down with bouillon. The food was enough for four men. They managed to jam two-thirds of it down their throats. On a mountain Willi happily gave up such measures of civility as brushing his teeth, changing his clothes regularly, or even taking them off to sleep. This night Hornbein decided that he too would sleep in his clothing, like Willi, taking off only his boots.

After dinner Willi dozed off breathing in just enough oxygen to feel comfortable. At nine, Willi woke up. It would be *that*. Willi was tempted to go in the big nylon bag in which he kept his sleeping bag. Jolene had sewed that bag for him. Somehow that didn't seem right. But at over 27,000 feet getting out of the sleeping bag would take a good twenty minutes, putting on his boots about as long. The simplest act wore him out. In this altitude each step was like bench-pressing two hundred pounds.

Hornbein still had enough of a physician's fastidiousness to want Willi to do his business outside. "You want a belay?" Hornbein asked. At least, his partner wouldn't fall off the mountain.

"No thanks," Willi said cheerfully. "A guide can handle these things himself."

Willi crawled out of the tent, poking the flashlight beam into the black night. He set his stockinged feet squarely on the nylon bag and wrapped his down mitten around the tent rope. As he squatted down he started sliding off toward the ledge. Willi felt as if he were on a skateboard. He held tightly onto the tent guideline, praying it would hold him. What a stupid way to go, he thought to himself, falling down the mountain with my pants down. The rope held. Willi laughed.

Back in the tent Willi nestled back into his sleeping bag, set the oxygen level on a meager one-liter flow, and fell asleep. Hornbein was still awake. Even now he had that same insatiable curiosity about how he acted. To see how his handwriting was affected by the altitude, he wrote a letter to his wife without using oxygen. Then, he too, settled down next to Willi and fell asleep.

For years Willi had been waiting for this morning. Yet May 22, 1963, began as any ordinary climbing day began, in that drowsy, half-conscious state where habit is the only sovereign. At about 4:00 A.M. the oxygen ran out and Willi and Tom woke up. They got the bouillon brewing on the tiny stove and started dressing. They already wore layers of clothing. They topped it with relatively lightweight wind parkas and stuffed their heavy down parkas into their packs along with the extra oxygen cylinders. They pulled on their felt-lined reindeer boots over two pairs of wool socks, strapped on their crampons, and put on oxygen helmets, wool balaclavas, and parka hoods. With down parkas, lemonade, oxygen bottles, cameras, and a radio their loads came to about forty pounds a piece.

Outside in the gray dawn Willi fiddled with his oxygen regulator.

"Even with the regulator turned off it hisses," Willi said, relieved that Hornbein was the expedition's oxygen expert.

"It's always the regulator," Hornbein said, knowing what had gone wrong before. "I've got a spare."

For twenty minutes Hornbein fiddled with the regulator. He double-checked the valves for ice, but the bottle kept hissing away.

"It doesn't sound too bad," Hornbein shrugged. "Let's just keep an eye on the pressure."

If that didn't work out, Hornbein figured, they could share as they did when they slept, using one bottle, the T valve, and long tubing. It was a measure of the toll the mountain had already taken on their judgments that the two of them thought climbing to the summit tied to each other like Siamese twins made perfect sense. They couldn't bring themselves to walk back even the forty feet to the tent to pick up the extra oxygen cylinder. Instead they decided to set the oxygen regulators at half the regular rate, only two liters a minute, turning them off entirely while belaying and resting.

Willi looked down. Below for a thousand feet lay the steps Corbet had cut. Above, the gully was only about ten to twelve feet wide, rising at a 45-degree angle, covered with loose, unstable snow. Willi led up the couloir, driving his toes into the snow, cutting steps with his ice axe. Below, Hornbein belayed his partner, bracing himself if Willi should fall. When Willi had moved up the hundred feet of rope, he belayed his partner up to join him and started out again.

Willi and Hornbein were in Tibet. Below to the east between the Rongbuk and East Rongbuk glaciers lay Everest's 23,000-foot North Col, the route the early British climbers had used. Above that, not far from where Willi was climbing now, and almost exactly parallel but hidden by protruding walls, was the place where Mallory and Irvine had been last seen, two black specks moving upward.

Four hours had gone by already. Willi had climbed only about five hundred feet. The couloir had begun to narrow. It became so thin that they had to climb sideways. It looked like a crack pointing up toward the summit. They were at the Yellow Band that girds Everest. Facing them lay the most technically difficult climbing anyone had yet done on Everest. For sixty feet they would have to climb a sheer cliff. It was not even solid rock, but a crumbling tawny slab rock surface covered with unstable snow. Tom saw that "the rock sloped malevolently outward like shingles—rotten shingles on a roof." It was a roof in which the last ten feet rose absolutely vertically, without a trace of a handhold.

"You want to lead this one?" Willi asked.

"Sure, I'll try," Hornbein said, not thinking.

While Hornbein waited, Willi drove a pin into the wall as a belay point and tied the rope through. Belaying was an almost automatic reaction for Willi. He switched off the oxygen. While Hornbein worked overhead Willi dozed. After a while Willi heard Hornbein hammering a piton into rock far above him. If his partner had to use pitons, then the pitch was really a bear. There was nothing he could do. Willi fell half asleep again. After close to an hour, he realized the rope was moving through his hands. Hornbein was right above him moving down through the air on the rope like a great spider.

"I couldn't do it," Hornbein said as he landed in the snow beside Willi. "You'll have to finish it."

First the two men sought an alternative route. They traversed onto the North Face itself, seeking some other way up. That looked even worse. It was the couloir or nothing.

"Tom, if you didn't do it, what chance do I have?" Willi believed that of the two, Tom was the better rock climber.

"No, you won't have any trouble," Hornbein said reassuringly. "Turn your regulator clear up."

Willi moved the oxygen gauge up to the full five liters a minute, feeling the rush of adrenaline. Then, wearing his forty-pound pack, Willi moved back up the unfinished pitch. Tom had gotten most of the way up the limestone, pounding a piton into the crumbling, rotten surface. It was the last ten feet that had stopped him.

Snapping the rope into the high piton, Willi surveyed what lay above. He would have to gut it. Taking off his mittens, he clawed his way up, using his frozen hands as if they were crude instruments. His fingers touched the edge. He felt for some kind of hold on the rotten rock. Then he thrust himself upward. His crampons scraped for a momentary hold, rock splintering and falling downward. He hurled his body upward, grasping a toehold, pulling himself over the top. He had made it.

Willi belayed Hornbein up the pitch. "Good lead," Hornbein gasped as he reached his partner. "That wasn't easy."

"Thanks. Let's roll."

From here the couloir widened and was not so vertical. After six hours of climbing they found a place to sit down. Willi discarded his empty oxygen cylinder, glad to be rid of the ten pounds. The rotten rock had about ended. Above lay gray rock, firm rock, *real* rock, and snow into which they could dig their crampons. The altimeter read about 27,000 feet, still 1,100 feet from the summit. It was one o'clock. A great bulk of mountain rose above with no hint of the summit or a route up.

Willi took the radio out of his pack.

"West Ridge to Base," Willi yelled into the walkie-talkie.

"This is Base here, Willi," Whittaker replied, his voice surging with excitement. "How are you? How are things going?"

"Man, this is a real bearcat!" Willi said. "It's too damned tough to try to go back. It would be too dangerous."

"I'm sure you're considering all exits," Whittaker replied. He knew what that altitude did to a person's brain. He knew how gung-ho the two climbers were. He was worried about how much judgment Willi and Tom had left. He felt they simply weren't being rational. "Why don't you leave yourself an opening? If it's not going to pan out, you can always start working your way down. I think there is always a way to come back."

"Roger, Jim. God damn it, if we can't start moving together, we'll have to move back down."

"Don't work yourself up into a bottleneck, Willi. How about rappelling?" Willi could tell that Whittaker was upset at this talk of being past the point of no return.

"There are no rappel points, Jim. Absolutely no rappel points," Willi said. "There's nothing to secure a rope to. So it's up and over for us today and we'll probably be getting in pretty late, maybe as late as seven or eight o'clock tonight."

The rock was so rotten that if they tried to rappel back down the pitons would probably tear out, sending Willi and Hornbein smashing down the mountain. If they had wanted to, however, they could have found a way back down the West Ridge. "It was not reasoning but desire that moved us," Willi said. "We had committed ourselves." How many times before had Willi thought that there was no turning back? It had not been true though. Out of the corner of one eye Willi had always looked back. Now all hesitancy, self-doubt, conjecture, reflection were gone, left below the Yellow Band. The only direction was up.

By three o'clock there was still no news of Lute and Barrel coming up the South Col. That meant that when Willi and Tom reached the summit they would probably have to find their way down the South Col route by themselves. Willi pushed onward, reaching the snowfield at the bottom of Everest's summit pyramid. They were at about 28,400 feet. From here they had been thinking about going up the northeast ridge. The West Ridge looked easier.

At 4:30 they stopped for a belated lunch. Out of his pack Willi pulled slushy lemonade wrapped in his down jacket and some frozen kipper snacks to share with Tom. After eating, Willi led onward again, moving diagonally upward, first on cruddy slate, then on snow. Though the wind was blowing close to sixty miles an hour, Willi was feeling the joy of climbing up here, alone with his partner and the mountain. For Hornbein it was fine too, like a day climbing in the Rockies.

They were at the crest of the West Ridge. A hundred and fifty feet above, Willi saw the south summit of Everest ablaze in the late afternoon sunlight. The main summit itself lay only 400 feet above. All that stood between Willi and his one great dream was a rocky spine.

Willi looked at the stretch of pure rock with anticipation. He and Tom took off their crampons and overboots. Willi headed up, the Vibram soles clasping onto the rock.

How Willi loved the feel and touch of rocks. Close to 29,000 feet in the sky, Willi moved joyfully up, choosing the tiniest footholds, feeling the rock through his down mittens, sensing the texture of the stone each time he grasped a new hold. He moved further and further out onto the face, into more danger, into more risk, further out than he had any right or reason to take them, further and further out, and it was pleasure, pure pleasure. Five thousand feet below to one side lay the Rongbuk Glacier that Mallory had ventured up so many years before. Below to the other side stood Lhotse and Nuptse. Eight thousand feet down lay the South Col and Advanced Base Camp. Willi did not have to be climbing out here so exposed, but he was beyond reason, and it was good and beautiful and fine. He was far beyond where he had ever been, and he moved upward and upward and upward.

Willi regretted when the rock ended in a snow belt. Willi and Tom stopped to strap on their crampons, taking twenty minutes. Willi headed up again. This was good snow, firm snow, the spikes digging in.

Willi stopped. He waved Hornbein ahead, coiling the rope as his partner moved forward. Hornbein drew up beside Willi. Forty feet ahead on a pure spire of snow was the tattered American flag that Whittaker had planted three weeks before. As the evening sun cast its last rays of light across the mountain, the two men embraced. Tears ran out of their eyes and down their faces. Holding onto each other they walked onto the summit of Everest, Chomo-lungma, the Goddess-mother of the World. Everest cast its massive shadows down across the bulk of Makalu, the mountain Willi had attempted so many years before.

It was 6:15, nearly dusk. No mountain cast shadows down on Everest's summit. The sun shone bright and pure, the sky so clear that it was as if they had risen beyond time itself, beyond dawn and dusk and darkness. The wind blew fiercely across Willi's face. Northward stretching for hundreds of miles, he saw the brown hills of Tibet, rolling on and on. Southward lay the gentle valleys of Nepal covered by a wispy white blanket of cloud.

Willi and Tom did not try to talk. They were full of an understanding beyond understanding. They turned off the oxygen and stood looking down on the world. Within the beauty of the moment they felt loneliness. Within the roar of the wind they felt silence. Within the glory they felt fear, not for their lives, but for the unknowns that weighed down on them. Within the triumph, they felt disappointment that this, only this, was Everest, the summit of their dreams. They knew that there were higher summits still if they could only see them.

The two men took pictures, including a shot of Willi holding the

Oregon State Mountain Club flag. Then Willi took a crucifix, given him by The Reverend Andrew Bakewell, a member of the 1951 Everest reconnaissance expedition; and two Buddhist prayer flags, a gift of the Sherpa Ang Dorje. He put them at the base of the flagpole tucked into a *kata,* a Buddhist ceremonial scarf that Gombu had left three weeks before.

"Buddhist prayer flags and ceremonial scarf, the American flag, and the cross of Christ all perched together on the top of the world—supported by an aluminum rappel picket painted 'Survival Orange'. The symbolic possibilities rendered my summit prayer more than a trifle incoherent. Feelings and thoughts melted and merged in our moment of climax. My thoughts were heavily weighted with history—the early drive and vision of such men as Mallory, Norton, Smythe, Shipton, and Tilman. And the later generations of Everesters led by Hillary and Tenzing. . . . Following these years of effort and achievement appears our own expedition and the tremendous output on the part of the entire team—sahibs and Sherpas alike—output and sacrifice without which our own summit moment would never have materialized.

"But dominating such thoughts were the surging emotions which colored them. Control is thinned by the altitude and the tears came readily—called forth by a wave of gratitude and a burst of comradely feeling for each member of the expedition—our wives and families—eliciting their own peculiar mixture of guilt and exaltation. Twenty minutes of emotional flux such as this and the marvel is that we still had the starch even to start the descent."

It was 6:30. They could stay no longer. They headed off the summit toward the South Col, Bishop's and Jerstad's fresh footprints their only guide.

"Want to go first?" Willi asked.

"Doesn't matter, Willi, either way."

As Hornbein uncoiled the rope in the gathering gloom, he watched Willi moving out ahead. Climbing down a mountain the man who went second had the tough belaying job to do. Tom wondered if Willi was finally tiring.

Fifty feet from the summit Willi stopped. It was 6:35. As he took out the radio, Willi looked down on a sea of shadows, only the summit of Everest still bathed in light. Willi told Maynard Miller at Advanced Base Camp that they had reached the summit and were on their way down.

"Have you seen any sign of Barrel and Lute?" Maynard asked.

"We saw fresh tracks on the summit so they must have been here."

Before ending the conversation, Willi spoke a few lines derived from Robert Frost:

> . . . . . *I have promises to keep,*
> *And miles to go before we sleep,*
> *And miles to go before we sleep.*

If they could only make it down to Camp VI where Dingman and Girmi were waiting, they would be okay. Willi moved downward as if intuition and instinct were one, without fear or apprehension, feeling his way in the gathering gloom, all he had ever learned in the mountains guiding him. He didn't need his goggles any longer. It was getting too dark for that. For a moment Willi caught a glimpse of Advanced Base Camp over 8,500 feet below. Makalu was all darkness. Lhotse too. The sun was setting on the summit of Everest.

Seven-thirty. All that was left of day was what Tom called "a dream landscape of feathery vagueness." Willi took out the flashlight. He had to see. He had scarcely begun to use it when the light dimmed. He leaned over and held the flashlight just off the snow, trying to find Bishop's and Jerstad's footprints like a blindman reading Braille. He couldn't lose them. He just couldn't.

"No tracks over here," Willi called.

"Maybe we should dig in for the night," Hornbein suggested.

"I don't know. Dave and Girmi should be at Six."

No one had ever survived a bivouac nearly this high. If they stopped they could end up frozen statues left forever on the summit flanks of Everest. Down they stumbled, groping their way along the massive slopes of the mountain. Nothing stayed the same. For a few feet the snow was firm. As soon as they got used to that, they hit soft snow. For a while the snow was deep, then so shallow that their crampons struck rock. The wind ripped at them from one side. When they caught on how to lean into the bitter gusts, the wind struck them from the other side, battering them down.

If only they could make it down to Camp VI where Dave and Girmi would have food and rest, and guide them down the mountain in the morning. If only. . . . *"Helloo."* Willi shouted, his shrieks picked up by the wind and cast off into the void.

"Hello!"

"Hello!" Hornbein shouted.

Willi yodeled.

"Hello."

"Hello."

The wind seemed to be answering, not an echo, but a taunt, a game.

"Hello."

Could it be?

"It's Dingman," Willi shouted. "He hears us."

"Then we're near Camp Six," Hornbein replied.

"But why doesn't he show a light?" Willi said irritatedly. "He could show us where the lousy camp is if he would just flash a light."

Willi moved on again, feeling his way down the mountain. Time and time again they heard the beckoning voice. It was like a warm embrace waiting below in Camp VI.

Hornbein moved cautiously following Willi's footprints, belaying his partner whenever necessary. *"Willi!"* Hornbein shot out into space. As the rope stiffened, he fell into the snow.

The wind picked up, tearing at them. The two men stopped, cut the climbing rope in two, and tied in close to one another. Even five feet away, Willi could hardly see Hornbein. Down and down they went, over hard snow and crunchy snow, firm rocks and rotten rocks, down and down, following the voices. The wind let up finally and they could hear words, sentences even, wafting up out of the blackness. If only Dave and Girmi had a flashlight to guide them. But they didn't and Willi's light gave off only a dull glow.

It was after nine o'clock. Still they continued downward. Willi ran out of oxygen. That slowed him even more. Nine-thirty. Still they kept moving.

"This way—come on," a voice sounded out of the dark. As Willi heard the voice again he fell five feet down a crevasse. "That's right—come on—you're going fine." The fall was nothing, nothing. He pulled himself up. Still they moved down the mountain, the voice appearing and disappearing, like a mirage.

"It sounds like a Sherpa," Willi said.

"Wait a minute, there it is again."

"Is that you, Dingman?" Tom shouted.

"HELLO. HELLO," Willi yelled. Then he muttered to himself, "Why doesn't he flash a light?"

A shout. A shout from below.

"Hear that?" Tom said. "They're still there."

"Come on. Let's go!"

They hurried onward with a rush of urgency, knowing that soon there would be sleeping bags, tents, and rest, and warm food.

"This way—come on."

The voices were so near.

Out of the black night two figures appeared, standing in the snow leaning on their ice axes. "Is that you, Dingman?" Tom asked, hugging the first man as if to reassure himself that he was real.

"No. It's Lute. Lute and Barrel."

Like children waking from a dream, Willi and Tom took awhile to realize just what this meant. They were not at Camp VI at all. They were 850 feet above, at the top of a knifelike snow ridge. They were not in the hands of two fresh climbers who would guide them down. They had two exhausted remnants on their hands.

That morning as Bishop and Jerstad had been preparing to leave Camp VI, their gas stove had exploded in a sheet of orange flame, burning their beards and eyebrows, devouring Bishop's sleeping mask. They had put the fire out and left two hours behind schedule, not arriving on the summit until 3:30. The two climbers had waited as long as they could, but seeing no sign of Willi and Hornbein had left the summit at 4:15. They were still moving downward when they heard the voices from above. Although they were terribly tired, the idea of continuing on down to Camp VI did not even occur to them. They believed that they had no choice but to wait and help lead Willi and Tom down.

If this would be what they called a "terminal experience," Jerstad and Bishop decided they would go out with dignity. They would not lie down. So they stood leaning on their ice axes, stomping up and down, using what energy they had left shouting up Everest. There were few things on earth below as tiring as standing waiting that high on a mountain. Bishop was not wearing the expedition boots but the lighter, more comfortable boots that the British had worn in 1953. He could feel his feet beginning to freeze, moving from discomfort, to growing numbness, to no feeling.

Willi and Hornbein thought that Bishop appeared as if he didn't care anymore, wanting only to be left alone. Jerstad's eyes were so hemorrhaged that he could hardly see, as was Bishop's left eye.

Here in these two men Willi and Tom thought they would find strength and succor. But while they were waiting so much had drained out of Bishop and Jerstad. Willi and Hornbein found weakness worse than their own. That truth became itself a gift of strength and succor. Jerstad had saved some oxygen for Bishop, but he had been too tired to change the cylinders. Hornbein took off his mittens and screwed the oxygen hose to the regulator, his fingers growing numb. Willi took the Dexedrine in Hornbein's pocket—and gave one tablet to Bishop, one to Jerstad. Even with the oxygen and the Dexedrine, Willi had to prod, to insist to get Bishop moving again.

"Get your ass in gear," Willi yelled.

"Let's go," Hornbein said. "This is no place to spend a night."

Hornbein led, followed by Jerstad, then Willi and Bishop about sixty feet behind. The rope jerked as Bishop collapsed in the snow. Willi helped Bishop up and tried to pump him with encouragement. Off they moved again. Lute was trying to find the route but his eyes were swollen shut. As they moved downward they kept stumbling. Willi and Hornbein pushed, and prodded, cursed and threatened. When Bishop fell Willi yanked him up.

"Anybody can walk a hundred yards, anybody!" Willi shouted. "No matter how tired you are, keep going."

Bishop could barely stand, but he stumbled downward. One by one the other climbers ran out of oxygen. Jerstad tumbled down, his fall stopped when his neck caught on the climbing rope.

An outcropping of rock appeared far below.

"Now where, Lute?" Hornbein asked.

"Can't see, Tom. Can't see a damn thing. We've got to turn down a gully between some rocks."

"Which gully? There's two or three."

"Don't know, Tom."

"Think, Lute. Try to remember. We've got to get to Six."

"I don't know. I just can't see."

It was after midnight now. In three hours they had come only four hundred feet. They had reached the rocks. But which gully?

They were at about 28,000 feet. They knew that no one had ever survived overnight at such a height. If they went down the wrong gully they probably would never get back. They had no choice. It was too dangerous to go on. They set their packs on a narrow fifteen-foot sloping outcrop of rock and perched there the best they could.

Willi and Hornbein huddled together. Bishop and Jerstad sat a few feet down to the right. Jerstad was so tired, his fingers so uncoordinated, that he couldn't even zip up his down parka. He knew that if he was going to survive he had to keep his circulation going. He kept hugging himself, banging his feet together. He couldn't stop. He wouldn't stop. Bishop's feet didn't even hurt anymore. His fingers were growing numb. There was nothing he could do. Nothing. Lying with his feet propped above, he drifted into sleep.

Willi's feet were numb. But that was okay. He wasn't worried about them. Hornbein had wanted to keep warm by hugging Willi. But Hornbein was shaking uncontrollably. Hornbein reached down and took off his steel crampons. In the 18-degree-below-zero weather they were conductors of cold right up into the soles of his feet. Willi noticed what Hornbein was doing. He came out of himself a moment and offered to rub his partner's feet. Then Willi helped Hornbein remove his boots and socks, slid the chilled feet under his parka and underwear, up against his stomach, held them there, and drifted off again. When Hornbein offered to do the same for his feet, Willi said no. He was okay. He was in better shape than Tom. He drifted off again.

If the wind had blown across the high ridges of Everest as it had the last ninety-three nights in a row, they would almost certainly have died. The wind had let up, though, and the four men settled into the cold, endless night.

Willi looked up and saw stars gleaming like icy diamonds. He looked down on the world. Far out on the Indian plains bolts of heat flared up, illuminating the low, distant sky.

Lying on the cold rock the four mountaineers had the same flashes of illumination. It was as if the landscape of their souls was the same, or the landscape of all men's souls was the same. None of them thought of living or dying. They were beyond that. Tom and Willi had gone through so much together; still Willi felt so far from his climbing partner that Tom hardly existed. Tom knew that he was completely alone too. So did Lute and Barrel.

Barrel "felt a speck in the universe realizing the tremendous insignificance of man." Tom "floated in a dreamlike eternity, devoid of plans, fears, regrets. . . . Death had no meaning, nor, for that matter, did life." It came to Lute that nothing mattered, not laws, not relationships, not even his children, nothing. He disappeared into nothingness and felt free.

Willi was the philosopher. Willi was the mystic. Like the others, he too was journeying beyond the summit. He was not even trying to encapsulate what he was feeling into mere words, mere thoughts. He lay there lost in time and space, peering out into the darkness.

Were the stars dimming? Or was that his imagination? It was only four o'clock. Were the rocks not quite so black? Or did they just seem so? In the eastern skies the great bulk of Kangchenjunga loomed up before his eyes. Tom's face was clear now, as gray as the mountain. Each minute the rocks grew lighter. Yet another peak rose up out of the darkness. The night had gone from black, to gray, to purple, to a pink alpine glow. A half hour had passed. Still, there was no sun.

The peaks turned golden. Light shimmered down the white mountains. The sun rose up above the Himalayan peaks, fiery and intense and alive. It was five o'clock, a new day.

"Wake up, Lute."

Lute opened his eyes too, as best he could, and saw the great fireball. Light passed down from the South Col. As the sun moved on up into the blue sky, it seemed to cool, to grow more distant. The rich colors of dawn faded away. The day was upon them, stark and real.

Hornbein strapped on his crampons. Then the four men set off as they had begun their journey, Willi leading tied to Tom, followed by Lute and Barrel on a second rope. Lute's eyes and Barrel's left eye were blood-red slits.

Willi and Hornbein trudged down the gully that they had been unable to find at night. Though he was not feeling as strong as his partner, Willi had no trouble making his way down Everest. Turning a corner Willi saw Dingman and Girmi moving up the mountain one hundred feet below.

Dingman ran up the mountain, reaching the two summiteers too breathless even to greet them. Looking at the faces masked in beard and frost, Dingman was doubly speechless. He was amazed that this wasn't Barrel and Lute, but Willi and Tom.

"There's oxygen," Dingman said finally, preparing to get out his extra cylinder.

"We're okay. Lute and Barrel will need it more."

Dingman and Girmi could almost certainly have made it to the summit themselves this day. Instead, they hurried on up the mountain to help Bishop and Jerstad.

Willi and Tom continued down the mountain. At Camp VI, Nima Dorje, another Sherpa, greeted them. Willi took off his boots. His feet were a deadly white, as hard as metal. Willi knew that he might lose his feet. He was so thirsty. He drank coffee, tea, hot chocolate, lemonade, anything.

After the other summit team arrived and rested, the seven men headed on down Everest. The South Col was a desolate, deadly place. For Willi the South Col was all new. As tired as he was, he drank it all in. At Camp V, the climbers huddled in a tent eating lunch, then moved out into gale-force winds. Further down the mountain the winds let up.

In the late afternoon Willi got out his walkie-talkie to see if he could reach Advanced Base Camp, still so far below. Willi told Dyhrenfurth in Base Camp the news of the dual ascents. Then Dan Doody, the radio operator, patched in Willi's walkie-talkie with the radio shack in Katmandu.

"We're all right—greetings—love," Willi said.

Jolene was immeasurably relieved. The previous evening when the radio message had been received at Katmandu that Willi had reached the summit, almost everyone waiting at the Royal Hotel had been ecstatic. Not Jolene. She was a mountaineer herself. She knew what Willi's chances were on a bivouac.

"Truly I promise this will be my last big climb," Willi said.

"This time I have a lot of witnesses," Jolene said.

Hearing Jolene's voice filled Willi with new spirit. He loved to come romping down a mountainside after a climb. Moving down now was "one long schuss." It was a long journey. By the time the group reached Camp III at the foot of the Lhotse Face, darkness had fallen. No one wanted to stop until Advanced Base Camp. The climbers slogged downward, guided by Dingman and his weak flashlight probing around the crevasses.

Life was returning to Willi, to his limbs. With life came pain. During the long night on the mountain, Willi's feet had become not a part of him, but an appendage that he sat back observing. Now he felt a certain vague numbness, then some tiny sensation. As his feet slowly thawed they began to ache. He moved more and more slowly. It was like walking on two open wounds, grinding the flesh into the ground with every step.

At Advanced Base Camp Auten, Corbet, Emerson, and the West Ridge Sherpas were there to greet Willi and Tom. To Willi it was like being reunited with half of himself. Try as he could to block the pain, his feet still throbbed. Dingman looked at Willi's and Bishop's frozen feet. He looked at Jerstad's as well, though Lute's were not half as bad. Only Tom, so disciplined, so determined, so relentless in his personal quests, had returned from the summit unscathed. Since there were not enough sleeping bags, Willi and Tom slept together.

In the morning they headed down again. Willi, Bishop, and Jerstad hobbled along like beggars on stumps. In Camp I, at the base of the Western Cwm, the climbers rested awhile. They were still terribly thirsty. No one had any water. Maynard Miller, the geologist, took some of the bottles of glacier water that he had been laboriously collecting for analysis in the States and gave them to the men.

Just below lay the Icefield. Even in the coldest weather the Icefield was a groaning, shifting, dangerous maze. In the warm weather it was like a gigantic white amoeba that never stopped moving. A large section of the old route had collapsed two days before, leaving a chasm bridged by a 150-foot rope.

Trying to cushion his throbbing feet, Willi wrapped his legs around the rope and slid down. As Willi shuffled slowly through the giant upheavals of ice, he tried to walk so carefully. But he kept stubbing his toes. Despite the codeine, he cried out in pain. Behind Willi walked Hornbein. Watching Willi stumbling on, Hornbein cried.

In Base Camp, Willi cried too, and laughed, shook hands and embraced his comrades, ate food and drank more liquids. His feet were hurting terribly. To try to save Willi's and Barrel's feet, the doctors decided that they needed immediate medical attention.

In the morning the entire expedition left the base of the mountain for good. It was a gray day, gently snowing. Willi put on a blue parka, climbing boots, and a gray felt hat shielding his sunburned, windblown face. He eased himself into a porter's cut-out wicker basket. The four porters who took turns carrying Willi were full of joviality, racing the porters carrying Lute and Barrel.

Willi was looking in the direction he would have chosen to look, but Everest was lost in mist, lost up there somewhere, almost as if the mountain had never existed. As he was jostled back and forth, Willi watched the snakelike procession. This was no triumphant parade. The American climbers were a motley lot, bearded, scrawny men retreating helter-skelter from the great mountain, the 250 low-level porters carrying what remnants of goods and equipment the sahibs had chosen to salvage.

Riding in the basket Willi had a good view, but the jolting became intolerable. After a while the porters began carrying the three injured climbers piggyback, like fathers lifting their children. It had been winter when Willi had come this way before. Now it was late spring, the twenty-fifth of May. The snow had turned to rain. Willi could feel the sweet juices of spring and see life everywhere, the little alpine flowers next to the glacier, the flowing water, the goraks.

At Gorak Shep, the sahibs filed silently past the large boulder where a Sherpa stone mason had completed his work:

IN MEMORY OF JOHN E. BREITENBACH
AMERICAN MOUNT EVEREST EXPEDITION, 1963

The expedition had taken eight days to walk from Namche Bazar to Base Camp. It took them only two days to return. The next morning Willi was lying in bed in Namche when he heard the whir of the helicopter engine sounding up the valley. No one had imagined the helicopter would come so soon to take Willi and Barrel out; Willi had no time to think. No time to reflect. He dressed hurriedly in gray wool pants, a gray wool shirt, gray hat, and climbing boots. As he stumbled into the sunshine his was not a young man's face any longer. The eyes were deep, narrow slits that seemed to look not out into the world but inward. His face was as red as an American Indian's. His red beard appeared to flow into his face.

Willi could have spent hours saying good-bye to the other climbers who would be trekking back to Katmandu and to those Sherpas staying in Sola Khumbu. But he had no time. One of the Sherpas wrapped a white *kata* around his neck. Willi could have spent days talking with Tom who looked not like someone who had just climbed the world's highest mountain, but a little old man, all bone and bristle and memory.

Before Willi knew quite what was happening he and Barrel were off flying back across eastern Nepal. Willi looked down on the richly contoured hills of Nepal, so verdant in the monsoon, as if green were a whole spectrum of colors. In only a few minutes the helicopter was flying over these hills that Willi had spent two weeks crossing.

The Katmandu valley opened before them. There was the United Mission Hospital. There stood Jolene in a blue cotton dress and white sneakers. And there were the children.

Suddenly the helicopter was down and Jolene was rushing to him.

The days had become weeks. The weeks had become a month. The month had become two months. Willi lay in bed staring at his black toes popping out of the hospital linen. The big toe and second toe on his right foot were so shrunken that a whole other toe could have been set in between. The knucklebone showed through the skin on his small right toe. It felt like a loose tooth. As much as he didn't like doing it, at night Willi often took sleeping pills. The first weeks had been worse. Then, even with the pills he couldn't sleep more than a couple of hours. Even today when Dr. Robert Berry, the missionary doctor, came in to scrape off the flakes of dead skin, Willi could hardly take the pain.

Willi stared at the blank wall. "Mirror, mirror on the wall, was it worth it after all?" he kept asking himself. Willi totaled it up. First of all, the negatives. Jake's death. The loss of Barrel's toes and the tip of his little finger, and probably Willi's toes too. The enormous amount of resources, over four hundred thousand dollars. All the time. All the energy. The months away from other human endeavors. Then he thought of the positive side. In retrospect the squabble with Dyhrenfurth and the South Col advocates seemed like nothing. To work for the common goal, these tough, strong-willed men had all given up at least part of their desires. "Against this many-hued background of human warmth and interaction there looms the uniting bond—the fierce drive and desire to penetrate the unknown . . . to push beyond one's ordinary limits . . . to stretch upwards toward new levels both of achievement and of sacrifice," Willi wrote from his sick bed. "Everest looms there as the perfect symbol of the heights to which the human spirit in all its diversity can aspire when seriously engaged in joint endeavor. For Everest it was clearly worth it."

Although Willi couldn't know it, the other expedition members regarded him as having come closest to, indeed, fulfilling that philosophy. On Lester's post-expedition questionnaire the climbers were asked which individual they most would like to have as their leader on a similar expedition. They were also asked which individual they would most like to have as their teammate. Although it is rare that a person wants his friend and his leader to be the same person, Willi stood first in both categories. Moreover, on the Everest expedition, he was judged by his peers as having been the most influential, the most concerned with group welfare and progress, the most mature, the person who made the greatest contribution to keeping the team moving ahead, and the member who most frequently tried to smooth out differences.

Jolene came out to the hospital every day. She hated the dirt and disorder, the flies in the kitchen, the unboiled water, the fact that there were no daily baths. Every day she washed Willi's feet and put fresh cotton between his toes. To her these toes shriveled up like dried pea pods symbolized her husband's heroic generosity. She wrote family friends that Willi's "frostbite was the result of . . . his unconscious solicitation of the other fellow partially as a result of his many guiding years but mostly just because that's the kind of mister I have. He helped Tom (his climbing companion) remove his gaiters and boots and for one and one-half to two hours massaged Tom's feet against his stomach sitting in a very cramped position which impeded circulation and froze his own toes. After he had warmed Tom's feet, he was too tired to make any attempt on his feet. That's my man and I wouldn't really have him any different."

When friends and volunteers came out to the hospital, they sometimes looked at the black toes as if they were relics of a religious pilgrimage that Willi had carried down from the summit of Everest. As much as he might talk cavalierly about the prospect of losing them being a small price to pay for having climbed Everest, getting used to the idea took time. Willi loved his body, the pleasure that it gave him. He didn't relish losing any of it.

As the toes turned blacker, Willi was sure that Dr. Berry's plan to do skin grafts to save them wasn't going to work. The toes were dead. Willi often fiddled with them. They weren't a part of him anymore. He could practically have snipped them off with a pair of scissors.

"I'll trade you my toes for your freckles," Willi joked to Ted Stone, the son of Howard (Rocky) Stone, the CIA station chief.

Stone and his son stood next to Willi's bed. Stone stared at Willi. The CIA station chief was a devout Catholic. The night of the bivouac Father Moran, the Jesuit priest, had led an all-night prayer vigil. As they were praying in Katmandu, the winds on Everest had stilled themselves.

"Did you pray up there, Willi?" Stone asked.

"Hell, no!" Willi said. "I got myself in the fix and I figured I'd get myself out!"

"You know it's funny, Rocky," Willi said, shaking his head at this man who looked more like an AID accountant than a top CIA operative. "You know what got me in trouble up there?"

"What, Willi?" asked Stone, one of the few Americans in Katmandu with whom Willi would discuss religion in depth.

"Tom knew he was hurting," Willi said, shaking his head. "But when I was helping poor Tom I was so darn proud my feet weren't hurting. I thought I was in better shape. I didn't even realize I was feeling no pain because my feet were too far gone for that."

The night of the bivouac was becoming the great symbol of Willi's life. Jolene saw her husband's act as one of perfect purity and beauty. But if love was the father of Willi's selflessness, pride

was its mother; Willi could admit as much. What Willi never could
see was that the most selfless act that night was Barrel's and Lute's.
Because of their concern for Willi and Tom, the two mountaineers
had waited long on the summit, and even longer after they heard
voices above them. In the end Barrel lost his toes and the tips of
his little fingers.

In climbing to the summit of Everest, Willi had done the one
thing he always wanted to do. He knew that it would be difficult
finding other meanings in his life. He was regarded in a different
way by people. He was receiving letters from all over the world,
mainly from strangers. He had even heard from the guru he had
stayed with in India in 1949. At times Willi felt almost sorry for
himself. He had gotten out of the hospital for a while. Then he had
come down with hepatitis. The day he was readmitted, he had cried
openly.

During the expedition, Bob Chase, a Washington staff man, had
flown in to take Willi's place in the Peace Corps in Katmandu,
followed by two other short-term people called "thirty-day wonders" by the volunteers. They were gone now, and Willi had been
appointed the new director of Peace Corps Nepal.

There was endless work. During the day he talked to volunteers
about their problems and wrote volunteer job descriptions. New
staff people were due. Nepal II, a group working in community
development, was arriving in October. Willi was worried about
what would become of them. As it was, there wasn't too much he
could do, sitting in bed day after day, absolutely drained by the
hepatitis. "Every now and again I still get a guilty feeling about not
doing a job," he told a reporter from *Time*.

Some of Willi's friends thought it important that Willi return to
the United States for treatment. Willi disagreed. "A basic principle
of the Peace Corps is that its personnel should live under the same
conditions as the people of the country they serve in," Willi said.
"I dislike the idea of going home when the risk in staying is only
the minor part of whether I lose one joint of my toes. Going home,
I feel, is admitting that my toes are more important than my Peace
Corps job."

What Willi didn't talk about was the other reason for staying in Katmandu: money. During the three months of the expedition, Willi had gone on unpaid leave. To tide the family over, he had borrowed money from the First National Bank of Corvallis. Willi was back on his Peace Corps salary now. With all the medical bills, though, if he hadn't been able to use the government health insurance, the family would have been in bad shape. One positive note was a letter from Dr. A. L. Strand, president of Oregon State University, offering financial help from friends in Corvallis.

Early in September Willi was wheeled into the operating room. Dr. Berry cut off Willi's nine toes, leaving only the little toe on his right foot. If the amputation didn't stop the deterioration, Willi knew that the doctor might have to cut off even more to right up behind the ball of each foot.

Willi was lying in the hospital, recuperating, his feet swathed in white bandages, when the September 20 issue of *Life* magazine appeared on the newsstands in the United States with the story of the expedition. Willi's picture of Bishop, wearing snow goggles, full beard, balaclava, and high-altitude regalia, was on the cover. He looked like a creature of the snow. Willi wanted to get up in the mountains again someday, but first he had to learn to walk again. When Charles Houston, the Indian Peace Corps representative, came to Katmandu to evaluate whether Willi could carry on, he ordered him home for treatment and further evaluation. Willi was scheduled to return to the States for blood and liver tests early in October. On the appointed day he was running such a fever that he couldn't get on the plane. Later in the month he finally felt well enough to travel. He settled into the Naval Medical Center in Bethesda outside Washington, D.C.

Willi was getting used to the idea of losing his toes. What he didn't like was paying out in the nickels and dimes of tedium. Hepatitis attacked not only his liver, it attacked his spirit. The disease robbed him of all his energy and strength. Anyone who had spent fifteen hours high on Everest without oxygen lost some of his mental edge. The hepatitis made that loss seem far worse.

Willi had many visitors, including Sarge Shriver. To the Peace

Corps director, Willi was an ideal representative of the Peace Corps, so much so that he put Barry Bishop's stunning picture of Willi and Tom slogging up the West Ridge on the cover of the first Peace Corps staff handbook. Shriver brought a gift out to the hepatitis victim: a bottle of Scotch.

The week after Willi's arrival a newspaper reporter, A. Robert Smith, came out for an interview. Willi told the journalist that he hoped to return to Nepal in December to finish up his two years. In the fall of 1964 he intended to resume teaching at Oregon State.

"My strengths are in teaching," Willi said, as if he had already had enough of administration. "But the Peace Corps is doing the same thing as the missionaries. We are testifying to our faith by performing social development work in the country where we serve." The volunteers were not experts but "human beings with some savvy and know-how to give the villagers some pointers." Telling stories about the work in Nepal, Willi made the role of a volunteer seem an exquisite combination of service and adventure.

Jolene had looked upon Willi's return to Katmandu as the beginning of a new life as wife of the Peace Corps representative, wife of a man who wasn't forever traipsing off on expeditions. Instead, Willi had returned burdening Jolene with even more family responsibilities. In June she had run a 103° temperature from what Willi felt was pure exhaustion. With Willi gone, Jolene picked up the pace even more. As Willi wrote in a letter, "she fights the loneliness of our separated family by embarking on flights of frantic business which steadily take toll on her resources."

From her letters, Willi learned of Jolene's activities. She was still putting on weekly spreads for groups of volunteers. She helped the wives of the new staff people settle in, set up meetings with Embassy and AID people, taught the women how to operate their kerosene-run refrigerators and where to shop. She was chairman of the Welfare Committee of the American Women of Nepal Club. She visited leprosariums, sanitariums, and schools and was thinking up other new projects.

Willi was worried about Jolene. As for the children, he was sure that they could take care of themselves. "The four children have always been a rather in-grown unit and hence relatively indifferent to environment," he wrote a friend at Oberlin. "They devise endless games together with only occasional frictional flare-ups. We wish there were channels for greater contact between them and their Nepalese contemporaries, but such relationships have proved very difficult to establish in any number."

The money problem loomed even larger. By mid-October Willi had exhausted all his sick leave and annual leave. His only income consisted of Workmen's Compensation benefits. Late that month when it seemed the Unsoelds were about to be dragged down in debts and hospital bills, Willi received a letter from Dr. Strand saying that he had already raised $1,561. "This is considerably more than I expected," the university president wrote. "I have been involved in a number of money-raising efforts, but none as pleasant as this one." Although Strand didn't say so, almost all the money had come in small contributions between $5 and $25.

The money was such a relief that Willi might have relaxed. How he hated being cooped up in the hospital, though, knowing that he didn't have enough energy to do anything else. Learning how to walk with no toes was at first like balancing on a pogo stick, a whole different way of moving. The weeks went by. November. The chill of Washington winter was already on the land. One day Willi looked out the window and saw the body of John F. Kennedy being carried into the hospital. December. The trees on the grounds were all bare. Still he lay there.

Reading Willi's mournful, lonesome letters, Jolene decided to come back with the children while he convalesced. She felt that if she didn't do so, Willi would return to Nepal too soon. The Peace Corps did not go for the idea. In situations like this the wives of Peace Corps staff members were supposed to sit it out, not come flying halfway around the world. The Peace Corps wasn't going to pay for one extra round-trip ticket, much less five. Jolene's love and concern were both a blessing and a burden. Willi cabled his wife telling her no, absolutely no.

Jolene came anyway, traveling on borrowed money. On December 23, the day Willi was released from the hospital, Jolene and the children arrived in Washington. The four children rushed up the quiet hospital halls to their father's room. Willi thought that they looked fine but that Jolene appeared worn out. The next day while Willi and Jolene watched, eleven-year-old Regon led his two sisters and brother onto a United Airlines flight bound for Portland, Oregon. There Jolene's parents met their grandchildren.

Willi and Jolene settled into a one-room apartment owned by a Nepal volunteer who had been a teacher in Washington. Jolene was so tired that for over a week she slept ten or eleven hours a night. Even then, she couldn't stay awake after 8:00 P.M.

Willi was in no condition physically or mentally to go back to Nepal yet. He wrote Dr. Strand that "a muscular weakness is the primary problem now after the long siege in bed, but there is also an apparent tendency toward excessive fatigue in the face of even nominal psychological tension."

While he convalesced, Willi worked with the Nepal III volunteers training at George Washington University in the capital. To the trainees this unpretentious man hobbling around them had heroic stature. The fact that Willi had lost his toes made the Everest conquest more than a mere climb. It was as if Willi had lost his toes for humanity. The Peace Corps, Nepal, courage, sacrifice, Everest, mountains, stoicism, idealism all seemed to blend together in Willi as they did in the talks he gave.

Whenever Willi lectured about Everest, he took his audiences right up the mountain with him, slide by slide, day by day. The audience shared his triumph, ohhing and ahhing at the beauty and majesty of Everest, awed at his courage. Then at the end he showed gruesome slides of his toes, leaving the picture up on the screen far longer than necessary. It was as if he wanted these people to share in the ugly, private aftermath as well.

What the volunteers did not see was how difficult a time Willi was having getting back to life after Everest. Other expedition members were having troubles too. Several climbers, including Jerstad, Hornbein, and Whittaker, ended up divorced. Of all of them Willi took the longest time to return to his normal life.

While Willi was convalescing, Shriver sent him around to colleges to recruit. Willi was a wonderful salesman, standing in his shoes stuffed with cork in the toes and lined with steel shanks. ("I have happily discovered that toes are just the vestigial remains of the time when we lived in trees. Man doesn't really need toes.") But it was not easy getting used to life below.

Not until May did the Unsoeld family finally return to Katmandu, eight months after Willi's departure. Shriver had made Willi into a symbol of the Peace Corps. Yet so far Willi had spent over twice as long climbing Everest and recuperating as serving the Peace Corps in Nepal. In added staff costs, medical bills, and other expenses Willi's climb had cost the government thousands of dollars and been partially responsible for the serious administrative weaknesses in the Nepal program. Shriver and other top officials believed that now that Willi was back and well he would do an exemplary job as Peace Corps director.

As Bob Bates' deputy, he was good old Willi whom the volunteers came to with their problems, good old Willi who always had time, good old Willi who left volunteers enthusiastic again about the adventures of the Peace Corps. Willi was still all for setting the volunteers loose, sending them roaring up into the hills to show their stuff, tromping back six months later full of wondrous tales.

It wasn't Willi's feet that held him back from visiting the volunteers. It was all the routine and rigmarole of bureaucracy. He had papers to fill out in triplicate; memos to write; staff meetings to attend; pesky little details to worry about; functions to go to wearing a coat and tie; endless problems to face.

The Nepal II program was a mess, even by Nepalese standards. Just before Willi returned to Nepal, Robert Hellawell, a Peace Corps official, did a month-long evaluation. In a lengthy report for Shriver and a few others, Hellawell called the Nepal II record "dismal." Often, the volunteers didn't have any work. Hellawell blamed the debacle "more than on any individual . . . on our failure to provide staff continuity during the critical planning period. And when it was apparent that there would be no staff continuity, on our failure to cancel the program.'' The evaluator pointed out that the district Nepalese officials weren't prepared for the arrival of the Americans; the ministry officials hadn't even been given a list of the volunteers' qualifications. Although the report didn't say so, as much as any single factor, Willi and his climb were responsible for the magnitude of the problem.

In their frustration and anger, the Nepal II volunteers turned for solace and advice to Dr. Jack Davis, the new associate representative. Davis was a husky, outspoken former navy doctor and psychiatrist. He and his wife, a doctor and Tibetan by birth, were very different people from the Unsoelds. Davis believed that the Peace Corps should work more directly with the government.

Willi didn't think much of that idea. It limited the volunteers' freedom. For the first time in his life Willi was faced with the prospect of working intimately with someone for whom he didn't feel affinity. Willi decided that he couldn't do it. Davis was asked to resign.

Up until then, to the thirty-nine Nepal II volunteers Willi had been simply the man who wasn't there. Now to many of them Willi was the man who had fired the one staff member who understood their problems. Will Newman, one of the more active volunteers, went straight to Willi.

"I'm resigning, Willi," said Newman earnestly. To him it had become a matter of principle.

"You can't resign," Willi said incredulously. "Do you understand what would happen?"

Newman shrugged.

"You're an experimental, elite group. You've had special training. George Carter, the regional director in Washington, is conservative. You resign and you'll take people over the side with you. These community development programs will stop all over South Asia."

Newman looked directly at Willi. "You have one degree in philosophy and one in religion. And I have one in rhetoric. And what you're saying doesn't make any damn sense."

Harry Barnes, the deputy chief of mission, talked Newman out of resigning. Willi, however, never regained his status with the Nepal II volunteers.

The administrative problems were getting Willi down. For several months he had been looking forward to the arrival of a full-time secretary who would relieve him of some of his duties. On a hot, dusty day in July Willi drove his open jeep out to the airport to meet Gwen Griffin, arriving on the flight from Delhi.

Two years before Griffin had been part of the annual migration of high school graduates to Washington from the small towns of Pennsylvania, New Jersey, Maryland, and places south. Griffin had come all the way from rural south Georgia. That would have been adventure enough for many, but she was excited about working overseas for the Peace Corps. She had a pert openness in looks and manner, and a bright curiosity and intelligence. She had a choice between going to Pakistan or Nepal. When she heard about the Himalayan kingdom and Willi Unsoeld, she immediately made up her mind.

Even before arriving in Nepal, Willi was one of her heroes. Seeing Willi *there,* taking the trouble to come out to the airport, a big grin on his face, an old canvas bag slung around his shoulders, she knew she had made the right choice. Willi plunked her bags into the jeep. Before she knew it they were driving through the narrow streets into Katmandu. She had never been out of the United States before. What she saw before her was an explosion of the exotic. When Willi drove into the Unsoeld compound, she felt herself enveloped in this loving family.

In the evenings everyone went in to supper and sat on long benches before the dining room table, passing the big platters of food around. Willi was full of stories. After eating, the family usually moved into the living room. If there were guests Willi showed his Everest slides. If not, there were Willi stories, and more Willi stories and laughter. With cotton stuffed in his sneaker, Willi's shoes pointed up like a pixie's, Griffin thought there was something magical about this man.

As for Jolene, Griffin considered her simply incredible. Jolene ran the house like a military base. She was the general. She had everything shipshape. She was worried about exotic diseases that might strike down her four children and was extraordinarily careful about sterilizing dishes, boiling water, washing hands. She wanted so much for her children. She worked with Regon, so quiet, so remote, as he built a butterfly collection.

Often someone else was staying at the Unsoelds, if not a volunteer down from the hills, then a mountain climber or somebody Willi had found interesting. Willi liked and needed people around. He thought of the Peace Corps as one big family.

The Unsoelds had many special times. One night Willi invited the expedition Sherpas over. He gave them a great feast. The Sherpas did a Tibetan line dance, their bodies snaking across the lawn. Willi walked among these men who had carried the supplies that allowed him to stand on the summit of the world. He was one of them, a man of the high mountains. Griffin thought that the Sherpas looked upon Willi almost as a god.

Even on the most ordinary of days, the Unsoeld house surged with energy and excitement. With the Himalayas in the background, Willi often had the kids rappelling off the front balcony. After a few weeks Griffin began to have different feelings about what was going on. She was only twenty-one years old, new to Nepal, new to this kind of life, and she didn't dare tell anyone what she was thinking.

It seemed such an ungrateful thing to think, but there was no privacy at the Unsoelds. Every night she had to sit at the dining table with the whole family. Every night she had to go into the living room and hear Willi's stories, or if there were other guests, see Willi's slides. In a month she had heard the stories and seen the slides so many times. She couldn't understand why Willi himself wasn't bored.

At the office, Griffin wanted to do things right. When Willi sat back in the afternoons and dictated four- and five-page letters to volunteers in the field, she typed them up right away. She was glad to be helping the volunteers in the field. The letters were full of philosophy, humor, and mountain lore. She was really interested in the volunteers. She started reading their letters to Willi. She realized that often Willi wasn't answering requests for information and services. She told Willi that. He shrugged and said that he hadn't noticed or had forgotten.

At the office Griffin felt that the important work wasn't getting done. Willi could spend an hour talking about boots with a volunteer who was a climber, two hours spouting off philosophy. But Willi had reports from Washington to fill out, volunteer requests to answer, memos to prepare, decisions about future groups to be made. Willi didn't even read many of the reports from Washington. When Willi's in-box piled up so high that she couldn't stand it anymore, Griffin went through and set some priorities. Here was a financial report that had to be done this week. This volunteer needed an answer on his problem. These other volunteers would have to wait until next week. And this request from Washington could go on hold a bit longer.

Gwen began siphoning off administrative matters to the associate representative, Lee Bomberger, a quiet, colorless, gentle professional administrator. She still had all Willi's letters to type. She sat beside her dictaphone, Willi's voice ringing in her ear, typing eighty words a minute, pounding the keys in her anger. She cared so much for Willi. Yet he made her so mad. He was such a wonderful man. Everyone loved and respected him. She felt so guilty.

"Willi wasn't very aware that he wasn't doing a good job in the office," Griffin said. "That's why he would get so nervous when I would keep trying. Willi just wasn't a well-rounded person. There was a whole big part of him that didn't work. He was very immature, and very fearful of getting into a realm that he felt so insecure about. He resisted with all his energies those whole other realms. He resisted with his physical being. He would tense up. He resisted almost the normality of a situation, the normality of life.

"He resisted dealing with conflict unless it was a happy kind of situation or something that was funny or bizarre. In the family it was the same way. Jolene was the disciplinarian. He was almost like one of the children. I'm sure from their perspective they were very conflicted over whether I do this because I want to do it or because Dad's so excited about it and obviously enjoys it and would like to be one of them. There was that pressure.

"Plus from Jolene. She was the intellectual. She really did push books on them. She pushed them to do things. There was this constant talk about it. You couldn't get away from it. And so the different kinds of pressures, Willi's physical enthusiasm and excelling in all those areas, plus Jolene's 'you've got to be smart. You've got to be intellectual.' How much they adored their parents and at the same time felt so pushed.

"The Unsoelds considered what you do spontaneously, emotionally, as the truth, but it had to be their spontaneity, not yours. The happy times I had with them were very good for me. But when I got away from it, I was so happy. It was a sad kind of thing. There was so much life there."

After Gwen left the Unsoelds, Ira and Ruth Kaye and their two children arrived. It would have taken a considerable search to have found a deputy director so much the antithesis of Willi as forty-nine-year-old Ira Kaye. Kaye was a New Yorker. He had spent most of his adult life in the South, primarily as a civil rights attorney. He looked like one of those pudgy, pallid New Yorkers who limit their calisthenics to elbowing their way onto the subway at rush hour and consider a pack not something you wear outdoors but a container for cigarettes.

Kaye was a Jewish monologist, whose sentences sometimes went flooding over other conversations; a sentimentalist, a sucker for a sad tale and a couple of tears, an intellectual for whom politics was the center of life. He had his own ego and a fierce sense of personal integrity. The previous summer Kaye had been in a training program for Iran, studying Farsi, and learning about the culture. One day the Peace Corps said they needed him in Nepal instead. Kaye was a good soldier. Though he knew nothing about Nepal, he went along.

From the moment the Kayes arrived at the Unsoelds to stay while finding a house, they felt uncomfortable. Ruth was as different from Jolene as Ira was from Willi. She was a Southerner with pride in her region and upbringing. She had not dropped out of college to marry Ira but had met him when she was working on her law degree at New York University. Ruth was used to setting a fine table and pitching in with the lady folks.

"I'd just looooooove to help, Joleeeeeeene," Ruth drawled.

"That's all right," Jolene replied curtly. "I'll do it. You're a guest."

To surprise Jolene by making breakfast, Ruth started getting up earlier and earlier. No matter what hour Ruth rose, Jolene was already up and in her kitchen. The longer the Kayes stayed at the Unsoelds, the more unwelcome Ruth felt.

Willi knew that Kaye was not in top physical condition. As his initiation Willi sent Kaye out to take a new volunteer to his post in Tansen. This was one of the most difficult treks, a two-day walk over the hills of western Nepal. Kaye did his best. He ended up blacking out and had to turn back.

Willi could have had Kaye work with volunteers in the Terai. For Willi, though, if you couldn't trek, you couldn't hack it. When Kaye returned to Katmandu, Willi called him into his office and told him point-blank: "We need a replacement for you." Although Kaye stayed on for eight more months before being transferred to India, he never let on what Willi had done to him. He tried to work developing new programs. Kaye was very well liked, particularly among volunteers who weren't committed to the hills and mountains. Gwen Griffin thought that Willi was jealous of the deputy director and his following among the volunteers.

Willi had his problems at home as well. He came home one evening late as usual. It was raining and Jolene was waiting for him in her fanciest dress ready to go to a big dinner at the American Embassy. She was at the dinner table carving a roast for the children.

"Well, Missus?" Willi began brightly. He had loaned the one covered Peace Corps jeep to another staff member so that his wife wouldn't get wet. "You don't mind, do you, hon?"

Jolene took the carving fork and threw it across the room, the prongs sticking into Willi's forearm.

If Jolene thought that her husband was going to change dramatically after the Everest climb, she was discovering that wasn't to be. Although Jolene was proud of her own accomplishments such

as serving as president of the American Women's Club in Katmandu, she was still living in good part through Willi. She helped
her husband with his paperwork. She had a better sense of the
politics of life in the American community than Willi; she knew
who had to be invited to dinner and why. As Willi turned Jolene
into the loving, bossy wife in *his* stories, so Willi had become a
character to Jolene. Her husband was a hero, her family and its
activities far larger than life.

In the Unsoelds' annual mimeographed newsletter, Jolene called
the family's trek to Dhankuta in eastern Nepal "the most memorable event of the year." The walk was as fascinating to a Nepalese
as a morning on the San Bernardino Freeway to a southern Califor-
nian. Even to a volunteer stationed in the eastern hills, the journey
was a mundane business. Writing about the day-long walk, Jolene
could have been describing a major expedition: from the "pre-dawn
filled with the big question of 'Will it go?'" through the "first
exultation over an uphill stretch well negotiated" on to the "growing weariness on the long, long last hill climbing to Dhankuta."

While Willi was walking on toeless feet, old porters journeyed
down the trail weighed down with eighty-pound loads of tangerines
or potatoes, unaware that they were involved with heroic endeavors.
Little children toddled along; girls in saris sashayed down the trail;
and fat merchants waddled ahead, followed by an entourage of
porters. "But physical exhaustion is not enough," Jolene wrote in
this missive to friends and relatives. "Within five minutes of taking
off sweat shirts, pulling on warm sweaters and removing heavy
boots from tired feet, Willi was swinging into his role as Peace
Corps director. . . . Sometimes I could cry for the way he flogs
himself to do more than a man's job."

Willi couldn't always avoid the Terai. It was at least better than
being stuck in his office. He flew down to Nepalganj. Most of the
Terai was bad enough, but Nepalganj was said to be the grungiest,
the grayest, the dirtiest place in God's creation. Terry Deklotz and
Peter Burleigh were Nepal II volunteers stationed there. They were
supposed to be working in community development, but things
were so hopeless they had turned themselves into high school and

college English teachers. Peter and Terry were not admirers of Willi's. They didn't think of themselves as gung-ho hairshirt types. Moreover, they were still mad over the firing of Jack Davis.

In every way Nepalganj lived up to its advance billing as the absolute pits. Mahendra College, the pride and joy of Nepalganj, had attracted as teachers a slew of unemployed Indians from across the border. In a society where men carried cards saying "BA Failed" to advertise the distinction of at least having taken the final exam, credentials were paramount. The Indian teachers all had masters' degrees, albeit from schools that if called second rate would be overpraised. Still they had the papers. They were raising an unholy stink because Terry and Peter had only bachelor degrees.

Willi went out to Mahendra College. The college looked like almost every other school in Nepal, a long one-story whitewashed building, a blackboard and wooden chairs in each room. The college had only twenty-six students but Pashupati Dayal, the principal, acted as if it were Harvard, Oxford, and the University of Tokyo all rolled into one. As soon as Willi learned that the man was an Indian Brahmin and had studied philosophy at Agra, his face lit up.

"I studied philosophy and religion too," Willi said, rolling out his knowledge of Hinduism as if it were yard goods. "Not only that. I have climbed the sacred mountain, the mountain you call Sagramata and we call Everest."

The darkset Indian began listening to Willi more intently.

"And not only that either," Willi continued. "I made a sacrifice to Sagramata. I left part of my body up there."

By now it was not only the Indian principal who was speechless, but the two volunteers. Peter thought, "My God, he's not going to take his shoes off." Without further preamble, Willi leaned over, pulled off his sneakers and socks, and stood there wiggling his one toe. Pashupati Dayal knelt down before Willi as if these feet were a religious shrine. For a moment it looked as if the Brahmin were about to kiss Willi's only toe. But the man pulled himself up and looked at Willi with holy respect.

"That was wonderful," the two volunteers told Willi as they

left, clapping him on the back. From then on the only trouble Peter and Terry had with the principal was to get him to stop sending so many cables asking Willi to return for another visit. Yet the more the two volunteers thought about Willi's act, the less they liked it. Pashupati Dayal was a pompous fool, but Willi had taken the man's most sacred beliefs and used them to manipulate the Indian.

The volunteers on whom Willi had the greatest impact were those the Peace Corps dubbed "high risk/high gain," a phrase that could have been used to describe Willi's philosophy as well as a category of volunteer. Willi had immense sympathy for such young men and women. It was as if he believed that they felt and saw more than their more easily adjusted contemporaries. In Nepal some of these "high risk/high gain" volunteers developed a rich, deep appreciation for life and its possibilities and did excellent work. Others failed miserably.

One young man who later became an artist was stationed in a dirty Terai town. When he discovered that his fellow teachers were cheating on a certification examination, he called them on it and was ostracized. Without telling the Peace Corps, he flew to Katmandu and was having a good time when Willi came upon him at a party. The next day Willi and the volunteer went to visit a high official at the ministry of education to discuss the situation.

As an individual Willi knew where he stood on a moral issue like this one. But as Peace Corps Director, Willi felt that he had to think of the whole organization and its future. Instead of creating a crisis, Willi agreed meekly that the volunteer would return to the school where life would go on as it always had.

As the two men left the office, Willi turned to the volunteer. "You can hit me if you want."

"Are you kidding?" the volunteer said incredulously. "What for?"

"For what I just did in there," Willi said, ashamedly.

12

Willi liked to believe that the Peace Corps wasn't a government agency at all but a glorious bunch of individuals. Like it or not, though, Willi was the head of a bureaucratic organization. In that formal capacity he was a dismal failure.

Seeds and medicines that volunteers requested often never were sent out to their posts. Preparations for a new group of community development volunteers were almost as inadequate as for the first. Graduate school applications that volunteers wanted mailed to the States in the special pouch sometimes arrived well after the deadlines. Nepalese officials who looked to the Peace Corps for serious help in developing their country were met by Willi with anecdotes and generalities.

In Washington, George Carter, the assistant director for North Africa, the Near East, and South Asia, didn't like the looks of the program in Nepal. Willi wasn't keeping things rolling, planning ahead, getting a good quota of volunteers, evaluating his programs and reevaluating them. Carter's boss, Sarge Shriver, believed that if one hundred volunteers were doing a good job, two hundred volunteers would do twice the job. Carter was doing his best to build up the numbers, but Willi was playing the game haphazardly, sending in requests for more volunteers too late or without much forethought about the programs themselves.

Carter was a wise, wily bureaucrat, one of the few blacks in a top position at the agency. Carter never forgot that Shriver was the boss. Shriver believed that Willi symbolized the Peace Corps at its best. Carter agreed that Willi was a great person, innovative, full of ideas. He looked good on film. He sounded great in interviews. But Carter considered Willi one of the "wild men." Running the Peace Corps was like running any other bureaucracy. The wild men had a place but it wasn't as directors of the Peace Corps.

The time of the "wild men" in the Peace Corps was over. Willi was not going to be reappointed director in Nepal. His successor, George Zeidenstein, arrived in Katmandu for a visit in the spring of 1965. Willi could not feel close to this small, intellectual, bespectacled New Yorker. Zeidenstein was a quiet, unassuming man with a personality as piquant as a plate of rice. To go to Nepal he had given up a lucrative position in a Wall Street law firm. He was deadly serious about the Peace Corps.

As he had done with Ira Kaye, Willi sent Zeidenstein on a trek to Tansen, shepherded by Dr. Steve Joseph, the Peace Corps doctor. Joseph was a young, impulsive, gung-ho devotee of Willi and his ideas. Though Zeidenstein had been doing Canadian Air Force exercises twelve minutes a day, he was in no shape for such a trek. Developing a case of "sahib's knee," Zeidenstein limped along, trying at least to keep Joseph in sight, a mile or so ahead.

When his Peace Corps assignment ended, Willi had been reluctantly planning to return to teach at Oregon State. Friends thought that Jolene would be far happier back in the States. Willi wasn't sure what he wanted. Since the Everest climb the hardest thing was finding something that Willi truly wanted to do.

Some of Willi's friends at the Embassy and AID began talking about what could be done for Willi. Although these men knew that Willi had been a failure as an administrator, they were themselves buoyed up by his innocent exuberance, his perpetual wonder at life. They wanted to do something for Willi, who in the words of Harry

Barnes, the deputy chief of mission, "needed help in making a transition, help in growing up." Harry Barnes had long conversations with Willi about his future. Barnes felt Willi realized that he should leave Nepal. Staying was not good for him, nor was it good for the new Peace Corps representative. Willi, however, could not find anything else he cared about doing.

A position was created for Willi at AID in family planning and rural development, two areas in which Willi had almost no experience. Making matters even more difficult, Willi was supposed to oversee a group of six former Nepal II volunteers, members of the group with which he had had so many problems.

Willi ended up standing on the sidelines watching Zeidenstein dismantling *his* Peace Corps, storing away the romance, battering down the freedom, changing once and for all the institution that had given Willi so much of his identity.

"The Nepal operation has made one important basic change," wrote a Peace Corps evaluator after a visit to Nepal in early 1966. "It has outgrown its mountain-man phase and acquired leadership based on something more down-to-earth than a mystique of the Himalayas."

In his own way Willi tried to do a decent job for AID. When his mother came for a visit in mid-1966, Willi was swamped with AID work. "All snarled in a big, annual documentation merry-go-round at the office," he wrote his sister Isabel after his mother left. "You'd never recognize your bureaucratic baby brother, Is . . . For me the 3 months passed in a flash since I've been so tied up in this lousy job as to scarcely have time or energy left to be aware of what's going on at home."

Although Willi tried to be a better administrator than he had been in his previous position, the job wasn't for him. At the Peace Corps he had been able to talk in glorious, glittering, amorphous phrases. When he waltzed in to see Nepalese development officials and tried bowling them over with his rhetoric, he found that they weren't impressed. After a while some of them didn't like to see Willi coming. The Nepalese didn't care that Willi had climbed Everest.

As for the six AID interns, they were not macho mountaineers ready to follow Willi wherever he chose to lead them. For the most part they were serious, rather introverted young men planning careers in international development. They knew the Nepali language far better than Willi. They understood the local culture in ways that Willi never would. They weren't impressed with Willi.

"I want you to go down to Nepalganj," Willi told Pirie Gall, one of the interns.

"It's bad timing, Willi," Gall said pointedly. "In the Terai it's their Holi holiday. Everyone's going to be stoned on *ganja*, throwing colored powders on each other. It'll be a wasted trip."

"No, Pirie, I want you to go."

"It doesn't make any sense," Gall said, shaking his head. "I'm not going."

Gall had been right. That didn't stop Willi from giving the former volunteer a bad rating for "cooperation" on his next evaluation. Although Willi rated him high in the other categories, Gall was upset enough to ask for a meeting with Willi's superior. Willi wasn't used to having his authority challenged. It was one of many unpleasantries with the AID interns.

Willi still had a way of drawing people to him. When five American couples decided to fly up to the new airstrip in Sola Khumbu and trek to the Everest Base Camp, Willi was the unquestioned leader.

Willi was still enthusiastically giving his Everest talk, showing the slides of his toes while some of the women squirmed with discomfort.

On Sundays Willi was part of a group that got together to discuss religion. Catholics and Protestants took part as well as those like the Unsoelds who didn't go to church. Willi was comfortable with a life of constant questing. His relentless probing and scrutiny could be unsettling to those who had lived their lives within a sanctuary of belief. As the Embassy physician, Dr. Robert Damn saw at least one couple who he thought were Willi's victims, people who in these discussion sessions had lost the comfort of certainty and found nothing to put in its place.

Willi wanted everyone to experience life at its fullest, especially his four children. He loved to have them rappelling off the front balcony, the Himalayas in the background, a whole platoon of Unsoelds running down the rope one after another.

Whereas other kids got a few bruises and scrapes growing up, the four Unsoelds sometimes took harder knocks. In the spring of 1967 the Unsoelds flew to Hong Kong and Bangkok for a vacation. Horsing around in the swimming pool at the Hong Kong Hilton, Krag stuck his toe in Regon's eye. The eye bled and continued to be blurry for a couple of days, but like the rest of the family, Regon was a stoic. Bob Damn remembered when Regon had just completed expensive orthodontics. In a Scout program Willi was leading a group of boys across a ravine on a rope. Regon followed his father. He fell. Regon's knee hit him in the chin, driving his teeth up into his jaw.

Friends of the family felt sorry for Regon. They were sure that Regon would have much preferred working on his butterfly or bug collections or reading. Devi, however, loved rappelling, jumping, playing, wrestling, carousing with her father. Devi was still a little girl but she watched out for her dad, as if that was why she had been put on earth.

Devi seemed such a joyous, carefree, exuberant child, so much Willi's daughter that it was as if she had been sired from Willi alone. She wore long skirts with shorts underneath to school, and carried a Swiss army knife. Though she appeared free and open, she was even more of a stoic than the rest of her family. Once in science class she became sick. She threw up and swallowed her vomit.

Devi's creative writing at Lincoln School had dark overtones that seemed to come from a different person. In fifth grade she wrote a story about Sal-ma, a crocodile taken out of the swamp and made to fight men while tourists watched. Sal-ma finally escaped, barely making it back to the swamp. "Now Sal-ma is dead. He was killed when he was fighting a man who was getting animals for a zoo."

For the school newspaper Devi contributed a story about a Christmas tree. "My boughs are filled to the breaking point.

Among the objects placed upon me are candy and candles. The candles' wax drips upon me burning hot. . . . I shall soon wither and die before my real time. . . . Sometimes I have dark thoughts about the person who thought up the idea of an indoor Christmas tree.'' Another of Devi's stories, ''How Rudolph Got His Red Nose,'' is far different from the contemporary Christmas classic. ''To this day Rudolph has a large red nose to remind him of the day when he quit showing off and got humility.''

Willi was very proud of Devi. But although he thought Nepal was worthwhile for Devi and his other children, he knew that it was no longer worthwhile for him. Through Bob Bates, his former boss, he was offered a position as executive vice-president of Outward Bound, Inc., in the States. He jumped at the opportunity. If ever there was an organization that fit Willi and his ideas, he was sure that it was Outward Bound.

Leaving Nepal, Willi missed not the job but his friends. During his time at AID, Willi had his most intense, deepest philosophical and religious discussions with Rocky Stone, the CIA bureau chief. It was a strange friendship, even more so because the Peace Corps was extraordinarily sensitive to any suggestions that it had links with the CIA. Although Stone looked like Walter Mitty and had a severe hearing problem, he was a legendary CIA operative. A Catholic liberal, Stone was a deep, intense man who could have been a character in a Graham Greene novel.

All the time Willi and Rocky talked, some part of Stone was standing back observing and analyzing.

''I felt that the only place Willi found real peace was in the mountains,'' Stone said. ''Willi was a very brave man but I think he was confused inside, afraid inside. He had all kinds of doubts and fears that resolved themselves in this theological search. Physically, they resolved themselves in his idea that you depend only on yourself. Although Willi liked people very much he didn't like to get in too encumbering a relationship. It was important for him always to be in control. Only there on the West Ridge with Tom Hornbein did he ever let himself become vulnerable, dependent on another human.

"He affected people so that they wanted to be like him. For some people that was dreadful. Since he was so physical, he had only one response to any problem: go climb a mountain. The trouble is that in trying to struggle with the difficulties of life, you don't have the same exhilaration as climbing mountains. Physical courage is almost a response whereas intellectual courage is far deeper. Intellectual courage takes more of a commitment.

"In knowing what your vulnerabilities are and putting yourself in the hands of another person, you are admitting your weakness. The paradox is that it takes strength and confidence to do so. I don't think Willi had that kind of strength and confidence. I think Willi's strength was primarily physical. He used that great physical strength and beauty trying to make it something spiritual. He never climbed the real mountain. He knew that in Katmandu. I don't know if he knew it later. In Katmandu I thought of him as a big kid."

13

Willi stood in auditoriums and lecture halls in cities across America talking about Outward Bound. He was a pied piper in a Pendleton shirt. Looking out at a roomful of parents he said bluntly, "I can't guarantee your son won't die. But I can guarantee if you continue to stifle him, his soul will surely die." The parents could see their sons' souls shriveling up.

When Willi talked about the development of Outward Bound, he led his audiences to places where they could see and feel ideas being born. He told about Kurt Hahn, the founder of the Outward Bound movement. Born into a family of cultivated Berlin Jews, Hahn had begun developing his educational theories at Salem School in South Germany after World War I. Imprisoned for his anti-Nazi views, he was eventually allowed to go into exile. At the Gordonstoun School in Scotland, he continued his quest for educational programs to help young people live lives of moral, spiritual, and physical fitness.

At the beginning of the Second World War, Hahn was asked to help with a more immediate, dramatic problem. Every day British merchant sailors were braving German submarines. When their ships were torpedoed, the old salts had a good chance of surviving. These senior sailors had been trained in sailing ships. They had felt the wind and the rain, the cold and the sun beating against their faces. The young recruits knew only modern ships. Suddenly, the cocoon of relative comfort and convenience in which they had always lived was blown away. Left in open boats or bobbing alone in the seas, they often died.

Willi could envision what these young sailors were like, kin to the young people that he saw wherever he went in America. Willi didn't need Hahn to convince him that in the modern world people no longer felt the fresh winds of experience in their daily lives. They could no longer see the sinews that tied them one to another and to one another's fate.

Life could not go back to what it had been, but an educator could create experiences. To prepare the sailors for the brutal world that faced them, Hahn created adventures to jolt, prod, shock, and stimulate young sailors into seeing and feeling life. Hahn developed the first nearly month-long Outward Bound courses. The program included training in small boats, rescue work, sports; and to conclude the four weeks an expedition in a small boat. The course proved a resounding success, not by Hahn's judgment, but out *there,* out on the cold, cruel seas. After the war he took the program that had worked so well with working-class sailors and developed it into a series of schools for young men. From Great Britain the program had already spread to Germany, Holland, Australia, Rhodesia, Kenya, and the United States.

In his eighty-eight years Hahn did very little writing. As a bona-fide philosophy professor, the new executive vice-president of Outward Bound took on the job of defining what the organization was trying to do in the States. On the blackboard, Willi drew four concentric circles. At the center he wrote "self-concept." The Outward Bound programs were full of "laid-back" kids who didn't think much of themselves. Willi believed that one of the best ways for them to test their limits and reach beyond themselves was on high rappels swinging down a cliff. The rappel was virtually a sacrament to him.

Willi labeled the second ring "compassion." To teach a person concern for his fellow humans he talked about group activities using ropes, boards, and harnesses. The third ring was "social service." Even Willi had to admit that this aspect of Hahn's thinking was undeveloped in the American Outward Bound programs. "Teaching a sense of social service is clearly limited to the duty watch at Hurricane Island Outward Bound School," Willi said, referring to the Maine school where participants scanned the horizon for ships in distress.

Finally, Willi reached the outer ring: "Serving man in a cosmic perspective." Outward Bound taught this by a solo in the wilderness. "Some of them come back with a turtle shell," Willi said, "and some of them come back with God."

This last category was more Willi than Hahn. Although Willi was sometimes criticized as a gushy nature mystic, he pushed his ideas with great intensity. Willi had returned from half a decade in an Asian land where the relationships between man and the land were symbiotic and certain. Willi believed that the villagers in the hills of Nepal understood their place in the universe; their whole lives were infused with the sacred.

In modern America, though, Willi saw a people alienated from themselves and from their bodies. Willi considered life a seamless web. To destroy the environment, to sully the wilderness, to mistreat things led men to mistreat each other, to sully what was nearest and dearest to them.

The answer, as Willi saw it, was to begin to heal these spiritual wounds of modern life by stepping out into the wilderness. Listen and feel once again the mystery of the sacred! If a person touched the sacred, he was scared. As far as Willi could see, kids of today weren't scared of anything. They needed a good tonic of fear. The wilderness was the place to get it.

It wasn't merely fear a person felt in the wilderness. It was joy! It was indescribable, immeasurable joy. That's what Willi found in the wilderness. That's what he believed anyone could find.

Willi's lectures fell on ready ears. When Willi left the United States in 1962 his belief in grasping experience and emphasizing the nonmaterial aspects of living had been unusual. Now late in 1967 a whole youthful community sought to live life immediately, directly, experientially. Along the roadsides Willi saw young people hitchhiking across the vast expanses of the continent. He listened to teenagers telling him they intended to *live,* not settle down into the routine and rituals of their parents' generation.

When Willi visited the five schools he seemed to personify Outward Bound as much as he did on the lecture circuit. What made the American schools different from their British counterparts was in part that they were set down in wilderness areas in Colorado, Oregon, Maine, North Carolina, and Minnesota. There was a brash pioneering spirit at the schools that was very much a part of Willi's personality. The instructors approached risk generally with care, but equally with delicious anticipation. At the Colorado school, day began with a mile-long run and a swim in an icy stream, as it had when Willi had been training there with Nepal I. The students faced tough physical conditioning, classes in first aid, survival techniques, outdoor cooking, and compass work. And there was Willi's favorite: rappelling.

Midway through the course came a seventy-two-hour solo in the wilderness, each student armed only with six matches, salt, a bit of wire, and some camping gear. At the end of the twenty-six-day program groups of four students went off together making their way through the wilderness for four days.

At the schools instructors and students alike were drawn to Willi. "Willi had penetrated to the center of what adventure was," said Robert Pieh, then director of Minnesota Outward Bound. "I felt there was a kind of understanding beyond words." Whenever he could Willi went out with the students. While teaching them how to rappel, tie knots, or do a Tyrolean traverse on a rope, he was teaching the instructors as well.

Once Willi went on a winter climb of 4,810-foot Mount Moosilauke in New Hampshire with an Outward Bound group. The students had no idea who this flamboyant, wisecracking man might be. As he stood before them talking about climbing, Willi slowly began taking off his clothes. First his wool hat, thick down jacket, and wind pants, then his old wool climbing pants and sweater.

"You gotta protect your hands and feet," Willi said. He had peeled down to his long underwear and down booties. "If you don't protect your feet, you're gonna have *real* problems." Not changing an inflection, he whipped off his booties and started dusting his toeless feet. "Yes, sireee, *real* problems."

The eyes of these tough Boston teenagers popped out. They nicknamed Willi "Dr. No Toes." Climbing Mount Moosilauke, they took good care of their feet.

When he was out lecturing, actively working with Outward Bound programs, or listening to the problems of the individual schools, Willi enjoyed himself immensely. Being stuck in the headquarters of Outward Bound in Andover, Massachusetts, was another matter. From almost the moment the Unsoelds arrived in this historic New England community, Willi knew that it wasn't for him.

Like most Westerners, Willi believed that space was the beginning of freedom. Andover was a traditional New England town where most people considered freedom to be like the old buildings themselves, a resource to be preserved with decorum and reserve.

At the far end of town stood the campus of Phillips Academy, one of the premier private schools in America. Willi didn't like the snotty quality that he thought emanated from many people at the prep school. Nor did he appreciate a dress code that had teenagers duded up in blue blazers and ties. When Willi walked across campus, he often wore an old shirt, jeans, and sneakers, looking like one of the janitors.

The Unsoelds had bought a big two-story wood frame house at No.5 Embassy Lane, a cul-de-sac on the edge of town. Most of the other men in the new development commuted to Boston or to managerial positions in the light industry that was rapidly replacing the mills and shoe factories in the nearby towns.

Regon went to Andover High School, a squat, gray building that looked like a modern factory. While most of the students affected a neat Ivy League look, Regon wore hiking boots, down parkas, and big sweaters as if that proved his authenticity. With his intense, earnest, serious manner he was unlike most of his comtemporaries. The family learned that their eldest son would be accepted at Phillips Academy, but Regon agreed with his father and mother that the elite school was not for an Unsoeld. The academy offered scholarships to a few blacks and a rebel or two, but it remained a boot camp training the American establishment.

Devi attended Andover East Junior High School on the other side of town. The day she arrived at the gloomy red building she was sure that everyone was looking at her. With her long blond hair, pearly teeth, big eyes, and pure complexion, she looked like an American Heidi. She wished that her hair could suddenly become longer, blonder. She didn't have loafers like most of the girls. She chastised herself for wanting the shoes and for not being up to date in style. She felt that she was being pointed at when she carried her pen in her blouse. She wanted to sock the students looking at her, but felt that if she did, everything would be lost.

During the Nepal years, walled off in their compound, the Unsoeld children developed a closeness far beyond that of most American families. They had no television, Little League baseball, junior high sock hops, or *American Bandstand* to distract them from the overwhelming presence of their father. In Andover, when Willi wasn't traveling or working, he and his family often went out climbing, canoeing, or trekking. Wherever they went, Jolene was usually along, watching out for Willi.

With his new job Willi was gone a lot. Even more of the burden of the family fell on Jolene. She poured her immense, nervous energy not only into raising her four children but into one cause, one pursuit or another, from the League of Women Voters to educational reforms in the public schools. Jolene had high standards for herself, her family, and her marriage. She insisted on Willi's attention. Willi had so many activities going that he was like an overworked short-order cook.

One day Willi invited Lee Maynard, the new business manager for Outward Bound, out to the house for lunch. Driving down the narrow, tree-lined street, Willi explained that he had another reason than mere hospitality for inviting Maynard.

"Lee, I'm in the doghouse," Willi said. "If I come home alone Jolene's gonna chew me out. The whole family's gonna dump on me. If I've got you, I'll be okay."

While Maynard was trying to digest the whole scene at lunch, Terres marched up and placed a pickle jar on the table. Maynard looked down and saw Willi's nine shriveled toes. He managed neither to gag nor fall out of his chair. That, he figured afterwards, had signaled acceptance.

Although the Unsoelds kept their distance from most of Andover's social life, they tried to be good citizens. At town meetings, Willi and Jolene sat together knitting mittens. No one in Andover had ever seen a man knitting before.

The Unsoelds often invited students and Outward Bound people out to their house. Elliott Fisher, a student at the Academy, was one of these young people who went climbing with the family and thought that Devi was beautiful, pure, and good.

Young people found it fascinating to be around the Unsoelds. They felt a tremendous vitality. At the Unsoelds everything was done with earnest intensity, from the way the family climbed together to the way they bought gifts for each other, or decided not to buy gifts. Most of these other teenagers came from families where life existed on a moral middle earth. At their homes everyday activities were matters of habit and not of ethical concern. In Willi's house, no issue large or small was unworthy of moral consideration. His family lived a continuous moral drama.

In the summer the family headed back to the Northwest. One night they stayed with the Emersons in Seattle where Dick was teaching sociology at the University of Washington. In the morning Willi was going to put Keti, the Unsoelds' ancient dog, in a kennel and drive the kids over to Jolene's parents. Then he and Jolene would go off to do a reconnaissance of a wilderness area for Outward Bound. As for now all he had to do was to enjoy the Emersons' good company.

"What about Keti?" Regon asked his father earnestly.

"What about her, Regon?"

"Would you put one of us in the kennel?"

"No." Willi shrugged.

"Then how can you put Keti!" Regon said as if he were summing up before a jury. His brother and sisters looked at their father as if he was on the verge of becoming a murderer.

Most other fathers would have allowed their children the illusion of democracy, debating with them before telling them point-blank that Keti was going into the kennel. To Willi life was one big classroom. He led the debate, drawing out every moral subtlety.

After several hours, Pat Emerson wearily headed up to bed, thinking to herself that this was not the way she raised her family. In the middle of the night she awoke and heard the sounds of fervent debate still reverberating from the living room. In the morning she learned the judgment—Willi and Jolene would take Keti with them, Willi packing an extra thirty pounds of dog food.

Whenever Willi went back to the Northwest, he knew that this was where he was meant to be. He might have gotten better used to Andover if his job had worked out differently. Every time he returned to the office, he knew that he would once again have to deal with Joshua A. Miner, president of Outward Bound, Inc.

In organizations such as the Peace Corps and Outward Bound, the egos are often as large as the ideals. Outward Bound was supposed to be creating a new man, free and open to life. Yet as far as many of those in the organization were concerned, Miner was so far from that as to make its bold, optimistic statements smack of hypocrisy.

Miner was a graduate of Exeter Academy and Princeton University, class of 1943. After serving in the Second World War, he had touched the holy grail, working at Gordonstoun School with Dr. Hahn himself. He returned to the States hoping to carry on the German educator's ideas. After twelve years as admissions officer, physics teacher, and housemaster at Phillips–Andover, Miner had his opportunity. To develop Outward Bound, he brought in, among others, a dozen Princeton men and a board of directors that with its blue blood, tweeds, old money, and noblesse oblige resembled a mainline Boston law firm.

The men who ran the five schools and came in now to help run the central organization were on the whole public school graduates, Westerners in spirit if not necessarily in fact, men who wanted the organization to soar, to cut away from the ballast of tradition in manners, to get away from the preppy world.

In part Willi had been hired to make peace between the headquarters in Andover and the five schools. He was as marvelous a mediator now as he had been back in his Peace Corps days. He salved egos that Miner had wounded, and he helped convince people that the central office cared about them and was not merely a publicity mill.

"We were in the ego business." Miner said. "It's a wonder we didn't all fly apart. We were going through our intellectual adolescence. It was all very emotional, all feeling. If we had had a smoother running organization, Willi could have been more creative."

Miner could be fervent, almost bombastic, talking about the glories of Outward Bound; he and Willi usually did not appear on the same television program together. At cocktail parties the two men staked out different ends of the room. The Outward Bound president had hoped that the Miner and Unsoeld families would spend time together. It never worked out. Miner thought that a coat and tie were what a civilized man wore in civilized surroundings whereas Willi delighted in dressing like a woodsman down from Maine. The Miner and Unsoeld children were equally different; Miner thought that he had selfless children but considered it a bit too much when the Unsoelds asked that instead of Christmas gifts money be sent to feed the starving in Biafra.

Willi believed that the greatest problem in the world was how human beings treated one another. He was working for an organization that was supposed to be changing the way people treated one another; yet Outward Bound, Inc., was a textbook example of what was wrong with human relationships in modern organizations. Almost everyone in the office believed that as long as Miner remained, the organization would never grow into a major educational force. To get rid of Miner called for some of the guerrilla warfare so common in corporate offices. That was not Willi's way. He helped to develop new safety procedures. He worked on an outreach program into the public schools. There were days when he didn't do much. He might talk to a visitor or another staffer for hours instead of tending to business.

"When I was young my one goal was to climb Mount Everest," he said to Lee Maynard. "You know it's very difficult to see yourself carrying on after you've achieved your greatest goal. How are you going to top it?"

"You must have known that you would accomplish that at a relatively early age," Maynard said. "There aren't any fifty-year-old Everest climbers."

"Well, it never occurred to me."

One day Willi drove over to East Junior High School to give his Everest lecture. Willi talked, gesturing with his hands, regaling the students with anecdotes. Suzanne Coates, the French teacher, watched Devi, her head tilted upward toward the stage, beaming with profound joy. She thought it extraordinary that a daughter could love her father as Devi did.

Willi loved Devi as much as she loved him. When she won the principal's award for the student with the highest personal standards, Willi was immensely proud. Willi looked at Devi and saw himself perfected. There was nothing self-centered about Devi, nothing biting in her wit, no feisty competitiveness. She was almost too good to be true, and she was his daughter.

Another day Willi gave his Everest lecture at Andover High School. Standing up on stage Willi cast a great shadow across Regon's young life. Regon had begun to seek out pathways that led where his father had not trodden. He was a thin, blond, bespectacled teenager. He carried all the complex burden and glory of the Unsoeld name, all the ideals and values, all the intensity and passion, unleavened by Willi's humor and philosophical detachment. Regon acted as if all the world's problems were his own.

Regon confided a great deal in Allison Guess, a pretty, miniskirted French teacher. He almost never mentioned his father. Regon was full of anger. He reminded Guess of Holden Caulfield in *Catcher in the Rye*. "He was the personification of all my youthful ideals," she said. "He was so pure, so idealistic, so principled. It's a torturous way to be. He was too vulnerable. He loathed the high school. It was like being a caged animal. It was so anti everything his family stood for.''

Although Regon often refused to do his homework, he was a fine student. Guess considered Regon brilliant, totally untrained, but brilliant. He wanted attention. He had to be an original. He had to be unique. To her he was a fawn in the woods that she didn't want to frighten away.

Guess was one of no more than half a dozen idealistic young teachers at Andover who sympathized with the few rebels in their classes. These were the teachers interested in forming an ecology club, teaching about black culture, learning in depth about the war in Vietnam. In their own haphazard way, they formed an open conspiracy against the entrenched, conservative town and the school that was its proudest public institution.

At Memorial Day ceremonies in May 1969, hundreds of students from the public schools as well as from Phillips–Andover Academy wore armbands bearing the Peace Symbol, an upside-down "Y" inside a circle. Nothing like this had ever happened in the patriotic all-American town. During the parade honoring the war dead, an enraged Vietnam War veteran slugged one of the protesters. Afterwards, the owner of the Coffee Mill refused to serve coffee to four women wearing armbands. Someone else called the women "Comies.'' A teenager socked one of the male protesters, giving him a concussion and a chipped tooth.

The Andover Townsman editorialized that what had happened was "a disgrace.'' As far as the weekly paper and most of the local people were concerned, the disgrace was not that the protesters had been attacked. The disgrace was that on Memorial Day a protest had taken place.

Many parents cringed at the idea of their sons and daughters taking part. They would have been appalled at their children becoming protest leaders. Willi and Jolene were enormously proud of Regon. Jolene was the more political parent. Like her eldest son, she could sound terribly moralistic, even self-righteous, but she believed in her son and his causes.

Willi wanted desperately to be close to his son. He tried to do things with Regon, to get him to confide in his father. On one of their summer trips to the Northwest, Willi discussed Regon with the Emersons, who had a teenage son.

"Jolene won't let Regon go," Willi said. "When Regon says he's going to a basketball game, Jo makes a whole expedition out of it. I don't know what to do."

Several years later Pat Emerson realized that wasn't true. "I saw Jolene was not a possessive mother," she said. "It was Willi who couldn't let him go. It's hard seeing your kids grow up and Willi needed an audience."

Regon had to go off on his own and climb his own routes un-roped to his father. With the family's deep love and concern for one another, and Willi's whole joyful exuberant philosophy, it was hard for Regon to admit any dark, ambivalent feelings that he might have had. Once Willi and Regon played tennis together, one of many ways Willi was trying to get closer to his son. Erik LeRoy, Regon's closest friend, and another student, were at the court too. Willi was not known as a tennis player. That didn't matter. He ran up and down the court, hitting the ball with strokes that had never been seen at Wimbledon. He and Regon beat Erik and his partner.

Erik considered Regon unbelievably lucky having Willi for a father. Erik was the son of a Gillette executive. He was a blond, handsome young man who could have been Devi's twin. He was as much a rebel at high school as Regon. He was far more disci-plined in his protest as well as in his schoolwork. He didn't have Regon's brilliance. He had a meticulous, careful approach to ideas. He liked to think things out. He loved talking with Willi.

Most teenagers would have felt jealous of a father usurping one's closest friend. Regon didn't seem to mind. Over the next several years Erik slowly became almost another member of the family, climbing with the Unsoelds, learning their secrets, profoundly con-cerned about each one of them. "Living with the Unsoelds was like sailing past the Isle of the Sirens," Erik reflected. "It is nearly impossible to resist becoming in some fashion a part of them. . . . When I fell in with them, if I could have I would have changed my name to theirs."

For his senior year Regon was elected president of the Student Council, a position that typically went either to a football player or to an adolescent politician with a touch of the Rotarian in his blood. Regon, though, had a daring that the other students admired. Moreover, Regon and the rest of the protesting minority had helped to bring reforms that pleased most students, ending the dress code, the locking of the restroom doors to prevent smoking, loosening up the curriculum, giving students more freedom.

Willi and Jolene went to the protest meetings and listened to their eldest son, a fine provocative speaker, as well as to Erik LeRoy and others. Regon believed in confronting the politicians and the polluters and the Pentagon with the battering rams of truth. Among the minority of students who cared about such issues as much as Regon did, he became a larger and larger figure. As the school year went by, however, Regon lost the support of many students.

If there was no limit to Willi's courage so that sometimes his bravery became foolhardiness, there was no limit to Regon's idealism. When he learned about an oil spill on the coast, Regon wanted to commandeer school buses and head out to save the birds. He didn't understand that a school didn't work that way, or if he did, he considered the birds infinitely more important than insurance regulations. Most of the students at Andover High School were more concerned about getting admitted to college or at least finishing high school than about the war in Vietnam or environmental issues.

Regon could not see a newspaper headline about Vietnam without becoming upset. Only one act was sufficient to register his protest: to go to prison as a draft resister. Regon was extremely well read, articulate, and determined. Only one person in the world had a possibility of talking Regon out of his decision. That was Willi.

"I think that Regon felt that his father in quiet ways ruled his life," Erik said. "And he did. He ruled it (in one way) by making all the best arguments he could about Regon becoming a conscientious objector and not a resister. He didn't want his son to go to prison. It would have been better for Regon to have become a resister. I think, though, that Willi's reason was pure love and caring and knowing that his son was not predictable and not knowing what would happen to him.''

In the end, Regon decided not to turn in his draft card.

If anything, the problems at the office were getting worse. By early 1969 Willi was fed up with Miner and Outward Bound. So were the directors of the schools. To placate them further, Willi and the school directors agreed to bring in one of their number, Murray Durst, as the top administrative officer. Anyone with a modicum of bureaucratic savvy would have seen that with Miner still president, and a new executive on board, Willi ran a good risk of being pushed out. That never occurred to Willi or if it did, he didn't appear bothered.

"Josh called each of us separately to suggest that Willi and I were in direct conflict over the position,'' Durst said. "Willi and I had the same identical reaction. We're not going to let this happen. My reaction was okay, I'll go back to North Carolina. Willi went right to Josh and talked to him about his ethics.''

Although Willi continued working at Outward Bound, he wanted out. It was a matter of finding the right position. At least, in the burgeoning environmental movement Willi had found a new focus for his energies and ideals. Willi had opposed the war in Vietnam, but that was a largely negative movement. The environmental cause was something he had felt, lived, and thought about all his life, a vessel large enough to contain his philosophical and religious ideas as well as his thinking about the wilderness and the need for risk.

For the first Earth Day, in April 1970, Willi flew out to Eugene, Oregon, and gave a riproaring speech before an audience of 3,500 at the University of Oregon. He told these sons and daughters of the people with whom he had grown up that there was this big American dream: productivity and consumption equaled prosperity, individualism was wholly admirable. That dream was going to end. Technology was no solution either. The good life as Americans had known it would have to change.

"When someone tries to shoot us down by saying we are against progress, I would answer that is correct. We are against progress in the terms in which it has been traditionally understood." As far as Willi was concerned, let the critics of the environmental movement call him and his kind fanatics. "If you define fanaticism as an enduring and stubborn enthusiasm for a goal, then I feel it is called for in this case."

While in the Northwest, Willi traveled to Olympia, Washington, to be interviewed for the eighteen-member planning faculty of The Evergreen State College. Willi liked Olympia. The state capital lies on Budd Inlet at the far tip of Puget Sound. The Sound is a hundred-mile finger of the Pacific Ocean cutting south from the Juan de Fuca Strait that separates the Olympia peninsula from the rest of Washington. Olympia is not only a political capital but a working town with lumber mills, a brewery, oyster fisheries, and a port shipping timber to Japan.

In the wilderness outside the city the state was building a new experimental public college. What excited Willi so much was that there would be no limits on anyone or anything at Evergreen. It was an extraordinary idea. Bring together eighteen of the most innovative educators in America and let them invent a new school. Although joining the planning faculty would mean an $8,000 cut in salary, Willi knew that this was what he wanted to do.

Willi was not the only Unsoeld involved in Earth Day. As a sophomore at Andover High School, Devi had her first chance to take part in a major political activity with her brother, Regon. She was quiet and reserved but she worked as hard as anyone. Regon was a leader. He decided that the students needed a symbol to show the townspeople how they were abusing the environment. In the parking lot next to the town hall, the students brought refuse from their town cleanup: heaps of no-return soft drink bottles and cans; pizza wrappings; aerosol cans and cardboard packing; beer bottles and broken glass. The mound of garbage grew higher and higher.

When William Seifert, the new superintendent of schools, looked at the garbage heap, he thought he understood the symbolism. "If Regon could create a mountain of garbage a couple of feet higher than Everest, he would do it," Seifert told two teachers.

When the family discussed the move to Olympia, Regon announced point-blank that he was staying in the East. That he had not become a draft resister, but had turned back part way up his moral Everest, he blamed on Willi. He wasn't going to college either. Willi was worried about his eldest son and the partial breakup of the family. There was nothing he could do. Since he needed someone to drive the U-Haul truck, he asked Erik LeRoy.

In the summer of 1970 the Unsoelds set out, heading westward toward home.

∧∧

14

At one of the faculty meetings of Evergreen State College, Willi arrived carrying a climbing rope. During the glorious freedom of Evergreen's first months, everything was possible and half of it was tried. The planning faculty followed Willi into the mountains. The teachers thought they were going off to learn to tie a few knots or watch Willi perform one of his acts of derring-do. Willi soon had the men rappelling off a cliff, jumping out into space, and shimmying down the rope.

The only person to refuse was Richard Jones. To come to Evergreen, Jones had given up a position as psychology professor at Harvard and chief psychologist at the Massachusetts Department of Mental Health. Jones liked Willi well enough, but didn't think that his mountain-climbing colleague was terribly academic. He wasn't about to jump off a cliff in the name of education.

"I told you, Willi, I have a pathological fear of heights," said the slightly built scholar for perhaps the tenth time.

"Now, Dick," Willi said soothingly. "You're a psychologist. You work with people with irrational fears. You gotta understand that."

"Oh, what the fuck!" Jones said, walking toward the cliff as if to certain doom.

Willi tied the psychologist in, double-checked the knots with great flourish. Jones sailed out over the side. He had never been so terrified in his life. Before he got down to the ground he turned upside down.

"Now don't you feel proud!" Willi said afterwards, bursting with pride himself.

"Fuck no. I'll never forgive you," Jones said. Soon afterwards, the two men were on good terms again.

At Evergreen Willi was his old ebullient self. He was in the thick of the debates over the new college. "Is Evergreen trying to prepare students for the 'real world'?" the eighteen men asked themselves repeatedly. Willi had a ready answer to that one. After lengthy discussions the entire planning faculty agreed: "No, we are trying to provide our students with a model of a better world, a world of human relationships of a higher quality than those to which they had become accustomed."

Members of the planning faculty had left schools that had gone through weeks of demonstrations, speeches, protests, and strikes. Kent State was no longer merely another state university but a great symbol. To some it was a place of martyrdom where in the spring six young, innocent victims had been shot down by the National Guard. To others, including President Richard Nixon, Kent State was the spot where life and all its responsibilities finally caught up with the childish, taunting throngs of protest.

Evergreen was far from that world. Here in these idyllic surroundings the college would be a utopian community. Students would gain strength, wisdom, and courage to face the broader world. For Willi, teaching at Evergreen would be similar to what he had done as a guide, leading his clients up into an isolated mountain wilderness to experience things that would help them in their lives below.

If the students were going to work together in groups, Willi believed that the faculty had better do so as well. He didn't recognize any of the barriers of discipline or approach that set some of his colleagues apart like a roomful of Maoists, Stalinists, and Trotskyites trying to plan a revolution.

As Willi sized up his new colleagues, he divided the eighteen male teachers into those concerned more with "content" and those concerned more with "process." Jones was one of the more content-oriented teachers. Though he was for innovation, he believed it imperative that the intellectual achievements at Evergreen be demonstrably higher than at a more traditional school. Willi was the most articulate defender of "process." To the "process people" what mattered was how a person learned. How he learned changed what he learned and how deeply he learned.

Even if Willi and Jones and the rest of the planning faculty had had a hundred years to debate the future of Evergreen, they would not have arrived at a consensus. As it was, they had less than a year. Meanwhile, they had to hire a full faculty, develop admission policies and academic procedures, and perform all the other work of starting a new institution.

The planning faculty agreed that there would be no departments, no faculty rank, no titles, and no tenure. With Willi leading the charge, the faculty knocked down most of the traditional guideposts that students used to judge their advancement. Grades, majors, required courses were all thrown away. In the place of all these structures team teachers would work together on year-long programs that ranged far beyond a single discipline or subject. Three year-long coordinated studies programs would be like climbing expeditions in which students and faculty, roped together, traveled toward a common goal.*

Even though Willi was extremely busy on the planning faculty he was always glad to give a speech somewhere. As the war in

---

*Such team teaching had originated with Alexander Meiklejohn in his experimental college at the University of Washington from 1927 to 1932. At Wisconsin, Meiklejohn developed a "moral curriculum" based on studying some of the great political works of western civilization with groups of teachers from various disciplines. Meiklejohn was trying to educate responsive, democratic citizens. Joseph Tussman, one of Meiklejohn's disciples, adopted a similar program at Berkeley from 1965 to 1969. Mervyn Cadwallader, one of Evergreen's three academic deans, had led a program at San Jose State based on Tussman's ideas. "So Meiklejohn's thesis of the 'moral curriculum' as being . . . the major channel for the transmission of social and cultural values definitely became one of the basic assumptions with which we started," Willi wrote later.

Vietnam slowly and bloodily wound down, the environmental movement became a central cause and Willi was very much in demand.

At the University of Oregon five hundred students had signed up for a course entitled "Introduction to Wilderness." Two hundred more were on the waiting list. In October of 1970 Willi traveled to Eugene to address the seminar. He stood before the students, his beard a fiery red, small blue eyes ablaze, looking as if he had brought his words down from the mountain. "I know that unless we preserve the spiritual values of what's there and what the wilderness symbolizes, man's future is bleak," Willi said, emphasizing each point with his hands. "When early man, being so close to nature, stood in the presence of a grand object, he especially felt the power and mystery and fascination of what he beheld. With the control of our environment and the artificiality of the modern world, man has lost his sense of mystery.

"My philosophy of mountain climbing is that a mystical vision leads the climber on, which often he is unaware of. The mystery which invests every climb is its necessary uncertainty. If you knew you could make it or not for certain, there would grow a feeling of so what if I make it, so what if I don't; it doesn't matter either way. Mountaineering allows a man to be out of circulation long enough so when he comes back he can better cope with the world's problems."

Later in the academic year Willi flew east to Bucknell College to give another talk. The invitation had come because Erik LeRoy was a freshman at the Pennsylvania school. That weekend Erik and Willi spent many hours talking together, much of the time about Regon. Regon had gone off to live in the slums of Boston. Later Regon returned to Andover to do custodian work in the school system from which he had graduated. Still later, he took a position with Dartmouth Outward Bound. Willi was almost psychic in his perceptions about other human beings but could not understand his eldest son.

When the two men weren't discussing Regon, Willi talked about his other children and Olympia. He was so proud of the way Devi and Krag were developing. They rode their bikes into school every day, twenty miles round trip. Devi was active in the Third Eye, a center in downtown Olympia for teenagers. She was a person that people in trouble called upon for help.

On the trip across the coast, Erik had begun to see Devi not as his best friend's sister but as a young woman. Erik had turned in his draft card and was every bit as idealistic as Devi. By the time Willi left to fly home Erik had decided to transfer to Evergreen.

Willi thrived on chaos, on disorder. As he picked his way happily around the scaffolding of the new buildings, so he picked his way around the intellectual scaffolding. At Evergreen, Willi was so strongly identified with Outward Bound that an early brochure about the college called him a founder of the organization. Romping around campus in jeans and sneakers, he exuded an energy and openness that personified what became the Evergreen spirit. As the first president, Charles McCann, said a decade later, Willi was "the spirit of Evergreen in the sense that he was this exciting person, full of ideas, whose enthusiasm was catching."

In the fall of 1971 just before the formal opening of Evergreen, everyone, the custodians as well as the deans, got together for a retreat at Millersvania State Park. They were all Evergreeners. For this occasion Malcolm Stilson, a librarian whose balding pate be-lied his youthful wit, had written a satirical play. Stilson based this play on an earlier Evergreen retreat when the faculty had first gotten together. He called his opus "Omnia Estares (Let It All Hang Out) or The Truth about the Events Occurring at Camp Chicken."

As the play opened President Cann and Billi Bunion sat together in the meeting hall of Camp Chicken discussing the latest crisis at Wintergreen College. The president had hired four new faculty members while budget cuts would allow him to hire only one. Cann asked Bunion to eliminate the three extra persons.

For the rest of the play Billi, or Hipp as he was sometimes called, got rid of unwanted faculty—taking one teacher over a five hun-dred-foot canyon and letting him fall; pushing another on his head during a log walk; and losing a third in the maze of the canyon. When that latter teacher found her way back, Billi was forced to make room for her on the faculty by becoming the Wintergreen mascot. The mascot was the geoduck, a large edible clam found in Puget Sound, whose siphon grows several feet beyond its shell.

At the end the combined Wintergreen faculty stood up and sang:

Omnia Exstares,
Omnia Exstares,
Alma mater, Wintergreen,
Omnia Exstares.

Go, geoducks go
Through the mud and the sand let's go
siphon high,
Squirt it out
Swivel all about,
Let it all—hang out!

That fall students wore sweat shirts with geoducks stenciled on them and the motto Omnia Exstares. It was not a case of life imitating art as much as inspired whimsy being transposed from one stage to another. "Let it all hang out," that archetypal slogan of the 1960s, was a perfect motto for the experimental college. The geoduck was right too. Willi made merry of the fact. The Evergreen Lions, Evergreen Tigers, or Evergreen Buffaloes wouldn't have worked. Nor would any name from the menagerie of menace where most colleges found their names. Evergreen didn't even have any intercollegiate athletics. Better the lowly geoduck, digging into the sand, looking like a phallic symbol and enjoying the enviable distinction of being able to have sex with itself.

The playful quality of Evergreen went far beyond the geoduck sweat shirt. As a short history of the school expresses it, "The first year was accented with an atmosphere of summer camp."

Willi coordinated a Himalayan range of a program called "The Individual in America." He loved the audacity of tackling such an enormous subject. This was all the 150 students and 7 faculty members would be doing for the academic year. They might soar to the heights. They might fail miserably. He believed that it was education without a safety net, education that was real.

Looking out on the students at the first group meeting, Willi saw young people dressed in jeans, T-shirts, old pullovers, climbing boots, sneakers. Since there weren't any chairs, the students were sitting crosslegged, with hands on their elbows, or lying down on their stomachs as if they were in front of a campfire. "The Individual in America" was not a subject to be knocked off in a fifty-minute lecture. The first meeting was vague and formless.

By the second meeting the new chairs had been installed. When some of the students sat down in the chairs, their peers hissed at them for reverting to "bad educational habits." The students wanted a more natural, open education. They were not, however, sitting in a grassy glen listening to Socrates. They were lying on expensive carpeting looking up at Willi and his colleagues refusing to lecture to them, refusing to tell them what they had to learn. "No longer do we, the instructors, get to stand at the front of the room as the Eternal Founts of Wisdom," Willi said. "It's a process that we're all in together. We're not producing knowledge so much as reproducing ourselves. We don't want to stamp them out in our image, no matter how godlike we might feel at the moment."

When the students went into the wilderness for two weeks working as trail crews for the U.S. Forest Service, Willi couldn't help but appear a little godlike. He had physical strength that had seeped out of most forty-four-year-old men. He did more work than anyone. He was full of an infectious joy and playfulness.

In the wilderness the students learned both to take care of themselves as individuals and to work with a group. "My portrait for the future of Evergreen, and for all society . . . is first of all a recapturing of the sense of group that's been lost in America," Willi said. In the wild Willi was confronted with one of the aberrations of affluence. Some of these young men and women had boots, packs, sleeping bags, and camping gear that could have gotten Mallory up Everest. Yet they would have been lucky to have survived a night in a tent in a state park. With Willi guiding them, the students began to learn and to have faith in themselves.

When Willi let people into his life, he meant all his life. In the evenings around the campfire, Willi talked openly about his colleagues and his own personal life, as if they were one big family.

Although they were not Evergreen students, Devi and Krag had come along. Many of the Evergreeners looked up to the two Unsoeld children as personifying Willi's ideas.

Although Devi was younger than the Evergreeners, she seemed more mature, and wiser. Devi had grown into a strong outdoorswoman. From daily bike riding her bare tanned legs, with their golden unshaven hair, were as tough as those of a competition swimmer. From climbing her arms were equally strong. Since coming to Olympia, Devi had put on considerable weight. One family friend felt that Devi had to shroud a feminine beauty that seemed to come from outside her family. More than ever, though, Devi glowed with a beauty that came from within her. Like her father up in the mountain wilderness, Devi was almost manic in her joy.

For all Evergreen's openness many students were as closed to ideas that challenged their preconceptions as were the old codgers in Olympia who considered the school a hotbed of sex, dope, and Communism. Blue jeans were the Brooks Brothers suits of Evergreen. Sometimes Willi wore a suit and tie to test the students. "They can't believe it," Willi said. "I almost feel rejected. We're as hooked on jeans and that image, just as locked in as we ever were."

Willi tried to make his students understand their own limitations and extend their sense of life. More than anyone else on the faculty, he was willing to work with the most marginal students, guiding them up new paths. When he went off climbing, the young, hotshot mountaineers at Evergreen would have traded their favorite ice axes for an opportunity to share a rope with Willi Unsoeld. Willi, however, bridled at the idea of any kind of elite. He wanted to take everyone climbing: his seminar members, his family, other Evergreeners including the saddest, most needy students at the school.

"If you go, you'll make it," he told students thinking about joining him for a climb of Mount Rainier, the premier mountain in the Northwest. The group became so large that heading up Rainier it looked like an Evergreen reenactment of the Jews leaving Egypt. Among the students slogging ahead, Willi had people whose major athletic accomplishment was learning how to walk. On the climb he set out once again to prove that anyone could do anything. As the group plodded upward he moved from student to student, teaching them about climbing. Twice as many students jammed in the tents as there should have been. To Willi that only made it more interesting. In the morning everyone went up to the summit, an achievement that the students never forgot.

Willi had hoped that the students would sail boldly into the classroom ready to plan what they wanted to learn. In Willi's section though, they sat and waited for Willi to tell them what to do. Willi wouldn't do it. They waited some more, class after class.

"Twelve years of lockstep education, being told what you ought to know, being told how you're going to learn it, and being told how you're going to know when you've learned it," Willi said afterwards. "Programmed. Just programmed right to a gnat's eyelash. Twelve years of it. And here they come, flooding into the Promised Land—Evergreen. And we're going to do it all different they're thinking. So we tell them. 'We're going to do it all different.' They answer us, 'That's why we're here.'

"Well we weren't quite that stupid. They couldn't handle it. We wait three more months and we hear them saying, 'What can we do? We don't have an assignment.' Before long we're molding and shaping just like the old days. 'Okay, here's what you do.' Or 'You could do this. Take your choice. That's freedom.' Then we have to back off and start again with what we really had in mind in the first place. It's a touch-go, for them and for us."

Evergreen had students who were for the most part the children of affluence. There were many young men and women at the college who stood poised to use the freedom that Evergreen provided them. They thrived at the school as they would have at few schools.

There were also those who without purpose or discipline had come to Evergreen. Many of them wanted the school to provide an instant replay of the sixties. Nineteen-year-old hippies who spoke breathlessly of love and peace and of a movement that had reached its peak when they were hardly in puberty. Twenty-year-old radicals who screamed at the slightest touch of authority on their young necks. Teenaged feminists who considered the women of their mothers' generation as little better than political prisoners.

The saddest of all, in many respects, were some of the students from Olympia and southwest Washington, the sons and daughters of mill workers and clerks, who came to get what they considered "an education," to study and move on. They simply didn't understand Evergreen.

Willi didn't mind that there was such constant evaluation of faculty by students, students by faculty, and faculty by faculty so that it seemed as if one's whole life stood in judgment. Students and faculty kept diaries that were exchanged and commented upon as if they were living their own biographies. Many of the students sought counseling from their teachers. The students talked to teachers about the most intimate details of their lives, for the most intimate details of their lives were part of their education.

For the seven teachers in the "Individual in America" the counseling load was, in Willi's words, "inhuman." It wasn't advising, helping students line up courses to be taken one semester after another, and plucking out those worthy subjects for graduate school. This "counseling" was more akin to therapy.

To have some time for themselves the teachers cut the hours of the seminar. The students filled up the free time with more of their problems. The teachers had no one to counsel them. Yet the teachers were as much the prisoners of freedom as any of their students. If it was all too much for a student, he just dropped out for a while, his record unsullied with F's and Incompletes. The teachers had joined a school without tenure, and with such schedules that they did not have time for scholarship. It was tough on marriages, tough on families. To save their homes, most faculty members learned to cut down.

As for Willi, if a student needed help, he was ready, even if it meant a late dinner or some course work that didn't get done. That was hard on his family too. Jolene and the children found it difficult criticizing Willi. He was not out carousing or working on an academic essay. He was helping people who needed him more than the family.

Even now, this busiest of years, Willi went off to lecture. He traveled down to the University of Oregon where he was becoming a yearly fixture. At a rally to protest the proposed logging of the French Pete National Forest in Oregon, Willi got up before 250 students outside the student union building.

The grand themes of Willi's life and ideas were well defined. He rarely prepared for a speech. He started talking, as much interested in what he was going to say as anyone in the audience.

It could have been a mystic guide standing there. His red beard and long hair curling up around his neck looked like a wild bush. He wore cheap black-and-white sneakers, dark work pants cinched at the waist by an ancient belt, and an old windbreaker. As he talked his hands seemed magical, kneading the words, caressing them.

"Man is a wanderer on the face of the earth," Willi said. "Where we walk now is on the pavement with carbon monoxide fumes and other pollutants. We belong to a lucky generation. We don't have to breathe with gas masks."

Then Willi helped lead the march downtown for a protest demonstration on the mall. At forty-four he was twice the age of the students, but Willi was one with them, and they one with him. At the end of the rally, Willi pulled out his harmonica and played "We Shall Overcome."

Although Willi's coordinated studies program was called "The Individual in America," it was a year-long experience in self-discovery. Without the pressure of grades and rigid requirements, each student developed his own learning experience. Some students took advantage of the freedom by not taking advantage of it. Such students Willi was willing to wait out until they were ready to take charge of their educations. Willi wrote that "a good proportion finally caught the dream and came alive to the academic mode strictly because *they* wanted to. This I saw as perhaps our most significant payoff."

Some students were at first mesmerized by Willi, but grew tired of his constant pushing about process and personal development. To others Willi and his ideas were a continual revelation. By the end of the year Evergreen and Willi Unsoeld were synonymous to many students.

Willi already was compelled to defend *his* conception of Evergreen. "I.A. ('The Individual in America') provided a certain atmosphere highly conducive to individual maturation on the part of certain kinds of students," Willi wrote at the end of the year. "My own worry is that this answering of the specific needs of such a large segment of those students who are drawn to Evergreen may be sacrificed (or at least radically reduced) because of the feeling that programs such as I.A. are not 'vigorous enough' or lack sufficient content."

In the summer of 1972 Willi headed back to the Tetons to film an episode of *The American Sportsman* television program. The program more typically had movie stars tarpon fishing off Florida or shooting big game in Africa, not mountain climbing. The producers were hoping to feature Willi and Devi, father and daughter.

Devi had graduated from high school a year early. She had decided not to go directly to college. Instead, she was working and saving for a lengthy trip to Europe and Asia. It would take many weeks to save what she could earn in a few days doing the program. Devi told the television people that she would do the show if they promised to include ideas on how to protect the environment. When Devi looked with warm blue eyes and spoke with her sincere, earnest voice, even the most jaded filmmaker would not skew the truth. She was told that once the film got to New York there was no guarantee how it would be edited.

When Devi backed out, the filmmakers decided to film Willi teaching climbing to David Ladd, the son of Alan Ladd, the movie star. Young Ladd, an actor himself, was full of youthful zeal. When the film appeared on television, it was clear how much Willi's ideas had affected the slim blond actor. "We were to spend a week together preparing for and finally climbing what appeared to be a frighteningly difficult reach . . . where I would learn to measure my progress by the inch and perhaps my self-knowledge by the yard," Ladd narrated. "For me it was an unforgettable learning process, punctuated by pain and plain fear, fueled by a drive to succeed and filled with wonder at a great man and an exceptional place.''

As Ladd began his narration the two men hiked up a steep trail, the younger man tentatively, Willi like an antelope, climbing as if there were no gravity. With his baggy shorts and big beard Willi looked like a giant elf. Suddenly Willi was glissading down an icy slope, using his ice axe like a rudder, his yodel splitting the air.

"Oh, this is great, Willi,'' Ladd shouted as he shot down the slope, his voice charged with exhilaration and fear, finally flipping over, stopping abruptly by digging his axe into the ice.

"That's the way it's supposed to be!'' Willi exclaimed, turning toward Ladd.

"It got a little bumpy there.''

"Yeah, it got a little bumpy there. It really went well, Dave.''

"Willi, tell me what is the fascination of something like Everest?'' Ladd asked, somewhat self-consciously.

"I guess it's a big conglomeration of fascinations, Dave. It starts out from the fact that you don't really know if you can do it. You know we're all lazy. Like everybody the big temptation is to just chuck it and say, 'Gosh, there's just no way this is justifiable.' And that's the fascination. Can you keep pushing when your body is saying 'Down, boy, down.' And then it gets wrapped up in the sheer immensity of Everest. It's so huge. And to be part of that hugeness even though you're just a tiny speck.''

"You tell me that you and Tom clasped arms just as you were about to get to the top. . . ,'' Ladd began.

"Yeah,'' Willi said wistfully.

". . . so that neither one could say the other was first.''

"There are other reasons for clasping arms,'' Willi said, his voice dropping.

"I'm sure that you must have a feeling that . . . I don't know that maybe brothers have.''

"Yeah,'' Willi said softly. "I guess that's it. It comes about the closest thing to the brotherhood of the battlefield. In a sense you really have been that close to the ultimate edge for a pretty long period of time and you know how you can depend on the other one.

A lot of people say, 'Weren't you the conquerers of Everest?' Together we added up to less than half a mote in the eye of the
infinite, a tiny speck. . . . That's part of the preciousness of it.
That you are a speck in the midst of the immensity.''

There was no better guide than Willi. In the film he taught Ladd
to tie a bowline, to move up over a rock, and to rappel. As with all
his students, at the same time Willi was conveying a higher knowledge.

''To me he really is a superstar both as a climber and as a man,''
Ladd said as the two men moved upward. ''From the beginning
you are aware of his great ability along with his complete lack of
irritant. And then he does it all with so little effort that you know
he's not just trying to prove something. My father was like that in
his work, always at peace with himself so that it was relaxing just
being around him. With Willi I felt that same kind of relaxation,
that same kind of rapport.''

Camera crew or no camera crew, Willi was enjoying this week.
The finale of the film and of the week was a climb of a peak. Willi
moved easily up the face, choosing his footholds as if they were
steps on a porch, then belaying Ladd up a pitch, encouraging him
with jokes or praise. ''As Willi began the next ascent I noticed for
the first time all week, I was beginning to relax just a little . . . I
was still afraid but the further I went up the deeper my commitment
until I was actually feeling a part of the mountain, a part of Willi.

''I was finding the cracks . . . and even the rock began to feel
warm, the rock texture pleasant to the touch. I was beginning to
trust it. . . . And the closer we got the harder Willi charged. He
was the tireless leader, pulling me up, straight up as if to the very
sky itself. And I followed eagerly with no fear now, just hard work
and concentration.''

From up above Willi's yodel sounded down the valley, and Ladd
moved up to join him on the summit.

15

At Evergreen Willi had found a place where he felt he belonged. From campus he bicycled home along a narrow, rustic road to a house that exuded Willi's personality. Up the long dirt driveway stood an open two-car garage jammed with climbing gear. The house itself could have been a climber's lodge. The great high-ceilinged combination kitchen and family room led through sliding glass doors to the garden and berry patch. The most coveted piece of furniture in the home was a dilapidated sofa in the family room.

The big living room looked out into a bramble of forest and undergrowth shrouding the house. In the living room hung Barry Bishop's stunning picture of Willi and Tom on the West Ridge. There were artifacts from Nepal too, a few Tibetan rugs, and non-descript chairs and tables. Downstairs the bedrooms and Willi's office were laid out like barracks rooms: cold and functional.

Willi was as much at peace with himself as he had ever been. Regon finally seemed to have found himself. He and Erik LeRoy were working in St. Louis at an Outward Bound-type program for juvenile delinquents. It was the kind of work Willi would have loved. Not only was Krag turning into a climber who might one

day surpass his dad, he was politically active in high school on the
environmental issues Willi cared about. Terres was a feisty little
fireplug of a daughter. She had as much energy as half a dozen
ordinary kids. As for Jolene she still thought it her duty to make
sure that no one took too much advantage of Willi's good nature.
When he went out climbing with students, she was not beyond
suggesting that they divvy up for the gas-guzzling Blue Jewel, the
Unsoeld's GMC suburban truck.

Willi was ever closer to Devi. She was working in an office at
the college earning money for her big trip around the world. Willi
loved being with Devi, talking to her, listening to her tell about her
life. Often each understood what the other thought without saying
anything. When Willi got into an argument with Jolene, Devi found
a way to smooth things over. The weak and hurting were drawn to
Devi for help, as they were to her father.

Willi tried to show equal concern for all his children. But he
could not hide how he felt about Devi. One time when Terres was
a little older, she came to her father and asked, "Dad, do you love
Devi more than me?"

Willi thought. "Well, in some ways I do, I guess."

Devi's friends were the kinds of people Willi particularly liked
too. For the most part these young people did not smoke, drink, or
date. They preferred climbing, trekking, or canoeing, sometimes
in the inlet only five hundred yards from the Unsoelds' house. Devi
had no desire to go out dancing, partying, cruising around Olympia
with somebody. Like her dad and mother she was seeking the one
soul mate with whom she could spend her whole life.

It came to Devi very slowly that the man she wanted, the man
who would be the vessel for all her love, was Erik LeRoy. At first
she confided her feelings only to her diary. When Erik came out
from St. Louis in the fall of 1972, she went climbing with him.
Even then she did not say anything. Only when it was time for Devi
to head off for her great trip, did she begin to express her feelings.

She decided to hitch with Erik to St. Louis and fly from there.
"Devi was heading east to Europe and Asia," Erik said. "I already
had a sense of interest. By the time we finished our hitch, I had a

sense of commitment. It was sixty fathoms down.

"We spent most of the night before she left talking about what it meant to be in love, talking about profundity of feeling, talking about how inappropriate to become lovers, inappropriate because things had just started coming together. It wasn't because she was leaving.

"As she was boarding the plane she said, 'I'm not going to change my mind.' She had a reputation for being flighty. Regon shook his head and said, 'There she goes again. What could she have meant by that.' She meant that she was going to remain committed, that she wasn't going to change her mind. And she didn't."

At the beginning of the new academic year, Willi and twenty-five students headed out to Flapjack Lake for five days in the wilderness. Even if the program had not been entitled "Wilderness and Consciousness" Willi would have found a way to get the students outdoors.

One of the students trudging along with Willi was Roger Mellem, a thin Northwesterner with a high, reedy voice. Mellem had heard Willi speak when he was still at Outward Bound. Later, while a student at the University of Oregon, Mellem had read what he considered a sensational new book, *The Greening of America* by Charles Reich. The best-selling book talked about a remarkable transformation occurring among young people. Reich believed that this new generation was transforming America by dropping out of the affluence and uptight life of the corporate/bureaucratic world and living more generous, less materialistic lives.

As much as he was impressed by Reich's book, Mellem was even more impressed by Willi's ideas. As Mellem saw it, Willi was quite literally talking about the greening of America, using the wilderness to change the way people thought about themselves and their lives. Although in the 1971–72 school year Mellem was a junior at Oregon, he had decided to transfer in the fall to Evergreen to work with Willi. In the spring of 1972 he had sent Willi a thick proposal for an "individual contract," the Evergreen term for a student studying a subject under the tutelage of one professor.

Mellem wanted to edit a book about "Wilderness and Consciousness" that would bring together the ideas that Willi and a score of thinkers and activists were developing.

In the spring, others of these students now walking with Willi to Flapjack Lake had seen Mellem's proposal. Some of the students were at Evergreen solely because Willi was there, young men and women who had been given up on—by other schools, by other teachers, even by the rest of Evergreen itself. There were students totally incapable of the kind of sustained intellectual effort that had produced Mellem's detailed outline. There were students who found their one solace in the wilderness and were bitterly disdainful of those who sought wisdom through books. There were students who were like sparrows with broken wings, hobbling around pathetically. Others were like young condors; given sustenance they might one day soar above the mountains.

To a few of these students even the minimal demands of Evergreen were too much. To them the coordinated studies programs were these gaudy, gypsy caravans creaking along the roadways while they wanted to climb the mountain peaks. A few of these students were about to drop out. But because of Mellem's proposal they decided to latch onto the project, or at least latch onto Willi. Instead of an individual contract, "Wilderness and Consciousness" became a group contract with Willi the sole faculty member.

In his own mind Willi divided the group between the Outward Bounders, who were all for challenge and risk, and the Blue Heron Watchers, who wanted to gaze at natural beauties. Willi's one mandate was that the students agree on what they wanted to learn. A week went by. They weren't getting anywhere. Two weeks. There were endless arguments and discussions. The strongest people, the real leaders, were the most irritated. Three weeks. Some of these students had come to *learn* and wanted to get on with the quarter. Four weeks. Some of the students considered the whole business absurd. Five weeks. The most upset were those few students who had taken the class for a specific purpose and didn't want to "groove" on group dynamics. Finally, six weeks, and the group reached agreement, writing a covenant. The 169-word covenant about which Willi was so proud began "We find the untrammeled places of the earth beautiful. We find in them a solitude that refreshes our hearts . . . We also see these lands, once wild, disappearing. We wonder why.'' The covenant then listed what the students hoped to accomplish: developing communications and wilderness skills, learning about wilderness preservation, building a philosophical foundation for a wilderness ethic, and exploring the wilderness. The document concluded: "As individuals, each of us proceeds on his own development—giving to the group—receiving from the group wherever possible, that the group may grow strong, compromising not sacrificing our differences and fostering our similarities.''

In most schools the covenant would not have been an adequate achievement for six weeks of a college education. Willi believed, however, that "a true group operation ought to be at or near the core of every group contract at Evergreen. This is the lesson so badly needed by our culture today.'' He was willing to sacrifice any amount of academic attainment to get students to work together.

Once the covenant was out of the way, the students met almost every morning and afternoon, spending more time together as a group than in any other program at Evergreen. They had twenty-four-hour marathons studying one book or one topic. That was akin to group therapy. They learned to speak extemporaneously. They improved their writing skills by writing letters to government agencies about the wilderness. They had spelling bees. There were workshops in knot-tying, photography, the identification of stars, mountain medicine, Outward Bound techniques, and other subjects. The best part of the program, as Willi saw it, was the field trips, which included rock climbing, snow climbing, and cross-country skiing. What the students were really majoring in during this 1972–73 academic year was Willi Unsoeld and Willi's concepts of group process.

Even after the students agreed to the covenant, there were still numerous arguments. The real leaders in the class were the most unwilling to sit around waiting for the whole group to decide something. These five or six students caused Willi the most trouble. In other circumstances, they would have been the young people whom

Willi might have most enjoyed being with, but not now. As one student wrote afterwards, "the most unbeneficial dissension . . . served to weed out a lot of the strongest individuals . . . those who were most committed to some purpose, and not willing to simply experiment with the group process to see where that went."

Willi was consumed with the idea that for civilization to survive, people had to learn to work together in groups. All his adult life Willi had been a guide, leading novices both in the mountains and below, responsible for them and to them, always moving above leading them on, with them but apart. Now it was as if he were trying to deny the basic aloneness of human beings, covering up his own isolation with one group after another.

At the end of fall term students took a field trip to a rainy Yosemite National Park in California. While there Willi appeared on *The Advocates,* the public television program that uses a trial-like format to discuss controversial issues. The question of the week was "Should your use of the national parks be drastically restricted?" The glorious Yosemite Valley had become so popular that on a summer weekend tens of thousands crowded into the park, clogging the roads. The great walls of Yosemite, upon which a new generation of climbers were dramatically raising the standard of American rock climbing, had begun to have their own traffic jams.

The Sierra Club and the more militant environmental groups wanted to shut down the roads and the concessions inside the park, leaving nature to those who enjoyed it on nature's own terms. On the other extreme were those who wanted to turn the national parks into little Switzerlands, planting hotels and other banners of civilization as close to the mountains as engineering could place them, running roads through the great virgin forests so that tourists could view nature in comfort.

Willi was not as militant as the Sierra Club. He would have provided buses to shepherd tourists through places like Yosemite, Yellowstone, and the Tetons. He didn't want them staying in fancy hotels or aluminum campers, roaring through the winter wilderness on snowmobiles or zooming across quiet alpine lakes on water skis. The parks were for *real* experience or they were for nothing.

"Mr. Unsoeld, what does the park experience mean to the boys and girls you bring in?" asked Howard Miller, the regular "Advocate." "What is that wilderness experience? Why do we need it?"

"My view of the wilderness experience has to be seen against the background of our national culture," Willi said, perfectly at ease with the camera. "We're a safety-conscious world today. You start with Mom herself fulfilling her God-given function. If you don't believe it, just ask her. She has to protect her children. So do the unions. So do the schools."

"And does coming into this park, does it provide an experience that all people need?" Miller asked, helping Willi lay out his position.

"It's that element of challenge which allows a young person or an old person to test himself against his own," Willi answered.

"What about you?" Miller asked. "You climbed Everest—the ultimate—one of the peak experiences of human days. What did climbing Everest mean to you?"

"The feel that I get about Everest is that sense of perspective on man's place in the universe and it's a very humbling one. We have the feeling that man is in charge and we could be in charge. That's the danger. We could put a hotel on the top of Half Dome [in Yosemite] and I think that would be tragic. What Everest tells me is the absolute need for harmony within the whole unity of things."

"Let's take the spiritual experience that you described and that you try to instill in your students for them to get when they go to the back country right behind Half Dome," said Eric Julber, a Los Angeles attorney advocating that the parks should be opened up even more. "Now spiritual experience is a subjective thing, isn't it? Something every man feels and it's not capable of being measured?"

"That's right," Willi nodded. This was one of his essential ideas. As his students sat there listening it was as if Willi were their surrogate, making all the points they had talked about in class.

"Suppose there is a couple in New York who have worked all their lives and have retired, not just for two weeks, but retired. They see the moon from their hotel room come up over Half Dome.

Do you feel, sir, that they don't feel just as much a sense of beauty as your young people who go up and backpack and sleep out in the wilderness?"

Willi was not about to back down. "I'd like to ask them the price that has to be paid for their enjoyment," he asked rhetorically. "And the price that we have to pay is the exposure of the rest of the humanity in this country to the wilderness experience."

The wilderness was Willi's church. He would like to have driven the moneychangers and concessionaires from his temple with the sheer warmth of his rhetoric. That there was bumper-to-bumper traffic at Yosemite; bears at Yellowstone that fed on garbage, candy, and crackers; and tourists who stood gaping on the rim of the Grand Canyon wondering what to do appalled him. The wilderness was there for anyone to go out and discover. It astounded Willi that most people missed experiencing even a few days of what was the central focus of the good life.

The idea of going off to Yosemite and watching Willi on *The Advocates* was enough to satisfy many students. But all the bickering and dickering had taken its toll. By the end of the quarter the students who were the real leaders were so fed up with the rigmarole of "group process" that they transferred out. In February, Mellem, the student coordinator, whom Willi called "our last strong leader," left to take a position with the Sierra Club.

The students who remained moved closer together. Willi told them how he had found the sacred in the high mountains. They could find it too, he said, not only in the mountains but in the desert or on the water. He told them of the *mysterium tremendum,* the power of the holy that had left him trembling. He told them, too, of the Yugan, the Japanese esthetic term for subtle profound beauty, a term religious in its overtones.

On a ski tour on the side of Mount Rainier Willi and the students looked ahead and saw a band of fog at the broken crest of the ridge. The mist parted. There breaking through the mists was Reflection Lake. It was like a Japanese nature print.

"Quick, what's the name of it?" Willi asked, as he stood on his old cross-country skis.

The students looked at the lake, then back at one another. Finally, someone spoke.

"Yugan."

"That's right," Willi said. "It's sublime. Sublime. Yugan."

Willi and the students stood silently watching the mists envelop the lake again. Years later Willi received letters from students saying what they had felt that day.

In April Willi and the group went for a month to Canyonlands National Park in southeast Utah. This realm of orange, brown, red, and yellow rock was like the bottom of the ocean, drained and dried in the desert sun. There were no great peaks to climb but an endless labyrinth of rocks, canyons, and hills.

"Why is a mountain climber coming here?" one of the tourists asked as Willi walked by with his students.

Willi stopped and talked for a while of his time in Nepal and how though the Nepalese had nothing they were happy, and though the Americans had everything they were not. Then he set out with his students leading them deep into the mazelike canyons as if there they might find the beginnings of happiness. As Willi explained later, their aim "was not biology, geology, hydrology, etc., of the desert, but rather the task of increasing one's sensitivity to the non-human environment."

When Willi went out in the wilderness he felt a great surge of life that stayed with him for days. Soon after Willi returned from the desert a correspondent for the youth page of *The Anderson Herald* came to see him. "Basically, I'm an optimist," Willi told the young man. "I enjoy living and life means energy and excitement. The one thing I'm really down on is apathy."

More and more Willi was reflecting on his life. "I've lived an extremely active and fortunate life, and I owe a great deal to the people that have made this life possible. I feel that I have an obligation to pass on to others what I've learned. Life includes struggle and for me, the tougher life is, the more meaningful and satisfying it will be. I used to be a competitor, but I'm down on competition at the moment. The toughness of life, in my book, means competition with oneself. This is perhaps the greatest test of all—how well you stack up against your own potential.

"As far as today's youth goes, I'm ambivalent," Willi said. "I see them on one hand with immense sensitivity, being much more aware of social issues than my generation ever was. On the other hand, I see them being typically 'youthful'—thoughtless, unaware, and irrational. Many simple refuse to face the issue of consumption in those areas where they are vitally involved. I also feel that there's still a large percentage who tend to cop out. They see the disagreeable aspects of the world, and they won't have any part of it.

"I guess what I look for most in today's youth is enthusiasm, and an enthusiastic attack on problems, with enthusiastic appreciation for the benefits of current-day life. All too often I find apathy. This apathy extends from broken ambition. The youth wants to go too far, too fast. And of course that is part of the culture that we live in today . . . instant everything. My view of the world is that this is an inaccuracy. You don't get things by wanting them a lot.

"The world is tough, and it takes endurance, and a long standing effort in any direction, if what you're after is really worthwhile."

Willi could have been lecturing his own students in "Wilderness and Consciousness" about their own faults. That he would not have done. Despite all that he had seen in his life, he still had a radical faith in the potential of each human being. He was willing to give people time and space to become what he knew they could become. This year he had often become discouraged with the students when they didn't try. But life to him was energy and excitement. He always managed to pump himself and the students up again.

As Willi looked back on the year, he wrote that "the success enjoyed in bringing the group together in a genuine working and living relationship was sufficient to justify the whole program." In part, Willi had liked the program because it had been full of risk.

Willi had refused to place fixed ropes to guide the students along. One quarter of the students' college education had depended on one teacher, one broad subject. Some of the students had gotten relatively little out of the year. They hadn't ever taken full advantage of the many workshops. Others had become excited about *their* education. They had worked hard because they wanted to work hard. To those students Willi was the greatest teacher they had ever had. Wherever they went they spread his legend.

The book of essays never was edited. There had been only four-teen books on the reading list, half of them fiction. Like most of his students, Willi preferred to be out in the wilderness, out with people, out living life.

"It was an unforgettable, unbelievable time," wrote one student in an addendum to a report on "Wilderness and Consciousness." "We finally made peace with ourselves as a group . . . and the most important single factor in making it what it is (oops! was) is Willi Unsoeld—but I guess you can't write that, Willi. So maybe if you ever learn to enjoy writing you can write a history explaining more of yourself and your philosophies of teaching."

Even Regon could not exist too long away from the energy, intensity, and warmth of the family home. Although he still re-coiled from too much contact with his father, Regon had returned to Olympia to enter Evergreen. Regon's sweet goodness and inno-cence had been soured after being touched by the vinegar of the world. Willi's own innocence and goodness was protected in a cocoon woven in part by Jolene, in part by Willi's gaudy strands of exaggeration. Regon had none of that. He was a political radical, a puritan who did not smoke or drink. Like Gulliver in the land of the Brobdingnagians, Regon held life up to such close, rigorous scrutiny that wherever he went he found the institutions of contem-porary society wanting. He was a student activist, fighting for the Evergreen ideals. In November 1974 he wrote a letter to the *Cooper Point Journal,* the college newspaper, talking about "the pervasive atmosphere of passivism that seemed to exist here at Evergreen, i.e., an absence of energy in the direction of a healthy, growing, self-critically developing community."

Willi was worried too that the Evergreen ideals might be slowly seeping away. He was even more worried about his eldest son. Erik had also returned to Evergreen, and Willi talked to Erik, trying to understand why Regon pushed him away. Willi was tired some-times, tired worrying about Regon, tired working so hard. He even sometimes felt like a man who had indeed lived four and a half decades. No matter how bad things got sometimes, he still found it sheer exhilaration getting up in the mountains.

Willi's attitude on a climb was changing. "I think the finest climb I did with Willi was the north ridge of Pinnacle Peak in the wintertime," Erik said. "Krag was along too. The outcome was always in doubt. There was a storm at the top. It was hard climbing, at least for me. We swung leads. Willi pushed us just enough so that it wasn't an easy trip.

"I had to hesitate a long time on a rock wall that was covered by snow. The snow felt as if it was going to slide. Willi said, 'Okay, I see that. I've got a good belay in. If you fall I've got you. Go ahead and try.'

"It was that kind of partnership. It wasn't competitive. It was giving, a sharing of knowledge that happens when you're really doing good work. It was always in my mind, 'Come on, Willi, you can make these decisions by yourself.' But he didn't want to make them by himself. That's how I learned judgment, by having a master come and ask me what I thought about that slope.

"From 1973–74 on, Willi wanted to share the lead. He wanted to share his vulnerability in decisions because his experience was enriched by that. He enjoyed it. We talked about how terrific it was for me climbing with him. And he kept insisting, 'Look, I'm the one that's reaped all the benefits.' "

Willi badly wanted Jolene to come along. On one climb Willi sat alone in his tent writing a letter.

"What you doin'?" one of the students asked.

"I'm writing Jolene."

"Why you'll see her tomorrow."

"I'm writing her because I wish she were here."

Jolene had become interested in other pursuits. She had lived her adult life not for the cosmic other but for the intimate other of family. She was disdainful of those proponents of women's liberation who tried to tell her that she had been a fool. She had been the one to choose Willi. Except for Regon, the children were emotionally closer to Willi, but she and Willi were partners, a team. Now that even little Terres was practically grown up, Jolene had more time.

Jolene had always been more interested in politics than Willi.

Watching how her own area of Coopers Point had been rezoned, she became curious about the relationship between money and political decisions. A 1972 law had forced the public disclosure of contributions to political candidates in the state. Jolene realized that nobody was digging in, figuring out where the money came from, where it was going, in what amounts. In her meticulous, energetic way, Jolene set out to discover what she could. To her "it was sort of like watching a river. Something started upstream and sort of spread and touched a lot of different places as it moved downstream."

It was a tedious business. Nobody else was doing it, not television or newspapers, neither journalists nor the reform groups that had lobbied so strongly for the law in the first place. Although Jolene was extremely high-strung, she sat for hours working at the long counter in the kitchen. She went for days with little sleep, then crashed exhausted. Day after day she kept up with the contributions. Willi and the rest of the family pitched in when they could, but the great burden of the work fell on Jolene.

Although journalists were at first skeptical about statistics compiled by an Olympia housewife, a Seattle newspaper and television station started using the information. On election day several candidates who had campaign funds bloated by special interest money were defeated. Though Willi was proud of Jolene, he was happy that life was finally getting back to normal. Then Jolene decided to put together a report on the fifty special interest groups that had poured the most money into the 1973 campaign.

Proud was hardly the word to describe how Willi felt about Devi's journey. As he read Devi's letters it was if she were living Willi's life all over again. Like her dad she had set out hitchhiking from the West Coast. Then she had traveled in Europe with women friends. She had not worked in a foundry in Sweden as Willi had but in a factory in Crete before heading eastward to Nepal.

Erik was getting letters from Devi too. Willi and Erik often talked about the woman whom they both loved. Willi knew that this relationship between Erik and Devi was no mere adolescent infatuation. His daughter didn't do things that way. After Devi returned she and Erik might one day marry and begin a new generation.

What came through in Devi's letters was only a flavor of her life. In Katmandu she wore Tibetan dresses of thick feltlike wool; Punjabi outfits, flared billowing white pants covered with a sheath-like dress. She walked the narrow streets trying out her Nepali once again, making friends with everyone from embassy people to rickshaw drivers.

Al Read, one of Willi's old guiding buddies in the Tetons, lived in Katmandu heading Mountain Travel, an adventure travel outfit. He thought that not only did Devi have all Willi's exuberance, but she was the most mature, outstanding young woman he had ever seen. What no one knew, however, was how lonely and isolated Devi often felt. She had terrible dysentery and stomach pains at times too, lying huddled in her bed. She decided that it was time to get out of Katmandu. In July 1973 she headed out to Sola Khumbu, south of Everest, to work on a tree-planting project.

When Devi received a letter from Willi or Erik, she surged with joy. Those months Erik and Devi wrote many letters to each other. In the time Devi had been gone Erik had become involved with someone else, one of Devi's friends, an outdoorswoman like Devi. Although Devi still cared deeply for Erik, her dream of one relationship pure in every respect was in danger. After she had returned from Sola Khumbu, at a party in Katmandu Devi met Andrew Laurie, a young English ecologist. Laurie was as blond as Erik. Devi spent a good deal of the evening with him. Devi was wearing a long, scruffy dress and flip-flops. She was decidedly not the kind of young lady that a Cambridge graduate was going to court.

Laurie hardly noticed Devi. He returned to Chitwan National Park, the protected jungle of south-central Nepal that serves as sanctuary for some of the last free rhinos and tigers. Devi came down, too, to work at Tiger Tops Lodge, a tourist facility. To Laurie she still seemed a big unkempt tomboy, keen to climb trees, walk in the jungle at night, and sleep out on the river bank without giving a thought to the danger.

Since he was doing research on the rhinos, Laurie knew how dangerous these lethargic-appearing beasts could be. When he helped Devi and a woman friend hire an elephant and mahout from the elephant camp, he warned them not to go strolling into the grasslands across the river. Several days later Devi and her friend talked a Nepalese worker at Tiger Tops into taking them across the river on foot. When a rhino cow charged the party, the worker helped the two women reach safety up a tree. Before he could get away the rhino tore into his leg with his horn, badly goring the man.

Devi left the park for a while, returning early in 1974. This time she had Krag with her. He had journeyed east to be with his older sister. Krag was the quietest and least articulate of the Unsoelds, a gentle, sincere young man who was closer to Devi than his other brother or sister.

Devi and Krag worked with Dr. Jack Seidensticker, a young scientist from the Smithsonian. He was studying rhinos and leopards. One day at dusk Devi was sitting in a tree platform near Seidensticker. She pointed toward half a dozen rhinos, then climbed down and walked through the herd. Another day Laurie was sitting on a tree platform on the south side of the Rapti River, near the spot where Devi had nearly been killed a few months before. As Laurie watched incredulously, Devi came running through the tall grass. A rhino charged, missing her by only a few inches.

In the summer of 1974 Devi and Krag traveled to Pakistan to meet Willi who was leading an expedition trip run by Mountain Travel. The three Unsoelds had a wondrous, boisterous, backslapping, tale-swapping reunion.

Some of the clients of this commercial expedition were far from first-rate climbers. The group wasn't supposed to climb a tough mountain. But with Willi along a real mountain it had to be. They set off climbing an uncharted, unclimbed 19,500-foot peak. Devi and Krag led rope teams along with Willi, and the three of them seemed a breed apart. Willi whooped and hollered the way he always did in the mountains, wrestling with Devi, the two rolling on the ground like a couple of bear cubs, telling stories of other climbers and other climbs.

After the successful ascent most of the participants flew back to the United States. Willi headed for Nepal for his first visit since leaving AID. His schedule was jammed, but he got together with Seidensticker to discuss how Devi could best pursue her interests in ecology and the environment.

While Willi journeyed eastward, Devi, Krag, and Roger Mellem, their Evergreen friend, set out overland for the west. The two Unsoelds were used to traveling so modestly that to many people it would have seemed not romantic adventure but hard penance. They moved across Afghanistan on creaking, dusty buses. To survive and prosper traveling this way required savvy and forethought. Devi and Krag thrived on this gritty diet of experience, though Devi, after so many months in Asia, had developed chronic stomach problems.

Willi got back to the States months before Devi and Krag and went down to Yosemite. There he spent a lot of time with William (Bill) Turnage, who was becoming one of Willi's closest friends. Willi had met Turnage when he was running a public affairs program at Yale University. Turnage had a ruddy complexion, pugnacious features, and an open, abrupt manner. Like Willi, Turnage had no use for mere chitchat. As a friend, he was capable of great intimacy. Now that Turnage was in California managing Ansel Adams, the photographer, Willi was seeing even more of his friend.

On their way to the airport at Fresno, Willi talked about his children. "Devi and Krag are just superkids," Willi said, puffed up with parental pride. "They have this incredible energy and positiveness."

"Yeah, I know," Turnage said, looking at the highway ahead. "But everything is up, up, up. Everything is smiles. I wonder how they deal with life's negative aspects?"

"That's not fair, Bill!"

"No, I really wonder," said Turnage, who thought that as positive as Willi was, he never forgot how tough life really was. "I don't believe Devi is as happy as she seems to be. She doesn't seem to express the negative side of life."

"You're wrong! They really do deal with the ups and downs."

‹‹‹

16

In the world of outdoor education, Willi had won great renown. He went off consulting and lecturing as far away as Germany. In October 1974 Willi gave one of three major talks at the Conference on Experiential Education sponsored by the Colorado Outward Bound School. While the two other speakers lectured on "The Role of Experience in Education" and "Outward Bound and Delinquency" in addresses studded with facts and figures, Willi stood up there gushing with emotion and energy talking about "Spiritual Values in the Wilderness."

"There are people who don't respond kindly to the Himalayas," Willi said, "but for others that's the sense of the fascination. . . . There is an attraction about it all, an attraction in the mystery, an attraction in the power. The sacred has always drawn man toward it, whatever it is. You are almost fatally attracted. You want to be near it and reach out and almost touch it. You don't touch it, of course, because of the taboos. But there's a fascination about the beauty and the solitude. There is a feeling of 'at oneness' where it's no longer you against the mountain or you against the wilderness, but you at home in the wilderness. . . . You go there to reestablish your contact with the core of things, where it's really at, in order to enable you to come back into the world of man and operate more effectively. So I finish with the principle: Seek ye first the kingdom of nature that the kingdom of man might be realized.''

Willi was ever more the iconoclast, the defender of the irrational, the spiritual, the mystical against the scientists, technicians, sociologists, and rationalists. In November of 1974 he traveled to the Horace Albright Training Center at the Grand Canyon, Arizona, to speak to a group about to become Park Service Rangers. "In true fanatical fashion I would like to emphasize your role as educators, the absolute necessity of training the public as to the proper value to be sought in the parks," Willi said. "You got to be pretty fanatical to take that stand. It's arrogant as hell. But I submit to you that you are the experts. And if you aren't, you better become so, experts on the legitimate use of national parks.''

Willi told of going up Mount Rainier with a group of students. There under the direction of the Rangers, the Evergreeners filled in the road going into Mowich Lake, forcing tourists to hike into the popular spot. To Willi the idea that people drove their cars into a high alpine lake was a virtual sacrilege, symbolic of the many ways in which modern man was alienated from nature and from himself. To Willi this training program itself was a perfect example of that alienation.

"My final invidious observation is that out of six weeks in the program for National Park Service how many nights did you spend out-of-doors? Come on! Three? Maybe four? Out of six weeks!! 'Well, you know there is something about this wilderness and maybe we aren't doing it justice. Oh I know, we'll bring Unsoeld here for a two-hour lecture. That'll take care of it.' That irritates me! Bring it up with your administration. We're indoors. We're artificial. We should be outdoors where it's happening . . . .''

When Devi and Krag arrived back in Olympia, they brought big news with them. While in Boston they and Elliott Fisher, an old Andover friend, had gone out to visit Ad Carter. Willi had known Carter since the 1950s when he had come to Jenny Lake looking for the young guide who had named his daughter after a mountain in India. Carter had been on the 1936 Nanda Devi climb that Willi considered one of the classic expeditions. He and Ad became friends.

Devi and Krag had been sitting in the Carter's living room looking at a picture of the northern view of 25,645-foot Nanda Devi taken by Chris Bonington, a prominent British climber.

"You ought to climb Nanda Devi in 1976," Devi said, "the fortieth anniversary."

"You too, Devi," Fisher said. "You should climb the mountain you were named after."

Thus the 1976 Anglo-American Nanda Devi Expedition was born. For Carter it would be a climbing life come full circle, his days of expedition climbing ending where they had begun. For Devi, how long had she thought of her mountain? Nanda Devi was Willi's mountain as well, a symbol of his first Himalayan climb, a symbol of his first daughter. He wanted to climb the Himalayan heights with Devi, to share the joy and mystery of Nanda Devi with her.

Willi loved having Devi back. It bothered him, though, seeing how much Erik's new relationship hurt his twenty-year-old daughter. The relationship was not a platonic one. She could no longer dream of a pure, perfect meeting of body and spirit with the first man for whom she had cared. As for Erik, for a while he thought that he was in love with two women. But the mere presence of Devi spilled over onto his new love killing it like too much water drowning a flower.

Willi tried to bring Devi and Erik back together again. "Look, you're playing your cards too long," he told Erik. "She's going to walk away. Now what are you going to do about it?"

Devi and Erik had long talks, not only about themselves but about politics and the environment. One night they sat in a boxcar on a siding, talking all night about their feelings. "Willi's trying to bring us together," Erik said.

Devi laughed. "Well, you know how much he likes you, Erik." Devi didn't know how she felt about Erik. One day she was sure she still loved him, the next day she had lost the feeling. For months she went back and forth. It was as if she were reaching out, catching something, then losing it again. A year or more passed before Devi realized that it was all over, finished. As much as she loved Erik, she would have to look elsewhere for her perfect mate.

Devi watched out for her dad as much as her dad watched out for Devi. She calmed him. She tempered his exaggerations. She watched his diet. When Willi and Jolene had their shouting matches, she was the one person who could mediate.

"You're just spending too much time in the legislature," Willi argued. Jolene had always been jealous of Willi's time. Now that she spent so much time in political work, Willi was equally jealous of Jolene's "I'm not even getting my sandwiches!"

"Well, Dad, you know what you're going to have to do?"

"What?" Willi asked, looking for a Solomon-like judgment from his daughter.

"You're going to have to learn to make your sandwiches for yourself."

"But I want my missus to make my sandwiches!"

"Well, you can't have it, Dad," Devi affirmed, her voice touched with love.

A person eavesdropping on the Unsoeld house during their arguments might well have imagined that Willi's next expedition would be to a divorce lawyer. But Jolene and Willi had always gone at each other like rustic refugees from *Who's Afraid of Virginia Woolf?* Devi had heard these sessions all her life. She knew the deep, intense feelings that her parents had for one another. Jolene made excessive demands on Willi just as Willi made excessive demands on Jolene. If there were those who couldn't imagine why Willi put up with Jolene, there were those who wondered how Jolene tolerated Willi.

As far as Erik was concerned, Willi and Jolene had a rich, remarkable, tenacious love. But even he thought the fighting was a bit too much.

"Jo, leave me alone!"

"Jo, let's talk about it!"

"Jo, don't do that!"

"Jo, you're being unreasonable!"

Erik had heard it all.

"Willi, you know I've been around you an awfully long time, but you know even I get tired of the quarreling you and Jolene go through," Erik told Willi. "I feel that it's getting even worse. Don't you want to do something about it?"

"It's not getting worse, Erik," Willi responded. "It's just like it was when I was finishing my Ph.D. Jolene has an uncanny ability to hit me at the worst spot. I mean she'd break down the night before finals. She'd make unruly demands on the last nights when the pressure was greatest. She's always done that. I can't tell you why."

Willi and Jolene were too busy now to spend much time squabbling. Nor did Devi spend much time refereeing fights. She was slowly getting used to living in the States. Upon returning from Asia she was more appalled than ever at the way the American society squandered the treasures of the earth.

Devi bought almost no new clothes. She made do with second-hands or hand-me-downs. Water was a sacred resource too. Devi and her family did not flush the two toilets in their house each time they used them. Devi didn't eat beef, not because she was against slaughtering cattle, but because beef is a less efficient source of protein.

For food there was a garden behind the house. More importantly, Devi and her brothers made forays down to the supermarket in the shopping mall. There they picked up wilted fruits and vegetables as well as milk and half-and-half tossed out behind the store. One time a patrol car came by, thinking that someone might be breaking into the supermarket. Devi and Regon gave the officers their first full-fledged environmental lecture, showing them all the food being wasted, and the police went away.

Willi would be forty-nine by the summer of the expedition. The doctors had told him that he had arthritis in his hips and a deteriorating fifth lumbar vertebra. He tried not to think of it. He tried to will the discomfort away. If he had a frantic schedule before, now he made it even more so. He wouldn't think about it. He wanted to get up there, to have another real climb while he still had time.

Willi couldn't get Jolene to go, but Devi and Krag were going. Maybe he could even get Regon to go, loosen him up, get him to have a good time. Willi kept thinking about his old heroes Shipton and Tilman. They had gone onto Nanda Devi the right way. No fancy hardware, no down jackets, no nylon rope, no crampons, no snazzy dried foods. Just Norfolk jackets and whatever food they could find along the way. That was the only way to do it, letting nothing stand between man and mountain.

The preparations for the climb had already begun. The Garhwal in India had been closed off from climbing expeditions for years.* It was a coup getting permission ahead of other groups. Carter would be one co-leader on the East Coast, Willi the other co-leader on the West Coast. Even planning a small expedition, the two men had many decisions to make: calculating expenses, getting donations of equipment and money from manufacturers and others, arranging shipping, and figuring the logistics. For Willi, though, choosing the team members was by far the most important decision. To him the group was the ultimate unit of human endeavor, and the members of a climbing expedition the ultimate group— ultimate because it was life itself that was at stake, ultimate because all the lessons of sharing and caring came together here.

A few definite names were already on the list: Willi, Ad, Devi, Krag, and Elliott Fisher, whom Willi remembered from the Andover days. In the summer of 1975 Willi traveled out to his old stomping grounds, the Tetons, and talked to Peter Lev, a guide, about going on a low-keyed, family-type expedition to Nanda Devi.

Lev was the kind of person with whom Willi liked to share a rope. The guide had started climbing back in the late 1950s in

---

*As Willi and Carter knew, the sacred sanctuary of Nanda Devi had been violated in the mid 1960s by secret CIA-sponsored expeditions. In 1965, a CIA-financed team of top American climbers tried to place a nuclear-powered tracking station on top of Nanda Devi to monitor Chinese nuclear and rocket tests. Two thousand feet short of the summit, the climbers turned back, leaving the nuclear power pack behind. The following spring a team returned to discover that the pack full of plutonium-238 had been swept down the mountain.

One climber soloed to the summit, but the CIA was left with a major problem. The plutonium-238 might one day begin to leak, flowing down from the headwaters of the Ganges, polluting and poisoning. Another expedition tried to retrieve the device, but it lies there still, buried under snow and ice, a potential danger for the next three hundred to five hundred years.

Yosemite. The Yosemite climbers of those days were an athletic counterpart to the Beat Generation, working a few months a year to get enough money to climb the rest of the time. Lev had never dreamed that he was picking up skills with which he would eventually make a living.

Lev had a long, sunburned face and crinkly, weathered eyes, the lean good looks of a Swiss ski instructor. He climbed and spoke with equal precision, testing each word as if he weren't sure it would hold his thoughts. In his mid-thirties, Lev was at an age when many climbers make their most daring climbs. The year before he had been on the tragic American Pamirs/USSR Expedition, a multinational climb in which fifteen mountaineers lost their lives. Lev was a fine climber. But like a good club fighter who has lost his killer instinct, Lev didn't have a deep visceral need to reach the summit. He loved the wilderness. He had what many people considered an enviable life. He was not that young anymore. He was glad that Nanda Devi would be a low-key climb. He was up for that.

After Lev decided to go, his friend Marty Hoey was invited as well. Hoey was a guide on Mount Rainier. A decade younger than Lev, she had brown hair, a narrow mouth, and eyes that made her look almost Asiatic. She was a strong-willed climber who did not let the fact that she was a woman stand in the way of her mountaineering ambitions. She, too, had been on the expedition to the Russian Pamirs. Devi was delighted that at least one other woman would be going along.

Then Carter invited Louis Reichardt, a neurobiologist doing research at Harvard. The scientist was in his early thirties. One expedition chronicler has described Reichardt as "weird" with "some kind of devils running around inside, which apparently were exorcised—and then I suppose only temporarily—by brilliant accomplishment." Reichardt didn't look like an outdoorsman but like a grumpy, bedraggled, preoccupied man of science.

Reichardt was not a man to sit around the campfire for hours swapping tales or happily lead a group of novices up for a weekend climb. He was a hard man. In 1969 during the first American expedition to Dhaulagiri an avalanche had swept down killing seven of the eight men in its path, leaving only Reichardt alive. Other climbers would have taken that as an omen. But on the 1973 expedition to 26,795-foot Dhaulagiri, he was one of the two Americans to reach the summit.

Carter showed Reichardt a grainy 1936 photo of Nanda Devi and pointed out the proposed new route on the North Face. Reichardt knew that this would be a serious expedition. A serious expedition meant serious equipment. It meant serious climbers too. Reichardt wrote John Roskelley, the young climber who at the age of twenty-three had gone with Reichardt to the summit of Dhaulagiri; he told him that if Roskelley wanted to go to Nanda Devi, he should write Carter.

Roskelley already knew Carter as editor of the *American Alpine Journal*. Roskelley had submitted a long, frank article about the Pamirs expedition to the journal, a publication in which reticence was still the king of the virtues. The two men had disagreed over the article, and Roskelley did not expect to be invited to Nanda Devi. Carter may not have been delighted at the prospect of sharing a tent with Roskelley, or sharing the pages of the journal he edited. But there was no hiding the fact: Roskelley was fast becoming one of the best climbers in America.

When Lev heard that Roskelley was going, he became upset. From both Dhaulagiri and the Pamirs he knew what Roskelley meant. Down below John often played the redneck yahoo, a northwestern hillbilly. Up on the mountain he became relentlessly determined, all his energy and strength focused on one single goal: reaching the top. On Dhaulagiri Roskelley had lost the tips of some of his toes to frostbite but he had reached the summit. In the Pamirs he had been almost swept away in an avalanche that killed another American climber.

Roskelley knew that it wasn't just any climb of 25,645-foot Nanda Devi being planned but an ascent by a new northern route. If the mountaineers spent too much time enjoying the scenery and companionship, they would not reach the summit. Reichardt and Roskelley were not going to India for mystical experiences or to listen to Willi play his harmonica. Roskelley, in particular, was in a hurry. Although still only twenty-seven by the time of the climb, Roskelley had to make his reputation quickly. He was not going to waste an expedition stumbling around the base of Nanda Devi.

In October the West Coast members of the expedition got together for the first time. Roskelley's home was in Spokane, in the eastern part of the state. He came to the Unsoelds' home as did Pete Lev and Marty Hoey. For all Willi's concern with groups and group process, when people were with Willi and his family, everyone played the Unsoelds' game—an intense, emotional, endless discussion.

This was the first time Willi and his family had met Roskelley. John was five feet ten inches tall, lean of build, with open impish looks, a face of youthful incredulity. As he spoke Roskelley had all the subtlety of a dump truck driver backing up into the Unsoelds' living room and unloading.

"I don't think we ought to have any women on this climb," Roskelley said.

This was a daring statement. Devi hadn't arrived back from town yet for the meeting, but the expedition had been in good part her idea. Nanda Devi was her mountain.

"What do you got against them, John?" Willi asked, not mad as much as fascinated.

"Look, I got nothing against them." Roskelley squirmed.

Roskelley had married a pretty schoolteacher from a Mormon family. She stayed home, taught school, and helped support him while he climbed, an arrangement that he thought not only inevitable but just. For a climber of Willi's generation such an attitude was common enough. But it was 1975 now, and the banners of women's liberation waved bravely not only over the Upper West Side of Manhattan, but over the suburbs of Olympia and even in conservative Spokane. Although Roskelley was criticized for his male chauvinism, he loved his wife, loudly proclaimed it, and was more loyal to her than were many of those climbers who professed the proper contemporary attitude like a catechism.

"But I have trouble just controlling my impulses at sea level, let alone at twenty thousand feet in a two-man tent," Roskelley continued.

Roskelly let this sink in while the Unsoelds looked at him as if his glands might suddenly explode. Then John tilted his head toward Willi.

"What does your daughter look like anyway?"

Willi was rarely at a loss for words. This time he was saved from that embarrassment by the timely arrival of Devi. She had pedaled eleven miles from Olympia and burst into the room wearing ragged cut-off jeans and a tiny halter that covered all that the law, if not decorum, demanded. She glowed with perspiration. She stood poised at the edge of the living room looking at the one stranger.

"Why you're Roskelley," she said in her exuberant voice. "I understand you have trouble with women."

Willi and Devi tried to enlighten Roskelley. "The macho image of climbing has got to change," Willi said, looking at his daughter whom he so badly wanted to see standing on the summit of her mountain, the highest any woman had yet climbed.

"It just doesn't work," Roskelley countered, shaking his head. Although he realized that it had perhaps not been right to challenge Devi's going, that was the way Roskelley did things. He was not ashamed or embarrassed. Nanda Devi was no place to fool around, no place for weekend climbers or women, no place for the less than committed.

Roskelley didn't want women along, but like everyone else that evening John agreed that on the expedition the Americans would live and climb modestly, not disrupting the environment on which they trespassed. Other foreign expeditions to the Garhwal had imported climbing Sherpas from Darjeeling or Nepal. These climbers didn't want that. On Nanda Devi they would carry their own loads. They didn't want a lot of equipment donated to them either, to squander, leave in India, or add to their own collections.

They intended to get all their food for the approach march and Base Camp in-country, not ship it from the States like the 1963 Everest expedition. They figured that they needed two or three six hundred-foot spools of rope to be fixed on the toughest spots on the climb. As for pitons to be used placing the fixed ropes, Willi had vintage World War II pins that he was delighted to offer up to the expedition. Beyond that everyone would bring his own gear.

For Devi the great joy of climbing was being out with people, not reaching for the summit itself. She badly wanted her climb to be right from beginning to end. After Hoey, Lev, and Roskelley left, the Unsoelds discussed the expedition. Things had gone fairly well at the meeting but Willi knew that Roskelley had a different attitude about climbing than the Unsoelds. Willi had worked with all kinds of climbers, though, and he was sure he could work with John. Jolene had no such faith in human beings in general or in Roskelley in particular. She wondered whether it made sense sharing an expedition with people with whom the Unsoelds had little in common.

The expedition received official sponsorship from the American Alpine Club. This was in part a fund-raising device. Donors, however, didn't give money and goods for chummy family expeditions, but for major endeavors, new routes, and new climbs. For his part, Willi wanted it both ways. He didn't want to go wallowing up the old milk route. He didn't want a relentless, joyless climb either, weighed down with tons of equipment.

Willi didn't have the time or interest to plow through applications for the expedition or to go out and find his kind of climber. He left that primarily to his co-leader on the East Coast. Carter chose a group of strong young climbers. As Reichardt recommended Roskelley, so Roskelley recommended Dr. James States, his favorite climbing partner from Spokane. Another strong climber chosen was John Evans, program director for Outward Bound in Colorado. Evans had climbed in the Yukon, Antarctica, and on Everest's southwest face. A big man, he had been on the Pamirs expedition where some of the members thought he was the strongest climber they had ever seen.

Andrew Harvard was invited too. He was an easterner, a Dartmouth graduate, who had gone on the 1973 Dhaulagiri expedition and coauthored a book about it. He had a good reputation and was Ad Carter's kind of person. To make this a truly international expedition, there would be two Indian climbers as well, Kirin Kumar and Nirmal Singh.

To Willi it looked like a good team though he didn't know most of these people. What bothered him though was that as the trip developed both Regon and Krag decided that they didn't want to go. For Devi that was a hard blow as well. She was very close to Krag. It hurt her deeply that her younger brother in his ponderous, quiet way had decided this expedition was no good. With Roskelley and the other hard men involved, this was no longer a low-key family climb. It was not the kind of venture with which Krag wanted to be associated.

By the time of the team meeting in Seattle in early December, the abstract philosophical question of what kind of climb it would be had come down to the nuts and bolts of equipment and detail. Of those most fervently in pursuit of the summit, only Roskelley showed up, along with Carter and Fisher from Boston, and Willi and Devi.

The meeting had hardly begun when the team members began to disagree. Although Roskelley had already accepted the idea of taking only minimum amounts of fixed rope, he and the hard men now felt that thousands of feet were needed. From the perspective of the hard men, it was not only prudent but mandatory to take sufficient rope to get the party up the mountain.

When Willi heard the figure of fifteen thousand feet, he joked later that he wondered whether they intended to place the ropes around the summit of Nanda Devi like a cargo net and climb up from all sides. Listening to Willi ridiculing the idea of taking a lot of rope, John thought that Willi was playing around, and it was a dangerous game.

It wasn't that Willi liked old or minimal equipment, skiing cross country on bindings that kept breaking loose, climbing with the same gear he had used on Everest. It was that he thought that fancy equipment often got in the way. In that opinion he was not unlike the old British gentlemen climbers who for so long had resisted crampons.

It was a day of compromises, on the amount of rope, freeze-dried food, medical goods, and practically everything else. These were not compromises where positions are honed down to their essences. These were compromises that left both sides discontent. Willi was a purist. Now he would be climbing Nanda Devi, that goddess of a mountain, weighed down with what he considered all kinds of modern junk and technology. Roskelley was a purist too. Now he would be climbing the mountain without enough rope and equipment to make him feel comfortable. He felt uneasy. If he hadn't so wanted to climb Nanda Devi, he might have packed it in. He knew that he would be okay. He was strong. But he believed these others in Seattle were cutting their own throats.

Roskelley represented the best of the new generation as Willi represented the best of the old. For John climbing was everything. Willi and his contemporaries sometimes looked disdainfully at these young climbers, calling them "professionals," their ultimate epithet. It was true that Roskelley hoped to make a living from climbing—giving lectures, selling pictures, writing expedition books, perhaps even endorsing equipment. It was a modest living that he aspired to, and so far he had earned very little at all. In order to succeed he had to reach the summit on most climbs. He had to make a name for himself. It was true too that up in the mountains Roskelley and his kind took far more risks than most climbers of Willi's generation would have taken. It was also true that down below they worked far harder in preparation.

They were the new breed.

Devi and her dad were such romantics that they sat together crying, watching *Cyrano de Bergerac* on television. But Devi wasn't always led by her romanticism. At Evergreen she might have been happier studying classical literature, traveling with Odysseus on his great journey, watching Lear and his madness, following along with Anna Karenina. Instead, she and Krag both took programs weighted down with politics and economics. As they started out, Jeanne Hahn, one of their teachers, considered them "uneducated radicals," Krag "more analytical," Devi "more emotional."

Devi cared for what was immediate and near to her in ideas and people. She believed in Evergreen as a place where students made their own educations. When she felt that one faculty member was far too traditional and rigid, she told him so. That might have seemed an act of willful arrogance, but like her dad Devi was devoid of that self-righteousness that sours idealism into smugness.

Devi worried about the expedition. She needed strength for Nanda Devi. It was so strange. When she sat with her family and friends she looked forward to Nanda Devi and yet at just those times she thought of not coming back. In her diary she asked herself if her life meant anything more than ripples. She wrote that she would like her image to disappear but wondered if some of her feelings might remain.

She had vague premonitions of death. She didn't like the way the expedition was developing. At times she didn't want to go to Nanda Devi at all. "When I look at the expedition the way it is now, I sometimes cringe inside because I know other people won't understand," she said. She took her responsibilities seriously. She thought that she owed it to Willi, Ad, and Elliott to go and see that it be the kind of expedition they intended.

The Nanda Devi expedition had already attracted the fascinated interest of one outsider, Worth Hedrick, a local journalist. Hedrick was a small, wiry man with an inquisitive, almost beseeching voice. The previous summer he had gone on a climb of Mount Olympus in a large group led by Willi. Hedrick had been an alcoholic. On the five-day trip he had often sat with Devi chain-smoking cigarettes, telling her about his problem. He was drawn to Devi and the family, seeking strength to stay away from alcohol for good. He decided to write a magazine article about Willi, Devi, and the mountain.

In one of his many talks with Devi, Worth asked why she wanted to climb Nanda Devi. "Part of it is being back in that part of the world," she said with sweet earnestness. "I've spent eight years over there altogether and it's a big part of my life. So being a sentimentalist at heart, I know what it means to Dad to go back to the area that he started climbing in, in the Himalayas. And since that part of the world means so much to me, it's in many ways a sentimental trip. And, well, Nanda Devi, being named after it, I've always had a desire to see it. I've heard stories about the Garhwal. I've never been to that part of India. And the opportunity to go in, not only to go in and see it, but to try to climb it, to spend some time with the mountains is very exciting.''

What did she seek in the mountains? Hedrick asked.

"It's through climbing that many of my best relationships with people have been formed,'' Devi said. "You become, you're dealing on some very elemental levels with life, and a goal is right there. Although the people are very complicated, you get some very good friendships in the mountains. It's always a time when you have time alone. You can look up on a hillside and look down on the world. I've come back from the mountains . . . and you feel better to face things.''

When Hedrick came out to the house to interview Willi about the climb, Willi rested on the sofa in the living room, his stockinged feet propped on a pillow. Jolene sat at the dining room table typing up the latest figures on campaign contributions, her fingers beating out a staccato rhythm on the old manual typewriter.

"This will be my last major expedition because of my increasing physical infirmities,'' Willi said solemnly.

"*Bullshit!*'' Jolene shouted, looking up, then returning to her work.

"I feel I have a chance at the summit—if my hip and back hold up. The feet are no problem, although sometimes they feel like red hot needles are pricking them—after violent exercise—because of the poor circulation. But that's a short-term thing and it goes away quickly.''

Hedrick asked how Willi felt risking his daughter's life.

"In Devi's case, I feel strongly that she has the kind of balance that looks at life similarly to mine—so I have no guilt or uncertainty about exposing her to dangers. I think you come out of experiences like the Nanda Devi expedition as a fuller, more secure human being for having been willing to go to those kinds of lengths, and I think it serves to stabilize you in your everyday relationships. . . .

"I'd love to [get to the top] because that's the way I'm oriented—and with the kind of knowledge we have of Himalayan mountaineering, I think we should get more than one team to the summit. I'm especially hopeful we can get Marty and Devi to the top. It's a feeling of mine that they deserve that, because women haven't had that opportunity. But my greatest hope is that we can get Ad up as high as possible.

"This will be the logical expedition for me not to reach the top. I also look upon it as my greatest challenge not to reach the summit—and to live with that fact gracefully. As I sit here now I think I can handle that."

It was not just the summit of Nanda Devi that Willi was trying to prepare himself not to reach any longer, but the summits of life itself. Through nearly five decades he had surged with energy, with a profound sense of well-being and strength. He still often felt good and strong. On the handball court he was a tiger. But he was tied down by his forty-nine-year-old hips. He couldn't be himself any longer. He couldn't be Willi.

"I have a fantastic body and I've made ultimate use of it," Willi said later. "And now it was beginning to rebel as it had every night. And so . . . because of the full circle which it comprised— where it had all begun in forty-nine [and also] now the fortieth anniversary of the first ascent, going back with Devi . . . she and her powers just coming into the fullness of her life, it seemed appropriate . . . to cast off the booster rocket. I was ready. I saw nothing particularly reprehensible about going out with honor.

"Now my eldest son is very sensitive to these things as he is to everything. . . . And he sensed this, was desolate, just most suspicious, raised this with me before I left. Challenged me.

" 'Dad, you don't have any screwy notions now, do you?'

"Ah, you mean my not coming back. The thought had crossed my mind.

" 'Yeah, I thought so. Just like you.' "

It was a perfect idea. Willi turned it over again and again in his mind like a jeweler examining a fine diamond. As he had written in his Ph.D. thesis, the rocket ship was Bergson's favorite metaphor, life blasting ever upward, the gray dross of spent life falling below. Devi, more like Willi than Willi himself, would go up the mountain. Willi would help lift her up to the summit. She would go on from there, climbing life's summits, high above the clouds. And he would stay on the slopes of her mountain, his body and beard as gray as cinders, stay there forever buried on the white flanks of Nanda Devi, the bliss-giving goddess.

As he contemplated dying on the mountain, there was a sense in the family that it was inevitable that Willi would die on a mountain. Maybe Nanda Devi was the mountain. Maybe the time was now.

It was a perfect idea. But it was only an idea. Willi loved to hear the sound of ideas, listening to them as if they were new melodies that he was trying out. The expedition, though, was not an idea. It was real and serious. In the East, Carter had been all for a modest climb, too. With Harvard's and Reichardt's encouragement, more equipment and food was shipped than anyone had originally envisioned. In the spring, while Willi was tied down with students and Devi was finishing up her first year at Evergreen, Roskelley was out by himself in the mountains preparing by running across high passes, soloing peak after peak.

For Willi the last weeks before leaving had left him little time to work out. At home Regon and Krag had set out to educate their father about socialism and economics. At Evergreen the faculty was supposed to be able to teach anything; Willi was an expert at improvising. He had a way of sucking up the essence of books and ideas, winging it intellectually as he did physically, getting himself in tight spots and working his way out. Regon and Krag knew all Willi's tricks. They went at their father furiously. At school Willi thought his lectures were often abstract and boring. By any standard but his own, they were not.

"I'm going to start my lecture like this," Willi said one day. He picked up a piece of chalk and drew a picture of a man holding something in his hand. Waves of giggling moved through the room.

"This is the crux of moral decision making. Anybody know what this is a picture of?"

"A Pilgrim?" a student said, looking at the hat on the cartoon figure.

"I don't know how Socrates stood it," Willi said, feigning disgust. "Hah, anyone can see that's a picture of an act. That's a hammer."

"A piton hammer!" someone shouted.

"Okay, this is a piton hammer," Willi said while the students were convulsed in laughter. "And it's stopped in full flight."

"Now we have a small difficulty: we don't know what the act is," Willi went on. "Now tell me, Karen, is it a moral or an immoral act?"

"It depends on the situation," the student said softly.

"It depends on the situation," Willi repeated. "She's read Fletcher. There's nothing I can tell her."

Willi led the group through a discussion of situation ethics. One of Willi's favorite books was Joseph Fletcher's *Situation Ethics*. Learning about aspects of situation ethics in books and essays by Barth, Bonhoeffer, or Niebuhr would have been tough going for most undergraduates at Evergreen. Fletcher's thin book was more radical and simpler. Written in a breezy, colloquial style, the book was one of the more popular philosophical texts of the day. Just as *The Greening of America* codified a lot of ideas that Willi had been thinking on his own, so did *Situation Ethics*. He had been delighted to find a book that put it all down clearly, uncompromisingly.

To the theologian Fletcher the New Testament idea of an *agapeic* love, a limitless love for all human beings, made Christianity "Christian." Fletcher wrote that "love *is* justice . . . they are one and the same. To be loving is to be just, to be just is to be loving." Thus "the situationalist holds that whatever is the most loving thing in the situation is the right and good. It is not excusably evil, it is positively good."

"Now let's make it a nail," Willi said. "It's a big nail, a big long one."

Looking up at the blackboard, the students laughed even louder at Willi's buffoonery.

"What's the nail going into?" one student asked.

"Is that relevant?" Willi asked rhetorically as several students giggled. "Well, it's going into a *hand*."

The students found that funny too.

"Is that moral or immoral?" Willi asked.

"It depends!" the students shouted.

"Okay, let's nail it down now, as the saying goes," Willi said slowly, looking at his handiwork. "Let's finish it off. Ah, I don't know . . . the hand . . . as a matter of fact . . . belongs . . . shall we slice it off there . . . belongs to Jesus Christ."

A few students gasped.

". . . And it's on a great big timber. Okay? Now. Moral or immoral?"

Suddenly Christ was there on the cross. Willi had manipulated the students. He had them where he wanted them. For the rest of the class he led them through the various moral systems, legalistic, Kantian, utilitarian, helping them figure out what each system would say about crucifying Christ.

When he had finished going over these moral systems, he talked about some of his own ideas. Willi said that for himself he considered all acts morally neutral until he had figured out their likely consequence. Only then did he act. That didn't always make it easy, Willi said, but it let a person perform a good act that ended badly, or a bad act that ended well.

"The tragic ones are when you do your very best, the best will for the best consequences and it just turns out miserable," Willi said. "Then what? You should always separate the person from his behavior when you're judging. Instead of judging the person you judge what he did.

"You can say, 'That was a bad show.'

" '*Oh, you don't like me.*'

" 'No, I like you very much but it was a bad show.'

" '*How can you like me if I do a bad show?*'

" 'Well, because that's one of the universals.' You always hold the person in high regard while you deplore his action. And even his motive . . . that one isn't easy to carry out either. That's enough."

It was a beautiful spring. As Devi and Willi made their final preparations, the June days were long, sunny, and fine, and nature glowed with goodness and warmth. One of those days Krag had been bicycling home when he tumbled to the pavement, knocking himself unconscious. When he awakened he appeared almost a different person. At times he thought he was God. He went for a walk and ran and ran and ran and ran and Regon had to go and find him. He made applesauce without peeling or coring the apples.

When Willi flew east to attend a conference, Krag was halfway normal. Devi couldn't stay any longer. She had to meet Elliott Fisher in New York City. From there they would fly together to New Delhi to make preparations before the other climbers arrived. On the night before Devi left, Jolene told her daughter, "I don't hold you responsible for what your father does."

The next morning Regon drove Devi to the airport. On the twenty-first of June, the first day of summer, Devi and Elliott left for India from Kennedy International Airport. Devi told Fisher that Jolene was confident that Willi might come back, not confident that he would, but that he might.

The more Fisher listened to Devi, the less sure he was that even that minimal confidence existed. As the plane soared eastward toward Nanda Devi, an image appeared in Fisher's mind. He saw a circle, a snake biting its tail. The mouth was the pilgrimage to Nanda Devi that Devi and Willi were undertaking together. The tail had begun back on Willi's first visit to India. Willi's climbing days were coming to an end. He had put his life in order. Perhaps when he returned to Nanda Devi his Karma would take him. To Fisher, it wasn't only a possibility. In its remarkable symmetry, it seemed inevitable.

17

When Willi got back from his conference, Devi was gone. Krag was feeling better. Jolene was working twelve to fourteen-hour days on her project. Except for his relationship with Regon, Willi felt that he had his life in order. Willi understood how Regon might still blame him for talking him out of draft resistance. Try as he might, though, he could not understand the intensity of Regon's bitterness. The two of them talked for hours. Willi couldn't figure Regon out.

The long Fourth of July weekend Regon worked on a pair of gaiters, outerboots for his old dad. That meant a lot to Willi. Again, Willi had a long talk with Regon. Though he often couldn't stand to have Willi touch him, Regon put his head on his dad's shoulder, tears welling up in his eyes. Willi thought that finally he was getting somewhere with his eldest son.

His last evening in Olympia, Willi accompanied Jolene to a party at the home of a local journalist. They got home very late. Regon was still up sharpening the edge of his dad's ice axe. In the morning Willi was too tired, and things were too rushed for him to say what he might have said, either to Regon or to Jolene.

Willi met Marty Hoey at the airport. Roskelley was already on board. In New York, Andy Harvard, Pete Lev, and Jim States joined the group. Though the six of them were together, there was still something tentative about the expedition. Reichardt had some research to finish up at Harvard; he wasn't planning to leave for a few days. John Evans wouldn't arrive until his wife had their baby.

On the morning the plane arrived in Delhi, an article about the expedition appeared in the *Times of India,* the premier English-language daily. A picture of Devi standing next to Carter accompanied the piece. With her golden hair and full large-boned frame, Devi looked like an Indian goddess. Nothing was as memorable in the *Times* as this story of Nanda Devi returning to India to climb her mountain. "I cannot describe it but there is something within me about this mountain ever since I was born," Devi said. The chief customs inspector at the airport was so impressed by the article that he let Willi and the others move speedily through customs.

Willi looked out on the hordes in the airport and saw Devi. They hugged and began talking as if they hadn't seen each other for months. Willi was exhausted. He hadn't been able to sleep much on the plane. Beyond that he had whole layers of fatigue, the usual end-of-the-year rush at Evergreen, the packing for the trip, the turmoil over Krag's accident, the partying and good-byes.

Roskelley looked as if he could at that moment have headed up to the summit of Nanda Devi. He didn't like what he heard when he got near Devi. She had a cough as did Elliott Fisher. The two of them had gone off to Katmandu for a week. This had been the result. Roskelley believed that in the close quarters of the tents the whole party might come down with colds.

"Elliott, you and Devi better get rid of those colds before you reach the mountain," Roskelley said, as if the coughs were debts that could easily be paid off. " 'Cause once we get up there you'll never get rid of 'em."

At the YMCA where the expedition was staying, Willi went immediately to sleep. The next day Willi was still tired. The deadly dry heat of the pre-monsoon wore him out. He and the others had much work to do. The fixed rope was the big problem. Willi had fought his battle over that one in Seattle and lost. Over ten thousand feet of nine-millimeter rope had been shipped over on six-hundred-foot spools. The plastic ends of many of the spools had broken, spilling the rope out into twisted piles that looked like enormous plates of spaghetti.

Untangling the rope in the heat was a miserable job. It took forever to sort out even seven thousand feet of the rope and wind it onto three hundred-foot spools that a porter could carry. By that time even Roskelley had had it. The rest was stored away. Willi felt a certain satisfaction that he had been proven right about not bringing so much rope. Still, it appalled him seeing the enormous excesses that had been shipped over, not only rope but food, equipment, everything.

Whatever potential divisions lay within the group, they were not obvious in Delhi. Neither Roskelley nor Hoey was interested in sampling much local cuisine or throwing themselves into India like the two Unsoelds, but that caused no problem. Both Willi and Devi enjoyed meeting new people. They got acquainted with Andrew Harvard, a twenty-six-year-old Dartmouth graduate. Harvard had recently broken up with a woman with whom he had been involved for several years. He was quiet, at times withdrawn, with an almost painful sensitivity to the world around him. Dr. Jim States was the other member the Unsoelds were getting to know. Unlike Harvard the expedition doctor was outgoing, full of fun.

Although Devi had almost lost her voice, Willi wasn't worried. To him she still glowed with life. Having a few extra days, she and Fisher had gone off to Katmandu. It had been as if she had never left. After two years, the rickshaw drivers and sweets vendors greeted her in the streets as if she had returned from a modest trek. As much as Devi enjoyed being back in Nepal, she had been faced with yet another responsibility. Fisher had told Devi that he felt ambivalent about the climb and was about ready to turn back. He was very much in love with a woman back home and was preparing to take exams for medical school. Fisher was the one climber Devi's age. She cared greatly for him. Devi talked Elliott out of giving up, but he was still undecided. In Delhi Devi cried when she read a long letter from Krag that in part told her to watch out for her father, to make sure that he didn't push himself too hard.

In the evening Willi was glad that they were finally leaving the furnace heat of Delhi. Captain Kirin Kumar, one of the two Indian climbers, arrived at the brightly colored rented truck with his wife and family. To Willi one of the real pluses of the climb was that this was an *Indo*-American expedition. He delighted in Kumar and his ways. With his army-style mustache, the bristles growing out like small flat brushes from the side of his face, and his typical army-style manner, barking out orders in a shrill voice, Kumar was a marvelous counterpoint to the American climbers. Kumar's wife, a shy wisp of a woman, applied colored *tikas* on everyone's forehead, and passed out sweets, the traditional Indian farewell.

It was after ten o'clock on the evening of July 9 when the truck finally pulled out. The vehicle lumbered northward through the warm night. The Garhwal district lies about two hundred miles northeast of Delhi in almost the exact center of the Himalayan chain. The Garhwal is filled with sacred shrines and holy places. To the Hindus Nanda Devi and the area around the great mountain is the abode of the gods. It was here that the *rishis*, the seven wise men of Hindu mythology, found their final sanctuary where no mortal would ever disturb them.

For Willi, Devi, Fisher, and some of the others this was a magical journey through the Indian night, talking, laughing, telling stories. Willi was full of tales. When it got very late everyone tried to make a bed for himself. Devi, States, Fisher, and Hoey crawled up on top of the load and strapped themselves in with manila cord. Carter, Lev, and Willi lay further back, jammed in together. Willi propped himself in a hole. He couldn't possibly doze off. Ad was a man of genuine solicitousness; at one of the stops he switched with Willi.

As the truck drew closer to the mountains, Willi drew closer to the source of his own spiritual reservoir. Shortly after dawn the climbers rode through Hardwar perched high on their throne of rope, gear, and boxed foods. In ancient times Hardwar was called

Gangadwara, Gate of the Ganges. The city lies on the banks of the Ganges, the holiest of rivers. The pilgrims were already down at the *ghats,* bathing in the water, doing their *pujas* near stones that were said to be the footsteps of Vishnu. The truck eased its way past *sadhus,* holy men, on their way to and from the holy city of Badrinath, unmindful of cars and buses, the mundane comings and goings of mortals.

It was still early morning when the truck wheezed into Rishikesh. Willi's bus had passed through here twenty-seven years before on its way up the Alaknanda Ganga toward Badrinath. Rishikesh had been visited by the Beatles and many other Western seekers. Rishikesh was much the same as when Willi had been here, the long, arching roofs on the houses, the cows strolling the narrow streets, the shrines lying along the Ganges.

In Rishikesh, the expedition had to wait hours to get a new truck and driver. Such delays were typical of India, but everyone was tired when well into the afternoon they headed off again.

Behind the town rose the first high ridges of the Himalayan foothills. The truck groaned slowly upward, moving back and forth across the switchbacks. The river barely contained the torrents of white water that roared down from the mountains above. If it had been hard sleeping the first night, that was mere training for this night's journey. By one in the morning there wasn't a person on the truck who didn't feel miserable.

Up front Kumar and Carter had the best seats. For them sleep was out of the question. They were making sure that the driver stayed awake; on a road like this one a moment's forgetfulness and they would all be swept to their deaths.

Kumar found good in nearly every situation. He wasn't bemoaning the long ride. He had recently read a book about the Second World War. He was having a fine time talking to Ad about the American climber's wartime experiences. Kumar's high-pitched, excited voice, as good as having an alarm clock ringing in his ear, kept the driver awake.

Suddenly Roskelley got up and began pounding on the back of the cabin. "I can't sleep," he shouted. "This is ruining my conditioning! We've got to stop!"

Willi thought Roskelley had freaked out. Willi jumped up, bolted over the tailgate, and ran alongside the slow-moving vehicle up to the passenger window. "We've got to stop a minute, Kirin!" Willi yelled.

"What's wrong?"

"John's upset. Can't sleep."

Kumar was relieved. He had thought someone must have fallen out of the truck. "We're trying to find a safe stopping spot, Willi."

Traveling all night two nights in a row was a dubious regimen for climbers about to attempt a new route on Nanda Devi. A few kilometers up the road the driver pulled over. The climbers finally fell asleep. Soon after dawn they were off again. The monsoon rains began to lash the truck. Up ahead landslides had covered the road.

By 9:00 A.M. on Sunday morning they arrived at Joshimath, the last main town before the high Himalayas. At 6,150-feet elevation Joshimath was surrounded by mountains. The gods that were worshiped here lay up above in the sanctuary of the Garhwal. *Bhotias* roamed the streets smelling of yak butter and smoke, back from journeys up toward Tibet. High above to the east, shrouded in mists, stood Nanda Devi. They could not see it yet, but it was there, a presence, mountain and god, an immense peak sovereign over earth and sky.

By the time the truck pulled into Joshimath, Nirmal Singh, the other Indian climber, had already arrived. An instructor at a mountaineering institute, Nirmal was a far more subdued man than Kirin. He was doubly introverted because he spoke little English. Willi and some of the others talked to Singh, but it was hard carrying on a conversation. Other than getting to know Singh and deciding on porters, there was not much to do on a Sunday afternoon but eat and rest.

Heading out of town by truck that afternoon for the final short haul, they found the road barely passable. As the truck bounced and jostled along the climbers sang songs, their voices sounding through the hills. The truck couldn't make it up out of one stream. Pushing did no good. The truck had to be largely unloaded, the wheels blocked with rocks, before the vehicle moved up the far bank. Then they moved on again, Willi, Devi, everyone singing.

A few hundred yards outside Lata, the last village on the road, they stopped for the night.

"Bhalu Sahib!" an old man shouted at Carter later.

It had been forty years since anyone had called him "Master Bear." "Sher Singh," Carter replied, remembering Tiger Lion, a porter on the 1936 expedition.

Willi, Hoey, and Lev slept in the back of the truck, the others at the nearby schoolhouse. As tired as everyone was, with the heat and flies it was hard getting to sleep. At 6:00 A.M. Carter woke everyone up, announcing that the truck had to be unloaded before the rain started.

No one jumped up with enthusiasm or energy. Even by the time the last straggler had arrived at the truck the driver hadn't shown up. Until he moved the vehicle further into Lata, they couldn't do anything.

Roskelley would have no more of what he considered ineptitude. Too much was at stake. Roskelley called a meeting. He read out a litany of error and negligence. He criticized everything from the ridiculous hour Carter had awakened everyone, the sloppiness of hygiene and health, to the lack of planning. He was furious that there wasn't even a list of what went into the boxes.

"Co-leadership doesn't work! One of you ought to start making the decisions!" Roskelley asserted. "Somebody has got to start making decisions around here! You're not doing any of that!"

"Now wait a minute!" Willi said angrily, thinking that John's performance was another example of his rigid way of operating. He looked directly at Roskelley with a look that John took as nothing short of vicious. "It wasn't Ad's fault the stuff wasn't packed with a list in Delhi."

Willi liked nothing better than to hone his rhetorical skills on a good argument, but this went beyond that. Roskelley rankled Willi. He let him have it full bore. "We just don't have the information to do things the way you want them, John!"

"But Dad," Devi interjected, "John is just trying to bring up some points." As Devi went on, Roskelley was amazed that she wasn't siding with Willi but was trying to be fair.

Devi helped to lance the boils of contention. This morning something had been lost. Carter was not used to being criticized in bitter words stripped of civility. Carter was co-leader but he would not be able to carry his full load high on the mountain. At sixty-one he was too old. What he had was authority and experience.

On another occasion Willi might have used his skills as a group leader to help the members work this out, to struggle through their differences. He was not used to dealing with a man like Roskelley who was just as tenacious in debate as Willi. John was a truthmonger unconcerned with how his words might affect people.

When the driver finally arrived it was decided that they would unload the truck right where it stood. Carter and Willi had arranged to hire eighty porters arriving early the next morning. The custom was to pay the porters 15 rupees (about two dollars) for each normal day's journey, as well as to provide food. To carry the porters' food, the expedition used 120 goats managed by herders known as *bakri wallahs*. While Willi and the others worked unloading the truck, the *bakri wallahs* poured about five pounds of flour, sugar, and other food into small woven bags to be placed two apiece on the goats like saddlebags.

In the afternoon when the work was done, Willi took a bath in the Dhauliganga River and relaxed. Willi was drawn to the children of the village and the children were drawn to him. They told Willi their names, and Willi told them his. They were poor, half-naked, running barefoot down the streets of Lata. To Willi energy was life; the more energy, the more life. When these children were well they were founts of energy: alert, engaging, eyes sparkling. When they were sick the energy drained out of them and the flies settled on their listless bodies like maggots. But as Willi saw it there was more life than death here, more health than sickness, and more happiness than back home.

The children led Willi and the others to the decrepit old temple of Nanda Devi. They scurried around the courtyard banging on the sacred drums, brandishing the sacrificial sword as if acting out a war story from Hindu mythology. Willi wondered if this religion had become so debased that only children performed the ceremonies. When he had about given up expecting anyone else, the head-

man of the village appeared with other adults. The children disappeared as fast as they had appeared.

To bring the expedition good luck the village men sacrificed a
goat. Willi ate a few pieces of the meat and left the temple knowing
that the journey tomorrow to the sacred mountain had been properly
blessed. Back at the schoolhouse Willi rolled out two foam pads on
the ground and lay down. He felt slightly chilled. When he fell
asleep, he had a strange dream. He was supposed to be giving a
lecture at Evergreen, on a subject about which he knew nothing at
all. Even after the lecture was to have begun, he was still rummag-
ing through his office trying to find some notes from which he
could speak.

In the morning the expedition moved out through a light drizzle,
a serpentine procession stretching along the verdant hills. Roskelley
and States marched at its head, unwilling to walk at the porters'
slow pace. Hoey pushed herself to keep up with them. The path
climbed steadily upward 5,000 feet, through forests of pine, rho-
dodendron, and birch trees.

To the porters these expedition treks were social gatherings. They
were a chance to trade gossip, to earn some cash, to get away from
the drudgery of farming their tiny hillside plots. Roskelley and
States had padlocked their personal belongings; they had little to
do with these hill tribesmen.

As the porters padded along Devi laughed and talked with them.
Didi, older sister, they called her though some were twice her age.
As they took pleasure in the warm sun, a plate of rice and *dal,* so
they seemed to take pleasure in *Didi,* pleasure listening to her
broken Hindi. She was Nanda Devi after all. And in India where
gods and goddesses are almost human in their glories and frailties,
that was no small thing. "Many may have suspected she was the
Goddess Nanda returning to visit her mountain," Reichardt wrote.
"The rest were captivated by her inexhaustible supply of good
humor."

The climbers had only started moving up through forests above
Lata when the monsoon rains began again. Three hours into the
journey the *bakri wallahs* unloaded their goats and sat down, say-

ing that they could not go on in the rain. Kumar burned their ears with a string of Hindu epithets, including the threat that if they did not move on they would pass through the anus of the gods. The *bakri wallahs* had suffered enough from Kumar's tongue for one day and moved on.

The rain stopped. It did not begin again until the expedition reached their first camp, at Lata Kharak, a high 12,000-foot meadow above the tree line. Next morning the rain was still coming down. The *bakri wallahs* refused to budge. The group spent a second night at Lata Kharak.

Whether it was meat from the goat that the porters had slaughtered or some other cause, in the night many of the sahibs became sick. Fisher had terrible cramps; he came dashing out of the tent at 4:00 A.M. States and Hoey had fevers, chills, and diarrhea. So did Harvard. Lev wasn't feeling well either. The climbers would better have spent the day in camp, but they had already lost one day. No one was in clear charge. States, the expedition doctor, hurried up the sleek, muddy slope to be with his buddy, Roskelley.

Even Willi had diarrhea now. Nonetheless, he and Devi stayed back to try to help the others. Except for Harvard and Hoey everyone appeared capable of walking without too much trouble. Harvard was suffering but moving stoically ahead.

By the time Hoey reached the over 14,000-foot pass, she was very sick. To relieve herself she squatted by the trail. She stumbled ahead on the wet, narrow trail partially delirious. When Hoey reached camp at 14,000-foot Dharansi, she was desperately ill. Lev was getting sicker too. So was Willi. There are few diseases as emotionally debilitating as the stomach illnesses westerners pick up in India; looking at Marty the others could imagine themselves soon lying beside her.

Hoey was semicomatose. That night Fisher, who hoped to become a doctor, and Devi, with her gift for caring, stayed with the sick. Whenever Hoey got up to relieve herself, Devi held her, steadied her, hoping that she could hold herself until they got off somewhere. Sometimes Hoey could not wait that long. Elliott helped Lev when he went outside. When States poked his head into the tent, Pete thought that the doctor finally realized the seriousness of the situation.

By morning Hoey was throwing up. She was dangerously dehydrated. Although Lev and Willi were feeling better, it was clear that Hoey would have to be moved immediately on down to the 11,000-foot camp at Dibrugheta where the altitude wouldn't be such a problem. Everyone worked as a team. Willi cut and tied a rope carry. Fisher hurried off down the grass slopes carrying a sixty- to seventy-pound pack to set up a tent for Hoey at Dibrugheta.

The rope carry worked fine until the route began a sharp 3,000-foot descent. The climbers took Hoey off the porter's back. With porters and sahibs surrounding her, propping her up, they moved gingerly down the tortuous path. Hoey was only half coherent, but she moved forward with the same kind of basic survival instinct that Willi had seen often in the mountains.

Dibrugheta was a beautiful campsite set among pines next to a clear stream, the earth graced with white anemones and red potentillas. Hour after hour Hoey lay unconscious in the tent. States had a grave medical crisis on his hands. He was not a seasoned practicing physician. He was a thirty-year-old medical school graduate who counseled juvenile delinquents and others in Spokane. He was literally days from a hospital or another doctor, days from sophisticated diagnostic techniques, without even the capacity to give Marty liquids intravenously.

States gave Hoey various medicines, working with Willi and Pete to get her to take liquids. Fisher wrote in his diary that States talked not "when" Marty survives but "if." Lev felt that the doctor believed his patient would die. It was decided that in the morning if Marty didn't improve, Dharam Singh, the head porter, would go back to request an Air Force helicopter to evacuate her. The climbers were all emotionally and physically exhausted. They hardly noticed that in the afternoon Lou Reichardt had trekked into camp.

Through the dark hours the doctor, Willi, Lev, and later Roskelley and Devi, stayed with Hoey, nursing her. Because of the possibility of cerebral edema, she was given oxygen. Marty did not stir.

Anyone who entered the tent smelled death in the air. Climbers knew death usually by fall or avalanche, not like this, a crumpled, stinking stick figure of a human form lying in a sleeping bag. The horror and dread was the everyday stuff of hospitals and old-age homes.

All night long they worked, but it was no good. Then at dawn, as the head porter prepared to set out to make the long journey back to Lata, Hoey opened her eyes and asked for water. It was as if Marty had come back from a distant journey. The climbers cried with relief.

Before setting out, Dharam Singh waited to see how well Hoey's recovery would go. The other climbers got some rest themselves. In the afternoon the expedition got together to discuss what to do about Hoey. States had been very shaken by the illness. For him there was no alternative to flying Marty out. Although she was eating Jello and drinking tea, she was still not completely coherent. The doctor didn't need to have a medical textbook before him to know that Hoey needed a series of tests for brain damage.

Willi wasn't about to let States puff himself up with medical authority, deciding for Hoey what she should do. He wanted to wait and then let Marty make up her own mind. When the doctor heard this he felt that Willi was playing with human life.

Everyone was tired. When Willi was tired he talked and talked. The argument went on for hours, Willi in one corner, States and Roskelley in the other. The rest of the climbers had their own positions but for the most part they were spectators. As Pete listened he thought that Willi was doing what he always did: using the situation for a philosophical and moral debate.

Neither man could best Willi in an argument. When Willi got tired battering at the two climbers, trying to get them to understand his position, he started tying their arguments up in knots. As Fisher watched the spectacle, he thought that Willi was being cruel, toying with States, who barely understood what was being done to him.

"I think the patient should have *some* say about her treatment," Willi said.

"She's got to take tests for brain damage," Jim asserted.

"It's the doctor's decision," Roskelley said. To him it was as simple as that. As far as he was concerned, Willi was inferring that Jim was incompetent.

"Well, I'm willing to take that medical advice and crank it into the general scheme of things," Willi said.

"Willi, you don't seem to understand," Roskelley countered, shaking his head. "That's a medical judgment."

As they spoke Marty trudged past, carrying a towel on her way to bathe in the stream.

"I recognize it as such," Willi said. "But Jim has very little data to judge from. It's him deciding for her when she's capable of deciding for herself. She's perfectly conscious."

"I'm sick of all these word games," Roskelley shouted and stomped out of the tent.

"I'm just saying perhaps we're being hasty," Willi said in conciliation. "If we send for the helicopter now it might be that she'll recover so that she can go on to Base Camp."

On and on the argument raged. "Anyway, Willi, you've got to admit that she made a simply miraculous recovery," States said, taking the debate into new territory. "And on those grounds alone she should be evacuated at once."

"Nah, Jim, I wouldn't call it a 'miraculous recovery,' " Willi answered, making yet another debater's point. "You know she just recovered. It wasn't miraculous. It's just one of those things that happen, ordinary run of the mill."

"If you want to kill her!" States shouted and ran out crying. As he burst out of the tent Marty passed by fresh from her sponge bath. She was still not normal. Her speech was somewhat disoriented. She had wanted to stay, or least wait to decide, but she saw what contention her presence was causing. She decided that she would have to go. She would not allow the expedition to split over her but would wait at Dibrugheta for a helicopter.

Outside the tent afterwards the bitter mood of the discussion hung over the camp. Suddenly Willi charged Harvard. The two men struggled in the grass, the forty-nine-year-old and the twenty-six-year-old. Harvard was amazed at the power of Willi's body, the two of them grappling on the stubbled turf. The porters formed a circle around the two sahibs, stunned at this fierce fight, the grunts punctuating the air. When the two men finally got up, their faces streaked with dirt and sweat, the foul mood seemed to have blown away.

Devi still saw a fine, organic group developing. "In the ten days we have been together we have become a group so that the absence of one member leaves a hole that is quite large," Devi wrote home. "We have not strayed into cliques and there is only one focus."

"The whole group is polarized," Roskelley told Lev. Roskelley was so irritated at Willi and some of the others that early the next morning he set off alone up through the pine forests "letting the rain wash the bitter taste of dissension from my thoughts." From then on when John thought of the "team" he put mental quotation marks around the word.

States had borne the brunt of Willi's attack and he was still upset. As for Willi he realized that he had not acted well in the tent. ". . . I performed poorly during the Marty discussions," he wrote home. "Lunged cuttingly at Jim States' naivete and sliced so shrewdly with words that Roskelley had to leap up and leave the tent and Elliott just looked up at me with the kind of horror Regon sometimes shows when most disappointed in me."

What Willi didn't mention in his letter was that at Dibrugheta States had examined Devi and told her she had a hernia. That was a worrisome diagnosis to someone planning to climb one of the world's great mountains. But Devi was a stoic, and Willi didn't think the doctor sounded very worried. Neither he nor Devi even mentioned the problem in their letters home.

Even before reaching the base of the mountain some members were thinking of turning back. Carter was staying with Hoey until the helicopter arrived. Though he was coming ahead later, the expedition was not turning out an idyllic return to his past conquests. Lev did not like the way the climb was developing. He had almost decided to go back in the helicopter. So had Fisher.

Fisher kept wondering why he had come to Nanda Devi. As he trudged along the slippery ridge above the raging Rishi River he

had hours to reflect. Fisher walked gingerly across a narrow, swaying bridge above the Rishi. At the lovely campsite by the river he
sat down next to Willi and began to unload his problems.

"You know, Elliott, when I was here in 1949 I had this feeling
of oneness with God," Willi said as if he hadn't heard Fisher.
"That's what brings me back to the mountains again and again."

Fisher told Willi about his love for a woman in America.

"Back when I was going to marry Jolene, I gave up climbing,"
Willi reflected.

That was not at all what Fisher wanted to hear. Willi usually
listened to another person's problems with absolute attention. He
was often almost psychic in his understanding. But Willi was off
in his own world. Fisher decided that if he made up his mind to
leave, Willi would not back him up.

Willi was returning to what he considered the source of his
being. He was casting off thoughts of dying up there. He was
girding himself to climb to the heights. He was young again.

On a long trek the days are much the same: up in the morning,
off and up the trail; up in the morning, off and up the trail; up in
the morning, off and up the trail. After a while the rhythm of the
trek becomes the rhythm of life, and a person settles down into the
routine. During the two days since leaving Dibrugheta the expedition moved on comfortably and well through spectacular scenery.
Walking along the south side of the Rishi gorge on a narrow trail
was dangerous. But it was beautiful. In most of the worst places an
earlier Japanese expedition had placed fixed ropes; where they
hadn't the American climbers did so.

On Thursday the twenty-first of July, yet another magnificent
day, the climbers slogged up a slope to a high ridge. There before
them, awesome in its magnificence, stood Nanda Devi. The summit was not a spire but an immense wedge. Below and to the
forefront lay the great buttress, a labyrinth of ravines and ridges.

John didn't waste any time rhapsodizing. He didn't enjoy mountains the way Willi did; he enjoyed getting up them and getting out.
What Roskelley saw was not only a formidable mountain but vin-
dication. If the trek had lulled some of the climbers into an almost

dreamlike state, what they saw in front of them shook them awake. Lev silently traced the planned ascent of the northwest face, up that sheer wall; he knew that they were in for the climb of their lives. Willi, still far below, had talked endlessly of Nanda Devi's beauty. Lev didn't see beauty. He was not a superstitious man; but even from here he thought that Nanda Devi was giving off "bad vibes."

"I don't like the looks of it," Lev said out loud.

Devi had been strangely quiet during much of the trek. Now she was simply joyous. This was her mountain. She looked at it as if it were a beckoning friend.

What was clear to everyone was that to climb *that* mountain by *that* route would take thousands of feet of fixed rope. They would have to send back a message asking John Evans to bring in the rest of the spools.

Devi was the only one Willi would listen to and believe. "Dad, Dad," Devi yelled as she ran back to where Willi and Kumar were paying off the *bakri wallahs,* "the group's decided that we need more fixed rope." To Willi the word group was sacrosanct. He reluctantly wrote out a note asking John Evans to bring in the fixed rope still in Delhi. Then he gave the note to the *bakri wallahs.*

Later Willi and Kumar pushed on. Willi wasn't feeling well. He had gas pains and mucous in his stools. Even when he was bloated with pain, he looked out on Nanda Devi, feeling the beauty and the mystery, and forgot the discomfort.

The next day's trek led into the Sanctuary, a benign, blessed area leading to the base of the mountain. Great flowered meadows and jagged granite spires bordered a path that was as gently soothing as the scenery itself. Paralleling the path, a couple of miles distant, stood the north ridge of Nanda Devi protected by a line of 4,000-foot cliffs.

While the others trekked on to Base Camp, Pete climbed to almost 16,000 feet to get a better look at Nanda Devi, its northern face completely protected by cliffs. Pete had an outstanding reputation as a climber. By rights he should have been more committed. But he had wanted a less ambitious climb, and he was afraid that this whole thing was getting out of hand.

In the afternoon when Lev reached Base Camp at Sarson Patal, he got into his sleeping bag next to Fisher. From the dour look on his face, Fisher knew that Lev hadn't brought good news. "It's just too dangerous," Lev said grimly.

That evening members of the group got together in a Bauer four-person tent to discuss the climb. "There is no way up the cliffs," Pete said. "Even if we could get up, we can't traverse above them to reach our route. The canyons cutting through the cliffs are impassable. The wall is really steep."

"We can always haul," Willi said, suggesting that they might try another route.

"We didn't advertise that we would climb this route," another climber chimed in. "We can be flexible."

Reichardt hadn't said much. He rarely did. But he thought to himself, "Not the regular route again."

In the morning Roskelley and Reichardt headed out through the dawn fog to try to find a way through the cliffs. A little later Andy, Elliott, and Devi hiked up onto the moraine, the glacial boulders, carrying a radio so that they could communicate with the other team. Willi joined them. Sitting there, Willi sketched out a route up the face. Fisher thought that it was positively suicidal.

At 8:00 A.M. the radio crackled alive. Roskelley and Reichardt had already discovered a way across the Rishi Gorge. It was an ice bridge, as neat a pathway as could be imagined. A couple of hours later they radioed down again. In thick fog the two men had moved up a gully. The gully ran straight into a vertical cliff, a dead end. To one side stood a half-mile-long catwalk leading behind the gully to a perfect spot for the next camp.

"We not only have a route; we have one for porters!"

Hearing that didn't make Fisher any happier. He felt out of control, like a child on a wagon rolling downhill toward a big road.

For Devi the climb meant people. She had felt the loss of Marty Hoey terribly, as if something precious and irreplaceable had been ripped away. She worried about Fisher. He was someone important to Devi, a friend, a traveling companion, the other youngest member of the expedition. When Elliott came into the tent to talk of his fears and started to cry, both Devi and Willi comforted him. Crying didn't seem to make Elliott feel much better. While Elliott's tears were still flowing, Willi poked his head out of the tent. He could hardly believe it. There stood Jaggat Singh, the *sirdar* of the porters, crying his eyes out too. The porters were scared. They didn't want to carry loads up any higher. The head man from Lata felt insulted.

For Devi and her dad it was human to care and to feel, so it was human to cry. When Fisher and Harvard were left in the tent, Devi turned to Andy. "Why are you so distant and detached?" she asked. "Don't you know how that makes me feel?" For Devi detachment was betrayal. To her it was terrible to see how far away Andy stood emotionally. Andy tried but he was not one to open himself up at will. Soon Devi was in tears.

"I want to climb Nanda Devi," she wept. "I want this expedition to be a good one. Why isn't it?"

After Harvard left to carry a load up above, Devi and Fisher worked together packing some more loads. "You people . . .", Fisher said, slipping into the second person when he discussed the climb. The others were depending on him. But he didn't want to die. It wasn't a shiny summit that stood above him any longer but a dark absurdity. He saw his future opening up for him at home, bright, rich, meaningful. He didn't want to die. He was scared, terribly scared.

That afternoon Carter arrived in Base Camp. He had walked a normal four-day trek in two days. He told the other climbers that by the time the helicopter arrived Marty had improved only marginally.

"I'm thinking of leaving, Ad," Fisher said, seeking some thoughtful counseling that he didn't believe Willi had provided him.

"You can walk out with me," Carter said. On his journey up the Rishi Gorge and through the Sanctuary, Carter had about decided after a few days photographing to head out. That wasn't at all what Fisher wanted to hear from Carter. Ad doesn't care about me, Elliott thought.

In reflecting back on the expedition, Lev said later that "what was most striking was that everyone acted out of character." As editor of the *American Alpine Journal,* Carter was one of the senior statesmen of American climbing, an ethical leader. Although Carter considered himself "the least useful member of the expedition," leaving in the middle of a climb was not usually done by the co-leader of an expedition.

The hard men, Roskelley most adamantly, believed that Carter and Fisher had no right to leave; they had no right to be here in the first place if they were so ambivalent about the climb. "I felt they were copping out," Roskelley said. "You don't go quit in the Himalayas. There are thousands of good climbers in the United States who want to go to the Himalayas who don't ever get a chance. If that's all he's going to organize, Ad should have stayed in the States and organized. If Elliott wasn't dead sure he was going to go in, we could have gotten some real good climber to go in."

Roskelley did not think much of Fisher as a climber. On a great mountain Roskelley considered other human beings the way he did crampons or climbing rope, as instruments to get the strongest climbers to the summit. Roskelley was not unfeeling, but he believed that they were waging war on the mountain. They had no space for slackers, for endless hand-wringing or handholding.

Willi and Devi wanted both Fisher and Carter to stay. They cared for them, not for what they could do or carry. Willi thought that Fisher would find it hard living with himself if he turned back. But Willi could not begin to understand how desperately Fisher wanted out. That night for the first time in his life Fisher took a sleeping pill.

The great Nanda Devi north glacier is an immense white body of snow and ice. It is like some ancient organism, moaning and rumbling and shifting. High on the mountain the glacier begins, a white swath clear across the face. As the glacier moves down the mountain it grows narrower until it becomes a snout pointing down into the Rishi Gorge. When the glacier shifts or the snow builds up, the avalanches pour down, enormous tides of snow and ice, moving faster and faster, an elemental force.

To climb Nanda Devi the expedition had to go clear across the avalanche basin to the new 17,800-foot Advanced Base Camp (ABC) on the other side. It was a half-mile distant, 100 feet higher, near enough but a fearsome business.

One day Roskelley stood by himself looking out across the avalanche basin. Suddenly two immense juggernauts roared down toward the basin. In power and size they were far beyond any of the avalanches the other climbers had seen. Though he often took risks most other climbers would not take, there was always cunning and calculation in the risks Roskelley chose. Roskelley was more frightened than he had ever been on a mountain.

For several days in a row Roskelley would not cross. "I've never turned around and not done something because I was scared," Roskelley said. "But the fear of the avalanches had me. I knew nothing I could do about it. I had no control."

Finally, Roskelley crossed. It was safer in the morning hours when the snow was frozen. Then Roskelley and practically everyone else made the run. The climbers tried to figure out a timetable. When they thought it was okay, they scrambled to the other side. Willi, however, walked across whenever he felt like it. If he was afraid it was a fear that he embraced.

Watching Willi walk jauntily across the avalanche basin, some of the other climbers thought that Willi was taunting fate. The hard men decided that Willi was a reckless climber. They didn't want to share a rope with him. Even Lev, who enjoyed climbing with Willi, was several times aghast at the time of day Willi was making his crossings.

Elliott Fisher was so spooked that he wouldn't cross at all. When Willi tried to shame him into going on, Fisher thought that Willi was cruel.

Devi tried a different approach. "I'm sorry, Elliott," she said, "you aren't going to be allowed to leave. The mountain is speaking to you." It was as if the rumble of the avalanches had brought a message.

"Okay, I'll go up," Fisher said later, though his fears were just as alive. To sleep he took another Dalmane. Reichardt, the climbing leader, decided that going across the avalanche basin was so dangerous that everyone would have to share the risk equally: six round trips apiece. If Fisher was staying, he couldn't postpone his first trip to ABC much longer.

Elliott spent hours looking across the avalanche basin, rejecting all counsel to risk it. The following morning dawned bright and clear. Fisher took a handful of hard candies for energy and walked down to the glacier. There had never been an avalanche in the morning. No one, not even Willi, had had any close calls. Fisher sat several hours. Finally, he moved quickly out onto the exposed glacier on steps cut into the ice. He got a third of the way. He heard a noise, a rumble. It was nothing, only a stream under the ice.

"Boom!"

"Boom!"

Looking up Fisher saw blocks of ice bouncing down the glacier. He had been walking as fast as he could. Now he started running, gasping for air. He darted across the ice.

"Boom!"

"Boom!"

The roar grew, moving nearer. Fisher ran on, chest pulsing with pain. He threw himself under a boulder as the tongue of the avalanche moved fifty yards behind him, covering his tracks. Then he laughed and peed in his pants with relief.

Advanced Base Camp lay on a sloping ledge at 17,800 feet, under the shadows of the northwest face on the edge of the great avalanche basin. It was the worst monsoon season in many years. The snow poured down on the mountain day after day pinning the climbers in camp. In their tents, the climbers heard the avalanches roaring down the mountain.

Willi had waited out the weather on Makalu, Masherbrum, and Everest. He would do it again. For Devi these days of bad weather were special times. She and her dad led the singing and talking. Willi played harmonica. He read *Dr. Dogbody's Leg* out loud; this was Ad's favorite book on expeditions, an endless compendium of stories in which Dr. Dogbody loses his leg in different ways. Out of his own rucksack of memories Willi had endless stories of his own. The climbers also had the long, emotional discussions that always took place when any Unsoelds were present.

The mountain was working its magic on Willi. He was feeling fantastic. "All I need is an annual expedition to keep completely in shape," he wrote the family. He loved being with Devi. "Find Devi's sunny certitude and simple joy in the terrain, the porters and the act of climbing itself a great comfort . . . just a joy to have around." He was "fascinated by the number of self-doubts among the members."

It was not "self-doubt" but doubt about the climb itself that affected the climbers. There was a dread so deep about what they faced on Nanda Devi that words like "fear" and "self-doubt" did not carry their meanings. Lev was all for trying another way or another mountain. Fisher was almost paralyzed.

States, who according to Fisher had thought of leaving, cursed the avalanches, swearing he would not wait much longer; it was as if by moving up the mountain he was fleeing himself. Roskelley, for his part, acted as frisky and touchy as an overbred terrier; he pushed the others to display more commitment, as if by their doing so they exorcised any doubts he had.

Willi and Devi could have sat it out indefinitely. Within the group tension was building. Though the climbers had had it with waiting, they could do little. At about 5:00 A.M. on the morning of August 1, Devi squatted outside the tent in her fishnet underwear. Suddenly, an avalanche exploded down the mountain. It was so fierce, so enormous that it moved outside the normal avalanche path, its way broken by fifty- to sixty-mile-an-hour winds. Devi clutched at a rock. She struggled to breathe in the snow-laden air. She listened to the tent ripping from its moorings, the center pole cracking in two. Then the air grew still.

Devi and Fisher ran toward the tent, crumpled on the edge of the cliff. A lumpy form moved around inside. As they approached States poked his head out of the wreckage, a pot in one hand, his beard streaked with Roman Meal oats. They laughed and laughed, but at 9:30 another immense avalanche struck, almost taking the tent away.

Early that afternoon Carter called from Ridge Camp. He had decided to go down. "Here you are abandoning the expedition that you organized," Roskelley yelled into the microphone. "How can you? You just can't do it!"

Carter thanked everyone, retreated into his armor of civility, and said good-bye. Two hours later when Carter was on his way down with two porters, another avalanche rolled down the mountain. Willi ran until he spotted three tiny specks. His exuberant yodel told the others that Carter was okay.

Two days later Fisher was carrying a load higher up the mountain when a rock ten inches in diameter sailed past him. For forty-five minutes he sat mute. Then he headed back to Advanced Base Camp to say that he was leaving. No one chided him any longer. As he left for good Devi played "So Long It's Been Good to Know You" on the harmonica.

"I'm not going to say good-bye," she said sweetly, hugging Fisher, "because I'll see you again."

Trudging down the mountain, Fisher came upon Roskelley returning from a trip to Base Camp. Roskelley was disappointed that the porters hadn't brought in any mail for him. Fisher said that he was leaving. Then, as Fisher wrote in his diary, Roskelley began to cry.

"Don't you understand," he sobbed beseechingly. "All of us want to go home. Why are you copping out?"

"I'm sor—" Fisher began.

"Don't say it. It won't make any difference. Don't you understand how I hate to go under that glacier too? I'm no different."

Roskelley headed up the mountain. When he was just a blue-and-red spot on the ridge above, Fisher heard an anguished cry echoing down the mountain. *"Tell my wife I love her!"*

Shaken, Fisher hurried away from Nanda Devi.

The real climbing was beginning. With Carter gone, Willi was supposed to be the leader of the expedition. In more normal circumstances he would have worked to create a consensus. It was too late for that now. Three of the climbers whose ideas about the expedition Willi shared were gone. One strong climber, John Evans, hadn't even arrived.

From the perspective of the "Dhaulagiri boys," as Willi sometimes called Roskelley and Reichardt, Willi's ideas could be partially blamed for the shortage of able climbers. Looking at the climbers who were left Willi could have suggested taking the old route up the mountain. The hard men, however, would have fought that suggestion. Equally, Willi wanted the new route for himself and for Devi. "I wasn't going to back off because we'd put in so much effort just getting here," Willi said.

Directly above ABC, Roskelley, States, and Reichardt moved upward along the edge of the glacier. Most of the time they were on cliffs sloping at a 40–45-degree angle. The snow was the consistency of sugar over sheer ice, ever ready to slide off. The rock itself was cruddy, forever breaking off. Along this route the three men strung a thousand feet of fixed rope. The rock was so bad in places that pitons were no better than nails pounded into rotten leather. The mountaineers ended up improvising, driving three-foot-long ice pickets into the rock. It was a dicey, frustrating business. "A continual 'hiss' to our right revealed these rocks were our only protection from continual avalanches down the face," Reichardt wrote later.

When they were finished the three climbers established Camp I on a narrow ledge at 19,990 feet. Up here on August 7, Willi, Lev, and States moved their belongings. The next morning they set out to forge a route up to a new high camp. Willi was almost twice the age of these two men. Off and on he was having terrible stomach troubles, but he was by no means weaker than Lev and States.

For a change the weather was decent. It became so hot during the day that the climbers had to start well before dawn. On Everest the mountaineers had put in fixed rope to help the heavily laden porters through the Icefield. Willi had never been on an expedition where the climbers affixed thousands of feet of rope like a handrail leading them up to the summit. The lead climber moved up above the last fixed point carrying about 300 feet of rope at a time. The climber behind belayed him. Where the route appeared particularly difficult or presented unusual problems, the lead climber pounded either a piton, ice screw, or picket into the rock or ice. Then he tied the rope onto a metal stake and moved further up Nanda Devi. When the sun got too high the climbers, drenched in sweat, hacked out a cache, set down their loads, and slid back down the rope.

For the climbers coming behind the leader, there was more to do than simply dodge ice and rock. Moving up the fixed rope, they practiced their jumaring techniques. The jumar is one of a number of mechanical aids that have helped to change the nature of climbing. It is a simple spring device that slides up a rope but not down it. The climber stands in a sling or harness. Whenever he wants to move up the rope he merely reaches up and pulls himself up the rope, then sits back down finding himself a good many inches up the rope. It is a boring, tedious, uncreative process, but with a good strong pair of arms and good technique the climber makes steady progress.

Unfortunately when the rope is wet or icy as so often happens in the Himalayas, when the jumar is acting cantankerous as is its wont, or when there's not enough pressure on the rope from below, the climber has to yank the jumar loose or pull the rope taut beneath him. To do this requires agility and athleticism, knees or chins or even sometimes a good pair of teeth.

One day high up the mountain while States was working above, some debris fell, knocking Willi unconscious. "I just suddenly came to and I was in self-arrest position buried in the snow and my head was ringing—more than usual—and I had just been glanced off by a piece of ice," Willi said. "You could tell the ice because it made a different noise from the rock."

One early morning moving up the ropes with States and Lev, Willi saw a moonbow, a night "rainbow" shining down on the valley clouds, the peaks attired in a misty gown. For Pete these were the first days of the climb that were memorably fine and good. It was a chance to climb with Willi, a chance to be away from the endless squabbles below.

Camp II ended up on a ledge only 900 feet above Camp I. After a day's rest Willi and Lev moved up to a high cache well above the new camp. Here on a narrow platform scooped out of snow and ice, they spent the night. In the morning they hoped to make the ridge above, to have that as their triumph. Below them Roskelley and States had been ferrying loads up to Camp II. They were waiting to show what *they* could do next.

Willi led slowly up Nanda Devi, fixing the nine-millimeter rope. Willi and Lev wanted to reach the ridge, to have that as *their* triumph. Willi was in the middle of a pitch when Roskelley arrived having come up that morning all the way from Camp I. Willi knew a fine climber when he saw one; it was simply incredible how Roskelley could move up a mountain.

Willi and Lev exchanged leads while Roskelley and later States waited impatiently below like sports car drivers caught behind a sluggish moving van. Before long Roskelley and States headed down to Camp II to wait their turn.

Willi thought that they would reach the ridge but they had to turn back. Willi was hurting. When he was young he was as strong and fast a climber as there was. He was suffering now, though he was not about to make excuses.

"It just keeps receding," Willi said when he got back down to Camp II.

"Our turn!" Roskelley replied.

The next day Roskelley and States took the lead. Before they could reach the ridge crest a blizzard fell upon the mountain. For six days the snows fell and the avalanches roared down Nanda Devi. At Camp I the snow that fell from the sky was mixed with snow blown over from the avalanche path. One day eight feet fell on the camp.

For Willi this was once again a chance to talk. The snow piled up around the tents. The wind whipped at the center pole. Willi discussed child raising with Harvard, mulled over Outward Bound with the newly arrived John Evans, chewed over situation ethics. He noted the conversations in his diary the way a first-time tourist to Europe writes down the names of museums and attractions.

Willi was proud that Devi was one of the team, as strong, as committed as anyone. If not for the blizzard Devi had been scheduled to go with Reichardt to fix ropes up to the ridge crest. When Willi had questioned Devi, since she had no experience fixing ropes, she had become a little miffed. But that was just Devi. Though still suffering from diarrhea, she was ferrying loads up the mountain as heavy and as often as anyone. There was just no stopping her.

Willi wasn't quite so sure about was what was happening between Devi and Andy Harvard. Back in Olympia he and Jolene had discussed whether Devi would find her mate among the men on the expedition. No one had seemed right for her. As it turned out, Willi considered Harvard a smart, interesting fellow, but there was something unfocused, almost cynical about him. As the expedition progressed, though, and as he watched Devi and Andy together, he saw that this was developing into Devi's first deep relationship since Erik. Willi wanted Devi to be happy, and if this would help, he was all for it.

The other climbers knew what was going on between Devi and Andy nearly as soon as they did. When Willi told Kumar the story of how he had fallen in love with Jolene and announced their engagement on the summit of St. Helens, the Indian thought that Andy and Devi might do the same on the summit of Nanda Devi. For those climbers to whom women on a mountain were anathema, however, this love was as much a distraction as an illness. Harvard, in fact, had so far not been up to par physically; he had not done what had been expected of him.

Lev still was talking about another route up Nanda Devi, a suggestion that rankled Roskelley. Lev was spending time thinking about why the expedition was going so poorly. It wasn't only the snow, though if that kept up much longer they might not have enough food to get them high enough for a summit bid. It was something more profound.

Pete enjoyed eating *chapattis,* flatbread, with the four high-altitude porters. He asked them, "Why are things not going well?"

"They will not go well until the sahibs stop eating beef," one of the porters answered.

Lev was not a superstitious man. He knew that the Hindus considered the cow a sacred animal. The only beef the climbers were eating were strips of beef jerky. It wouldn't be much of a loss simply to give it up. If anyone on the climb would understand that, it was Devi. But when Lev told her, she laughed.

"The porters think the weather is bad because we are eating beef on the mountain," Devi radioed the climbers up at Camp I, as if she had heard a new joke.

"Ignorant porters!" Kumar sputtered. "What blasted insolence! I'm eating it and I'm the highest caste of Brahmin. In adversity, you can eat anything."

Lev, however, stopped eating beef jerky.

$$\wedge$$

On the twentieth of August the snow stopped. The final push to the summit began. A large expedition goes through metamorphosis after metamorphosis shedding porters, equipment, and climbers, turning into smaller, sleeker versions of itself. Like modern combat, getting up the mountain was a matter of logistics as much as courage. If enough loads had not been carried up, enough food, rope, and gear, then even the possibility of a summit attempt was out of the question.

On this brilliant August morning the mountaineers began moving loads up to the high camps. Climbing up toward Camp I Willi once again was feeling pure exhilaration. As she moved up behind her dad, Devi, too, was ecstatic. It was a fine day. The distant rumble of the avalanches only emphasized that. On his way down to ABC in the afternoon Willi cleaned the fixed ropes, pulling them out of the ice. The next day while Willi puttered around camp, Devi headed up with another load. She was suffering from diarrhea again. She had to stash her load part way up.

When it came to carrying loads Devi and Willi were stalwarts. No one said or thought any longer that Willi was "an old man" and Devi "just a girl." Even Roskelley was impressed with the loads Devi was carrying up Nanda Devi.

On one of those fine, clear days as they were carrying loads Willi and Devi met States hurrying down the fixed rope. They learned that Kumar was above by himself still struggling up to the ridge crest. This was the kind of thing that Willi hated about fixed ropes. They took most of the immediate danger out of climbing, but as far as Willi was concerned, they took away much of the joy too. No longer were climbers tied to one another literally and figuratively. Instead, climbers latched onto the rope and traveled up and down by themselves like lone commuters in their cars. Gone was the responsibility for one another that was one of the glories of climbing. Gone, too, was that basic rule of climbing: you never climbed alone.

Willi and Devi sat waiting for Kumar. As they began talking, snow was coming down. Finally the sun came out. It was a glorious afternoon. Willi and Devi discussed what was bad about the climb and what was good. In analyzing the expedition, they were like chemists working with elements labeled "good" and "bad" that they believed could be readily defined and separated.

"It's been a strange climb," Devi said. "I wish the group could have been together. I wanted that so much."

"I know," Willi said.

"It's just so wonderful being here on the mountain."

Willi and Devi both had their illnesses, but at a moment like this one, all that was forgotten. They were with one another, one with the mountain.

Then Devi talked of Andy. Willi knew that his daughter would seek her happiness as he had sought his: with one loving relationship. He knew how hard that had been for her. With Erik she had been hurt. She sought much more than most people. Willi liked Andy. He saw much good there. He saw how good Devi was for Andy, how she helped him to affirm life once again.

"I'm not going back to school in the fall," Devi said. "I'm going to travel with Andy, see what we have to build on, see if there is enough."

"It has potential," Willi said. "It's worth the risk."

Sitting talking with Devi was, as Willi said later, "one of the most precious memories of my life." They had not sought out this time together. It was a gift to them because they had decided to wait for Kumar. After three hours they headed up the fixed rope to find out what had happened to the Indian climber. At about 21,250 feet Willi yodeled. Kumar's tenor voice split the air. He was moving slowly down the rope. He had still not learned to jumar properly.

On August 22, Roskelley and Reichardt finally reached the ridge crest. This wide, relatively flat strip was a fine place for Camp III. To the north lay the arid brown hills of Tibet, to the south the yellow plains of India. All around them at this same height were Himalayan peaks. Below this balcony lay the face that the two climbers had ascended. Above rose the great buttress of Nanda Devi's north side, a still steeper 1,200-foot sheer face. "You can pick out a possible route, so all is not lost," Reichardt said as he looked upward, "but the whole thing is plastered with snow and ice. Frankly, it is pretty horrendous."

On August 26, Roskelley and States set out to climb the buttress. In their own way the two men were as perfectly matched a team as Willi and Tom had been on Everest. Lev sometimes referred to States as "Roskelley's belayer." He was not the climber his partner was. He accepted that. He spent his days standing below Roskelley, protecting him if he should fall. He was as comfortable belaying as Roskelley was leading.

When Roskelley looked up at the massive buttress, he saw not only ice, snow, and rock but a blank canvas that with crampons, pitons, and pickets he would cut his name across. The two climbers set out. For the first 150 feet or so the going was not bad. Above that lay ice-covered vertical rock without any cracks or handholds. As Roskelley worked his way up he had to clean off the snow and ice and hammer in more support. Though States was belaying his partner, in case of a fall, the sharp protruding rocks were stone knives that might sever the rope.

Finally, Roskelley hung beneath a small, overhanging ledge. He had to drive some metal into the rock but could not support himself. He took his fist and jammed it into a crack. Then, his weight resting on his arm, his crampons chewing frantically at the ice, he reached back, grabbed a three-inch-wide piton called a bong, and pounded it into the rock with his hammer. Hanging there a second, he pounded another piton, and using these new steps pulled himself up on the ledge. He tied in the fixed rope, and calling it a day, rappelled back down the rope.

While States and Roskelley were on the buttress, Willi talked on the radio to Reichardt about the complaints of the group below. Lev, in particular, was livid, believing that everyone else was being used to glorify John. Lev wanted to try another route. When States and Roskelley got back from the buttress, the two groups had a second discussion on the radio.

"Some of us would like to do some of the buttress, too," Pete said when he learned of Jim's and John's progress.

"I don't want anybody else fingerpainting in my painting," Roskelley fumed and then went on to lambaste Lev for his ambivalence. "Willi, tell Pete to get off the mountain. I don't want to argue with him anymore."

The next day while the others ferried loads below, Roskelley and States moved up again to the buttress. Once again Roskelley made incredible progress, arriving finally at a snowfield of rotten rock covered by sugar snow. He nicknamed it Sugar Delight, the only irony he permitted himself.

After a day's break the two climbers headed up to finish their job. This time Reichardt went with them. It was the easiest of the three days. Finally, John pulled himself up on the ridge below the summit block of Nanda Devi. When the three men got back down to Camp III all the other climbers were there waiting for them except Willi and John Evans, who were below carrying up the last of the loads.

Whenever Willi had been on a Himalayan peak before, he had been up at the heights testing whatever lay strong and great within himself against the strength and greatness of the mountain. But it was Roskelley who was up performing what Willi considered a great feat. Willi was down below shackled with logistics, paying off the last of the high-altitude porters, deciding when he wanted the regular porters to return to Base Camp to carry the expedition out, and ferrying up loads himself.

In the spring Willi had said that it would be his "greatest challenge not to reach the summit—and to live with that fact gracefully." He had said it as if it would be *his* choice. Where once he physically transcended the ordinary limits of life, here he would transcend them spiritually.

On Everest Willi had moved up to physical, moral, and spiritual heights beyond anything he had ever known in his life. Physically, what more could a man do with a body than what Willi had done with his on the West Ridge. He had lost nine of his toes but considered that a small price. Morally, the climb had been as much a triumph, the right route done the right way by the right people. It was a beacon that shone above Willi's life as it shown above Himalayan climbing in general. Spiritually, too, he had experienced much on the summit and during the bivouac. Willi had great love for Dick, Tom and Barry. Dick and Tom lived in Seattle. He still saw them, though not as often as he liked. When Marc, Dick's sixteen-year-old son, died in a climbing accident, Willi had comforted him. Dick was a prominent sociologist at the university, Tom equally successful as a doctor. Willi wasn't as close to Tom as he had been right after the climb, but every year, no matter where they were, they always talked on the phone on May 22, the anniversary of the day they reached the summit. As for Barry he lived in Colorado. Willi still felt bad that Barry hadn't reached the summit, especially bad since the accident. Barry had been making a film when the helicopter he was in crashed, leaving him a paraplegic. Barry hadn't let that stop him though. He even went kayaking.

The memories of Everest stayed with Willi, the memories of his friends. They were like the hot coals that Kashmiri peasants carry next to their bodies in the winter cold, warming them wherever they went.

On Nanda Devi, a mountain of his spirit, he had been plagued by ugly, earthbound illnesses like hemorrhoids and diarrhea. Morally, he had set out to make this the right kind of climb, setting a new standard here as he had set one on Everest. But this was not a group climbing here. This was no moral equivalent to the expedition thirteen years before. This was a pack of isolated individualists, the very anathema of what he thought the world should come to. For the first time in his life, Willi had met a group of people he couldn't work with well or, more accurately, lead. Title or not, he was not the leader of this expedition. It was being led by pride, machismo, guts, and sheer drive. Spiritually, though, Willi had had some sublime moments on Nanda Devi. He had felt the joy and wonder of the mountain.

Willi wanted Devi to reach the summit. That would justify the climb: physically, morally, and spiritually. For all that Devi had done physically, for all that she had carried, she deserved the summit. She was a woman. For that fact alone and for all that she had helped others, it was morally right that she should be up there. Spiritually, too, it was as right as her name that she should have this mountain.

On the last day of August, Roskelley, States, and Reichardt set out from Camp III for the final assault on the summit. Lev accompanied the summit party carrying extra food, doubling the fixed ropes where they had become dangerously frayed. When Lev turned back Reichardt felt that the Teton guide had a perfect right to be continuing. It was a long, difficult journey. Reichardt did not reach Camp IV at 24,000 feet until after dark.

In the morning the three men got out of their little tent and looked up at the peak of the great mountain. It was as fine a day as they had had all summer, warm and windless. There was almost always a plume around the summit that the Garhwalis said was smoke from the goddesses' kitchen. Today Nanda Devi stood bare, unguarded.

The climbers dressed hurriedly and moved up the final ridge, up to their waists in sugar snow. They exchanged leads and continued plodding slowly skyward the 2,500 feet to the summit. They broke the thick crust of the snow. Suddenly, the snow to their left simply slid away, falling 3,000 feet. They stood motionless, afraid that they would start another slab avalanche. Then they slogged upward again, and at 2:30 P.M. reached the summit.

While the three climbers stood on the summit of Nanda Devi, Willi, John Evans, and Jitendra, one of the four high-altitude porters, were moving slowly up to Camp III to join the other climbers. Willi had spent much of the climb worrying about other people. If it wasn't Kumar and Singh not knowing how to jumar properly, it was listening to Lev and his problems with the "Dhaulagiri boys." Willi liked the four high-altitude porters immensely; they weren't as well trained as good Sherpas, though, and he had been watching out for them. Now jumaring up to Camp III for the last time, Willi had to think about not only Jitendra but John Evans too. Evans was a strong climber, but he had arrived late and had never acclimated. Willi thought it amazing that Evans was leading much of the way today.

When they were almost at Camp III Kumar and Lev came down to help them. Jitendra arrived in camp exhausted. He lay in a tent panting for breath.

"Oh Jitendra, *idhar ao, pani lyo,*" Kumar shouted, ordering the porter to bring him water. "You now go, melt snow."

"That's enough, Kirin!" Devi shouted, matching the Indian decibel for decibel. "We're not going to say anything at Base Camp. But up here it doesn't go. Go melt snow yourself!"

Though Devi and Willi had tried, no great brotherhood of the axe had developed on Nanda Devi. The hard men didn't think Nanda Devi was any place to run a training school for Indians or Americans. They hadn't been willing to spend time teaching Nirmal and Kirin how to jumar. Willi had tried to help the two Indians, but as far as he was concerned, they had matched the Americans ethnocentricity for ethnocentricity. They hadn't done their share. Moreover, though woefully inadequate on the fixed ropes, Kumar was hoping to reach the summit.

In the morning Willi broke trail as Devi, Harvard, and Lev marched toward the base of the buttress to move up to Camp IV for their summit try. It was as dark and menacing as the previous day had been bright and promising. Before they were even halfway to the great vertical wall, Devi's hernia popped out. It was enough to upset even Devi. She had psyched herself up for this final challenge. This was too much. Harvard and Willi comforted her, telling her she would be okay. It was turning into such a miserable day that they gave up and walked back to camp.

As they turned back the day cleared. The first summit party descended from Camp IV. Roskelley, States, and Reichardt were bone tired. When they got to the base of the buttress with their heavy packs, they had expected that someone would be waiting to greet and help them. No one was there, and when the summit party reached the camp they did not receive the reception they had expected.

The other climbers got out of their tents to meet the summiteers. Roskelley felt that the other expedition members were acting as if it took an enormous effort to get off their dead rears. He shook hands with Singh and Kumar; at least the two Indian climbers seemed enthusiastic. Roskelley felt that these people seemed glad to get him and his buddies off the ropes so now they could go up themselves.

No matter what Roskelley thought, Willi for one took pride in their accomplishment. But it was not what he had felt when Big Jim came down off the South Col of Everest. There was no joyous, backslapping conviviality, not from Willi, not from anyone else. Some of the climbers still thought that they had been used by Roskelley so that he could glorify himself. Roskelley on the contrary thought that he, John Roskelley, was the one who had been sorely used. What rankled him particularly was that he had led putting in the fixed rope to be used by people who didn't appreciate what he had done for them. He had put up the scaffolding and they would climb up it, trampling all the way to the summit, painting over his work of art with their clumsy strokes.

One of the axioms of climbing had always been: "The mountain decides who will reach the summit." But any climber who could latch onto the fixed rope with his jumar had a shot at reaching the top. "They only needed to jumar," John wrote bitterly afterwards.

Later that day everyone got together to discuss the rest of the expedition. Roskelley thought that Devi was being pushed to reach the summit, either by Willi or by her own ideas.

"Any of you that aren't fit shouldn't even try to make it up there," John said bluntly. "A lot of you don't have the jumar technique. You're not gonna make it. Devi, you're in no condition physically to go up there now. You have no business going up. Andy, you've never even carried above this camp. You've got no business either."

Listening to Roskelley, Kumar wondered whether Roskelley wanted anyone else to reach the summit. Lev didn't like John's words, either. He wanted someone to go with him to the summit. With John Evans still dragging, the two Indians fairly hopeless, it was only Devi, Harvard, and Willi. Willi wanted the summit for himself and for his daughter.

"Could I have the peanut butter can?" Devi asked as Roskelley continued talking. Below, Devi had probably been less interested in the summit than any of the climbers; now she too felt the pull of Nanda Devi. She yanked off the lid on the peanut butter can, stuck her fingers into the glutinous mixture. Then staring at Roskelley she licked the peanut butter off her fingers.

"I've told you a thousand times about that!" Roskelley exploded. He had warned Devi about hygiene. She wiped herself with water like an Indian. Then she did things like this. No wonder she was sick.

Devi gave Roskelley the finger and a look that he translated as "you son of a bitch." It was the first time he had ever seen her lose her temper.

"You're just hurting yourself, Devi," Roskelley said, almost speechless. Roskelley knew he was correct. But he had no support. Willi had a right to his philosophy. But Lou was the climbing leader; he should have chimed in. And Jim was the doctor; he should have said no way was Devi going up the buttress.

Jim examined Devi and told her that he thought she should not go up. But Devi shrugged it off. When she had been carrying those heavy loads lower on the mountain nobody had said anything. Jim didn't have much authority left.

For Roskelley this day at Camp III had filled him with bitterness. The expedition was ending as it had begun in Olympia many months before: with foolhardy compromises, blundering bravado. Roskelley knew that he was right, but his honest, heartfelt judgment had been shoved in his face. In the end he gave the remaining climbers what they took as his blessing. There was no stopping them anyway.

It was Willi's dream that all of them should reach the summit: Willi; Devi; Lev; Harvard; Evans; the two Indian team members, Singh and Kumar; and Jitendra, the high-altitude porter. It would be a magnificent victory for all the unmet, unfelt possibilities in life, a victory over the hard men and the hard and narrow life. It would be a victory over pain, over the bowels and the stomach, over Devi's hernia; a victory over age and inexperience; a victory over all that tied men and women down to the mundane and the ordinary.

Early in the morning when Devi, Harvard, and Lev headed up to Camp IV, Willi could have gone with them. He was stronger than Harvard or Devi, more experienced than Lev. By the logic of the hard men Willi should at least have been sharing the lead of the party. But Willi was the old guide, and if they were to reach the summit, all eight of them, he had to stay below to shepherd up the least experienced, the worst acclimated.

John Evans had broken trail for the summit party. By midmorning when Willi, Kumar, and Singh arrived at the base of the buttress, Evans was waiting half frozen. Evans and Willi were planning to spend the day teaching jumar techniques to the Indians on the buttress while ferrying up another tent and more food. Jitendra wasn't feeling well. He walked back to camp. Evans, Willi, Kumar, and Singh moved up the ropes.

By all rights the summit party should have been far above. But on only the third pitch Kumar reached Harvard. In front of him Devi was moving very slowly up the fixed rope. It was taking her an hour to do a 300-foot pitch.

That wasn't like Devi. By midafternoon it was snowing. Willi decided to cache the supplies and head back down with the others. Moving down the rope, Willi was awed by what Roskelley had done to put in the route. He worried about Devi too.

Early in the evening Lev called from Camp IV saying that he had made it, but Devi and Harvard were still on the buttress.

"If they have to bivouac tonight I'm going to order Devi down," Willi remembered Jim saying.

"Yeah, Jim," Willi replied. "She'll probably tell you to stick it in your left ear."

Willi figured that it couldn't be that dangerous for Devi and Harvard. Jumaring was a delicate, tiring business though. They had big packs. It was cold, black, and wet. Willi sat in the tent waiting for the radio call saying that Devi and Harvard had arrived. It was eight o'clock. Nine o'clock. Still they were out on the buttress. It was pitch black and snowing. Willi could imagine what it was like for Devi alone on the rope, only the darkness and the cold as her companions, struggling upward. Ten o'clock. By all odds they should have made it long ago. Eleven o'clock.

"Andy's here," Lev radioed. "Devi's behind."

Another long hour passed before Devi finally dragged in. Far from his daughter and whatever was happening above, Willi slept uneasily that night. The morning dawned beautiful and clear, a summit day if Willi had ever seen one. In the high camp he knew Devi and Andy would be too wiped out to try for the summit. A new chill had come into the air too. The warm monsoon season was ending. The expedition was ending too. The urgency Willi felt to get the second and third team to the summit stood against the urgency Roskelley, States, and Reichardt felt to get out and away.

Willi didn't like doing it, but he told Jitendra that he had better go down; the high-altitude porter knew better than Willi that he wasn't up for a summit try. Roskelley headed down to Base Camp too, with a letter asking the porters to return between the twelfth and fifteenth of September.

Reichardt had decided to leave as well. He wanted to see if he could make it home in time for the birth of his first child. Willi wrote a final letter home. "I am ready for it to be over now and only hope most fervently that Devi pulls herself together sufficiently to go to the top," he wrote. Willi's letter surged with the pride he felt in his oldest daughter and the way she carried loads. Now it would be a sweet victory indeed for Devi to reach the top. Roskelley had said that Devi had no business on the rope. Jim States had said that for medical reasons Devi should come down. Now it was all almost over. Willi wrote that he was eager to get home and tell the stories of the expedition. Willi's feet were hurting him. His thumbs were bad. He didn't write that home.

In the morning for what he was sure would be the last time, Willi trudged to the bottom of the buttress with John Evans and the two Indians. It was another nasty, sleety day. Each day was colder. Kumar was dragging badly. From previous expeditions the Indian had everything from a much dislocated shoulder to frostbitten toes. Kumar knew that he was having one of his bad days. But he was a man of such blissful optimism that he made even Willi seem like a Cassandra.

Willi shouted at Kumar. He warned him if he did not hurry, they would never make it to Camp IV. "Kirin," Willi yelled finally, "if we're not at Sugar Delight by three o'clock we're gonna turn around. Understand?"

"Oh, yes," Kumar replied, moving slowly up the rope. Willi watched as Kumar flipped upside down in his jumars. Weighed down by his heavy pack, the Indian rested like a turtle flipped on its back. Kumar struggled desperately for a while, then lay not moving. When Willi had about given up hope that Kumar would ever do anything, the Indian righted himself and headed slowly up the rope.

Willi stood freezing, waiting for Kumar. "Kirin, we've got to make Sugar Delight by three."

"Oh, yes, Willi."

The Indian flipped over again. Kumar was used to this by now. To regain strength in the thin air, he rested for a half hour upside down. Willi decided that he had better shimmy up the nine-milli-meter rope and give the Indian another lesson in jumaring. As Willi got there, Kumar righted himself and headed up the rope.

It was getting late. Willi looked below and saw that Evans and Singh were still behind. Willi hooked into the rope above Kumar and shot rapidly up to the Sugar Delight cache, a duffel bag hanging on the side of the mountain. When Kumar finally reached the cache around four o'clock, Willi told him they were going back down.

"But, Willi, we can put tent here and stay tonight," he argued in a high-pitched voice, "if you don't want to go further."

"No way, Kirin," Willi said, looking at the twelve-inch ledge.

"Well, then, we can bivouac out tonight. I'm game."

"No, Kirin, we're going down."

For Willi, going down with Kumar was about as discouraging as going up. Everyone wanted to get back to camp. Kumar was unbelievably slow. At the bottom of the buttress they yelled and yelled and yelled. Kirin was still up above. While the others went ahead, Willi waited for Kirin. It was nine o'clock before Willi finally trudged into camp with the Indian.

Talking on the radio with Camp IV, Willi was relieved to know that Devi was feeling better. But Lev, the old Teton guide, had done something inexplicable. He had tried to go to the summit by himself. He had gotten halfway there, had fallen, had turned back. Climbing by himself he could very easily have died.

In the morning when Willi came out of the tent to squat and relieve his diarrhea once again, the day burst upon him. It was magnificent. There was not a cloud in the sky. He had been so tired last night, but he looked at the sun, the snow sparkling in the sunlight, the buttress above, and he knew that he was ready to give it another go. Even before he asked John Evans if he wanted to go up, he knew that the big Colorado mountaineer was feeling too low to do much climbing. He stopped at the Indians' tent.

"Kirin, I'm going up."

"You should have told us, Willi," Kumar said, stunned at seeing Willi all dressed. "You said today was holiday. We're fit."

"I know."

"You're ditching us!" said Kumar. For his own reputation, the Indian had to reach the summit.

"No, you and Nirmal will come up tomorrow with John."

"You can climb with us too!"

"No, Kirin, I'm going up to be with Devi."

"But wait!"

"I want to be with Devi."

For Willi climbing alone was the sin against the Holy Ghost, the unpardonable sin. But he was so tired of all his responsibilities. This once he wanted to be by himself, to climb at his own pace up to his daughter, then to climb with Devi to the summit of her mountain.

All Willi's life he had been roped to someone, one way or another. Today he was free. He could rest when he wanted, climb when he chose. No one was on the rope above whom he had to wait for, no one below pressuring him, no one to think about. In less than three hours he made it up to Sugar Delight snowfield. At the cache he picked up another tent and more food.

He felt his muscles working beautifully. He was carrying an enormous pack. He was proud of that. He could still carry more than anyone. Sitting in his jumars, he stopped and photographed icicles and looked at the details of the rocks and the sky above. He had complained about jumars but it was not bad, not bad for an old-timer, not bad being in such control. It was as fine a day of climbing as he had ever had.

Willi had taken his time, but it was only seven o'clock, just getting dark, and he was already up at the final pitch. The last problem was to make it up onto the ledge no more than twenty feet from the tents. He yodeled up to have someone throw him a rope. Without some help it would be a risky business unhooking himself from the fixed rope, then throwing his body out and onto the ledge. He yodeled again. No one heard him. In one final act of exertion, he heaved himself up onto the ledge.

Willi burst into the two-person tent like a visitor from lower earth. The climbers hugged and whooped and shouted. Though she was still feeling low, Devi pulled out her harmonica and played some tunes. For Willi it had been great climbing by himself; now it was doubly great being up here with these people: Devi, who would soon have her mountain; Andy, whom Devi loved and Willi had come to accept; Pete, who had wanted this to be a different kind of expedition.

Willi lifted spirits immensely. Devi hadn't expected her dad; his presence was like a wondrous gift. Lev was happy seeing Willi for another reason. He had become worried about Devi. Today outside the tent he had seen Devi's bloody stools, stark against the white snow. He couldn't ignore Devi's condition any longer. He had told Devi that it didn't look good to him; it was up to Devi or her dad whether she went up or down.

The four climbers spent the night in the two-person tent, their bodies pressed closely against one another. In the morning Willi had planned to set up the tent he had carried with him. It was a blustery, snowy day though. The four climbers huddled in the one tent together. No one was going to the summit this day. Lev had brought up different teas in his pack. He brewed them one after another. They talked of other climbs, other times, memories falling out like loose pictures from a scrapbook. Willi loved being here, talking up a storm that more than matched what was going on outside.

Though Devi was still weak, her diarrhea had stopped. "I hope you all go to the summit and leave me here," Devi said.

Devi never wanted to be a burden. If there was any way to get her to the summit of her mountain, Willi was going to do it. By afternoon even Willi had to admit it. Devi probably wasn't going to make it.

That was hard to accept. First, it had been Jitendra who wasn't up to it. Then, despite what he had told Kumar, he doubted whether John and the two Indians would ever get up the buttress. Now it was Devi. Everyone agreed that if tomorrow, the eighth of September, was a summit day, Devi would wait while Willi, Harvard, and Lev went up. Then in the afternoon all four climbers would go down together to Camp III.

Willi dozed off that evening looking forward to climbing to the top of his third and last Himalayan peak. Suddenly, Willi woke up. Devi was sitting up. She had gone to sleep huddled in the middle of the tent, the other bodies pressed against hers. She had wanted to belch. But she couldn't get it out and had to sit up, waking everyone else. She didn't want to bother the others but she couldn't help it. "Blllllaaaaa," the gas exploded out of her. "Blllllllaaaaaaaaaa."

Willi was used to this. For years Devi had been having chronic stomach trouble. If it wasn't the runs, it was gas. "Blllllaaaaaa." Devi finally lay down again, and Willi fell asleep. After what seemed ten minutes, but was more like a half hour, Devi sat up again. "Blllllaaaaa." By now the whole tent stunk. Outside a great storm had fallen upon the mountain, shaking the tent, the winds roaring down Nanda Devi. "Blllllaaa." All night long Devi kept sitting up to belch. "Blllllaaaaa."

At dawn, Lev woke, his feet resting against Devi's head. Looking at Devi's face, he was shocked. Her face was bloated, distorted. Her countenance had an icy blue tinge. When Willi saw Devi he realized that they would have to take Devi down the mountain. She had been up at 24,000 feet for five days already. They would have to get her down today. Now he would not have the summit, not for himself, not for Devi.

This was no remnant of a monsoon storm beating at their tent, but the first great storm of the new season. Outside the wind screamed its challenge. Devi was weak. Willi took his time preparing to depart. Lev and Harvard were in no hurry either. If they left by noon, they would be fine. Devi was having trouble sitting up, but she said she could go down the buttress.

At 11:45 Willi unzipped the tent, pushed his way out into the violent wind and storm to relieve himself before the long journey down. Inside the tiny tent, Devi was sipping tea.

"Take my pulse, will you, Pete?" Devi asked.

"I'll do it a little later, when I'm ready with this," Lev said as he tied his bootlaces. The storm had picked up even more. Lev was hurrying, realizing what a job it would be helping Devi down the fixed rope.

Devi turned her head and stared in Lev's eyes. Where before a fevered struggle had been written across her countenance, she looked at Lev now with calm awareness. "I'm going to die," she said quietly. Then she pitched forward.

Willi unzipped the door and pushed back into the tent.

"We're in bad trouble," Harvard said, leaning over Devi. "Something's happened."

"She just said she was going to die, Willi," Lev said.

Willi rushed to his daughter, pressed his lips to hers, and started mouth-to-mouth resuscitation. He turned her body on the side and fluid drained from her lungs.

Willi tried to blow his life into Devi. "Oh, please don't go," he begged. "Please. Please. Don't leave, Devi!"

Only the rhythmic pace of the artificial respiration kept Willi from collapsing in agony. What in the name of God had happened to Devi? What could have done this to his Devi? He felt her lips growing colder and colder. He tasted Devi dying.

Lev took over to try cardiopulmonary resuscitation, pushing on her chest with his two hands. As Willi watched his daughter lying so still, he thought he saw one eye open. But at 12:30 even he had given up hope. The three men clutched at one another.

They cried. They wept loudly. They panted almost soundlessly. They moaned.

"What are we going to do? Should we leave her in the tent?"

"No." Willi shook his head.

"Take her down, bury her in the Sanctuary?"

"No. Commit her to the mountain. The law of the seas."

The three men wrapped Devi in Lev's sleeping bag. They half carried, half dragged her out of the tent. As they pulled the body toward the edge of the cliff, the fierce winds nearly uprooted them. On the edge of the ledge above the fixed ropes, the wind tearing at them, they fell to their knees. They linked hands forming a circle around Devi's body. Then Willi gave a prayer:

"Thank . . . you . . . for the . . . world . . . we . . . live . . . in . . . thank . . . you . . . for . . . such . . . beauty . . . juxta-posed against . . . such risk . . . thank . . . you. . . ."

The words were barely audible, carried away on the wind. Then the three men, the father, the lover, and the friend, rolled the body over the edge and Devi disappeared into the storm, into the depths of Nanda Devi.

The storm had become even fiercer. It was madness to descend through this fury. But to get away from the tent at Camp IV and the horror of what had just happened, Willi would have rappelled down into hell itself. What was left within him was that same pure, primitive instinct to survive that had led him down from the summit of Everest. But even that was numbed.

Willi strapped Devi's heavy Lowe pack across his own, an incredible load, and followed Lev down the fixed ropes. Lev did not strap on his crampons. Yesterday he had sent Harvard down to untie the end of the second rope so that they could pull it up to use as a climbing rope on the summit try.

Suddenly, Lev was swinging free, his feet clutching for some hold on the immense buttress. While Willi moved slowly down the pitch above, Lev began to swing back and forth, a giant pendulum, back and forth against the snow and rock, his crampon-less boots slipping against the icy face, back and forth in a 25-foot arc, his foot catching against the ledge, then pulling himself up.

Willi moved down the rope next. Lev pulled him up onto the ledge and then helped Harvard. It was midafternoon. The wind and snow lashed at their bearded faces. Willi waited while Lev moved down the next pitch and then followed him. The two ropes were coated with ice, frozen stiff. Willi went along slipping, sliding, jerking down the rope.

Below at Sugar Delight snowfield, while walking across to the next fixed rope, Willi stumbled and fell face down into the deep snow. The packs were so heavy that he was starting to suffocate lying there. He couldn't get up. Finally, he managed to pull himself to his feet and move on.

Willi was going last now. As he struggled downward below the cache, he found the ropes all twisted up. With his gloved hands he tried to untangle the mess. He wiggled in his jumar. The two packs were very heavy. They held him down. The harness that he was sitting in began to tighten. It was squeezing the very life out of him. Willi looked fifteen feet below where Andy and Pete stood on a ledge looking up.

"Help me, Andy," Willi begged, knowing even as he said it that it was too far.

"Do it, Willi, do it!"

"Don't give up. For Christ' sake, don't give up."

Willi was afraid. In a few minutes he would be dead. His bowels let loose. With a final burst of energy, Willi pulled himself up. It was late. Willi couldn't carry the two packs, or even one pack. He strapped the two packs to a piton and jumared slowly down to the base of the buttress.

The three men trudged through the dark, bitter night. Ahead was the solace and warmth of their companions in Camp III. After ten o'clock when they finally arrived, the camp was dead, deserted, the tents crushed. Willi, Harvard, and Lev stood in this graveyard of a camp, stunned and disbelieving. They entered one tent that was still standing. Using the radio they called down the mountain. They learned that the others had left because Evans and Singh had become sick.

Sitting sipping tea Willi was shocked beyond even pain. While Harvard and Lev zipped the two sleeping bags together, Willi stared into space. In the brutal cold, Lev and Harvard took off their boots and got into the double bag.

"I left my knife up there, Pete, it's my good knife," Willi said.

"Come on in, Willi."

Willi just sat there.

"Willi, at least take your boots off."

All night long Willi lay by himself wearing Lev's long down pants, his own parka and boots. He didn't seem to care any longer.

In the morning Willi had hoped to go back up again for Devi's pack. Great mounds of snow covered the ground, though, and everyone was terribly drained.

The next day the three men headed down the mountain, Willi stumbling ahead. He had frostbitten fingers. His feet hurt. At about 22,000 feet he saw a crow fly past. It was like the gorak that he had seen after Jake died on Everest. He took it as a sign that Devi's spirit lived on. Lev thought that Willi seemed to want to go on now, to seek meaning in whatever he had left.

At Base Camp Willi began talking about Devi's death, to fit what had happened into his philosophy. "If we can accept reality as it is then we have to accept death," he said, sitting in the sun. "We wouldn't repeal the laws of gravity, would we, even though we know gravity can kill you."

Roskelley couldn't understand how Willi could make such sense of Devi's death. He hammered at Willi, shoving his face in the rude realities of what had happened above. Willi was the most articulate, most loquacious of men. Before Roskelley's assault he stood mute. He turned from the climber and his words. He nursed his diarrhea with Lomotil. He read his mail. He read letters in which Devi was still alive.

On the journey back to Lata, Roskelley and States and the porters raced each other away from the mountain. Behind them trying to keep up came Willi, still suffering from frostbite; Evans, staggering along, his eyes yellow as egg yolks, a sign of hepatitis; and Lev, coughing with what he thought might be strep throat.

As much as Roskelley and States wanted to escape from the mountain and the expedition, Willi wanted to remain. Every bend in the trail, every high point, Willi turned back to catch a glimpse of Nanda Devi. Each time, thinking it might be the last, he stood gazing back, taking a picture before moving on. Then somewhere further on he turned, saw the mountain again, and took yet another picture before trekking down the trail.

As Willi moved toward Lata a great, gray numbing pain settled in, a pain that neither tears nor words could soothe. Even the porters, to whom death was as ordinary as night and day, knew that something awful had happened up on the mountain, awful in the way Willi used the word: awesome, fearsome, moving, and profound. They were a religious people, a superstitious people. Devi may have been the goddess herself, returning to the mountain. Or perhaps the goddess had taken young Devi to protect her. It was also possible that the goddess had been angered, threatened, and had struck Devi down. The goddess was not to be trafficked with by mortals.

When Willi and the last of the sahibs trudged into Lata, the porters took them and led them to the temple of Nanda Devi. The climbers were very tired, but the porters insisted. A large crowd had gathered in the temple courtyard. The porters held Willi by the arm and took him to the dark door of the temple. Then they brought a goat to be sacrificed to appease the gods.

The porters set the animal before Willi. It is the custom in the

Garhwal that before a goat is sacrificed it must nod its assent. The goat stood staring at Willi, its head still. After a while one of the old men threw water in the goat's ear. The goat shook its head. Another man lifted the ceremonial sword and in a single stroke severed the head of the animal, bathing the ground in blood.

Part Three

WWWWWWWWWWWWWWWWWWWWWWWWWWWWWWWWWWW

Willi stood before the reporters at a press conference in New Delhi. He was exhausted. His small eyes were set within deep circles of fatigue. A crescent-shaped beard ringed his face. He was as thin as a rail.

"Do you have any regrets?" an Indian reporter asked.

"No," Willi said in startled reply. Then he stopped a moment. "To do so would be denying reality."

His "no" that day was the beginning of a theme that came to dominate his life. He carried it from that room in India to his family in Olympia, to Devi's memorial service, to large public talks. It became his obsession. He wove it into everything he said, wherever he said it, with whomever he happened to speak.

Again and again the family went over all that had happened as if they were looking at a reel of film hoping to find something there they kept missing. They read Devi's diary. It was like opening up a cave from which darkness spewed forth. This Devi Willi had thought carefree and joyous often expressed profound loneliness and despair. Lyricism and exuberance abounded, too, but there were days when Devi had black moods, days when she was cynical, days when she was as different from the Devi she had showed the world as night from day.

Willi was terribly tired. Yet he could not as much seek solace from his wife and family as give it. Again and again he had to justify himself and his actions on the climb. According to Willi, at one point Jolene angrily blamed him for Devi's death. That was a dreadful, poisonous thought that if allowed to grow would kill everything Willi had ever been, or could be. Those who cared for the man and his life tried not to allow themselves even to think it.

Jolene believed that Willi would probably die on a mountain one day. She had accepted the idea that her husband might not return from Nanda Devi. But it was Devi who had been left up there. It was unthinkable. It was not only Willi's role in Devi's death that was in question. It was Willi's whole philosophy, Willi's life, the life that Willi and Jolene had led together. Whatever doubts the Unsoelds may have had, it became an act of faith to all of them—to Regon, Krag, and Terres as well as to Jolene—that Devi's death did not refute Willi's philosophy, the family's philosophy, as much as prove it.

In December Willi journeyed to Berkeley, California, to address the American Alpine Club dinner about Nanda Devi. Roger Mellem, Willi's old student, came by to see Willi. "You got a little time, Roger?" Willi asked a few hours before the evening speech.

"Sure, Willi!"

"Well, come on upstairs."

Willi had a hard time pulling himself up the stairs. "I used to be a mountaineer and now I can hardly walk," Willi said, hobbling ahead. Month by month his arthritis was getting worse.

It upset Mellem seeing Willi in pain. Willi and Mellem talked a long time. The hour for the evening program drew near. Mellem walked with Willi out to his car to get a tape recorder.

"There's this idea in evangelical Christianity that you don't have to struggle," Willi said, limping through the parking lot. "You accept Christ and that's it. Well, I reject that idea. Life is a struggle, Roger. It's continual struggle. A religion's got to have that in it."

As the two men walked back into the building, Mellem thought that the talk must be weighing on Willi. Mellem wanted to say something but as soon as they entered the lobby, Willi was surrounded by people.

At the AAC banquet Carter and Roskelley spoke first about their experiences on Nanda Devi. Ad had written an article for the *American Alpine Journal,* "The Goddess Nanda," a strange piece among all the expedition accounts. This evening, Carter described the goddess in some detail. Then while slides played on the screen behind, he told the story of the trek into the base of the mountain. He ended with exquisite slides of wild flowers.

Roskelley got up next. He was still extraordinarily bitter about Nanda Devi. Roskelley was not much of a speaker. He went on in a largely toneless voice detailing the climb. Except when he talked about Carter and Fisher leaving ("Those two we felt like we needed but not if they didn't want to stay"), Roskelley avoided controversy.

"The next team to go up would be Andy, Devi, and Peter, which didn't seem quite right to me," John concluded. "And I did argue the point about Devi and Andy going because they hadn't acclimated well. They hadn't been above this particular point. And Devi had been fairly ill the entire way up. So I think Jim States, the doctor, checked her out and said also that she had been ill and he recommended that she didn't go up from there. . . . This is where I descended to send out for porters and this is where I'll give you over to Willi Unsoeld."

Willi waited for the applause to die down. "I'm just here to pick up the pieces." He spoke in a warm voice that vibrated with controlled emotions. He was usually a flamboyant speaker, flapping his arms, going from seriousness to humor and back to seriousness. This evening's talk was stripped of rhetoric and flourish.

Willi told this audience of climbers how he thought the jumar affected the way climbers treated one another. He praised Roskelley's climb. He said how Devi had been happy on the mountain. She had given much. He told how Devi had died, how he had felt her lips grow cold. As he spoke his voice caught. Then he stopped.

"So how does one handle the death of one's daughter?" Willi

concluded, almost in tears. "Well, I'll tell you. You don't. It handles you. It rubs your nose in the reality of your mortality. It impresses upon you who's in charge. And it's not us. . . .

"Why Devi? Why not me who was old and decrepit and supposed to die on Nanda Devi? Why did it have to happen? Well, those two questions, I simply label illicit. You don't ask them. You don't allow them. You shut them out at the source because there are no answers and that way madness lies.

"And in the final analysis I guess all I can hark back to beyond the philosophical is the sheer visceral enjoyment of the world in which we live. And I offer you that joy . . . which gives one the courage to go on, the confidence that whatever lies beyond that tragic break in our awareness can only be better than ever than that which we've already experienced."

Willi could cry about Devi in front of a thousand people, his voice quivering. But in private Willi found no solace in tears. Many people had come to Willi for help with their own private agonies. Now he had every right and reason to seek help in facing his torment. But there was no one who could lessen his burden.

Often Erik bicycled over to Willi's office. The two men sat silently. "I was just thinking about something, Willi," Erik would say and tell a story about Devi.

When Erik finished Willi would look up. "Well, she's gone, Erik. What can I say? You got to get on." He smiled gently, a tear in his eye.

Willi was teaching a year-long outdoor education program. His programs had become practically a career track for those interested in working for Outward Bound or other outdoor programs that used risk as other disciplines used dictionaries, computers, microscopes, or other tools of learning. Willi had one phrase he kept repeating over and over now: "It has to be real enough to kill you."

In Willi the students saw a man who had lived that philosophy and whose daughter was a martyr to those beliefs. To them he was a vital, forceful figure. But one old friend, visiting for the first time since the Outward Bound days, saw that much of the sheer exuberance had gone out of Willi. The man left Olympia saddened, burdened with his memories.

Willi was having a terrible time with his arthritic hips. It was only a matter of time before he would have to have an operation that might leave him a cripple. "If I'm left in a wheelchair, well I'll just take up kayaking," he said on those days when it was most difficult to walk.

Willi was looking for a way out. When he was down visiting Bill Turnage in Big Sur, California, the two men walked through a field at Andrew Molera Beach. "You know, Bill," Willi said as they wandered through the tall grass, "my climbing days are coming to an end. I got to find something else, got no choice."

"What are you thinking about?" asked Turnage.

"You're a master at making things work," Willi said. Turnage was managing the myriad business affairs of Ansel Adams, the renowned photographer. "It's really important to be able to do that, to have that ability. I tried it at the Peace Corps and AID and I'm just no good."

"Come on, Willi, that's not everything."

"No, it's not. And the world needs both kinds of people. People like you. And people like me. I'm a catalyst, a healer, an individual force."

"Then you've got to find something new where you can use that."

"Well, they're looking for a new provost for Evergreen," Willi said excitedly. "It's the number two job after the president and I'm interested."

"My God, Willi," Turnage said incredulously, turning toward him. "After what you just said? You're not serious. You'd hate it. You know that. It's bureaucracy. It's all those things. You know what it is."

"No, I'm growing," Willi said earnestly. "I think I can bring together both kinds of people within me, at least enough to do the job."

"You *are* serious, aren't you?"

"Darn right."

"Well, Willi, I think it would be a mistake for you—and for Evergreen."

Willi couldn't lead his students into the mountains the way he once had. He became more of a classroom teacher. This year he was not so overwhelming. There was plenty of room for other teachers and other approaches.

Willi grew particularly close to one of the other teachers, Barry Williams, a gentle, serious outdoorsman. "Barry, these kids don't know how to put two and two together," Willi said disgustedly. For the college's guru of experience, Willi was growing more critical of many Evergreen students. Try as he could to stimulate them, to fire their interests, many of them were intellectual deadbeats.

The two teachers had many long talks about outdoor education as well. Williams was trying to decide whether he wanted to continue working in such programs. In making a life from the outdoors, he wondered whether a person deteriorated spiritually and intellectually when he started to deteriorate physically. He wondered what he and Willi were doing turning young people on to the wilderness, sending many of them roaring up into the mountains to work in adventure- and Outward Bound-type programs. Where would they be when they hit forty or fifty?

"I'm like Peter Pan," Willi said. Williams thought that Willi was right. He looked like a grizzled old trapper in from checking his line, but Willi was an eternal youth, a boy who would never and could never grow up. Like Peter Pan standing at the window of the playroom, Willi appeared in the classroom and took anyone who would go off on fantastic adventures. Willi had been there. He was the guide. If you would come along and undertake the discipline, he would lead you wherever you dared to venture. For an hour lecture he would take you out of yourself. For an afternoon he would take you off rock climbing and lead you places you had never gone before. Or he would lead you up a great mountain. Or he might even lead you higher than a mountain, higher even than Everest.

Williams was not the only one who worried about what the increased interest in the wilderness, climbing, trekking, and the outdoors was doing. Pete Sinclair, the other prominent climber at Evergreen, had once spent his summers guiding in the Tetons. He had given it up. So many people were out in the mountains now that they were destroying what Sinclair considered the wilderness to be, debasing the very idea of wilderness. He wished that the wilderness, the unpeopled places, could be reserved for people like Willi, saints and heroes, and for the learning of the heroic virtues.

The sheer numbers of risk-takers and adventure-seekers had profoundly changed the nature of risk and adventure. At one extreme stood Disneyland where four times a day a man attired in lederhosen climbed a 220-foot Matterhorn while tourists snapped pictures. In the middle were the hundreds of adventure travel tours: boat rides on the Amazon, treks in Nepal, climbs in Pakistan, safaris in Kenya, white water canoeing in the States. Willi looked rather disdainfully at his old Everest mate Lute Jerstad, who made his living running adventure-type trips. But Willi, too, was part of this institutionalization of experience. Outward Bound and Evergreen itself were packaged experience. At Evergreen, Willi was training people to create experiences for others.

At the far end of this spectrum stood the climbers themselves. Climbers by the score had reached the top of Everest. They had skied down the South Col, and hurled up a dozen climbers at a time. Climbers were "doing" things like the World Trade Center. Rappelling was not unknown on *The Wide World of Sports,* shown live and in living color. Out in the Tetons, Pete Lev thought that more and more of his clients were "stimulation junkies," looking to get zonked on risk. Willi was trying to use this supercharged *Life* to lead people into themselves and onto other kinds of mountains. But often he was just giving them stimulation fixes.

As soon as Willi returned to Olympia from India, Worth Hedrick came to ask to write a book about Devi. Willi knew that Roskelley was setting out to do his own book, one that would portray Willi and the climb in dark terms. Willi was concerned with immortalizing Devi in a positive book, as well as helping Worth. It was as beautiful an idea as the Nanda Devi expedition had first seemed. Here was Worth—needy, unfulfilled. Here was Devi—good, giving. Now Devi's goodness would live on not only in a book but in Worth's life, in what this project would mean to him, how he might transform his life. Willi still believed in the limitless potential of human beings. He was sure that Worth could do it.

Although Hedrick was not able to get a book contract, he did get a top New York agent. He let his job slip away to devote full time to the project. He realized that the Unsoelds were going through a period of great trauma. He knew, though, that he had to do this properly: to write a book that would shine with truth, idealism, and beauty, a book that would please all the family and the world as well. The more Worth probed, the more questions he asked, the more he became a thorn in the Unsoelds' side. Only Willi cooperated with him willingly.

When Hedrick was given sections of Devi's diary to read, he could hardly believe it. Part of it was like the blackest writings of Mark Twain. Worth thought that Devi must have been a tormented woman in many ways, and nobody knew it. Here were statements full of pessimism and cynicism right next to passages surging with idealism, hope, and joy.

Worth was present at many of the Unsoelds' long discussions. One evening when Worth was there with a friend, Eve Johnson, Willi was lying on the living room rug, his ankles and arms crossed. Johnson heard words burst out of Willi: "I killed Devi. I know I did it." Hedrick wasn't sure what had happened that evening, what it all meant. This wasn't something he wanted to deal with.

Willi had a range of emotion concerning his daughter's death, the peaks and valleys of which were so profound that Worth could not possibly contain them in a book intended to be a beautiful, pure memorial to Devi. Hedrick sought solace in detail. He had to know what Willi had said on a given day, what Devi had said, what they had worn, what they had thought. He bought a Greyhound bus pass and headed across the country interviewing those who had known Devi and Willi. He talked to people for hours filling up tape cassettes and notebooks with a mountain of detail.

It was not only Devi's death that consumed Willi but the prospect of a terrible physical decline. He talked to one doctor who suggested that he try a radically different diet, but Willi wanted to be himself. He talked often about the various kinds of hip operations and what the chances were that he would ever climb again.

In March 1977 Willi and Barry Williams went out one afternoon to the Olympic Mountains to check on some students who were going on a climb. Once Willi got in the mountains he decided that they should go on a little climb themselves. Though nothing was said, Williams knew that Willi felt this might be his last climb. It was nothing really, moving up a series of couloirs, working their way around a pinnacle. Nothing.

Willi was pushing it. Suddenly Williams realized that this was a real climb. He felt that he was only tagging along with a man who had an extraordinary relationship with the mountain itself. The fog closed in. They ran into a seeming dead end, a sheer wall that led nowhere.

"Well, we better turn back," Williams said. "Try somewhere else."

"Just a little more," Willi said.

Williams wanted to find another way. But Willi was leading. Willi trusted in the mountain. He moved on.

The sun broke through. Ahead lay a way around the pinnacle.

Like most arthritics Willi had his good days and his bad. Later that spring Willi was able to go up Mount Rainier with a group of students. He had been on the great American mountain dozens of times. The group was coming down Cadaver Gap, one of the routes leading to the summit, when Willi saw a raven. He sat down and began to cry.

"A raven meant something special to Devi and me," Willi sobbed uncontrollably. "Regon believes I can't cry, but I can cry." The students came up to Willi and put their arms around him and comforted him as best they could.

Since the marathon sessions soon after Willi returned, Regon and Krag had not talked to Willi much about the meaning of Devi's death. They came over to the house frequently to discuss political issues such as the inequalities in the world. For hours on end they went at their father in fierce, unyielding debate. He tried to deal with such subjects as he tried to deal with them in the classroom, but it was not Willi. His two sons pounded away at their father, beating him with fists of rhetoric. Observing the endless, fevered debates, an outsider might have thought that it was only Devi's death that could arouse such passions. If only Regon and Krag could talk about it openly.

As for Willi's marriage, when it had been good it had been very good, and when it was bad it was godawful. But it wasn't one or the other anymore. Willi and Jolene no longer seemed to have time. Jolene had stepped up her political activities, hardly giving herself time to think.

As a self-styled public interest lobbyist, she threw herself into a variety of issues. Some of the politicians in Olympia at first found this intense woman little more than a curiosity. But she was well prepared and dedicated. No longer simply "Willi Unsoeld's wife," Jolene was becoming a person to be reckoned with in liberal political circles.

Regon and Krag had stayed in Olympia. Only Terres had gotten out, moving to Seattle to study drama at the University of Washington. Terres was the proud inheritor of Willi's theatrical abilities. She was a tiny, vivacious young woman who appeared likely to play ingenue roles for years. She was the least purely idealistic of the Unsoelds—ambitious to be a successful actress; full of an impish, irreverent charm; usually with one male admirer or another. Still, she was an Unsoeld. When she arrived at her college dormitory, she asked to borrow her roommate's toothbrush. That was the most natural thing in the world to an Unsoeld. Her roommate threw a fit.

The spring after Devi's death Terres went to hear her father give a talk on education. Sitting looking up at Willi, she realized how similar the lecture was to what Willi had said years ago. The more she listened the angrier she became. All these people were hanging on to Willi, sucking him dry. What he needed was a sabbatical, a chance to read, think, learn, and study. His words had become a kind of pap. She couldn't stand to see that happening. She decided not to go hear Willi anymore.

Willi's speech had not changed in part because his ideas had not changed. At Evergreen he remained the guru of process, the most articulate, impassioned defender of the old ideals. In a speech about the college given in October 1977 Willi concluded: "There have been some disturbing signs of recent regression (which I haven't time to detail) but even so it appears that we have enough innovative momentum to carry us through at least another three or five years before the laws of educational entropy begin to overtake us."

Willi could step back and see that innovative education was a migratory species, staying nowhere forever. That didn't mean he liked seeing what was happening to the school.

The state legislature had thought it was funding an institution that would rocket upward in students and stature, fueled on the reformist energies of the sixties, recruiting legions of youth. But just as the mortar was drying on the first buildings, the baby boom generation was ending. Soon afterwards so did the fervor and idealism of the previous decade. Although Evergreen was supposed to grow to 12,000 students by the early 1980s, the school had reached peak enrollment of only 2,636 students in 1976 and had started to decline.

This new generation of teenagers was interested in going to college to find not themselves but a good job once they got out. They didn't understand Evergreen's catalog. One state legislator, author of a bill to dismantle Evergreen and turn it into the state capital campus of the University of Washington, noted that only seventy-nine students in the class entering in 1976 came directly from Washington high schools. Conservative legislators took no pride in the fact that such a high percentage of Evergreen students came from out of state. They considered that a dubious achievement, particularly when Evergreen was roughly twice as expensive per student as other state schools.

Evergreen had begun to change in part because the students themselves were demanding change. That glorious first year practically every student at Evergreen (97 percent) took one of the Coordinated Studies Programs that were supposed to be the center of the Evergreen experience. In 1976–77 less than half the student body were involved (41 percent). The kind of education Willi wanted at the college was intense, fiercely involving; it was one thing to have that kind of learning during the first year when practically everybody was full-time, harder these days when many students went part-time.

Willi believed that Evergreen should serve the local community. But Willi wanted to teach values, not how to coach a high school football team. He wanted to teach how to live, not how to get a graduate fellowship in philosophy. As Evergreen threatened to evolve into a far more traditional school, Willi fought for the old Evergreen. There were dozens of places where a student could get that other kind of education. But Willi felt there was only one Evergreen where students who couldn't make it anywhere else had a chance not only to survive but to flourish.

It was a measure of how beleaguered the experimental school had become that even Willi and some of the most reform-minded faculty took the arrival of former Governor Daniel J. Evans as president as a positive sign. Although Evans was a politician, not an educator, he was a progressive politician with considerable clout in the legislature.

On a trip to Washington, D.C., that fall Willi met Fleming Heegaard, a Nepal I volunteer, near Dupont Circle, a tiny park from which the great avenues of the city radiate. The two men walked slowly up Connecticut Avenue, past the boutiques, restaurants, and stores toward Heegaard's home a few blocks away.

"Jolene has really changed, Fleming," Willi said proudly, moving along barely lifting his feet off the ground. "She's not like the woman I married. She's dealing with the legislators. She's drinking and swearing and she's getting the legislation through."

Heegaard could tell that Willi was in pain, having to twist his hips even to walk. "I've chosen this operation that'll at least give me the prospect maybe of walking," Willi said, looking down at his hips. "But I'll never be able to carry any loads anymore. It would be easier to take if I'd gotten this arthritis from carrying heavy loads over the years. But it's not that, Fleming. It's a virus, some kind of bug."

Willi shrugged and walked a few more feet. "I've got to call a cab," he said, stopping suddenly. He appeared absolutely crushed. "I can't make it."

As Heegaard hailed a cab, he thought that there were two Willi Unsoelds: the flamboyant public man, the self-sufficient mountaineer he had seen so often, and this man he was seeing today, this private Willi, suffering and vulnerable.

Many of the people to whom Willi had given so much were deeply concerned about what he would do now that his days as a climber were probably over. One of these was Dee Frankfourth, who as a student at Evergreen had been touched by Willi and his ideas and, like so many others, had gone on to make her own independent life. She had learned to climb with Willi and to love the wilderness in ways that she never had before. From Willi and Evergreen she had taken away a belief that a person could do almost anything with his or her life.

A month after arriving in Washington in the fall of 1977 to work for the Alaska Coalition, she wrote a letter to Margaret E. Murie, the naturalist and member of the governing council of the Wilderness Society, one of the leading environmental organizations. She proposed Willi's name for the Society's eighteen-person council. "Though his [Willi's] heart is tied very much to the mountains, and always will be, sometime in the next year he is to undergo a hip replacement operation, which will restrict the activities he loves so much," Frankfourth wrote. "He must look, in his words, not in the direction of Mount Rainier any longer, but to other directions."

Frankfourth believed that Willi could find one new role for himself drawing together the wilderness preservers at the Society and elsewhere with the wilderness users: the climbers, trekkers, outdoor- and Outward Bound-type of group. "Willi is the essence of vitality and spirit, and I'm sure, just because of his limitations that may crop up in the future, his wisdom, perseverance, and love for the wilderness will not diminish, only intensify."

At the next meeting of the Wilderness Society, Willi was chosen for the council.

Willi wore the masks of a hero. It was hard for him to find new paths worthy to venture upon. It was doubly hard finding paths that would satisfy those who adored him. No one in Olympia even knew this Willi Unsoeld who could confess openly a desire to be provost of Evergreen, who was proud to be one of the top five candidates, disappointed when the school decided to reopen the selection process.

Willi continued giving his talk about Nanda Devi wherever he went. Members of the audience sometimes rushed forward to hug and comfort him. He received letters saying how much his talk had helped others to handle their own losses. Some people, though, were appalled that Willi could turn Devi's death into a continuous public purging. They wondered what in the name of God he was doing.

Dick Emerson knew and loved Willi deeply. Emerson's child had died in a climbing accident, too. When that had happened Willi had been there with all his strength and love. But Emerson was left mute before Willi. He could not relate to him any longer. He could find no thread of continuity between himself and the way he had handled his loss and the way Willi was handling his. He could not understand how Willi could be so articulate. He vowed one day to go to Willi and talk to him.

Willi said that he felt an obligation to use Devi's death to impart what he had learned about life and living, death and dying. A public lecture was his favorite forum. "I believe I do it for several reasons," he told one reporter. "For one thing, I have a need to deal with my emotions, and I find it easier to do it in public than in private. I'm not atoning as some might think. Rather, the lectures are my form of catharsis."

As an actress Terres understood why it might be easier to cry in public than within your own family. She appreciated the sheer dramatic power of Willi's lectures. She discussed with Willi how "even while breaking down and crying he knew that for him to do that would leave a greater impression." To her that was not manipulation. That was an art that led people to feel profound, emotional truths. Yet even she had her doubts.

"You're trying to make a goddess of Devi," Terres told Willi one day, as they stood downstairs by the dryer.

"You're overdramatizing," Willi countered, cutting his daughter off.

Willi wasn't the only member of the expedition haunted by what had happened on Nanda Devi. John Roskelley had spent months writing a book that he said was about "victims not villains," a book that exorcised much of his anger. Although Roskelley was now considered America's outstanding Himalayan climber, the manuscript had not found a publisher. Pete Lev had been frequently depressed for nearly a year after the expedition. He was still guiding. Andy Harvard had gone on to law school, but the memories of Devi and the climb were still much with him. Although Ad Carter's expedition days appeared behind him, he remained editor of the *American Alpine Journal*. Willi had thought that Elliott Fisher would have terrible regrets about leaving Nanda Devi early. Yet of all the expedition members, he had moved furthest beyond the events on the mountain. He was very much in love with the woman who was one of the reasons he had left the climb; they were medical students at Harvard.

In March and June 1978 Willi went to Seattle to have operations installing plastic hip joints. Learning to walk again on what he called his "bionic hips" was the kind of challenge Willi understood. At the Mason Clinic, Dr. William G. Boettcher noticed that while Willi had beads of sweat on his forehead, he had a big smile on his face as well.

Even as he was recuperating, other, more nebulous problems filtered into the room. For over a year and a half Worth Hedrick had been working on his book about Devi, a project that had become an albatross both to the writer and to the Unsoelds. Not only had Hedrick quit his job, but he had taken money out of his retirement plan and gotten himself in financial trouble.

Talking with Hedrick was a kind of catharsis for Willi. Like his lectures, though, it did not touch the center of his pain. For the rest of the family, dealing with Worth was unbelievably vexatious. Each time he visited seemed an eternity.

Hedrick produced part of this book that was supposed to make the Unsoelds happy. The manuscript was positively adoring of the family. When Worth showed the pages to Willi, he was delighted with the one scene Hedrick had invented—Devi at the Greyhound bus terminal in Manhattan on her way back from two years in Asia. She was in the ladies' room with her pack, showing prostitutes how to use an ice axe. Willi could see it happening! When the rest of the family saw the manuscript, they were upset over such a liberty. Worth felt they tore the manuscript apart, criticizing tiny errors and misplaced details, not appreciating what he was trying to do.

Worth was a capable writer but the 250 or so pages were often stilted or sentimental. The manuscript was rejected by various publishers in New York City. So this venture that Willi thought might help Worth, filling his life with new meaning, had ended up cursing him, dragging him down even further. For months, years even, Hedrick had been spreading his problems and weaknesses before the family. Even now he did not give up on the project. And he did not go away.

In September of 1978 Willi traveled to Lost Creek Ranch in the Tetons to attend a Wilderness Society meeting. The newest member of the Council, Willi already had a large impact on the group. When he learned that the Society was looking for a new executive director, he had approached Bill Turnage and talked him into applying for the position. The Society was in deep trouble financially and organizationally. Willi thought Turnage was the person for the job. Sixty other candidates had applied but Willi lobbied actively. Turnage got the position.

At the Council meetings Willi dealt with all the details of administration, outlining the real, immediate crisis that faced the Society. Mardy Murie, who had been on the Council for years, was amazed at the grasp Willi had of the problems, and how quickly he had gotten it.

The Tetons were Willi's youthful stomping grounds. He wasn't about to leave before seeing old places and old friends. He spent more than half a day talking with Jake Breitenbach's widow, Lou Breitenbach. Since Jake's death on Everest, Lou had had some bad years. Willi always had time for her.

"Will good triumph over evil?" Lou asked as they sat in the library of the Climber's Ranch, the bunklike accommodation run by the American Alpine Club.

"It has to do with Karma," Willi said, launching into a soliloquy about life and justice.

Rick Lou, the manager of the Climber's Ranch, sat listening. He couldn't imagine how anyone could ask such a question or try to answer it. He didn't take Willi's ideas seriously. He considered Willi a nice man but in some ways an anachronism.

Willi also went out to see Glenn Exum. Glenn was in declining health. They sat talking and reminiscing. Many years had passed since Willi had first been an Exum guide. They discussed Devi, raising a family, and how much the world had changed. When Willi was about to go he turned to his old boss and said, "You know, Glenn, my sons consider me a square."

Before leaving the Tetons Willi wanted to climb a mountain. He had been off crutches only a few weeks. The last thing he was supposed to do was go climbing, but Willi decided to give it a go. One morning Willi and Krag, who was already in the Tetons, went out to climb Baxter's Pinnacle. It was not an easy climb.

"Bill, I did it!" Willi exclaimed to Turnage upon his return to the ranch. "I can still do it! I can climb!"

"Jesus, that's not easy!" Turnage replied.

"No, it's not."

"How'd you do it, Willi?"

"I did it on my arms! My arms, Bill, my arms!"

Willi always began the academic year with a week in the wilderness. In September Willi took the new outdoor education program up to Mount Rainier for a retreat. Willi drove the Blue Jewel. The GMC Suburban wheezed its way up the asphalt highway. The old vehicle was crammed with as many of the eighty students as could fit in, the others piling in other cars. It was about seventy miles up to Rainier. They soon left the shopping centers of Olympia, the McDonald's, Pizza Huts, and Kentucky Fried Chickens stamped on the landscape; the mobile homes and little frame houses of the rural poor; the farms and ranches.

Ahead stood 14,410-foot Mount Rainier, rising almost 8,000 feet higher than any nearby peak. The Blue Jewel moved through the classic northwest forests of Douglas fir, red cedars, and western hemlock standing a good 200 feet above the damp, mossy fern-laden valley floor. Driving upward into the park itself, they felt the air grow cooler. The students with Willi could feel the great mystery and magic of the mountain wilderness.

At times Willi got tired always doing the outdoor education programs at Evergreen, but it was great getting up in the mountains again. Willi was excited because after enormous prodding Evergreen had hired a full-time outdoor educator to work with him. Lynn Hammond had the strong, lean, healthy look of a young outdoorswoman and a sweet, soothing manner. From the moment she had arrived on campus, and Willi had invited her over to share some of Jolene's fresh apple cake and tea, the two had talked for endless hours.

As much as Willi liked having Lynn Hammond, Willi figured that he could take on any faculty member and work him or her into what was *his* program. In the spring Willi had talked Diana Cushing, a psychologist, into joining the program for the year. Cushing appeared in her early forties. She was an attractive, nervous, cigarette-smoking woman who dressed with far more care than did most of her fellow teachers. In her life, the educator had gone on only two hikes, one of six miles, the other three miles. But Willi was the most persuasive of men. He had told Cushing that the outdoors was only the bait. Most of the time Cushing would be able to sit safely ensconced on campus. Willi also had lined up Frank Motley who was taking a quarter off from his work as a librarian. Motley was as shy as Willi was outgoing.

Willi's idea on these retreats was to get people to work together. To foster this he had developed service projects for the park. Near the park headquarters at Longmire, the group dug a ditch. Willi worked beside the students, wearing his old red wool shirt from Everest, his brow wet with sweat. Those Evergreeners who had done little physical work before soon had blisters.

"In Europe they put sap from trees on their hands," Willi said as he swung the pick again, plunging into yet another story about his first trip abroad.

The students tried keeping up with him, but no one did as much as fifty-one-year-old Willi. He was always there, telling stories, watching out for people. At night after supper he had even more stories to tell. Each day before dawn Willi woke up, turned on the Coleman lantern, got out of the tent, and let out a gigantic yodel.

One day after finishing the eighty-foot-long ditch, the group was sitting having lunch. Willi was discussing his hip operation in excruciating detail.

"Are you a man of steel, Willi?" a student asked.

"Only the hips," Willi said, gnawing on a salami sandwich.

"That sandwich is not only unorganic, Willi, it's unhealthy!"

Willi took another bite. "Some Evergreeners go organic. I've gone bionic."

Digging ditches was one thing. But Willi had come up with what appeared to be an impossible task. The Rangers had a number of enormous pyramid-shaped concrete blocks that had to be moved up the mountain as a foundation for a cabin. They had decided no one or nothing could move the blocks up six miles along a narrow trail. Until Willi came along, the Rangers were planning to use a helicopter. To Willi, though, this was the perfect project. It looked impossible. To do the job, people would have to work together.

The different ways people tried to move the blocks fascinated Willi. Among the Evergreeners were strong young men and women. But there were some rather frail students as well. Even for the strongest, carrying the two hundred-pound blocks proved a formidable job. Some of the students attempted dragging the blocks. Others carried them on two poles—four or five people on a pole. One young man tried hefting a block by himself. Another banged up his knee. One did not get back to camp until late in the evening.

Willi lifted as much as anyone. "What is Willi doing?" the students asked themselves. "What is he teaching?" "What is he trying to prove?" Some of them were incredibly impressed. Some were simply amazed. Some were amused. Some thought that something was wrong.

Hammond positively bubbled with enthusiasm. Cushing helped carry one of the blocks, but even as she did so, she felt less confidence in Willi and his judgment. She started to leave early, as she had told Willi she would. Willi tried to talk her into staying. She departed even more irritated. Watching her go Hammond thought that it was Cushing who wasn't playing fair, running off, not giving in to the experience, not doing her share.

One of the first things the group did on campus is what is known in Outward Bound as a "quiet walk." Everyone joined hands. Willi led the students around the wooded campus. The previous Saturday he and Lynn had scouted the territory. Willi took the students and the three other teachers along the tops of walls, moving across high railings, trying to scare them a little. Then he plunged off course into the wood, leading the group through a thicket of brush.

"My God, I'm lost," Willi said, plowing onward through the dense forest.

"Willi's lost," the word filtered down the line. "Keep your eyes out. Willi's lost!"

They were still on the Evergreen campus. They could not possibly get lost. But Willi made it seem as if they had wandered into a dark, unknown jungle.

Lynn and Willi were becoming very close. Each knew what the other was going to say. They broke into each other's sentences at will. Hammond had the ebullient, breathless enthusiasm for the wilderness that to Willi was the essence of life, an enthusiasm that back in the early days he and Jolene had expressed openly.

"I think every day at four we should have an hour of physical activity," Hammond said at the weekly outdoor education morning faculty meeting. She looked as if she were ready to jump up and do a hundred jumping jacks.

"I've got to be home with my daughter," Cushing said.

At these meetings Hammond and Willi rambled happily on about outdoor education. They didn't edit their exuberance. As often as not, when the noon hour rolled around, not all the important decisions had been made.

Cushing and Motley had other commitments, and they wanted to go. It irritated Cushing that so many of the decisions were made after she left. Although she mentioned this to Willi, things never seemed to change.

On one side, Willi had Hammond as full of optimism and energy about the program as Willi ever had been. She kept pushing him to get the students out in the wilderness, to live and learn experientially. On the other extreme he had Cushing. He had promised her she would not have to do very much outdoors.

Willi did very little but make promises. Hammond grew increasingly irritated at the psychologist, who she thought simply wasn't doing her share. Cushing couldn't understand what was going on.

She kept coming to Willi thinking they had worked things out, but finding out that he had gone ahead and done it his own way.

At Evergreen Willi offered his services to the most bedraggled and forlorn students. He spent hours with individual students coaxing, listening, sympathizing, guiding. This year, when Willi himself was sometimes feeling so low, they lined the corridor outside his office waiting to tell him their problems. On the weekends Willi had little respite. With Cushing and Motley lacking in outdoor skills, Willi and Hammond ended up leading most of the field trips.

In his seminar Willi said again and again that if the human race was to survive people had to learn to work together. The students might be learning climbing, volleyball, fencing, or gymnastics. What they really would be learning was how to live, how to care, and how to watch out for one another.

When two of the seminar members didn't show up for class, another student, Frank Kaplan, heeded Willi's message. He went and found the two students. Kaplan had dropped out of the State University of New York at Binghamton. He thought that Willi was wonderful, but couldn't understand what the man was doing teaching this program at Evergreen. "Why is Willi burdening himself with this crummy shit?" he asked himself. "These interminable big meetings with people talking for hours on end about learning how to learn. All the needy students. Much of the reading." Kaplan had never seen anyone living such a crisis-oriented life as Willi. He wanted to go in and talk to Willi, but the line was too long.

One day a group of students was out simulating a rope fall on one of the buildings. They had no acknowledged leader. There was danger involved. The Evergreeners decided not to risk it. Willi came by. "The problem is not the danger," Willi said even before hearing what had happened. "The problem is the egos of the group."

One of the students, Sean Downey, a dropout from Cornell, was amazed that Willi understood. Downey was very shy. The program was helping him get out of himself. He thought that all the hugging, feeling, caring, emoting was exaggerated enough to be insincere. But it made up for something lacking in most people's lives.

For all Willi's concerns for groups, in many respects he was alone at Evergreen. He almost always ate lunch with Hammond in his office. He brewed up some soup, scrounged one of her cookies, or the rest of her apple, eating it seed, core, and all.

"Lynn, this parenting is something," he exhaled one day.

"What do you mean, Willi?"

"Oh, Regon was over until one A.M. talking. I never can get him to come at reasonable hours. He always comes at ten and stays till one."

"You never ask him to come at reasonable hours," Hammond said earnestly. "You don't know how to draw a limit on your own son. You don't even try."

Willi talked a great deal about his colleague, Diana Cushing. Personally the psychologist was going through a difficult emotional period. Moreover, she felt the pressures of working in a program where she knew she didn't belong. She felt that Willi was a shameless manipulator. It was too much for her. She went to see Jeanne Hahn, the dean, to complain about Willi. Hahn was a great believer in Willi and his approach to outdoor education as well as a close personal friend of the Unsoelds. Even before the end of the quarter, Cushing dropped out of the year-long program that Hahn later called "the most troubled in our curriculum."

In November Willi flew to Los Angeles to do his Nanda Devi lecture for the Sierra Club. Close to a dozen American climbers had already died in the Himalayas in 1978. Willi criticized this new generation of climbers who "haven't learned or seemed unwilling to learn that there is as much gratification in the ascent as there is in the summit itself." He said that these devotees "seemed not to want to learn the basics of mountaineering, such as map reading, compass work, and survival skills."

Then, as he had done so many times before, Willi told the story of Nanda Devi. He stood alone on the dark stage. When he said how Devi had died his voice cracked. The audience sat in stunned silence broken only by the soft sobbing of a mother whose child had died on a mountain. Afterwards, Willi told a reporter for the *Los Angeles Times* that "his wife once held him responsible [for Devi's death] in a burst of anger."

On his next trip to Washington, D.C., Willi sat up all night at

Turnage's apartment in Alexandria talking about his life. He said that he now found a certain warmth and tenderness lacking in his marriage. He talked about what he might make of the days he had left.

"I don't know what I want to do now, Bill, what I can do?"

"Good God, Willi, that's ridiculous! What a book you could write, getting your ideas down. There are all kinds of possibilities!"

"I don't know," Willi sighed. "At Evergreen with these students. I don't know. I've got to find something."

"You've got so much!" Turnage said, bolstering Willi, thinking, however, that Devi's death had trivialized everything Willi believed. "Look what you're doing for the Wilderness Society and the environment. Don't you realize how much your presence means?"

"Well, yeah, I can appreciate that."

"Well, then what?"

"One thing's these kids at school. Everygreen's not the real world. That's all there is to it. And they don't realize it. What you're doing's the real world."

"Maybe." Turnage smiled. "But my staff's loaded down with these kids. They're so laid-back. The fact that we're about bankrupt doesn't faze them. It's no good. I've got some tough decisions to make and the first is going to be to unload a lot of them."

"That's not the way," Willi said adamantly. "Hold off. They'll catch on."

"I don't like it," Turnage said, shaking his head.

"You know if Devi were here. . . ."

Willi talked on and on about his daughter and his life.

"Jolene is fighting mad over that quote in the paper," Willi said.

"What about it?" Turnage asked.

"That I'd say that to the press."

"Well, does she?"

"Does she what?"

"Blame you for Devi's death."

Willi sighed. "I don't know. I'm just bothered that she might. I don't know. I just don't know."

Turnage felt the sadness pouring out of the man. Nothing in Willi's life seemed to be going for him the way he wanted. Turnage thought that as bad as things may get, Willi can't appear down; if he does he's afraid that Jolene and the family will think he's blaming himself for the death. UP! UP! UP! All Willi's life. UP! UP! UP! It wasn't Outward Bound. It was Upward Bound. Now Devi was dead and Willi was growing old.

Whenever the family got together, they spent hours discussing what to do about Worth Hedrick and his project. Hedrick had been in contact with film people in Los Angeles. Columbia Pictures Television wanted to make a feature-length television film about Devi. There would be a book involved as well, and Worth saw this as his salvation.

Over the Christmas holidays Regon, Krag, and Terres sat in the family room discussing what to do. They realized how much Willi had manipulated the family over Worth, pushing them into cooperating. Now when it came to the film, Willi had grown silent. He wandered in and sat down on the old sofa.

"Why haven't you said anything?" Terres asked, looking up from her pink cushion on the linoleum floor.

"It's not really very important, whether it comes out or not, whatever it is."

"What do you mean, Dad."

"I've transcended the whole thing," Willi said. When it came to dealing with human pain, Willi thought some people were like ostriches, sticking their heads in the sand avoiding it. Other people were like ducks in the rain, not avoiding pain but transcending it, letting the pain run off them.

After talking about Worth and the film for a while, the conversation turned to Devi and her death. It had been over two years since the accident. Never had the family sat down and openly discussed their own pain and agony.

"Why haven't you talked about it, Dad?" All these months Willi had bared his pain in public. "Why can't you cry *here?*"

"I just can't share it with you now."

"Why not?"

"I had to deal with the immediate pain when I was there, when Devi died in my arms, when I had to fight my way down the mountain. When I got back I talked with Mom a lot, but I've already worked that out now. I'm through it all. I'm on a new level of consciousness."

"Is this one of your philosophical techniques, playing the guru with your emotions?"

"Aren't you just copping out with your real feelings?"

Listening to this conversation, Terres felt immensely sad. When they had talked to Willi about taking a sabbatical and having time for himself, he hadn't seemed very enthusiastic. "Dad, are you waiting around to die!" she asked.

"Yeah, in a way that's what I'm doing. I'm waiting to die." Willi thought a moment. "Only it's not that I'm sitting around. I'll continue working at Evergreen. Day-to-day things are still important. But I've reached all my lifetime goals. I've reached the physical goal of climbing, of working my body to the limits. I've reached the spiritual goals, the most important being how I communicate with people, how I give myself in trust and support. I can't be any more sensitive or any more giving than I am now."

As Terres heard these words, she began to cry. Normally, she would have given Willi a hard time for sounding conceited. But what he said rang true.

"But I would like to share this experience of Devi's death with one of you," Willi continued, looking down at his daughter. "I do look forward to that, but none of you are ready for it now."

"Yeah, I don't think any of us are ready yet, but I think I'm pretty close," Terres said.

Willi smiled.

Willi began the new year by flying east to the annual Wilderness Society staff meeting held at Coolfont, West Virginia. Normally he enjoyed these trips, but he had a lot of work ahead of him for the new quarter at Evergreen. Moreover, he knew that he would have tough business to deal with at Coolfont. Bill Turnage was the fifth executive director of the Wilderness Society in thirty-three months. The organization had been sucked dry financially and was becoming the weak sister of the environmental movement. Turnage had entered office two months ago with a mandate to clean house, hire new staff, and end the horrendous deficits. Willi had asked Turnage to give the old staff a chance and hold off firing anybody until the employees had ample opportunity to prove themselves. Willi was the one person trusted and admired both by council members and by the young staff.

Dee Frankfourth, one of Willi's former students, was a leader among the staff at the Wilderness Society. Many of the staff would have fit in at Evergreen. They looked upon Willi as their savior. They knew enough about Willi's philosophy to believe that he would abhor what Turnage was doing. The staff had worked long and hard for little pay; now they felt Turnage was pushing them aside. People at the Society had always worked together; now they believed Turnage was taking all the power into his own hands. They considered the new executive director secretive and arbitrary, an elitist of the first order.

Willi believed that what was going on was a fundamental debate over what kind of organization could best serve the goal of saving the wilderness. Turnage had strong elements of Willi's idealism in him but he was equally a practical, ambitious man in a city of practical, ambitious men. He wasn't about to run the Wilderness Society like a commune where everyone had an equal say. To Turnage the laid-back breathless style of the young staff might have been fine at Evergreen, but it was preventing him from creating a lean, efficient organization.

At the meeting, Willi got up to make his position clear. "What the Wilderness Society is experiencing is a loss of innocence," he said, lining up firmly behind Turnage. Not for a moment would the young staff members tolerate that. They came back at Willi.

"You're reminiscent of people at Evergreen," Willi replied. "You're living in an ivory tower."

Dee Frankfourth could hardly believe what she heard. She felt betrayed. She had been responsible for suggesting Willi's name for the council. Then Willi had worked to get Turnage appointed. She waited to talk to Willi privately.

"You've brought in this man who's a czar, Willi," she cried. "That's what you've done."

"Don't you understand?" Willi countered. "Evergreen's a laboratory. It's not the real world. It's a fantasy land. It's make-believe."

"You're looking at the ideal sort of person Evergreen turns out," Frankfourth continued. "They're dealing with a tough reality. They're taking these hard knocks and doing good, creating more wilderness. They're adults who're putting a lot of Evergreen ideals into reality."

"You're evading reality," Willi said, not pulling back an iota. "The Wilderness Society is not a family. It's an organization trying to do a political job. It requires a very different sort of system and operation."

"You're wrong, Willi."

With Willi's support Turnage began to get rid of the old staff, bring in new people, and turn the Wilderness Society into a growing, efficient, financially solvent organization where the spirit of Evergreen wasn't relevant.

To catch his plane Willi had to leave the conference early. Putsie Jackson offered to give him a ride to Dulles Airport in Virginia. Jackson had just gone to work for the Wilderness Society. Meeting Willi for the first time she was impressed by his enormous *joie de vivre*. They were of the same generation. As she cruised along country roads leading to Virginia, they exchanged life stories.

"My father coached a women's ski team from Denver," Jackson said. "He was caught in an avalanche once."

"What a horrible way to die!" Willi exclaimed.

Willi talked about his early life and then discussed his children. "I wish they were happier," he said. "Regon, the eldest, cooked Christmas dinner for a bunch of deadbeats. I was proud but it was kinda sad. He just hasn't put his life together. Krag, the younger one, hasn't either. I'm happy for Terres, though, she's an actress. And, Devi, why she's just so special, so full of happiness and joy." Willi went on talking about Devi.

"What's she doing now?" Jackson asked.

"Well, I guess I have to tell you. She's dead," Willi said, tears flowing from his eyes. Choking up he told about the accident.

When they arrived at Dulles, Jackson pulled the car up beside Saarinen's glassed terminal. Willi continued talking about his dead daughter with infinite tenderness. "Devi was an achiever, and she'll always be an achiever because she died so young," he said.

As Willi got up to leave, he turned toward Jackson. "I hope I wasn't boring you, but it makes me feel better talking about Devi." Then he patted the woman on the shoulders and walked into the terminal.

At Evergreen the outdoor education program headed out for a retreat to plan the new quarter. One new student, Ian Yolles, had come all the way from Antioch College in Yellow Springs, Ohio, to study under Willi. Willi told the students that their first and biggest task was to accept the new people, to make them feel a part of the group.

One of the new faculty members was James Gulden. A few years back Willi had defined Gulden as "the boat builder." Although Gulden had a master's degree in counseling psychology from the California State College at Los Angeles, he was indeed a boat builder, as much a man of the earth and water as Willi was a man of the mountain and sky. Whereas in recent years Willi had fought to return Evergreen to its high utopian ideas, Gulden was all for bringing the school down to earth, teaching things like vocational education, practical courses for the people of southwest Washington.

Gulden was thirty-eight years old. He was of moderate height, with flaxen hair, a small mouth, large blue eyes that looked like tears set on their side, a squat nose, and a body that appeared both hard and soft. He had worked as a laborer and logger, taught at the penitentiary, built his own house. Though he was comfortable sitting downtown in a bar lifting a few Olympia or Rainier beers with some of his working-class buddies, he also had a refined, almost feline quality as well.

The big decisions at the retreat involved the major field trip projects around which much of the learning for the quarter would center. Inevitably, Willi decided upon a trip to the mountains. With Gulden's interest in boats and water, it was natural for him to lead a group going to Vancouver Island. Hammond decided upon a desert trip to the Canyonlands National Park.

The other new faculty member, William H. Brown, signed on for a visit to Baja California. Brown was a quiet, handsome black geographer with a Ph.D. from Berkeley. He was very academically oriented and not particularly interested in the outdoors. Willi had told Brown that what they were teaching in the program could be taught anywhere.

By far the most popular project was Willi's mountain journey. The students discussed where the group might go. "It's important to have a goal," Willi said. "The goal itself is not important."

"What about a winter climb of Mount Rainier?" one student suggested.

"Well, that would be an Himalayan-type experience," Willi said, nodding his head. "Pretty close to an Himalayan climb."

The more Willi talked about Rainier the more the students were drawn to the idea. It would be almost like climbing Everest, or part of Everest.

"We might get up to Rainier and spend ten days in the parking lot at Paradise," Willi said. "That's a real possibility."

While Willi talked, one of the more experienced climbers in the group whispered: "You know how dangerous this is? There's a real chance someone could get injured or killed."

Those students who decided to go on the climb knew that they were doing something real. Some of them were so gung-ho that they would have strapped on their crampons right then and there, grabbed an ice axe, and headed up. Others listened with dry-mouthed excitement and fear that made them feel alive and vital. Bob Dash, who had transferred from New Hampshire in part to study under Willi, felt scared. What worried Yolles was that as passionately and eloquently as Willi was speaking, the students could have no idea what was involved in a winter climb. It was an incredible challenge. Enormous amounts of snow fall on the mountain each winter. The weather is fierce and unpredictable. There are avalanches and whiteouts. It was a major undertaking even for an expert mountaineer.

The first piece of reading for the quarter was a short essay lauding the virtue of risk. Hammond had chosen the piece. She did not consider the idea of challenge and risk the end-all, be-all of the program. But it was important. She believed in it. Willi believed even more in a philosophy of risk, and both he and Hammond led seminars based on the reading.

Gulden attacked the whole idea passionately. "It's an upper-middle-class point of view," Gulden told his students. "It shows what a decadent society this is that people can't find challenges in their own lives and have to go seeking them."

No idea stood so opposed to everything Gulden was and felt as this one. He would have been against the idea anyway, even before the events of the previous year. The past spring he had taught in a program designing and building a scientific research vessel. At a party, a student had drowned when he had paddled out to help a floundering sailboat and his canoe overturned.

Gulden had spent much of his time and energy in the fall building a new house. In December a driver arrived with a load of cinder blocks. Gulden watched as the driver maneuvered a boom load of blocks with a control box. The boom struck a 7,200-watt power line. Flames and smoke flared up from the driver's hands.

Gulden picked up a two-by-four and hit the box. The shock carried up the board and almost knocked him out. Gulden smelled the seared flesh. He hit him again and again. When the man dropped the box and fell to the ground Gulden knelt beside him and applied heart compressions on his burned chest. The man lived on as a vegetable.

In previous years Willi had worked with people whose ideas

clashed with his at Evergreen, but never had he faced such an antagonist as Gulden. Though he had an ego of his own, the psychology teacher fancied himself one of life's little people. Hammond wanted to do something to bring the faculty team together. She suggested at a faculty meeting that was attended by students that Gulden and Brown move their offices down next to Willi's and hers.

"I've been in my office for six years!" Gulden said. "And I'm not about to move."

"You don't understand how that helps us work together, Jim," Willi said.

"You're just trying to dictate."

"Hey, I'm the one who brought this up," Hammond said finally. "What I'm realizing is that you guys are trying to work out your pecking order and I don't even count. I'm female."

Never before had so many unhappy students camped in front of Willi's door as this quarter. He had little respite at home. Jolene was busier than ever. Neither son had been much interested in studying, but Regon was finally close to getting a degree. He went ahead and took an individual program in forest management. Krag couldn't make up his mind which program he wanted to take. Willi had spent hours counseling him. Terres was still in Seattle working in a natural foods store to earn enough money to study drama at New York University. She had been making only about $300 a month.

Willi knew that he had to get in shape for the Rainier climb. But he hadn't had time even for one workout. In January he had made another trip to the Wilderness Society in Washington, D.C. At the end of the month Willi went up to spend a weekend with some students at Reflection Lake on Rainier. He hadn't wanted to go, but Gulden had raised a fuss about the students going up alone. Willi had decided that he had better make the journey. He had carried a pack and slept in a snow cave.

Willi was having all kinds of arguments with Gulden. The psychology teacher could still smell the stench of death. Again and again he took on Willi over the issue of risk. For Gulden it was one thing to play games of risk in an Outward Bound program where people knew what they were getting into. It was quite another matter in a college program. He didn't mind the students taking risks per se, even climbing a mountain, as long as they were not going out to experience risk as a pedagogical tool.

Although Gulden attacked Willi and his ideas, he felt sorry for the man. In all his teaching days, he had never seen such a sad group of students as in the outdoor education program. He watched them feeding off Willi, insisting that he be their hero, always witty and charming, insisting that he pump them up until he was empty inside.

Gulden came to Willi one day. "I love you, Willi," Gulden said. Even as he said it, he was amazed at his words. He didn't even say such things to his own family. "Look, Willi, you're one of God's children and you're having a hard time. You got these kids on you. You're unhappy and you're in a real jam."

"Jim, I don't think you understand."

"Willi, I see you trying to cope. I know how much you feel. I care for you. It's your ideas and strategy I object to. You have to understand that."

"Jim, I like the way you stand up to me. I'm glad you care."

At 10:00 P.M. on the twelfth of February 1979 Willi typed a letter to his eighty-five-year-old mother on some stationery he had taken from Lost Creek Ranch in Jackson Hole. "Oh Mither o' Mine—but Ah'm just plain tahrd! Somehow things have kinda gotten away from me here during these last two months." For a single-spaced page and a half, Willi ran down the litany of problems, everything from faculty and students, the Wilderness Society, to the situation at home with Regon and Krag. He told his mother that he was very tired but that as long as he could remember he and Jolene hadn't been to sleep before midnight. He said that he was becoming too old to keep such a pace.

The next evening Willi gave his Everest lecture at Evergreen. "I'd really like to wind this one up, the 179th occasion for this sterling presentation," Willi began, his voice streaked with fatigue. "The peculiar thing about Mount Everest is that once you've climbed it you're never allowed to forget it and it hangs around your neck

like a great leaden albatross. Everywhere you go you're talking
Mount Everest. It presents you with something of a challenge to
keep any anticipation in you alive at all.''

Willi looked at the audience. ''Stevens suggested to me that I
might want to make a——'' Willi stumbled. ''What was it, Tom?
I'm getting so old.''

''A comparison between your expedition and the 1978 expedition
of K2.''

''Ah, I remember now. K2. Now what I'd really like to talk to
you about,'' Willi went on over the laughter. ''Well, you gotta come
for some reason because Mount Everest is fifteen years old, sixteen
years old. That's ancient history. I suspect we can't even remember
what it was like . . . and back in 1963 the mountains were very
young comparatively.''

Willi talked about the way the climbers had been chosen for the
Everest expedition. It was not merely raw climbing ability but character that had mattered. ''I feel there is a definite shift in, I don't
know what you call it, the underpinnings, the automatic standard
assumptions that you bring with you to the mountain,'' Willi said.

The 1978 American expedition to K2 was led by Jim Whittaker,
who of all Willi's comrades on Everest had the most affinity with
the new generation of mountaineers. Two members of the Nanda
Devi expedition two years before were on the climb: Lou Reichardt
and John Roskelley. When Reichardt and Jim Wickwire, a Seattle
climber, reached the 28,250-foot summit, Reichardt headed down
by himself long before his partner. Wickwire had to bivouac alone
at about 28,000 feet, the same height at which Willi, Tom, Lute,
and Barrell had spent the night outside on Everest. Staggering down
the next morning, beard caked with ice, face haggard, Wickwire
ran into Roskelley and Rick Ridgeway, a California climber and
writer, heading up to the summit.

''Jim Wickwire is now going snow blind,'' Willi said. ''. . .
He's munching down, really in sad shape . . . and here comes the
second team going up.

'' 'Oh, Jim, how are you doing? You're going to make it down.
Is the high camp okay?'

"What do you expect a guy like Wickwire to say? 'Help me.' No, in a pig's eye—'I've got one leg left. I can hobble. It's okay, guys, I'll make it.'

" 'Good. Glad to hear it. We'll see you when we come back . . .'

"I can't help but comment on that. I think times have changed. We'll see a similar situation on Everest . . . and an extremely different resolution. Somehow the social matrix has been altered and the day of the individual has become rampant, even in Himalayan climbers. I merely make an observation that has cosmic consequences."

Brown and Gulden were sitting one day talking with Willi about the impact he had on students.

"This society needs heroes and you're it," Gulden said. "With it comes all the responsibilities."

"And all the tragedies," Brown said, thinking that Willi seemed to like the idea that even Gulden considered him a hero.

"So many of these kids are devoid of a sense of meaning," Willi commented. "They look for it anywhere. I know that. It's something I deal with all the time."

"You've got an enormous responsibility," Brown said.

"Yeah, society puts people in these big shoes and they begin to believe it," said Gulden, taking another neat jab at Willi and his vanity.

Hammond also looked to Willi as a hero. "I don't want your agapeic love that's an act of will," she told him. "I want to feel validated as a person. I don't want to feel you're giving the same kind of agapeic love to me that you're giving to everyone!"

"How pompous of you!" Willi exclaimed. Even members of his own family doubted a love that went not only to them but to all humanity.

"Don't you see, Willi? What we're trying to do is create happy people who then can reach out with love toward other people. But if we create this false sort of love that people *will*, they won't be able to sustain it underneath."

"It's a training, a discipline, it doesn't come easy," Willi said.

"It becomes manipulative, Willi. Look, I can't tell how straight you are with me. How much I'm just one of those people you tell what you think they want to hear or what you think they need to hear. I can't tell how much your affection for me is this agapeic stuff and how much is for *me*."

As the quarter went on Willi was opening up to Hammond as he had not before. They had much to talk about. Their problems with Brown and Gulden loomed even larger than those with Cushing in the fall. From their perspective Brown was not doing his job; not only wasn't he interested in the subject, but he was putting in less than the minimal effort. As they saw it Gulden was working harder but was so bitterly antagonistic to Willi that he dissipated whatever positive impact he might have had.

As the month of February moved ahead, Willi had less time to deal with Brown and Gulden. The climb was almost upon them. As Willi thought it would, the climb had gotten many of the Ever-greeners moving. Students were sewing outerboots. Others were getting the food and equipment together. Students were working out. But, as he wrote his mother, he "rate[d] their preparation as still marginal."

Greg Thayer came to see Willi. The twenty-two-year-old student was probably the most experienced climber in the mountain group. He had attended two climbing schools, the American Avalanche Institute and climbed in Alaska and Colorado. He was one of the people Willi would depend upon on the mountain. He was strong and outgoing. He was getting worried. Thayer thought that Willi seemed distant. Willi had left so much to the group and Thayer didn't think there had been enough physical conditioning.

"You think they know what they're getting into, Willi?" Thayer asked. "You think they know what's involved in a winter's climb of Rainier?"

"It's up to *you*, Greg," Willi sighed. "Up to *you*, not just me to see that they know. It's a group."

"I'm worried about the group's momentum. You know, 'wow, man, gonna climb Rainier.' "

"Well?"

"I think they're being carried away by the whirlwind of your experience."

"That's a given!" Willi said emphatically. "I try to play that down."

"I know you do," Thayer said, shaking his head. "These are my friends. I don't want to get stuck up there. I don't think I'm gonna go."

"Don't be a crumbhead!"

"No, I'm not going."

Thayer was in Gulden's seminar. All quarter long he had heard the psychology teacher harping about risk. Gulden had an ominous sense about the winter's expedition. The trip epitomized everything he disliked about Willi's ideas, everything he disliked about many of the students. As the days went on, he became obsessed with Willi and the climb. On a Sunday drive three weeks before the weeklong trip, he turned to his wife: "I know somebody's gonna die up there."

Over half the students scheduled to go on the climb had, by their own admission, no or limited practical climbing experience. Only about six of the twenty-five or so students had good or intermediate experience; they, for the most part, made up the leadership cadre. Willi could reasonably have turned down a dozen of the students for one reason or another, but that had never been his way.

Willi would like to have spent more time with the group before the climb the last weekend in February. But he was swamped with work and students. He never got away until late. After dinner he had correspondence, student papers, letters of recommendation to write, Jolene and her endeavors to discuss, Regon and Krag to talk with, as well as speaking engagements.

When the mountain group headed up to the Nisqually Glacier on Rainier the next to the last weekend in February for some last-minute practice, Willi was tired. Skiing toward the immense 300-foot thick glacier, he kept falling further and further behind. Hammond, who had joined the group for the weekend, asked two of the students to fall back with Willi, but not to let him know what they were doing. She didn't want to hurt his pride.

"The Cascades are the death of the individual in the winter,"

Willi told the group when they reached the campsite. "You can't do it alone."

The weekend was cold, blustery, miserable. Willi spent a lot of time with Hammond in a two-person tent. Willi was having problems with his hips and shoulders. "I could swallow this strongest pain pill, if I wanted to," Willi said. "But I like having it in reserve. I know I can still take it as long as I don't take the strongest one."

The dampness penetrated into the tent itself. Hammond's sleeping bag became wet and clammy. "You better take a pee before we sleep," Willi said.

"*I* don't have to take a pee," Hammond said, thinking of Willi who prided himself on being able to hold his bladder all day.

"No, go ahead," Willi said, pulling down the zipper on the tent. When Hammond got back Willi had exchanged sleeping bags so that she could be warm and dry.

"Lynn, if I make it up to Muir next week," Willi said, referring to the cabins part way up Rainier, "I won't come up the mountain again. I'll turn in my hat. And then those academicians are gonna get me in their clutches. And it's gonna be horrible. It's so much more fun to work with people's bodies than their minds. And I know it doesn't work as well."

On the trip back to Olympia, the group stopped at a restaurant outside the park gates for Willi's favorite: homemade blueberry pie à la mode. When he had finished Willi licked the plate and looked up.

"Pass 'em down," Willi said, proceeding to lick over a dozen other plates, cleaning them like a kitten.

"You got a method, Willi!" Hammond laughed. "You start from the outside and work in so you never get your beard dirty."

"Yep," Willi said, licking away.

Driving home, Willi held forth. Yolles sat next to Willi. Since Yolles was spending only one quarter at Evergreen, he always tried to get next to Willi in the Blue Jewel. With a beard that tufted his chin and cheeks, narrow-set eyes, large nose, and delicate birdlike bones, Yolles looked like one of the Smith Brothers on the old cough-drop packages.

Yolles listened as Willi quoted something from his favorite philosopher.

"Who is your favorite philosopher?" asked a student.

"Old Webb."

Yolles thought of all the philosophers whose names he knew. He couldn't place Webb. He wasn't about to ask either.

Willi cocked his head toward Yolles. "I can tell your problem, Ian." Willi winked.

"I know. I know. I don't know who old Webb is."

That set Willi off telling about old Webb from the fine Western novel *Moontrap* by Don Berry. Webb was one of the last of the free mountain men. He had lived in harmony with the earth and the spirits. He had killed only what he could eat. He had moved alone through great forests, trapping for a living. His friends were either dead or had settled down. Life as he had known and loved it was all over. New men were taking over the Oregon territory—shopkeepers, lawyers, farmers, politicians. "It was something that he could not understand, this mindless violation of what existed and was good; the insensate drive to make the world conform to man's size and comprehension."

Webb was only forty-five, but he was an ancient graybeard of the mountains. He had lived a rich, deep life, joyous and dangerous, free as an eagle. But his kind of life was over. He decided it was time to die. He killed one of the new men and climbed a mountain from which he could see clear to Mount Hood and Mount Rainier. The new men followed him up the mountain. On the summit old Webb charged the new men and they shot him dead.

When Willi and the students got back from Nisqually, they had a meeting. Though he didn't say it openly, Kaplan was upset that everyone was being allowed to go on the Rainier climb. Moreover, he felt that there hadn't been enough preparation. "I think we should have stayed up there another day, Willi," Kaplan said.

"I'm tired," Willi answered, his voice tinged with disgust. "If you wanted to stay up there you should have done it."

Kaplan realized that he wasn't giving a positive suggestion. Like so many of the students, he was only draining Willi.

The group would leave on Sunday. Willi needed time to relax. But he had so many students coming to him. Willi could never say no. On Tuesday he gave his Masherbrum talk at the college. He told the students that he had promised Jolene he would be at home and asked them to write her a letter. Nobody did it, though. Willi gave a rip-roaring, emotional speech that transported the audience to the mountain. On Thursday he agreed to chair a panel discussion on the Forest Service. He hadn't wanted to do it but the students said they were stuck.

As the day for the departure drew near, Gulden became even more obsessed with Willi and the climb. Again and again he discussed the expedition with Brown. Gulden decided to call Pete Sinclair, the other top climber at Evergreen.

"I wonder about Willi," Gulden said. "I wonder whether he should be going up there with all those students. I want you to check it out," Gulden went on, his voice cracking.

"I'm not prepared to make that judgment," Sinclair said evenly. Willi was one of Sinclair's heroes. He thought that Willi had become trapped in his role at Evergreen. Willi was scheduled to teach with Sinclair in the fall in a marine studies program. That was one new direction for Willi.

"I'm worried, Pete," Gulden said, starting to cry, "worried what may happen up there. I want you to talk to Willi."

"Okay," Sinclair said, though he was not about to second-guess a man of Willi's stature.

Thursday at their faculty meeting Willi and Gulden got into a fierce discussion. While Brown and Hammond listened, Gulden pounded at Willi, tearing away at his ideas of risk, Willi hammering back, pounding at Gulden. When Hammond left to take a long distance phone call, the three men hardly noticed.

"What will happen if something happens to you up there?" Gulden asked, relentless in his argument. "Have you ever thought of that?"

"I've got a leadership cadre," Willi said, spitting out the names of the students.

"Willi, it is wrong. It's wrong for you to use your charisma, your authority as a teacher to lead these kids into risk!''

"I know what I'm doing," Willi said. "I've been doing this all my life, and I know what it does for people. I know what it gives people. You are just incapable of understanding!''

"My God, Willi, haven't you ever been wrong? Haven't you ever made a mistake?''

Willi looked at Gulden a moment. Then he began sobbing. "My daughter's dead! Devi's dead! I watched my daughter dying in my arms!''

As Willi continued weeping, Gulden noticed that Brown was staring at him as if he were some kind of a monster. Gulden had been thinking of going to talk to Jeanne Hahn, the dean, or even to Dan Evans, the president, to see about stopping the climb. But Gulden began doubting what he was doing. There was nothing else to say or do. Soon afterwards, Brown and Gulden departed.

While Willi sat alone writing a few notes on a pad, Hammond returned to the office. "Oh, they've left," she said. "Well, I've got a meeting of our group right now, packing the food for our trip.''

Willi looked blankly at Hammond. "I need you to sit down and listen to me. Close the door.''

"Okay, Willi.''

"I just did something you're not gonna believe," Willi said, shaking his head.

"What?" Hammond asked, suddenly serious.

"With Jim I wanted to win so badly, so badly.''

"I don't understand.''

"I told Jim about Devi. I said I watched my daughter dying in my arms. I used my daughter, Lynn. I've never . . . I would never . . . never. . . .''

In the evening, before moderating the panel discussion, Willi walked into the college cafeteria and had dinner with Yolles. "Jim and I just had another one of those discussions, Ian," Willi said.

"What happened?" the former Antioch student asked. He had thought that listening to the faculty discussions was going to be one of the best parts of the program. But about all the four teachers had done was to argue.

Willi told Ian how Gulden had criticized the trip. "You're my ace in the hole," Willi said.

On Friday, the last day on campus before the climb, Willi had many details to worry about. It was even later than usual when he left. Walking out he passed Richard Jones.

"Dick, I got this situation," Willi said, telling the psychologist about a former Evergreen student who was getting a divorce, coming up from Los Angeles to get help from Willi.

Jones thought that Willi was a natural as a counselor. But he had a few suggestions. "That's terrific," Willi said excitedly. "I'll do it."

Saturday morning the Unsoelds sat in the living room discussing Worth Hedrick and the movie project. A few days before, a contract had arrived from Columbia Pictures Television. Terres was down in San Francisco auditioning but Willi, Jolene, Regon, and Krag were all taking part. It would be terribly disappointing to Hedrick but the Unsoelds were going to give Columbia a flat-out no.

To come to that decision was a draining, exhausting, endless process. When Bob Dash appeared at the door to borrow some boots for the climb, he waited for a break in the discussion. Then Willi and Regon led him downstairs to go through the climbing gear.

"Here's a note for Jolene, Willi," Dash said, pulling out a card. Willi read the note that apologized for all the times the students had pulled Willi away from Jolene: "The amazing thing is Willi's willingness to give to others (in the true agapeic sense that has become clear this quarter). This provides a heartwarming model for any to admire, though I'm afraid it can at times be rather challenging to both him and you."

"Why don't you take it up?" Willi said.

"Okay, Willi," Dash said, though this was the first time he had met Jolene.

As Jolene read the letter, she began to cry. Willi stood behind his wife holding her in his arms. Jolene walked forward and hugged Dash. When the student left Willi gave him a big salute.

As the rain picked up outside, Brown had become more and more worried. He was no climber, but he was a meteorologist. It was going to be a very bad storm. He hadn't said much before, but he shared Gulden's misgivings. He decided to call Jeanne Hahn.

"Jeanne, I'm really concerned about the weather," Brown said. "It just doesn't look good."

"Willi knows what he's doing," the dean said. "If it's bad, they'll stop."

ᎳᎳᎳᎳᎳᎳᎳᎳᎳᎳᎳᎳᎳᎳᎳᎳᎳᎳᎳᎳᎳᎳᎳᎳᎳᎳᎳᎳᎳᎳᎳᎳᎳᎳ

The caravan of vehicles wended its way up toward Mount Rainier on a gray, hazy Sunday morning. As the vehicles neared the park entrance at Sunshine Point, they passed Roger's Golden Age of Mountaineering, Nisqually Park cabin sites, stores, motels, restaurants, and other forms of commerce that had not been there when Willi had first climbed 14,410-foot Rainier, the mountain the Indians call Takhoma, the mountain that is God.

The mountains of the Northwest had mothered Willi, nourishing his ideas and feelings. It was late winter now, February 25, a time of change. From the long, cold months the snows lay heavy and deep on Rainier. The winter storms were dying but they could blow themselves out in one last convulsive rage of wind, snow, and blizzard.

From the Nisqually entrance (elevation 2,003 feet) the road turned abruptly upward the last few miles to the Ranger station at Paradise. Rainier is the center of the largest glacier system in the continental United States, more than thirty-five square miles of ice, the fourteen glaciers reaching out on all sides of the volcanic cone like the legs of silver spiders. Six of the glaciers begin at the cone of Rainier. The others begin lower down where they feed off the heavy winter snowfalls and the avalanches that thunder down from higher on the mountain.

This late in winter so much snow lay on the ground that the snow and the glaciers blended into one another. The park was a universe of white, the snow heaped in great drifts, the road tunneling through the whiteness like a thin, black serpent.

Arriving at the Visitor Center at Paradise (elevation 5,400 feet) Willi and the group saw that the three-story-high building was covered up to its roof in snow. In the parking lot Willi met Yvon Chouinard, the best-known ice climber in America and his old friend.

"It's bad up there," Chouinard said. "We're coming on down."

"We're going up the mountain, Yvon," Willi said to the diminutive climber dressed in down jacket and rain gear.

"These are some of the worst avalanche conditions I've ever seen," the climber said. As Chouinard spoke, he looked at Willi's group and thought them a pretty ragged-looking lot to be going up Rainier.

"We've got food for eight to ten days," Willi said. "We'll just wait it out."

It had been snowing for days. The snow had become wet and heavy. Chouinard had heard avalanches going off all around. As he headed out of the park, his car was stopped when an avalanche spread across the road.

In the wilderness of snow, the circular Visitor Center appeared a beleaguered outpost. The group tromped inside, the snow melting from their boots and parkas. The park Rangers, in general, viewed these Evergreen mini-expeditions with less than total delight. Large, inexperienced groups were always potential problems. But there was something about these "Greenies," breathless, bright-eyed, full of themselves, that rankled some of the Rangers. In a previous year there had already been a close call with people from Evergreen.

A dozen of the students followed Willi into the small room that served as the Rangers' office. Willi told Ranger William W. Swift, a park naturalist, that the Evergreen expedition intended to go up Rainier by one of the standard routes. First, they would trek to Camp Muir, a group of buildings sitting on a rock saddle at the beginning of the upper Cowlitz Glacier. From there they would traverse the Ingraham Glacier to Disappointment Cleaver, an island of rocks to the far side of the glacier. The route led up Disappointment Cleaver, moving up to the crater rim.

"What kind of shape is the group in?" asked Swift, who loaned Willi a five-watt Park Service radio.

"I'm probably the worst, Bill. I haven't worked out in about a year."

"Have you thought about the direct route through Cadaver Gap?" Swift asked, mentioning the passage directly from Camp Muir through an indented, snowy notch to Gibraltar Rock.

"Yeah, I've considered it," Willi said. "Just have to decide when we get there."

"You should consider the possibility of avalanches," Swift said. "That way the danger's extreme."

Willi got the group together to talk about what to do in an avalanche, swimming with the snow, getting rid of packs. The students listened as if their lives might be at stake. Winter climbs of Mount Rainier were relatively new. In the period between 1922 and 1965 there had been only two recorded winter ascents of Rainier, one of them a solo climb ending in death. Since then many climbs had been made in the winter but it was still, as Willi suggested, about as close an approximation to a Himalayan climb as one could find in the continental United States.

In midafternoon Willi, the twenty-seven students, and Nancey Goforth, a former student, moved up out of the parking lot. Goforth, a close friend of the Unsoeld family, was coming up as far as 10,000-foot Camp Muir to watch out for Willi. She was supposed to carry his pack and see that he didn't push himself and his hips too far. The U.S. Forest Service had called the avalanche danger "extreme."

In the summer, the four-mile journey up to Muir took three to six hours. This afternoon the group moved only several hundred yards and pitched their tents. It was snowing hard, the wind blowing. During the night the center pole of one of the tents snapped.

Morning dawned foggy and blustery. They headed upward, pushing through the foul weather. Suddenly the day grew even grayer until it was as dark as night. Willi and the students near him stood there ohhing and ahhing at their good fortune of being up here during an eclipse of the sun.

The second night the expedition slept in snow caves near Panorama Point, still less than halfway to Muir. Inside the white caves the world was muffled, warm, and damp. Goforth, Janie Diepenbrock, and Willi shared one cave. Diepenbrock had been planning to go to the desert, but Willi's presence had drawn her to Rainier. As Willi had learned in his seminar, Janie was a strong young woman who had grown in confidence and self-awareness. She had written that her ultimate goal was "to come to terms with death because all fear stems from the instinct of self-preservation. If we can lose that fear, we will gain ultimate freedom." When Janie was outside, Willi told stories about her and how she had grown these past months. When Willi was outside, the two women talked about him, drawing from the endless repertory of Willi stories.

The next day it was snowing too hard to go on up toward Muir. But a small group led by Willi decided to take a toboggan loaded with supplies further up the mountain. Wearing his old green parka, orange hat, his beard laced with ice and snow, Willi looked like the old man of the mountains. Suddenly, Willi's whole face flashed with joy. Above for a brief moment the clouds had parted, revealing the round summit of Rainier.

In the morning when the whole group headed up once again toward Muir, one of the students left and walked back to Paradise by himself. The young man was one of the most troubled of the students. Willi had thought the climb might do him some good. Instead, he had copped out, jeopardizing not only himself but the whole group. Even Willi was angry. Later in the day Goforth turned back, taking with her three other students who had also had enough of Rainier.

Slogging up toward Muir, Dash and two other students led the party, moving through the swirling, trackless snows. Dash was wearing the boots Willi had worn on Masherbrum, and the over-boots he had worn on the top of Everest. Dash felt they had a special, magical energy.

"Wearing your boots I feel like I'm floating, Willi," Dash said as he moved upward through the storm.

"Yeah, they can smell the summit."

When the lead party reached the entrance to the public cabin at Muir, Willi went back to help the slower students. By the time he returned with the last stragglers, the day had become bright and brilliant, the sun sparkling on the pure snow. Willi and four of the students stood outside the cabin, looking upward, their arms around one another.

All it ever took for Willi was to get above 10,000 feet to feel right with the world. He went stomping through the cabin, telling stories of other climbs and other climbers, stirring up the students with his great good humor. Soon the dank old cabin was cluttered with drying socks, cans of food, packs, ropes, and happy chatter. In the morning some of the strongest students, including Diepen-brock, headed down to bring up the supplies left below on the toboggan at Moon Rocks.

It was such a marvelously clear day that in the afternoon Willi and six students did a reconnaissance. They moved up the upper Cowlitz Glacier to the top of Cadaver Gap. Up here they could see to the crest of the summit, and all the way down to Muir.

Dash was stunned by the beauty of the mountain.

"Let him stay there awhile," Willi said. "He's drinking in the wondrous sights."

Then the seven of them headed down Cadaver Gap, whooping and hollering, running down the mountain. That evening almost everyone was in an exuberant mood. While they sat in sleeping bags preparing to go to sleep one of the students kept thinking of all those slides of his toes Willi had shown during his Everest lecture.

"Hey, Willi, let's see your feet!"

"Sure, I'll show you my feet!" Everyone crowded around Willi laughing and giggling as he whipped off his socks.

The climb had started out five days before under fierce unwelcoming conditions. The students had survived. They felt increasingly at home on Rainier. The avalanche danger had lessened. Friday morning dawned bright and clear, the second perfect day in a row. The weather was so good that when two more students decided that they had had enough of the mountain, Willi felt confident sending them down alone. Willi radioed the Ranger station at Paradise saying that the avalanche danger was very low and the group would be ascending directly up Cadaver Gap. Then Willi and twenty students headed up Rainier, leaving behind still another student at Muir suffering from the altitude.

The group pushed slowly up Cadaver Gap, the same route that the reconnaissance party had descended the day before, traversing high enough to avoid the crevasses. They carried a three-day supply of food. Yolles walked last placing many three-foot-long wands into the snow to guide them back down during bad weather. When the group stopped for lunch near Gibraltar Rock, Willi talked about the alternatives.

"We could hightail it up to the summit today and bivouac in the caves up there."

"Wow!"

"Far out!"

"Or we could slog on up to the Ingraham Flats and then maybe some of us go on up to the summit, some of us stay there."

"I don't like the idea of splitting up the group," Yolles said, "diminishing our strength."

"Well, the third alternative is to go up to the Flats and camp there tonight."

Postponing a decision until later seemed to make the most sense. The group headed up. Beyond Gibraltar Rock the snow became softer in places, the climbers sinking in up to their knees. Some of the students had nausea and headaches from the altitude and were in no mood for further climbing. At about 12:30 the group stopped and pitched their tents at the 11,800-foot level, within striking distance of the summit.

It was a fine day, a summit day if there ever was one. "Who wants to go up and recon a route?" Willi asked.

Yolles, Dash, and Rowland Zoller were game. They pushed upward with Willi through the deep snow exchanging leads, fifty or one hundred feet at a time. The route became steeper and more icy. They pushed upward. They came to a foot-wide crevasse. Willi jumped across, the others following. Still they pushed upward.

Yolles led now, the others followed talking with Willi about the Sherpas. Willi was going more slowly. Yolles sat down in the snow and waited for his fifty-two-year-old-teacher.

"You move beautifully in the mountains," Willi said.

Yolles said nothing.

"You move like the Sherpas move," Willi said and moved out ahead breaking trail. The route got steeper and more icy. Willi was going even more slowly now. Yolles and Dash moved into the lead. They were over 13,000 feet.

"Can you believe we're up here?" Yolles said in absolute ecstasy.

"Yeah, I know," Dash said, equally in awe.

"Can you believe we're up here with Willi?" Yolles said, kicking steps in the icy snow, trying to catch a glimpse of the sun setting behind the peak of the mountain.

"That's enough for me!" Willi yelled, a hundred yards behind.

On the way down to high camp the four men were as full of joy and comradeship as if they had reached the summit of Everest.

"There's this guide in the Tetons," Willi said, trudging downward, "who's one heck of a good climber. But he's reached the end of his rope as a guide. He's got the knowledge, the skills, but he's lost his feeling for people. It's just too bad."

As he talked Willi was walking painfully slowly. Yolles thought that because of his physical problems Willi was at the end of his rope, too. Willi stopped for another rest. Yolles turned to his teacher. "How ya feelin', Willi?"

"I feel my hips, Ian, and I'm not supposed to feel them."

When the four men finally tromped back into high camp, dinner was ready. Willi was tired, but it had been a fine day. In January he had told the students that they might not even get out of the parking lot at Paradise. Now they had every chance to reach the summit: all of them. There had never been such a group to reach the summit of Rainier in the winter. It would be a victory for everything in which

Willi believed: for the magnificent potential within each human being; for experiential education; for the virtue of risk as a tool in opening and shaping the human mind and spirit. It would be a victory over age and decrepitude; over these plastic hips; over those doctors who said that he would never climb again; over Jim Gulden and others who had harassed Willi, nipping at his heels.

As Willi went to sleep, the sky was perfectly clear, the summit beckoning above. When the group woke up at about 3:30 A.M., the sky had a pristine clarity. As Willi and the students bolted down breakfast and got dressed, the sky slowly disappeared, covered by a blanketing mist. By 5:30 when the six rope teams began moving out, snow had begun to fall. The steps that Willi and the others had kicked into the snow the day before had largely disappeared. Minute by minute, foot by foot, the storm worsened.

Some students were yelling for the sheer joy of climbing to the summit with Willi. Other students were yelling simply to be heard, their voices carried away on the rising winds. Finally two of the women, Marjorie Butler and Sheri Gerson, got their message across; they wanted to go down. One of the more experienced climbers, Peter Miller, a thin, bearded, twenty-six-year-old Pennsylvanian who had come west to study with Willi, led the women down to high camp. The others continued upward. But the storm was too fierce. After reaching about the same height as Willi's party the previous day, the rope teams turned back and struggled down to high camp.

By 9:30 A.M. when the group trudged into camp, the storm had developed into a full-scale blizzard. The weather forecast on the radio predicted three days of deteriorating weather. They were low on food and fuel. Some of the students were getting wet. Snow was drifting around the six tents, the wind shaking at the center poles. To prevent the snow from piling up, burying the tents, the people in each tent had to go out into the wind to dig trenches around the tents.

In the afternoon Dash took his turn digging a trench. Willi was outside at the same time.

"What do you think about the objective danger?" Dash asked, terribly worried about avalanches and piled-up snow.

"Oh, this is nothing!" Willi yelled over the wind. "On Everest I was in hundred-mile-an-hour winds. All we did was pull the tent down and wrap it around us."

Later Willi sat in his tent with Diepenbrock and Miller, members of his rope team. "I feel I keep shrinking," Diepenbrock said.

"You're not shrinking, Janie." Willi laughed exuberantly. "It's just the amount of growth people do in the mountains."

Willi talked about himself and what he had found in the mountains. "When I was a kid I wanted to be Peter Pan," Willi said, sitting in the tiny tent, the wind rattling the nylon. "The only never-never land I ever found was up here, up above ten thousand feet."

It was a long, exhausting night. Everyone took turns shoveling the drifting snow away from the tent. The wind blew furiously, tearing Willi's tent. Several of the students heard the boom of an avalanche. Some of the Evergreeners were as blissfully unconcerned as children on a picnic. Others realized that the group was in serious trouble.

By morning three feet of snow had fallen. The wind was blowing at sixty miles an hour. It was fearsome weather, but with food and fuel so low, the wind ripping away at their cloth habitats, the snow threatening to bury the tents, Willi had little choice but to lead the group down. Willi was up and around cheering people up, getting the group moving, singing songs about flapjacks and hairy marmots. He told the students that they would go down by Cathedral Gap to the Cowlitz Glacier, then traverse across to Muir. It might have been tempting to take the direct, short route down Cadaver Gap to Muir. But Willi said that the new snow had created avalanche dangers.

At about 10:00 Sunday morning the six rope teams set out, feeling their way through the blinding, shifting snows. Leading the way, Willi and Yolles couldn't even see most of the three-foot-long wands that had been placed only two days before. As the two men walked back and forth trying to find the route down, the others waited shivering. The students no longer thought of Willi's hips or his humor, but only that he was the one person to lead them out of this white, frigid fury.

Willi and Yolles had gotten off route. The group had to work their way down through an area strewn with crevasses. They be-layed each other over the crevasses, waiting in places close to an hour. It was noon before the first two rope teams stood at a flat area beneath Cathedral Rocks, just above Cadaver Gap. The wind was fiercer than ever. The climbers in the first two rope teams huddled together to get warmth from each other and protection from the rocks.

"We're gonna go right down Cadaver Gap," Willi said.

"What about avalanches?" a student asked.

"What about them?"

"Are you worried about them?"

"Some people worry about avalanches, and some don't," Willi shouted, the words carried away in the raging storm.

When Dash's team finally reached the small, huddled group, he too asked Willi about avalanche dangers. "The wind has been strong enough to blow away some snow and compact the rest," Willi said. "It should be safe."

On Nanda Devi and other mountains Willi had treated ava-lanches as if they were acts of God. They could take a climber when and how they chose. The route down Cadaver Gap was dan-gerous, but Willi had few options. He had wanted everybody to make the summit; now he had people who hadn't trained physically for the climb the way they should have, and they were doubly hurting. Several people were on the verge of hypothermia, their body temperatures dropping. To go down the far longer Cathedral Gap route, the group would have had to traverse through some more nasty crevasses, a long, tough business in this weather. Thus Willi decided to do as he had done so many times before: to trust in the mountain.

"I want the rope teams spaced one hundred feet apart," Willi shouted into the wind. "And keep your distance." When Yolles heard that he figured that no matter what Willi said out loud, he took the possibility of an avalanche seriously; Willi wanted to make sure that a single avalanche didn't wipe everybody out. What Willi did not do was to tell the students to undo the straps on their packs, a basic precaution in an avalanche-prone area. Nor did he do it for himself.

Willi led, followed on the same rope by Diepenbrock, Miller, and Kaplan. Before heading directly down Cadaver Gap, Willi and his rope team traversed a seventy-five-foot stone ledge. The blasts nearly knocked the climbers off their feet. Willi dug his ice axe into the frozen snow. He fought his way across as if he were combating a physical opponent, moving each time the wind let up. Behind him Diepenbrock struggled, hardly able to see Willi; she had spent some wonderful hours with Willi on Rainier, and she trusted him completely. Miller pushed ahead, too, guided by the rope and by Willi. In the rear Kaplan kept yodeling back to Yolles, the leader of the second team, guiding him through the whiteout.

Almost a half hour had passed, and they had come across only the ledge. Willi turned directly down the steep slopes of Cadaver Gap, not keeping to the side. Step by step Willi moved down Rainier.

The mountain began to move, the snows sliding slowly, silently, picking up momentum and strength, rolling down Cadaver Gap. The great mass of snow and ice traveled down the mountain silently, the thundering sounds of the avalanche buried under the roar of the storm. Willi had feared dying in an avalanche, lying alone in a snowy coffin, slowly suffocating. Suddenly he was cast into the endless, enveloping snow. Diepenbrock was jolted off her feet, pulled ahead by the rope, flung into the swirling whiteness. When Miller saw Diepenbrock falling, he plunged his ice axe into the snow. But he too was yanked forward. He had to get his pack off, but it was impossible.

The rope grabbed Kaplan, dragging him down into the snow. It was smooth and slow and dreamlike, floating through time and destiny. Kaplan turned over and over again, moving through the weightless, shifting snows. He tried to get out of his pack, but couldn't. He started to swim, a backstroke, then tried a stroke like treading water, but his legs were still trapped. He remembered what Willi had said: as soon as the avalanche stopped the snow became like concrete. As the avalanche slowed nearly five hundred feet down the slope, he pulled his pack off and swam upward, plunging out of the hardening snow.

Kaplan thought, "My God, I've been in an avalanche." He

wanted to get out of there. Then he saw his pack and Miller's mitten sticking out of the snow twenty-five feet away. Kaplan ran toward his friend and housemate and began digging with his hands. Almost as fast as he dug a hole, the wind covered it up with snow again. Up ahead all Kaplan saw was an endless panorama of snow, nothing of Willi and Janie. Hearing Miller's moans, Kaplan grabbed a shovel from his pack and dug frantically. He got Miller's head out, but the snow kept covering him up.

Yolles moved slowly down the steep slope. On the traverse he had had trouble with Wanda Schroeder, who had started to cry and wouldn't move. But she was all right. Yolles moved down the steep slope of Cadaver Gap. Step by step by . . . gone . . . nothing . . . nothing . . . he stopped his fall with his ice axe. Turning back he saw the ragged fracture line of an avalanche, three feet deep in the middle, running the whole length of the gap. He had heard nothing. Seeing some rocks at the side of the gap, he ran, tugging the rope. Standing at the side panting, he heard great gasping screams drifting in and out of the storm. The storm lessened a moment. He saw someone waving. Kaplan. Yolles figured that Willi's team must have gotten off route. As he ran toward the shadowy figure he realized that Willi's rope team had been caught in the avalanche.

When the second rope team arrived at the accident scene, Bruce Clifton and Wanda Schroeder helped Kaplan uncover Miller. Yolles pulled the climbing rope out of the snow, following it until he came to Diepenbrock's body. He had no shovel. With his hands, he began digging. David Ridley, the other member of the second team, dug too, moaning, "Oh my God, oh my God."

Yolles dug even more furiously. A bit of blue pack appeared. The two students had no idea which way the body might lie. Yolles finally uncovered Diepenbrock's upper body. She was face down two feet deep in the snow. He couldn't turn her over. He cut her pack off. Still, Yolles couldn't turn her over. She was totally encased in snow. On his knees, the storm swirling, Yolles dug around Diepenbrock's thighs. He turned her over finally. Her face was the purple-blue color of the suffocated.

Grabbing the rope from Diepenbrock's stomach, Yolles jumped up. He yelled at Ridley, "Take this rope and find Willi!" Then Yolles began mouth-to-mouth resuscitation on what he was sure was already a dead body. Ridley pulled the rope out of the snow until it held, anchored to Willi's buried form.

After Kaplan and Schroeder freed Miller they moved over to help unbury Willi. With their hands they dug down to his thighs, three feet deep in the snow. Each minute decreased dramatically the possibility that he might still be alive. Using a shovel they uncovered Willi more and cut off his pack.

Kaplan pulled the radio out and handed it to Miller who appeared to be okay.

"We are Unsoeld party at Cadaver Gap and have been caught in an avalanche," Miller shouted into the radio at 1:55. "Unsoeld and another person have been buried."

J.P. de St. Croix, the Ranger on duty at Paradise, thought Miller's voice sounded frantic. "What is your location?" the Ranger asked.

"One hundred yards down from Cadaver Gap."

"When did this happen?"

"About fifteen minutes ago," Miller said, though it had been almost three times that long.

"What you have to do now is dig them out."

"They're unburied now and we're attemping to get them breathing."

When Willi was finally turned over, one of the students began mouth-to-mouth resuscitation. As he saw the purplish-red face, the nostrils packed with snow, and smelled death, he recoiled screaming. The other students took turns attempting to blow life back into the chilled form. Again and again they tried but the body grew colder, the snow drifting anew around the body.

"I think Janie's dead," Downey said, feeling hopelessly sad, starting to cry, then restraining himself.

The students were alone. They were cold. They were wet. Some were on the edge of hypothermia. Some were on the edge of hysteria. People were turning to Yolles now.

"Are they dead?" the students asked Yolles as he knelt over Willi's body. For the longest time he could not say no. Finally, Yolles turned from Willi's mute form and looked up at the group.

"They're dead. I think they're dead. And we're in a dangerous situation."

"We'll take them with us, the bodies," one student blurted out.

"No," Yolles said. "We can't do that."

So they lifted Diepenbrock's body out of the snows and put her in a sleeping bag and laid her there in the deepening snow. Then they took Willi's body, half buried still, and covered it with sleeping bags. They put bright wands around the two bodies and began to prepare to leave.

Yolles realized that he was terribly tired and cold. He knew that he needed help. He turned to Jeff Casebolt, the leader of the third team. "Will you lead us down?" Yolles shouted, struggling to make himself heard.

"What about you?" Casebolt shouted back into the wind. If they ended up too low they might miss Muir. If they went too high, they could set off another avalanche.

"I'm just really exhausted," Yolles said.

"I'll do my best," Casebolt said.

When the fourth rope team arrived, Yolles turned to Bruce Ostermann. "Will you help lead the party?" Yolles asked. Ostermann stared blankly at what he considered a scene of mild chaos. "Willi and Janie are dead."

"I'll try," Ostermann said.

"We've got to stay together," Yolles told the group. "If we split up, that'll be the end."

By now Miller was on the verge of shock and hypothermia. He could hardly stand up. He had what appeared to be broken ribs. Yolles tied Miller into the rope behind him. As they headed out, Bob Dash, leader of the sixth and final rope team, appeared out of the storm.

"What's happened?" Dash shouted as Yolles moved out. "What's happened! What's happened!"

Yolles turned back. "Willi and Janie are dead. We've got to get to Muir."

Dash shook his head disbelievingly. He felt as if he were floating. Now with Willi gone who would lead them?

"A lot of us are tired and exhausted," Yolles said. "We need your strength."

So they set out, the two other members of the last rope team not even knowing what had happened. The wind and storm were fiercer than ever. Setting their faces into the storm, the students moved downward, plunging through an ocean of whiteness. They were half blinded by the hammering volleys of wind. Ice coated their beards and faces. The wind picked up their packs, slamming them down again.

Out front Casebolt felt his way down Rainier, guessing by the angle of the steps he was kicking into the deep heavy snow whether he was going right. The rope teams kept losing each other in the white maze. The wind ripped at the students, blowing them off their feet, smashing Miller to his knees.

"Get up," Yolles shouted, looking at the dazed figure lying there.

"I can't do it."

"You've got to."

Up Miller struggled, vomiting as he staggered forward, only to be knocked down again a hundred feet down the mountain. Some of the students dropped their packs, with that dropping almost any possibility that they could survive if they did not reach the confines of the cabin at Muir. Butler and Gerson fell to the ground crying that they could not go on.

"You've got to go," Yolles pleaded, putting his hands on the two women. "You've got to use everything. You've got to get to Muir."

As Downey moved along, he thought that some of the students were being too self-indulgent, letting themselves be weak. Up ahead Casebolt pushed on. In his whole life he had never prayed. But with that terrible vision of Willi's grotesque face before him, he prayed for Willi. He prayed for Janie too, and for all of them, prayed that he see some sign that he was going right. Step by step he moved, step by step . . . falling downward . . . falling. . . . Casebolt tumbled down, his feet sliding on ice. Another avalanche fracture! This one was 4 feet deep, 150 feet wide. One by one the eighteen students moved across the ice as if they were slipping on a skating rink, knowing that if they had come earlier this avalanche could have carried them away, knowing that there might be a new avalanche at any time.

The group stopped to confer. It was 4:30. The deep shadows of dusk had begun to appear.

"Do you think we're going in the right direction?" Ostermann asked. If they did not make it to Muir soon, they would not make it today. If they did not make it today, other people would die this night.

"Should we be there on the ridge?" Ostermann asked urgently.

Yolles, Casebolt, and Ostermann agreed that they should move up the slope a little. The three men walked about twenty steps. A few rocks appeared out of the gathering gloom. Casebolt noticed wires sticking out of the snow. They rushed forward. A small door appeared out of the endless white panorama, all that was visible of the stone cabin at Muir.

The students hugged each other. They danced across the stone floor. Thawing out, they began to realize that something had happened on the mountain that they could not begin to understand. They cried. They laughed. They kept waiting for the door to bang open and Willi to come stomping into the dark cabin, yodeling with all his might. Wherever he looked Yolles saw Willi's face; whenever he swallowed, he tasted Willi.

While the storm raged outside, the Evergreeners talked of Willi. They talked also of Janie. She was strong and courageous. It seemed right that she should be the one to rest up there with Willi. At night many of the students dreamed of Willi and of his spirit and knew that he was alive. The second night almost all the students slept pressed together on one long bunk. It was as if they would have liked to believe that there were not the strong and weak among them, the leaders and the led, but one human organism.

On the morning of the third day at Muir the rescue party of Rangers and guides reached the cabin, breaking the sanctity. The students felt that these intruders did not understand and could not possibly understand. Later that day as the students headed down

Rainier, many of them dreaded what might meet them below. They dreaded the media and their questions. They dreaded the possibility that people wouldn't understand what Willi had done, what Willi had been, how they had fulfilled Willi's philosophy, becoming what Willi wanted them to become.

When the party reached Panorama Point, a small group was waiting for them including Nancey Goforth. She suggested that as the students reached Paradise, they might want to sing a song, and she told them the words. Even before the students saw the cameramen and reporters they began to sing. They looked straight ahead, their eyes off somewhere beyond the horizon:

> *You can't kill the spirit*
> *It's like a mountain*
> *It's old and strong*
> *It goes on and on.*

As they passed through the gauntlet of onlookers, the Evergreeners sang louder and louder, drowning out the questions and the doubts, death and pain, the mediocre and the mundane, drowning out everything but Willi and the mountain.

> *You can't kill the spirit*
> *It's like a mountain*
> *It's old and strong*
> *It goes on and on*
> *You can't kill the spirit*
> *It's like a mountain*
> *It's old and strong*
> *It goes on and on*
> *You can't kill the spirit. . . .*

Author's Note

Willi was always teaching. He used his life as the lesson book, reading from it as if it were a profound text. When Willi died his whole life lay there, a tome that a person could read and ponder, in wonder and awe, regret and sorrow, joy and horror, taking from the testimony of his days whatever one could.

I have sought to write a book in which the reader can truly experience Willi's life, to go along with him on his spiritual and physical quest. The dialogue in *Ascent* comes directly from Willi's own recollections and the recollections of others who were present at various gatherings and discussions. In taking a lengthy discussion and putting it down in a few pages in a book, one is inevitably highly selective. What I have done is highlight that part of the dialogue and debate that Willi himself considered important, and that elucidate Willi's own quest. For instance, when the Nanda Devi expedition members got together at the Unsoelds, they spent most of the hours talking about the mundane, minute detail of planning their climb. But it was the drama of that evening that Willi remembered and told about in his Nanda Devi lecture. And it was the drama that made the evening unique and important. And so it appears in *Ascent*.

People love talking about Willi Unsoeld. I have reams and reams of anecdotes, stories, and remembrances that did not find their way into the text. But each interview added to my understanding of Willi and to this book, and I want particularly to thank those whose names don't appear in the text.

Many people contributed more than interviews. Mrs. Isabel Unsoeld decided that if I was going ahead writing a book about her son, I should be as free and unfettered as the ideals for which Willi lived. I will always remember my visit with Mrs. Unsoeld and Willi's sister, Isabel Chrisman, in California.

Bill Turnage was the friend to whom Willi could talk most freely in his last years; I am honored that I too now think of Bill as my friend. Barry Williams and I had long conversations on the telephone; he pointed the way to Jung's archetype of the *puer eternis,* the eternal youth. Erik LeRoy led me up the Grand Teton; Willi couldn't have done better. Rod MacLeish wrote a letter that helped more than he knows. Bill Robinson steered me toward the book the way we used to steer each other home on evenings in Dhankuta, Calcutta, and points east. Dr. Steve Cole and I traveled together returning from Nepal; every time I see Steve I feel that we are still traveling together. Judith Starr provided endless sound comment.

On the publishing side of this venture, I have a large number of people to thank. My agent, Carol Mann, saw the potential of this before anyone else. When I was starting out a number of editors and others contributed their ideas: Patrick Filley, Erwin Glikes, Fred Graver, Joyce Johnson, Juris Jurjevics, and especially Susan Bolotin. Good friends of mine read the first draft: Judith Starr, Bill Turnage, Carol Mann, Kitty Kelley, Mike Edgley, and Peter Ross Range. Barry Bishop read the Everest chapters. Patti Pancoe typed the manuscript. Then Alice Mayhew edited the manuscript with the skill and dedication that is her standard.

In my research I have read the books Willi read, from the Bible to Ken Kesey, Plato to Kierkegaard, Bergson to Otto. One of my happiest discoveries was Willi's favorite novelist, Don Berry, whose books far transcend the category of western novel. I was not nearly so impressed with another of Willi's favorites, Joseph Fletcher's *Situation Ethics.* Willi's Ph.D. thesis, *Mysticism,*

Morality and Freedom: The Role of the Vital Impetus in Bergson's Theory of Ethics, was helpful.

Among the other books I found useful were: Joseph Campbell's *Hero with a Thousand Faces;* Ernest Becker's *Denial of Death; Puer Papers*, edited by Cynthia Giles; Roderick Nash's *Wilderness and the American Mind;* Reinhold Niebuhr's *Moral Man and Immoral Society;* and Miguel de Unamuno's *The Tragic Sense of Life in Men and Nations.*

Of course, I read and profited from climbing and outdoor books including Tom Hornbein's beautiful *Everest: The West Ridge*, recently republished by The Mountaineers. James Ramsey Ullman couldn't leave the Katmandu valley in 1963, but his *Americans on Everest* is still a major achievement. John McCallum's *Everest Diary* was useful as well. So was Leigh Ortenburger's *A Climber's Guide to the Teton Range;* Fritiof Fryxell's *Mountaineering in the Tetons: The Pioneer Period 1898–1940;* Robert Craig's *Storm and Sorrow in the High Pamirs;* Rick Ridgeway's *The Last Step: The American Ascent of K2;* Showell Styles' *Mallory of Everest;* Dee Molenaar's *The Challenge of Rainier;* Joshua L. Miner's and Joe Boldt's *Outward Bound USA;* and Chris Jones, *Climbing in North America.*

Willi loved to talk about himself. Accounts of his speeches were invaluable. In my opinion the best single article about Willi is Worth Hedrick's piece published in 1976 in Seattle's *The Weekly.* I gained much information from articles in *The Oregon Daily Emerald, The Daily Olympian, The Eugene Register-Guard, Off-Belay, Summit, Outside, The Anderson Herald, The Cooper Point Journal, The Seattle Post-Intelligencer, The Seattle Times, The Los Angeles Times, Life,* and *The National Geographic.* The accounts of Willi's expeditions and experiences in *The American Alpine Journal* were immensely useful as was *The Sierra Club Journal's* article on the Makalu expedition. "You Can't Kill the Spirit" by Terry and Harriet King in *The Reader's Digest* is a vivid account of Willi's last climb.

The National Park Service inquiry into the accident on Rainier was a serious, detailed investigation, extremely helpful to me in writing this book. The Evergreen State College investigation was not so detailed or helpful.

Finally, let me thank John and Cristina King, in whose apartment this book was written, and Mary Glenn, who with gentle goodness put up with all my papers and manuscripts.

Glossary of Terms

acclimatization: the process by which the body becomes accustomed to living at high altitudes

agape: the all-encompassing love that Willi Unsoeld thought the essence of Christianity

avalanche: a large mass of snow and ice moving rapidly down a mountain

bakri wallah: goatherd

base camp: the lowest and major supply camp on an expedition. The other, higher camps are usually numbered consecutively.

belay: the crucial safety system of roped climbing. While the lead climber moves upward, the second climber has anchored the rope to a piton or rock. When the second climber moves up, the lead climber anchors him from above. Thus if the belay is sound, the climber can fall only a limited distance before the rope becomes taut.

bivouac: a night outside on the mountain without tent and other camping equipment

Chomo-lungma: the Tibetan name for Mount Everest

col: a snowy pass or high valley between two peaks

couloir: a gully of ice or snow

crampons: steel spikes that are strapped onto climbing boots to grip into snow and ice

crevasse: a crack in a glacier that is like an earthquake fracture

cwm: a Welsh term for valley

élan vital: the term that Henri Bergson, the French philosopher, used to describe the creative life force

Everest: Standing between Nepal and Tibet, this 29,028-foot peak is the highest mountain in the world.

fixed rope: rope that is anchored along a climbing route

Garhwal: This Himalayan region is a religious sanctuary to the Hindus of India. Here the seven Rishis, the saintly sages of Hindu mythology, retreated to live within the Sanctuary, protected by Nanda Devi. Indeed, the gorge into the base of Nanda Devi wasn't penetrated until Shipton and Tilman made their epic journey in 1934.

glacier: a great flow or river of ice

high-altitude porter: human load bearer able to carry supplies high up on a mountain

icefall: that portion of a glacier which has fallen down a mountain forming a mass of broken blocks of ice

jumar: a simple spring device which slides up a fixed rope but not down. The climber sits in a harness; when he wants to move higher, he merely stands, reaches upward and pulls, raising himself a good many inches up the rope.

Karakoram range: a 300-mile-long mountain system between the Indus and Yarkand rivers. The range is the greatest barrier between India and Central Asia.

lead: in mountaineering parlance, the first climber. This is the most challenging position, to some climbers the only real climbing.

Masherbrum: a 25,660-foot peak in Pakistan's Karakoram range

monsoon: the warm, wet season in South Asia, bringing with it often torrential daily rains. To Himalayan climbers it usually means the end of the climb. Some expeditions, however, are made during the monsoon.

moraine: earth and stone carried and deposited by an avalanche

Nanda Devi: Nanda, in Hindi, means bliss-giving, and Devi means goddess. Nanda Devi is a Hindu goddess, as well as a mountain. The 25,645-foot peak is the highest mountain in India.

Nepal: This 500-mile-long, 100-mile-wide Himalayan kingdom lies between India and Tibet. It is home to the world's highest peak, Mount Everest.

Nilkanta: This beautiful 21,640-foot peak is located in India's Garhwal.

pitch: This is the distance between two belay points, the distance a team of mountaineers climbs at one time. It can be the length of a climbing rope, 150 feet, or much less.

piton: a metal spike driven into rock or snow to hold a climbing rope

porters: In Nepal and the other Himalayan regions of South Asia men and women are the main beasts of burden, carrying loads that sometimes weigh almost as much as they do.

Rainier: This 14,410-foot peak is located in the state of Washington. It is the highest mountain in America's Northwest and is often called simply "the mountain."

rappel: the technique a climber uses to descend on a rope. The climber sits in a harness, then applies or relaxes friction to let himself slowly or rapidly down the rope.

sahib: Though literally meaning "master," as the term is used by the Sherpas it has a friendlier quality.

sirdar: the head man

slog: a hard trek or walk

Sola Khumba: the northeast region of Nepal, home of the Sherpas

Sherpas: the word in Tibetan means easterner. These are the mountain people living in northeastern Nepal. Of Tibetan origin they are famed as porters, high-altitude porters and climbing partners on expeditions.

trek: a long hike

wand: a long, thin stake placed along a climbing route so that even in stormy conditions climbers can find their way back along the route